Human Communication in Everyday Life
Explanations and Applications

Jason S. Wrench

SUNY New Paltz

James C. McCroskey

University of Alabama, Birmingham

Virginia Peck Richmond

University of Alabama, Birmingham

PEARSON

Boston   New York   San Francisco
Mexico City   Montreal   Toronto   London   Madrid   Munich   Paris
Hong Kong   Singapore   Tokyo   Cape Town   Sydney

i

Editor-in-Chief: Karon Bowers
Assistant Editor: Jenny Lupica
Marketing Manager: Suzan Czajkowski
Production Supervisor: Karen Mason
Editorial Production Service: WestWords/PMG
Composition Buyer: Linda Cox

Manufacturing Buyer: JoAnne Sweeney
Electronic Composition: WestWords/PMG
Interior Design: Anne Flanagan
Photo Researcher: Naomi Rudov
Cover Administrator: Joel Gendron

For related titles and support materials, visit our online catalog at www.ablongman.com.

Between the time website information is gathered and then published, it is not unusual for some sites to have closed. Also, the transcription of URLs can result in typographical errors. The publisher would appreciate notification where these errors occur so that they may be corrected in subsequent editions.

Library of Congress Cataloging-in-Publication Data
Wrench, Jason S.
  Human communication in everyday life: explanations and applications / Jason S. Wrench,
James C. McCroskey, Virginia P. Richmond.
      p. cm.
    ISBN-13: 978-0-205-43501-2
    ISBN-10: 0-205-43501-7
      1. Communication. I. McCroskey, James C. II. Richmond, Virginia P., III. Title.
    P90.W69 2008
    302.2—dc22   2007013457

Printed in the United States of America

10 9 8 7 6 5 4 3 2 1   RRD-VA   11 10 09 08 07

Photo Credits: 1, Photodisc; 4, David Young-Wolff/PhotoEdit; 9, Bob Daemmrich/PhotoEdit; 32, Photos.com; 48, Scala/Art Resource; 58, Corbis RF; 59, Liaison/Getty Images; 87, Tyler Mallory/AP Images; 101, Bill Bachmann/ PhotoEdit; 112, Corbis RF; 120, Corbis Digital Stock; 125, Stone Allstock/Getty Images; 132, Corbis RF; 141, Joe Marquette/AP Images; 151, Efrem Lukatsky/AP Images; 160, Joyce Dopkeen/New York Times Agency; 164, AP Images; 177, Photodisc; 179, Matt Campbell/EPA/Corbis; 189, James Marshall/The Image Works; 199, Frank Siteman/ Omni-Photo Communications; 220, Rick Gomez/Corbis; 233, David Karp/AP Images; 236, David Kennedy/AP Images; 255, Ariel Skelley/Corbis; 264, Fernando Llano/AP Images; 279, Ron L. Brown/MIRA; 282, Yoav Levy/Phototake; 303, Simon Marcus/Corbis; 314, Michael Newman/PhotoEdit; 322, Dennis Cooper/Zefa/Corbis; 335, Jon Feingersh/Zefa/ Corbis; 344, David Butow/SABA Press/Corbis; 352, Will Hart/PhotoEdit.

Contents

Prologue

In 1973, Mark Hickson became the first editor of the *Journal of Applied Communications Research (JACR)* and ushered in a new era of communication research that was more practically focused. Prior to the publication of *JACR*, most research in communication studied the effects of various public speakers, from Abraham Lincoln to Richard Nixon. Although classical research on public speaking was useful, a group of scholars during the late 1960s started to question the applicability of communication research to the real world. The ultimate result of this conversation was the creation of *JACR*. Hickson defined *applied communication* as "the investigation of human communication events by a participant/observer of those events into a communication artifact that will help bring about communico-social change" (1973, p. 3). To analyze this definition, let's break down what Hickson was describing. First, applied communication research needs to involve communication events that happen in the real world today. Again, much of the early research in communication was analyzing the texts of public speakers—most of whom had been dead for a very long time. With the ushering in of applied communication, Hickson realized that researchers in communication needed to focus on actual communication that people could see in their day-to-day lives. Second, Hickson believed that research in the area of applied communication should have the ability to bring about changes in both communication and one's social environment. For communication change, Hickson believed that communication research had the ability to actually help people learn to communicate more effectively. As for social change, Hickson believed that communication research could actually have an impact on society at large.

Since the publication of the first issue of the *Journal of Applied Communications Research* (or what is today called the *Journal of Applied Communication Research*), much research has actually been published, having been designed to fulfill those two requirements of Hickson: (1) the research must be occurring today and (2) the research must have the ability to change people's communicative and/or social lives. More simply, Frey, Botan, and Kreps (2000) defined applied communication research as "[r]esearch conducted for the purpose of solving a 'real-world,' socially relevant communication problem" (p. 409). The authors of this textbook believe when students see how communication research has the ability for solving real-world, socially relevant communication problems, students will be more engaged in learning about communication. For this reason, *Human Communication in Everyday Life: Explanations and Applications* is not laid out in the same fashion as other textbooks in the communication field.

Human Communication in Everyday Life: Explanations and Applications covers much of the same content traditionally seen in lower-level, introductory textbooks; however, this textbook takes teaching communication concepts to an applied level. In essence, this textbook is designed with two primary units.

Unit One

The first unit is titled "Communication Principles" and consists of the first eight chapters of the textbook. In these eight chapters, we will introduce you to the basic concepts in communication. In these chapters, you will learn about various communication variables. A variable is "any entity that can take on a variety of different values" (Wrench, Thomas-Maddox, Richmond, & McCroskey, 2008). For example, the word *happy* can be a variable for social scientists because there are various values of happiness. You can be semihappy because you got a *B* on an examination you thought you failed, or you can be ecstatically happy because you just won the lottery. In other words, there are varying degrees of happiness. In the same way, communication is filled with variables. For example, in Chapter 3 we are going to analyze the communication variable *shyness.* As I'm sure you're already aware, there are some people in the world who are clearly shy, some people who are moderately shy, and others who are not shy at all. In other words, there are various degrees to the concept of shyness, or the level of shyness varies from person to person, which is why we call it a *variable.*

Throughout *Human Communication in Everyday Life: Explanations and Applications,* we will often talk about two statistical concepts that are extremely important to communication researchers: relationships and differences. Because these concepts are extremely important, we are going to explain these two concepts very briefly here.

Relationships Relationships between variables typically fall into one of three categories: positive, negative, or no relationship. Positive relationships exist when an increase in one variable corresponds with an increase in the other variable. An example of a positive relationship can be seen between a physician's use of humor and patient satisfaction. Research has shown that as physicians use humor, their patients tend to be more satisfied. Increases in one variable (humor) relate to increases in the other (satisfaction). This relationship is visually represented in Figure 1a.

A negative relationship exists when a decrease in one variable relates to an increase in the other variable, or vice versa. Studies examining the relationship between commu-

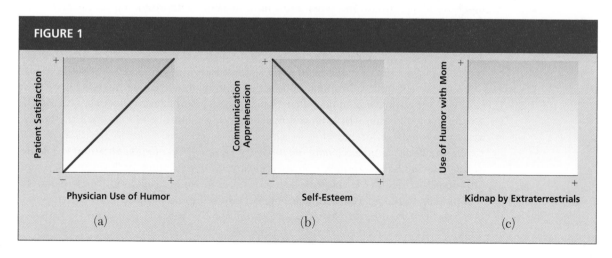

FIGURE 1

(a)   (b)   (c)

nication apprehension (anxiety associated with either real or perceived communication) and self-esteem have found that lower levels of communication apprehension are related to higher levels of self-esteem. The converse would be true as well. Individuals with lower levels of self-esteem would likely report higher levels of communication apprehension. Figure 1b depicts a negative relationship.

In some instances, a researcher may discover that the variables selected for a study are not related to one another. Figure 1c provides a visual representation of two variables that have no relationship to one another. For example, we can be pretty sure that there is no relationship between someone's reporting of the number of times he or she has been kidnapped by extraterrestrials and her or his use of humor during interactions with her or his mother.

Differences In addition to looking at relationships, researchers also examine differences. In research, differences fall into one of two categories: differences in kind and differences in degree. Differences in kind occur when two or more groups do different things associated with their groups. For example, football players play football and cheerleaders lead the crowd in cheers. The two groups (football players and cheerleaders) are fundamentally different and exhibit different behaviors. Although it may be entertaining to some, we really do not want to see a 90 lb. cheerleader being tackled by a 350 lb. defensive lineman, nor would we want to see the 350 lb. lineman trying to execute a flip or toe touch. Although differences in kind are interesting, they generally are not studied often in human communication.

Instead, *Human Communication in Everyday Life: Explanations and Applications* is interested in differences of degree, or when two groups have differing degrees on a variable that they both display. For example, perhaps we wanted to determine if females and males differed in their levels of smiling. We could watch a group of females and males and count the number of times each group smiles during an interaction. After counting the number of times each group smiles, a researcher could then perform statistical tests that would allow the researcher to determine whether one group smiles more than the other group. In Figure 2, we have two curves representing the average number of times the group of males smiled and the average number of times the group of females smiled. The curve to the left represents the average number of times a male smiled during an interaction, and the curve to the right represents the average number of times a female smiled during an interaction. Although eyeballing the two curves may make it appear that females smile more, researchers cannot use the eyeballing technique, which is why researchers use statistics to determine if the two groups are really different.

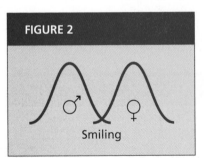

FIGURE 2

Smiling

Throughout *Human Communication in Everyday Life: Explanations and Applications,* we will discuss a number of research studies that examine both relationships and differences of degree. If you ever become confused while reading this book, please do not hesitate to reread this section to help get yourself back on track.

Unit Two

The second unit in *Human Communication in Everyday Life: Explanations and Applications* is called "Communication in Applied Contexts." In the second unit, we are going to take those basic communication elements discussed in Unit One and show you how they are actually seen in the "real world." Specifically, we are going to examine the real-world contexts of public speaking, interpersonal relationships, intercultural communication, health communication, mediated communication, organizational communication, and instructional communication. Through these eight different real-world contexts, we will see how communication concepts can be applied in a variety of different ways.

Use of Research Measures

Since the beginnings of social scientific research studying attitudes in the 1940s, researchers have had to use a variety of tools to measure human behavior. Unlike how chemists can put two chemicals in a beaker and receive the same result every time, social scientists are working with a rather inexact science because humans do not always respond the same way in every situation. To aid in the process of measuring human behavior, researchers started using a variety of research scales and questionnaires to analyze behavior. Communication researchers have also been creating and utilizing research scales and questionnaires to conduct research since the 1960s. Included in this book are over forty different research scales that have been created and used by communication researchers to analyze human communication. These scales are talked about in the textbook and can be found in the appendix at the back of the book. We opted to place these scales in the appendix to make the reading of the chapters flow as smoothly as possible. However, it is our strong recommendation that you fill out the research scales as we talk about them throughout the book. The more active you are while reading this textbook, the more you will learn about communication and yourself.

References

Frey, L. R., Botan, C. H., & Kreps, G. L. (2000). *Investigating communication: An introduction to research methods* (2nd ed.). Boston: Allyn & Bacon.

Hickson, M., III. (1973). Applied communications research: A beginning point for social relevance. *Journal of Applied Communications Research, 1* (1), 1–5.

Wrench, J. S., Thomas-Maddox, C., Richmond, V. P., & McCroskey, J. C. (2008). *Quantitative research methods for communication: A hands-on approach.* New York: Oxford University Press.

Acknowledgments

First, I would like to thank Karon Bowers and Jenny Lupica at Allyn & Bacon for their help and support on this project and for walking me through this process. Second, I would also like to thank Melena Fenn from WestWords/PMG, for her help on this project. Third, I would like to thank my Ohio University family: Sarah Mahan-Hays, Eileen McCormack, Candice Thomas-Maddox, Sheida Shirvani, and Shannon Brogan. Last, I want to thank my family, Bill and Karen Wrench, Roy and Virginia Horn, and Rick Wrench, for their love and support.

—Jason S. Wrench

We would like to acknowledge the work of Karon Bowers at Allyn & Bacon for her guidance and support in the publication of this book as well as many of our other books. Without Karon's guidance, none of this would have been possible.

—Virginia Peck Richmond and James C. McCroskey

We would also like to thank the reviewers of this text:

Jerry L. Allen, University of New Haven

Angie Marie Seifert Anderson, Anoka Ramsey Community College

Peter J. Bicak, Rockhurst University

Shirley Crawley, Fairfield University

Robert Dixon, Meramec Community College

Darin Garard, Santa Barbara City College

Thomas J. Knutson, California State University, Sacramento

Deborah K. London, Merrimack College

Aysel Morin, University of Nebraska, Lincoln

Jason J. Teven, California State University, Fullerton

UNIT I
Communication Principles

1

The Process of Human Communication

OBJECTIVES

- Explain the difference between human communication and mass communications.

- Define and explain the definition of *communication* provided in the chapter.

- Explain the three types of communication.

- Differentiate between verbal and nonverbal messages.

- Explain the rhetorical communication model.

- Explain the interpersonal communication model.

- List and explain the seven critical components of human communication.

- Understand the ten misconceptions of human communication.

*C*ommunication has become one of the most commonly used words in the English language. Communicating with others is a very important reality. There are now *three* things that are certain in life: death, taxes, and communication. Of these, only communication may be expected to enhance our lives.

Humans must communicate with each other to survive. However, simply communicating with others is not enough. As potentially harmful as no communication can be, if we express the wrong thing, or in the wrong way, we might be much better off not communicating at all. Unfortunately, many of us do not know how to communicate effectively in many situations. Frequently, our ineptness at communicating is rooted in our lack of understanding what communication is and how it works. Because we must communicate to carry on our lives, we need to understand communication. Ideally, the better we understand it, the more effectively we can use it.

The purpose of this chapter is to consider some basic matters that provide the necessary foundation for developing an understanding of communication. First, we will look at the two general ways in which people use the word *communication* and discuss how we will use it in our definition of human communication. Next, we will discuss three types of communication as they relate to our definition. Then, we will examine two models of communication. Lastly, we are going to look at ten common misconceptions of human communication.

▣ DEFINITIONS OF COMMUNICATION

What communication means to you and what it means to the person near you may be very different. What communication means to one communication *professional* may even be different from what it means to another communication professional! *Communication* is like any other word: it means whatever people who use it think it means. When we take a careful look at how people generally use the word, however, we find that people use *communication* in two very different ways. One way refers to the process of transferring messages from place to place, in which case it is often used in the plural form (that is, communications). Beaming television signals from Los Angeles to New York City via a communications satellite is an example of this meaning. Telephone companies also use this meaning when they advertise their "office communications systems." All electronic and print communications industries make use of the term in this way. This form of the word is also the basis of the phrase *mass communications*.

The second way of using the word refers to the process of stimulating meaning in the mind of another person by means of a message, which is how *we* will be using *communication* in this book. We define human communication as *the process by which one person stimulates meaning in the mind(s) of another person (or persons) through verbal and nonverbal messages*. Unlike the first use of communication, which emphasizes the

The man on the right is clearly the primary message sender.

exchange of messages, this definition of the term emphasizes *meaning*, and is concerned with three types of communication: accidental, expressive, and rhetorical.

TYPES OF COMMUNICATION

Accidental Communication

Each of us has had the experience of having a close friend or relative tell us something we were unaware of about ourselves. For instance, assume you have always considered yourself reserved and quiet. Imagine how surprised you might be if your date informed you that he or she admires how talkative and outgoing you are! Your surprise results from your lack of awareness that you come across to your partner in such a way. In essence, you have *accidentally* communicated this talkative, outgoing aspect of your personality to your date. When we reflect on experiences, it probably comes as no surprise that we are often unaware of what we communicate to other people. In fact, there are times when we are completely unaware that we are communicating anything at all, although we are. There are, of course, other times when we are very much aware that we are communicating and of what we are communicating. When we are consciously in control of sending messages to the other person, we engage in purposeful or intentional communication, which is the opposite of accidental communication. Most of our actions and words stimulate some meaning in the minds of other people. In short, people attribute meaning to our behavior even when we have no intent of stimulating meaning in them.

Accidental communication and purposeful communication are very much alike in their essential processes. Both are the result of one person stimulating meaning in the mind of another person through some type of message. The difference is that accidental communication often interferes with what we *want* to communicate to another person. A humorous, but potentially tragic, example of this occurred when former Vice President Richard Nixon stepped out of a plane in South America and extended to the awaiting crowd the hand signal meaning *OK*, which he famously used in the United States to signal unity and pride. Mr. Nixon obviously intended to express a positive, warm greeting to the crowd. Unfortunately, in much of South America, that particular hand gesture has roughly the same meaning for people as an extended middle finger does in North America! Vice President Nixon accidentally communicated an insult to his South American greeters. A similar example is provided by Hall in his book *The Silent Language* (1959). Hall notes that many Latin Americans stand closer to people in conversations than do North Americans. This difference manifests itself behaviorally when people from these two different cultures stand and talk with each other. The North American continually backs away from the Latin American, and the Latin American continually moves toward the North American. Both individuals are unconsciously trying to establish and maintain what is, for them, a comfortable conversational distance. At the same time, each person may be accidentally communicating certain feelings and attitudes to the other. The North American may perceive the Latin American as pushy and aggressive, whereas the Latin American may perceive the North American as cold and unfriendly. Neither person intends to express these feelings to the other; rather, the feelings are communicated "accidentally."

These two examples of accidental communication suggest that nonverbal messages can have a very strong impact on interpersonal interaction, which is often stronger than that of verbal messages. Although it is important to remember that communication can be accidental, in this book we are more concerned with purposeful communication. Thus, unless otherwise stated, when we use the term *communication* from this point on, we mean the process by which one person *intentionally* tries to stimulate meaning in the mind of another person.

Expressive Communication

If we are sitting quietly in a library and hear a loud noise of books falling on the floor behind us, we will probably turn toward that sound. We may then hear a person near those books muttering something we probably should not print here! That person is exemplifying *expressive* communication. Expressive communication is characterized by messages that *express* how the sender feels at a given time. More simply, expressive communication suggests a person's emotional state. Intention, or purposefulness, is a common, but not essential, characteristic of expressive communication. For instance, when we want to communicate affection to another person, we do so by intentionally saying certain things ("I enjoy being with you") and performing certain behavior (patting the person on the back). When taking a test, we may unintentionally communicate frustration by blaring out a four-letter expletive or "bad" word in response to running out of ink or breaking a pencil tip. Although this may not be our purpose, our outburst will stimulate meaning in the minds of others in the class.

Two other frameworks in which to view expressive communication are the *content* and *relational* levels of messages (Watzlawick, Beavin, & Jackson, 1967). The content level of a message is simply what we say; it is the words comprising the message. The relational level is an expression of how we feel about the other person or our relationship with the other person, and suggests to the other person how he or she should interpret our message. For example, your instructor might say, "The class average on this exam was seventy-four," imparting to the class an explicit bit of information. There can also be a relational level to your instructor's spoken words because you may interpret your instructor's message as saying, "I am very disappointed in your work." If this were the way you interpreted the person's message, it would stimulate in your mind some meaning about the nature of the relationship between your instructor and you and your classmates. Of course, the relational level can often result in accidental communication. Communicating that he or she is really upset with the class may be purely unintentional on your instructor's part; but the way that the instructor looks at the class and uses the voice and arms while speaking could be misconstrued as anger. Fortunately, we do have control over much of our expressive communication. We can reword an utterance or regulate our voice and movements to convey our emotional state without causing accidental communication.

Rhetorical Communication

Rhetorical communication is exemplified by the salesperson attempting to persuade a customer to buy a particular product, by politicians trying to solicit votes from the citizens of their district, and by parents when they attempt to get their children to spend less money. The major difference between rhetorical communication and accidental and expressive types of communication is that rhetorical communication is goal directed. The intent of rhetorical communication is to produce a specific meaning in the mind of another individual. Therefore, the salesperson, the politician, and the parent communicate rhetorically with a *specific* goal in mind: buy a new TV, cast a vote, or save money.

When we read or hear the words *rhetoric* and *rhetorical communication*, our first response may be to think of a public-speaking situation, a news item reporting on a congressional filibuster, or a defense lawyer briefing a jury. Although rhetorical communication is often associated with these kinds of situations, it is also an integral part of everyday interpersonal situations. We use rhetorical communication almost every day. Our goal may be as trivial as getting someone to pass the butter at the dinner table, or our goal may be as urgent as talking our neighbor into giving us a ride to work or school when our car won't start. In either case, the process that allows us to reach that goal is rhetorical communication.

Rhetorical communication assumes that we have intent to achieve a certain goal by stimulating specific meanings in the mind of another person(s). This suggests that rhetorical communication cannot be accidental but only purposeful. It does not suggest, however, that we will always achieve our goal by communicating rhetorically. Often, when we try to change another person's mind about something or attempt to get the person to do something for us, we may continue transmitting different messages until we discover the message that attains our goal. On the other hand, we might learn that nothing we say will get the task accomplished, so we give up. There is nothing accidental about this process, only successful or unsuccessful intent.

We also need to distinguish between the terms *influence* and *persuasion*. When we "influence" someone, we cause that person to alter her or his thinking or behavior. This may occur because of accidental, expressive, or rhetorical communication. On the other hand, when we "persuade" someone to alter her or his thinking or behavior, we do so with conscious intent. Thus, persuasion always involves rhetorical communication. Despite these differences, the two terms are frequently used interchangeably by mistake.

Rhetorical communication can take an expressive form. Often, we play on someone's emotions to stimulate a specific meaning in the mind of another person. We can do this by communicating sadness or pleasure, liking or love, or even anger or fear. Our intent is to make the other person feel that if we don't get what we want or need, our positive feelings will cease or our negative feelings will linger. Younger children are expert at communicating rhetorically in this fashion. When they get something—say, a new toy—that they desperately want, they can be as sweet as honey. However, if you deny them the new toy, they can throw a temper tantrum to end all tantrums. The "sweetness" expressed in the former case is, of course, the child's way of saying, "Thank you." The violent outburst in the latter case is the child's way (often, a successful one) of expressing her or his displeasure with our behavior.

Clarifying the Definition of Communication

Now that we have discussed accidental, expressive, and rhetorical types of communication as covered by our definition of human communication, we can consider the definition of communication in a bit more detail. We defined human communication as *the process by which one person(s) stimulates meaning in the mind of another person(s) through verbal and nonverbal messages*. In order for us to comprehend this definition fully, a few of its parts need some clarification. The word *process* suggests that interpersonal communication is dynamic and changing. Berlo (1960) suggests that communication is much like the river spoken of by the Greek philosopher Heraclitus. Heraclitus said that you can't step in the same river twice—from the moment you take your foot out of the water until you put it back in, the river changes so much that it really isn't the same river. As we change over time during our lives, our communication with others also changes; therefore, we can conclude that we can never communicate in the same way twice.

In our definition of communication, the words *stimulates meaning* convey that it is through communication with others that we develop, cultivate, share, expand, and reshape ideas. Rare is the occasion when we develop an idea completely on our own. The very thoughts that lead to an idea are the fruit of our experiences of reading various literatures, simply observing the world around us, and communicating verbally and nonverbally with others. By *verbal messages*, we mean language. Language, simply put, *is a system of symbols or codes that represent certain ideas or meanings*. The use of these symbols is regulated by a set of formal rules, which we call grammar and syntax. We transmit these messages either in spoken or in written form. *Nonverbal messages*, on the other hand, refer to *any messages other than verbal*. These messages include such things as tone of voice, eye movements, hand gestures, and facial expressions.

This examination of our definition accentuates the complexity of human communication. It is little wonder that so much intellectual and scholarly energy has been, and continues to be, expended in endeavors to learn more about this human phenomenon. The past five decades have witnessed many endeavors aimed at explaining the process of communication in pictorial or diagrammatical form. In the next section, we turn our attention to two diagrams or "models" of communication, each of which depicts a different view of the communication process. However, before we can discuss the rhetorical communication model and the interpersonal communication model, we need to examine the critical components of human communication.

CRITICAL COMPONENTS OF HUMAN COMMUNICATION

The Source

The source is the person who originates a message. In a broader view of communication, the source could be any individual or collection of individuals. Examples include one person (a man who wants a date with a woman), a dyad (a couple who wants another couple to come to dinner), a group (a city council that wants to explain to its constituents a new municipal tax), or even an organization (a national food chain that wants to explain to consumers why its food is better than its competitor's). Whether an organization, group, dyad, or individual, the source has three functions in communication: (1) to decide what specific meaning is to be communicated, (2) to encode that meaning into one or more messages, and (3) to transmit the message(s). In communication, it is typical that one individual does all three of these functions, but it is not uncommon to see each performed by a different person. Consider this example: Tom is having some problems in his relationship with his supervisor, Lisa. He has a specific idea and meaning to communicate to Lisa. He goes to his friend, Nicole, to ask advice on how best to state the message to Lisa. Then he goes to his and Lisa's mutual friend, Karla, to ask her to carry the message to Lisa.

When communicating, sources go through the *encoding process*. When it is our intent to stimulate a specific meaning in the mind of another, we attempt to convey that meaning by transmitting a message that we feel represents that meaning. Thus, borrowing directly from McCroskey and Wheeless (1976), encoding *"is the process of creating messages that we believe represent the meaning to be communicated and are likely to stimulate similar meaning in the mind of a receiver"* (p. 24; emphasis added). More simply, encoding involves translating ideas and information into messages. Encoding requires some degree of accuracy and precision in order for effective communication to take place. Inaccurate and imprecise encoding often can lead to accidental communication or, worse, total confusion. Therefore, it is very important that, as sources, we select messages that have similar meanings for us and our receiver.

The Receiver

The source in communication is the person who originates a message, and the receiver is the person who gets the source's message. Like the source, the receiver can be an individual, dyad, group, or organization. Also, like the source, the receiver has three functions in human communication. These are (1) receive the source's messages, (2) decode those messages into some meaning, and (3) respond to the messages. Again, it is typical in human communication for one person to do all three of these functions. However, it is not uncommon for more than one person to be involved. For example, Lisa could receive Tom's message, have Karla interpret it for her, and have yet another person, Don, respond to the message.

In a discussion of the receiver, the term *decoding* needs some explanation. Because meaning cannot be transmitted, neither can it be received. We must receive messages that are transmitted to us and assign meaning to them. Decoding, then, is the translation of a message into ideas or information. The meaning we assign to a given message depends to a great degree on previous messages we have received from the source and on our

The woman on the left is clearly the primary message sender.

previous experiences. Often, the meaning we get from or assign to a specific message may be nothing close to the meaning intended by the source. For communication to be effective, it is necessary for us as receivers to consider our background and experience compared with the background and experience of the source. This may require that we "put ourselves in the other person's shoes."

The Message

By now, you probably have developed a good idea of what a message is. To be on the safe side, though, we want to make another try at stimulating in your mind what we mean by *message*. We noted earlier that our major concern in communication is meaning, not messages. So what is the difference between a message and a meaning? Simply put, a message is any verbal or nonverbal stimulus that stimulates meaning in a receiver. Whatever it is that Tom wants to convey to Lisa, whether or not he uses other people in the process, he has to convey it through some message.

The easiest way to distinguish between verbal and nonverbal messages is to think of verbal messages as being composed of words. The nonverbal messages are anything else that can stimulate meaning. This oversimplifies the distinction a bit, but it makes a good starting point. The fact that verbal messages are composed of words tells us a great deal about them. We know by this characteristic that any given word has the potential for stimulating meaning in a receiver. We can even make up a word, like *chudnuk*, and assign some meaning to it, like "stupid person;" we can then share this word and its meaning with a friend. Later, both of us will know that when either of us uses the word *chudnuk*, we mean "stupid person." In essence, what the word *chudnuk* has become for us is a *code* for stupid person. We can now use that word, that code, together with other words to construct various messages aimed at eliciting certain meanings in our friend (for example, "That chudnuk couldn't walk and chew gum!"). We could not use chudnuk when talking with other people, however, because they would not know what we meant when we used the word because it would not be a *shared* code. We can only use shared language codes to communicate effectively. If two people know different languages—say, one knows English and the other knows Farsi—they will have difficulty communicating effectively because they do not have a *shared* language code.

Nonverbal messages are more difficult to characterize. All we know from the word *nonverbal* is that such messages are not verbal. This tells us what nonverbal messages are *not* but not what they *are*. Nonverbal messages are *any stimuli other than words that can potentially elicit meaning in the mind of a receiver*. As concrete examples, such behavior as winking, pointing with the index finger, fidgeting with a pencil, tugging at your hair, twiddling your thumbs, sighing, sticking out your tongue, wrinkling your nose, being late for class, and sitting with your right ankle resting on your left knee may stimulate meaning in the mind of an observer (a receiver) and thus are nonverbal messages. Some of these examples raise an important point: not all messages, particularly nonverbal messages, are consciously encoded. Very seldom do we intentionally, consciously sit at our desk fidgeting with our pencil; nevertheless, this behavior may be seen by someone else as a message, and it may communicate many things to that other person.

The Channels

Messages are not self-mobilizing; they are carried from the source to the receiver by one or more channels. A channel, then, is *the means by which a message is carried from one person to another*. Channels come in many forms. Apparently, any of our five senses can function as channels. In human communication, we typically think of sight and sound (or light waves and sound waves) as the most common channels of communication. There are many instances, however, when we send and receive messages through the channels of touch, smell, and taste. Moreover, in most of our face-to-face interactions, we use a combination of these channels. We hear each other's voices and see each other's movements. We also tend to touch each other at various times during our interaction. We may even take note of how pleasant (or unpleasant) each other smells. The messages conveyed over each of these channels gives us a much broader repertoire of stimuli to which we can assign meaning, which potentially allows us more understanding of the particular communication event.

Communication channels often occur in forms other than our physiological senses. In organizations, for example, supervisors function as channels for upper management by carrying management's messages to lower-line employees. There are mass-mediated channels, such as television, radio, film, and billboards, which carry messages from one or more sources to many receivers. On an interpersonal level, the postal system can be considered a channel through which written messages are carried. Electronic channels allow interpersonal communication via telephone, cell phone, fax machine, and computer. Even music and art function as channels for messages, often expressive ones, created by a source that can reach receivers centuries later or momentarily. To reiterate, a channel is *any* means by which a message gets from a source to a receiver.

Feedback

Feedback is a receiver's observable response to a source's message. Such responses may take the form of specific verbal messages, like "I don't agree with that, John." Even more commonly, however, feedback messages are nonverbal. A frown, a smile, the turning away of the receiver, crossed arms, or nervous fidgeting may all be taken as responses to the source's message. For the electronic media (radio and television particularly), in which there normally is a time lag for feedback to reach the source, the absence of such responses often is taken as the strongest feedback of all!

Feedback is very important in all communication. The source can carefully observe the receiver's responses to judge the success of the messages being sent. When feedback is negative, and is observed by the source, new messages can be formed in an attempt to improve the chances for successful communication. Truly, feedback in communication is the method we use to regulate the messages we send and those that are sent to us.

Goals

One component of communication, which we have referred to primarily in the realm of rhetorical communication, is goals. In our discussion of rhetorical communication, we noted that the source who communicates in this way does so with the intent of stimulating a specific meaning in the receiver—this is the source's goal. Generally, there are three major goals in interpersonal communication: *developing interpersonal relationships*, *gaining compliance*, and *gaining understanding*. We will first consider each of these goals individually and then discuss their interrelationship.

A fundamental goal of human communication is the development of relationships with others. Communication not only is essential to *relationship development* but also, some argue, *is* the relationship. In his book *Social Intercourse*, Knapp (1978) notes that communication contains the forces that "bring people together, keep people together, and divide and separate them" (p. vii). Most people have a very basic need to like and be liked by others. The fulfillment of this need is one reason we develop relationships. We also develop relationships out of our need for companionship, sharing, and love. Sometimes, we may feel we are not getting out of a relationship what we need from the relationship. Or we cannot put into the relationship what it requires, so we are motivated to end the relationship. Whether our goal is to develop and maintain a relationship or to end it, we must communicate to achieve that goal.

Another fundamental goal of communication is to gain the compliance of others. By *compliance gaining*, we simply mean getting another person (the receiver) to engage in some behavior that is wanted by the source. Our motivation to gain another person's compliance derives from our desire or need for changes in our environment, in the immediate situation, and in our relationships. For example, if it is your turn to wash the dishes at home but you have a very important test to study for, you may try to get your roommate to wash them. You will try to talk to your roommate so he or she will comply with your request. You could simply ask your roommate to wash the dishes, you could demand that he or she wash them, or you could offer your roommate something in return. Your only goal in this instance is to get your roommate's compliance in doing the task. To obtain her or his compliance, you must communicate in a way that fulfills your intentions and meets your goal.

A third fundamental goal of communication is to *gain understanding*. We all have a need to know and understand. To know and understand, we need information. To get information, we must engage in communication. Thus, our need to find information, so that we can know and understand something, may motivate us to communicate with others. If you are not reading this textbook only because you have to, you are probably reading it to gain some information about communication. Possibly, you hope that by having this information, you can get a better understanding of how and why people communicate with each other. We talk to other people to get information, clarify certain issues, expand our knowledge of events, and understand why the world operates as it does. Other people talk to us for the same reasons.

Although relationship development, compliance gaining, and gaining understanding are three separate goals of communication, it is a rare occurrence when they are achieved independently. In other words, to achieve one of these goals usually requires that the other two also be achieved. Relationship development is a good example. When we first meet someone, we often need or want to know how the other person is going to respond to us. Our desire for this knowledge may motivate us to communicate with the person. Berger and Calabrese (1975) have termed this process "uncertainty reduction." Our desire to know how another person will behave toward us in a given interaction creates a need for information. This need can only be met by communicating with that person. When we have gained that knowledge, we have reduced our uncertainty about that person and their actions. In this way, the goals of relationship development and gaining understanding function together in motivating us to communicate with the other person.

To maintain, or even to end, a relationship often requires compliance gaining. For example, in any relationship we are routinely faced with interpersonal differences, many of which can threaten the survival of the relationship. Perhaps the person is not spending as much time with us as we would like. Although our primary goal is to save the relationship, our secondary goal is to get them to spend more time with us. Our primary and secondary goals motivate us to communicate in a way that will gain the other person's compliance. Maybe the other person wants to end the relationship, but we do not. Their goal may be to get us to leave her or him alone; thus he or she spends less time with us, hoping that we will "get the message," which can be a very successful compliance-gaining tactic. You can think of other examples that illustrate the interconnections among relationship development, compliance gaining, and gaining understanding. It is nearly impossible to think of one occurring without the others. All three are potentially powerful motivators for communication. Our primary goal may be the achievement of only one of them, but the accomplishment of that goal virtually requires the achievement of the other two as well.

Context

We will conclude our discussion of the critical components of communication and focus on the "context" of communication. We use *context* to refer to the circumstances within which communication takes place. Context is an important concern in communication because we do not communicate in the same way with any two people in a given situation, or even with the same person in two different situations. Thus, even when we are communicating with a particular person, how and what we communicate are likely to change as the context in which we communicate changes.

Context centers on two important variables: *roles* and *rules*. That is, how and what we say to another person in a given situation or context depend on (1) the roles each of us take on in that situation, and (2) the rules that govern our interactions according to those roles. For example, we interact with classmates and instructors in the role of student, with certain friends in the role of boyfriend or girlfriend, with physicians in the role of patient, and with servers in the role of patron. Each of these different interactions involves a different communication context.

Not only do the different people and different locations of each interaction separate it from other contexts, but also each interaction is regulated by a unique set of rules. These rules are unique for a given context of interaction in that they are associated with our particular role within that context. Rules of this sort are not always of the "written on paper" variety. They are grounded in social and cultural norms. Some people maintain that how and what we express in any conversation are decided entirely by such rules. For example, when we are in the role of patient interacting with a physician, the "rules" say that we should communicate in a more formal and stylized manner than when we interact with a friend in the role of roommate. Thus, we might say that the function of roles and rules is to help us make predictions about how to behave in a given context. The roles and rules help us to reduce uncertainty about the other person and the situation, and coordinate the meaning of our messages with the meaning of the other person's messages.

We can get a clearer picture of how roles and rules affect interpersonal communication by considering five different contexts of communication in which we all have been or eventually will be involved. These are family, peers, school, work, and intimate relationships. Rather than treating each of these separately, we will look at their relation to each other compared with the roles and rules of interaction that each calls for in life.

In the family context, all of us take on the role of child, we usually take on the role of sibling, and many of us will someday take on the role of mother or father and husband or wife. Depending on which role we are in, our communication with other family members is governed by certain rules. Some rules are unique to individual families; others are common to most families in our culture. As children, we interact with siblings differently from the way we interact with parents, and with a sister differently from the way we interact with a brother. As parents, our interactions with our spouse will be quite different from our interactions with our children. We will probably interact differently with each child depending on her or his age, order of birth, individual needs, and personality.

Whatever our family roles, the rules of interaction will change when we talk with our peers. We can easily draw from our own experiences many examples of how our communication with friends differs from that with members of our family. Try to imagine what conversations are like between your mother and other mothers, or your father and other fathers. Perhaps you have overheard such conversations. They are vastly different from the conversations we are accustomed to having around the family dinner table. The difference may lie primarily in the change of roles and rules as we move from the family context to interacting with peers. We simply say and do things with our peers that we do not say and do with members of our family. Most of our communication in this context involves social matters and many interests that form the basis of our friendships.

The school context also requires that we take on roles that are different from our family roles. Many of our peer roles, however, may be most active in the school setting. When we are enrolled in the same class as a friend, we may interact with that person in the role of friend but with other members of the class in the role of student. As the roles change, so do the rules of interaction. Even in the classroom, communication with a friend may involve our mutual social interests. With another classmate, the interaction may center on only class-related topics. Our interaction with instructors is highly rule oriented. As the instructor enters the classroom, we tend to cease any ongoing interactions and focus our attention on that person. Communication in the classroom is typically quite ritualized and flows according to the instructor's individual teaching style. Even when we interact with an instructor one-on-one, we tend to avoid communicating on a "social" level.

Interactions on the job are similar to those in the school setting. We may have peers at work whom we consider to be good friends, and we communicate with them on a social level at work. With other coworkers, our interactions may depend entirely on our work roles and the rules associated with them, so that most of our communication with those people is task related. Moreover, organizational rules, and even some societal rules, dictate that we interact with coworkers differently than we interact with superiors, and with superiors differently than we interact with subordinates. Often, organizational rules and roles totally restrict us from interacting one-on-one with certain others in the organization. For example, although the president of your college or university may follow an "open-door policy" in her or his office, it may be highly unlikely that you could visit at any given time. Your role as an individual student is simply too far removed from the role of university president.

Finally, there is the intimate context. By the *intimate context*, we mean a context that is highly conducive to sharing with another person our private and confidential thoughts, feelings, and attitudes. We can much more easily conceive of such a context occurring in family and peer contexts than in school and work contexts. We often tell very private information about ourselves to certain family members and not to others, and discuss other confidential information with close friends outside our family. That is, we reserve intimate information about ourselves for those people we can trust and for those contexts in which trust is least likely to be violated. We also expect in an intimate context for the other person to share themselves with us and to have a mutual degree of trust in us. Our role in intimate contexts may be close friend, confidante, or lover.

We emphasize context to prove the fact that what and how we communicate with others are dependent on our roles in a given interaction and on the rules associated with these roles. Communication is a dynamic and change-oriented process. Much of this change is manifested in the vast differences in which we communicate across contexts and with various people. Although we have discussed only five contexts, there are many other contexts in which communication takes place (for example, the dating context, the religious context, the political context, and so on).

Culture is the largest, and often the most important, aspect of context. Imagine if in 2,000 years someone finds a book from today and reads the phrase "out in left field." What would he or she think? This simple phrase could have three distinct meanings depending on which context the phrase is placed. If a teacher says your essay was "out in left field," he or she is probably saying that it seemed odd or that it did not pertain to the topic. If someone playing baseball says, "Go stand out in left field," he or she means a specific geographical location in relation to the baseball diamond. Lastly, if a farmer says that she has some potatoes "out in left field," she is referring to a specific location on her property. It is amazing how even a simple four-word phrase can have three very distinct and different meanings depending on the cultural context in which the phrase is said.

It is very important that you understand the context in which this book is being written. We are writing from the position of the general culture of the United States. Therefore, many readers will need to adapt what is presented in the following chapters to the cultural context in which they live. The norms or rules in one culture may be very different from those of another culture. The constant is that all cultures have norms and rules. People learn the norms and rules of their culture informally by living within that culture. When one needs to talk with people from a different culture, it often is necessary to study that culture in a formal manner.

In this section, we have explained a variety of terms necessary for understanding human communication. In the next section, we are going to examine two distinct models of human communication: the rhetorical communication model and the interpersonal communication model.

MODELS OF COMMUNICATION

The Rhetorical Communication Model

The rhetorical communication model (McCroskey, 2006) centers its concern on intentional communication. This model (Figure 1.1) includes the source, message, channel, and receiver as essential elements in the process. The model distinguishes what occurs during communication from what occurs in the source before communication and in the receiver following communication.

A source, before communication, undertakes what is referred to in the model as the *investigation process*. Through this process, the source must conceive an idea, decide

FIGURE 1.1   Rhetorical Communication Model

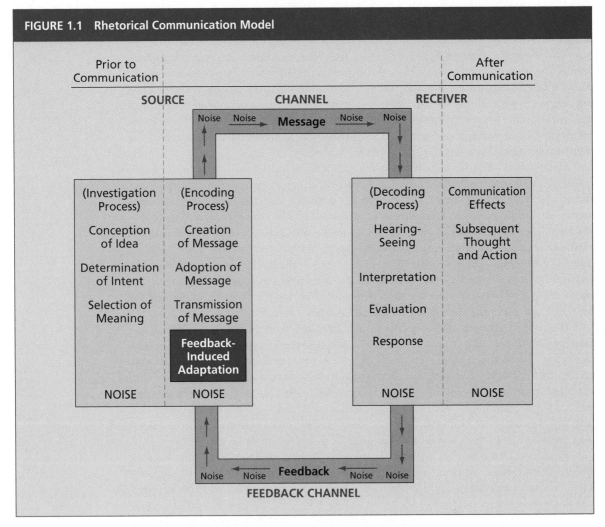

Source: McCroskey, J. C. (2006). *An introduction to rhetorical communication* (9th Ed.). Boston: Allyn & Bacon.

her or his intent, and select some meaning to be stimulated (intentionally) in the mind of the receiver. During the actual process of communicating, the source undertakes an "encoding" process. This process involves creating a message, adapting it to the receiver, and transmitting it across some source-selected channel. Also during the actual communication process, the receiver undertakes a "decoding" process. This entails sensing (for example, hearing or seeing) the source's message, interpreting the source's message, evaluating the source's message, and responding to the source's message. Feedback is the receiver's response to the source's message.

After communication, certain "communication effects" occur for the receiver. These effects are any thoughts or actions on the receiver's part that occur after communication with the source. If the subsequent thoughts and actions of the receiver are those the source wanted, then the source has succeeded in her or his intent: rhetorical communication has taken place.

Finally, this model includes noise. Noise is anything that prevents a receiver from accurately being able to interpret a message. Typically, researchers refer to two types of noise: internal and external. Internal noise is noise that occurs within an individual, and can also occur as two types: psychological and physiological. Psychological noise occurs when an individual's psychological state prevents her or him from being able to accurately attend to a message. For example, maybe a receiver was just dumped by her or his significant other, and is trying to have coffee with another friend. The receiver's mind may be trying to figure out why her or his significant other just terminated their relationship, and not on what her or his friend is trying to say over coffee. Physiological noise, on the other hand, is noise that occurs within an individual as a result of some biological process. For example, maybe it's noon and you're sitting in a lecture and you're stomach starts to growl because you haven't eaten all day. The hunger pains you're feeling may prevent you from focusing your attention on your teacher's sent messages. External noise, on the other hand, is noise that occurs outside of an individual. We are surrounded by thousands of messages (e.g., people talking loudly) and other auditory occurrences (e.g., a lawn mower outside your window) going on around us at all times. Often these other messages prevent us from focusing our attention on a sender's message. Note, however, that noise is not restricted to the channel. The model shows that noise can occur at any point during, and even before or after, the exchange of messages.

The rhetorical communication model considers many elements of the communication process. Specifically, by looking at what happens before, during, and after communication, this model includes such elements as encoding, decoding, and feedback. Based on this composite of elements, and particularly concerning the notion of feedback, this model shows *interaction* between the source and receiver. That is, the model illustrates that by communicating in a specified and intentional way, the source produces a certain response from the receiver.

The Interpersonal Communication Model

The basic model of interpersonal communication that we have chosen to consider was first presented by McCroskey, Larson, and Knapp (1971). Their model (Figure 1.2) depicts communication as it occurs between two people, and thus may be considered a *dyadic* model (as can the rhetorical model of communication). A most important

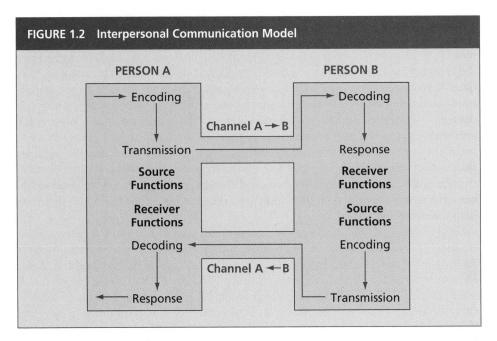

FIGURE 1.2   Interpersonal Communication Model

Source: McCroskey, J. C. (2006). *An introduction to rhetorical communication* (9th Ed.). Boston: Allyn & Bacon.

feature of this model is its treatment of the two people as both source and receiver. Also included in the model are the components of encoding, transmission, channel, decoding, and (although not labeled as such) occurrences before and after communication.

We can begin an analysis of this model by starting when Person A forms an idea. Person A encodes this idea into a message and transmits it across channel A → B to Person B, who is serving as a receiver. Person B decodes the message and emits a response, which contributes to subsequent idea formation in Person B. The process of idea formation in Person B may cause this person to function as a source, at which point he or she encodes a message and transmits it across channel A ← B to Person A. Now, Person A begins to serve as a receiver by decoding the message from Person B and emitting a response to the source's message. This response may effect Person A's idea formation, at which point he or she may again begin to serve as a source.

The process depicted by this model is essentially a perpetual and cyclical one. In this sense, communication is truly a process that is susceptible to change at any given point. Moreover, to the extent that each person can serve simultaneously as both source and receiver, we may say that this model depicts communication as a *transaction* between two people. Time and proximity play important roles in the interpersonal communication model. If Person A and Person B are separated by 2,000 miles and several time zones, Person B may encode and transmit (via e-mail) a lengthy message to Person A. In such a situation, of course, any response from Person A to Person B is delayed by time and distance. In a face-to-face encounter, however, the roles of source and receiver shift more rapidly. The same can be said for communicators who are separated by great distances but are electronically connected via telephone, Internet chat rooms, or text messaging. Any message from one person can be responded to almost immediately by the other person. Any message that is received by either person may alter any subsequently transmitted messages. In Figure 1.2, the communication from Person B, as source, to Person A, as receiver, may be considered the feedback component that is depicted in the rhetorical communication model. Feedback is really irrelevant here given that in human communication, the person who starts out as receiver is unlikely to remain only a receiver in the communication transaction because at some point he or she will become a source.

Examination of the interpersonal and rhetorical models has pointed out several basic concepts inherent in human communication. Although most of these ideas have been mentioned in our discussion to this point, we will treat each aspect of the models individually by focusing on its role in the human communication process.

THINKING ABOUT COMMUNICATION

Any time you take a course in a new subject area (chemistry, art, music, creative writing, etc.), you enter the course with certain ideas about the subject. As the course progresses, you realize that many of your earlier conceptions were inaccurate. Similarly, you are likely to discover that you have many misconceptions of human communication. Thinking straight about communication is the most important communication skill a person can develop. Unfortunately, most people in contemporary society have been taught some very fuzzy thinking about communication. People reading their first book or taking their first course in communication often bring this fuzzy thinking to those tasks. The rest of this chapter will be directed to clearing up some very common misconceptions about communication. But first, let's see how accurate your current perceptions of human communication are. Please take a second and take the following Communication Inventory seen in Figure 1.3.

TEN COMMON MISCONCEPTIONS

1. Meanings Are in Words

The idea that meanings are in words is perhaps the most common misconception about communication.[1] The most important and vexing problem with this misconception is that it can lead to much misunderstanding between two people and thwart the effectiveness of communication. What a particular word means to us may not be what it means to someone else. The word stimulates a meaning in our mind that is different from the meaning it stimulates in the mind of our receiver. Many examples of this derive from the jargon used in various industries and academic disciplines. Thus, *communication* means one thing in the telecommunications industry and something much different in the social sciences. Even the word *science* has different meanings for people in different fields, which is exemplified by what it means to physical scientists as compared to social

---

FIGURE 1.3   Communication Inventory

Directions: The following is a short quiz evaluating your knowledge about human communication. Please answer each of the following questions true or false.

_____ 1. Words have meanings.

_____ 2. Communication is a verbal process.

_____ 3. Telling is communicating.

_____ 4. Communication will solve all of our problems.

_____ 5. Communication is a good thing.

_____ 6. The more people communicate, the better.

_____ 7. Communication can break down.

_____ 8. Communication is a natural ability.

_____ 9. Interpersonal communication = intimate communication.

_____ 10. Communication competence = communication effectiveness.

Scoring: To determine your score, complete the following steps.

Step 1. For each answer your marked true, give yourself one point.

Step 2. Subtract your total number of true answers from the number 10.

Step 3. Each answer you marked true is an incorrect perception of human communication.

---

scientists and behavioral scientists. Even within the field of human communication, researchers and scholars often have different meanings for some ideas.

The point we wish to make about words and their meaning is that *no word has meaning apart from the person using it.* Because of the way we are educated about words from early in life, we fail to understand that words are merely codes or symbols for meanings we have in mind. The meanings we have for words are the products of our culture, ethnic group, social class, and experiences. Thus, no two people share precisely the same meanings for all words, because no two people share the same background and experiences. *Meanings are in people, not in words.* For effective communication to occur, we must realize that what we say to others may not stimulate in their minds the meaning we want or intend to be stimulated. This requires us to adapt our ideas to the background and experiences of our receivers so that they can adapt to our ideas. When we can successfully make these adaptations, we are more likely to create shared meanings for words (and also for nonverbal symbols and actions). As our definition of communication implies, shared meaning is what communication is all about.

2. Communication Is a Verbal Process

When people think about communication, they typically think about words, either written or spoken. Our focus on communication as a verbal process is due in large part to our educational experience. From preschool education up through college, much attention is paid to verbal learning and language usage. Many children's television shows, like *Sesame Street*, *Blue's Clues*, and *Bear in the Big Blue House*, emphasize the learning of words and language, and often these programs allude to the importance of words for communication. However, despite what formal and informal educational systems have taught and continue to teach us about words (and what they teach is correct in many respects), communication is *more* than a verbal process because it is also a nonverbal process. We may go as far as to say that most of our communicative behavior is nonverbal in nature. This is particularly true of oral communication in interpersonal contexts. In fact, neurologically, infants develop the ability to understand nonverbal messages earlier than they can understand verbal messages.

What we say or write (the verbal message) is important to communication. How we say it and the nonverbal context in which we say it are of equal and often greater importance. Recall the discussion of expressive communication and the content and relational levels of communication. It is our nonverbal behavior that comprises much of our expressive communication and the relational aspects of our messages. To a very large extent, our nonverbal behavior is *the* determining factor in whether the words we use convey the meanings we want them to. Thus, *the process of communication is both verbal and nonverbal*.

3. Telling Is Communicating

Many people believe that simply saying something is communicating it. This is an unfortunate misconception because it is the basis for much conflict and misunderstanding. Communicating with someone involves far more than only telling. As our model of interpersonal communication illustrates, encoding a message and sending it (telling or saying something) are merely the beginning of the communication process. People have the "telling is communication" misconception because they fail to acknowledge the active role played by the receiver in communication. Again, meaning is the crucial variable. Telling does not consider that a message's meaning is determined by the receiver's own background and experiences. In writing this book, for example, the authors realized that you probably have little technical knowledge about human communication theory. However, you have had much practical experience in actual communication. Therefore, we had to encode and structure the information to be communicated (the content of this book) to the background and experiences of its intended receivers (college and university undergraduates). This was done so that the information is relatively basic and both practical and applicable to our receivers. Had we attempted to achieve the goal by simply telling (writing) you what communication is and how it functions without considering your probable knowledge and experience in communication, the book would be difficult to read, at best.

4. Communication Will Solve All Our Problems

At one time or another, each of us has been told that to solve our interpersonal problems, all we need to do is communicate. Periodically, delegates from Israel meet with delegates from Palestine along with U.S. government officials, with the idea that "if we can only sit and talk with each other, we can iron out our differences." Similarly, so-called management communication consultants sometimes give business managers and executives the idea that if they would only open lines of communication with subordinates, production and profits would automatically increase steadily. Whether our problems are interpersonal, international, or organizational, it is a misconception that those problems can be solved by communication alone. The basis for this misconception is that many of us believe that *whether* communication occurs is more important than *what* is communicated.

Obviously, the occurrence of communication is essential to any of our problem-solving efforts. Yet often communication itself is the spark and fuel that ignited many of our problems. For example, presume you suggest to a friend that he or she should change hairstyles. Your motive for making that suggestion may be purely for your friend's own good. However, communicating that suggestion could easily be the source of much interpersonal conflict. Although communication does occur in this instance, and although its intention is positive, *what* is communicated can be misconstrued by your friend as a "cheap shot." By the same token, whenever two people, groups, or even countries have irreconcilable differences, any communication between the two parties may serve only as a catalyst to bring these differences to the surface. This may result in more problems than were there at the start. Furthermore, communication may emphasize some insignificant differences between two parties, the recognition of which may present more serious problems. Thus, effective communication may allow us to solve some problems, but it cannot be expected to solve all problems. Ineffective communication may create more problems, or make already present problems worse than if no communication were attempted at all. *Communication can either create or help solve problems.*

5. Communication Is a Good Thing

Ask any politician, community leader, or school administrator, and chances are they will tell you that communication is a good thing. This misconception is ominously pervasive in our society. It probably stems from another misconception about communication, particularly that communication will solve all our problems. As we have already noted, however, it will not solve all our problems. Moreover, communication is neither a good thing nor a bad thing. *Communication is a tool*. Like any tool, communication can be used for good or bad purposes. Take a chalkboard eraser, for instance. If we use this tool for its intended purpose—to clean chalkboards—we can say that it is a very useful device. However, put that same eraser in the hand of an irate teacher so that he or she can throw it at a student, and most will agree the eraser has become a bad thing. Has it? Not really. It is simply being used in a bad way. Similarly, communication can be misused, and even abused, so that it appears bad.

If a teacher were to ask a failing student to visit the office to discuss the student's academic plight, one of two things could happen. The teacher could openly and sympathetically point out that the student needs to focus attention to improve her or his grades. If this meeting (which would probably be more complex and involved than depicted here) were to result in marked improvement on the student's part, we could say there was good communication between teacher and student. More appropriately, we should say that the student and teacher used their communication with one another well. Conversely, if during their meeting the teacher were to degrade and chastise the student for doing so poorly, it is likely that the student would do no better, and maybe do worse. Then we might say that there was bad communication between teacher and student. More appropriately, we would say that the teacher misused her or his communication with the student so that the results were bad. Therefore, *communication is neither good nor bad; it is a tool* we can use to help us solve our problems and to get along better with others.

6. The More Communication, the Better

A common stereotype concerning the value of communication in American society leads to the fact that the more a person talks (up to a point), the more positively that person will be viewed by others. The talkative person is perceived to be more competent, more friendly, more attractive, more powerful, and a better leader than the less talkative person. This is a fact that has been confirmed repeatedly by many laboratory and "real-world" research studies. In our society, it seems, the people who talk a lot are seen as the better people. Nevertheless, it is a misconception that the more communication, the better.

The problem arises in that people tend to equate quantity (more) with quality (better). Although more may be better in many of life's endeavors, such as in making money and scoring points on tests, there are many instances in which more is worse. One instance is golf; the more shots you take, the worse your score. In golf, it is the quality of your shot that counts. Thus, the better you shoot, the fewer shots you have to take and the *lower* (or better) your score. In many ways, communication is like the game of golf. Often, it is not how much we say or for how long we say it, but the quality of what we say that counts. Often, it is not *how much* people communicate but *what* they communicate that is essential. In communication, *quality is more important than quantity*.

7. Communication Can Break Down

Perhaps the most socially prevalent misconception about communication is that it can "break down." We consistently hear the phrase *communication breakdown* whenever people feel a need to place blame for their poor communication. Blaming our failures on communication breakdowns is a copout. Communication *cannot* break down. People can be ineffective and poor communicators, but their communication will not break down. Machine communications (like telephones) may break down, but human communication does not.

When people refer to communication breakdowns, they are usually implying that communication is unsuccessful and has been stopped. However, in many such situations communication has been highly successful. Each party involved may have developed an excellent understanding of how the other person thinks and feels. The parties just don't agree. In other situations, the breakdown refers to circumstances when communication was attempted but really was a failure. In either instance, the people involved may stop talking to one another. This does not mean that communication has stopped (much less "broken down"). The absence of talk often communicates more than talking itself. In a very real sense, *one cannot not communicate.* The double negative is intentional because it illustrates a very important idea about communication. The absence of verbal communication only emphasizes the importance of nonverbal communication. Remember, communication is both a verbal and a nonverbal process.

8. Communication Is a Natural Ability

Very few basketball coaches will state a person is born with the ability to be an effective outside field goal shooter. Shooting field goals from anywhere on the basketball court, let alone from beyond fifteen feet, is a learned ability. We are born with the *capability* (the potential) to become an effective field goal shooter. However, the *ability* to become one is learned through years of observation, coaching, and, as the saying goes, "practice, practice, practice."

Communication, like shooting a basketball, is not a *natural* ability; it is a *learned* ability. Barring any pre- or postnatal maladies, we all are born with the capability to become effective communicators. We are born with the senses necessary to transmit and receive messages. As we mature and develop, we can expand our mental and physical capacities to decode and encode various interpersonal and environmental messages. This process is one of acquiring the intellectual, psychological, emotional, and physical skills that allow us to communicate with others. It is the process of shaping our natural communicative capabilities into learned communication abilities.

The misconception that communication is a natural ability is attributable in some part to educational and governmental entities. For most of the twentieth century and all of this century, the three Rs have been recognized as basic skills that every child needs to learn. Hardly anyone will argue that reading, writing, and arithmetic are *natural* abilities! Only in the last decade or so have speaking and listening been recognized as essential basic skills to be included among the three Rs. We note that, although it may be obvious to most of us (it isn't to some educational and governmental leaders), reading, writing, and even arithmetic are communication skills. Recognizing them as such, and including speaking and listening along with them, will enable our schools to better prepare children *and* adults to become more effective communicators. Most children are born with the capacity to learn these skills. Careful instruction, personal observation and experience, and "practice, practice, practice" are required for a child to develop much ability in any one of them. The fact that many of us may be lacking in our communication abilities is thus more a result of previous educational (and perhaps interpersonal) inexperience in these areas than of some innate limitation. One purpose of this text is to help you overcome any deficit you may have in communication skills. The most important communication skills are those relating to analysis and understanding of how communication works and the determination of appropriate behavior for a given communication context.

9. Interpersonal Communication = Intimate Communication

A common idea is that interpersonal communication and intimate communication are the same, so whenever we communicate interpersonally we communicate intimately. This, of course, is not the case. Obviously, not all interpersonal communication is intimate. When we ask the service station attendant (if we can find one!) to "fill it up" or ask the telephone operator for a particular phone number, we are communicating with those people interpersonally but not intimately. Most of our daily communication with others is of an interpersonal nature, and little of it is truly intimate. On the other hand, whenever we communicate intimately with someone, we are communicating interpersonally. The idea we wish to express here is that *some* interpersonal communication is intimate, but most is not. The difference lies at what level of communication we engage in with another person. It is important, therefore, that we distinguish among the various *levels of communication*.

We can communicate with others at a cultural, a sociological, or a psychological level. When we communicate with others at a *cultural* level, we adapt our message sending and receiving processes to predictions we make based on the culture to which they belong. When we are introduced to someone from a foreign country and begin to get acquainted with that person, much of our communication is at first based on what we know (or what we *think* we know) about people from that individual's own nation. We can predict with some certainty that if the person is from the Middle East, he or she most likely has religious (Islamic) and political beliefs that are different from our own. We can also state that this person's beliefs are probably very different from those of someone from Argentina, South America, whose beliefs we can predict are also unlike our own.

In our American culture, we share many common beliefs, values, and characteristics that are unique to us. This shared identity allows us to communicate among ourselves as a cultural entity, and it helps to distinguish us from other cultures. We can talk, write, and sing about Old Glory, baseball, and apple pie so that they stir our emotions and patriotism; the same words simply will not have the same effect on citizens of New Guinea. This process also operates within co-cultures surrounded by the larger American culture. These co-cultures (cultural groups not necessarily below or suppressed by the larger culture, but existing inside of a larger culture) arise from such diverse areas of the country as Appalachia, a Sioux reservation, the Louisiana Bayou, and the beaches of southern California. Individuals from each of these subcultures share common beliefs and values. These are different from those of other co-cultures, and this sets them apart as unique even within the American culture. Effective communication on the cultural level requires that we make accurate predictions of commonalities among persons in these cultures. We should attempt to adapt our encoding and decoding processes to these predictions. When we are communicating at this level, we usually are operating with cultural stereotypes, a very dangerous basis on which to attempt to communicate. Nevertheless, in the initial stages of many communicative relationships, this is the only level open to us.

At the *sociological* level of communication, the predictions we make about other persons, which we use to make our encoding and decoding decisions, are based on our perceptions of the sociological subgroups to which people belong. At this level, our concern is with the various social institutions that comprise a society. Some of these are professions, occupations, political associations, religious affiliations, sororities, fraternities, and even more discrete roles like students, professors, children, and parents. When we talk with others at the social level, we communicate with them according to their roles in society. The predictions we make at this level about people are based on commonalities they share with others who act or function in the same societal role. Although we are still operating with stereotypes, these stereotypes are less likely to cause us serious problems than those based on culture alone. We communicate with one teacher, one police officer, or one doctor in pretty much the same way we would communicate with any other teacher, police officer, or doctor. We expect bank tellers to behave in certain ways, ministers to hold specific values, and politicians to have particular beliefs; we say things to each of these types of people and interpret their messages according to their respective roles. Obviously, we may communicate differently with different people who function in the same role. However, effective communication at the social level requires that we make accurate predictions of commonalities among persons in the same societal roles. We adapt our message-sending and -receiving processes to those predictions.

When we communicate with others at the *psychological* level, our communication is adapted to the unique characteristics of each person. It is only at this level that we move beyond primitive stereotypes. Our predictions about a person's beliefs, values, and behavior transcend cultural and social expectations and derive from the person's unique psychological, emotional, and personality traits. To communicate with someone at this level requires that we know the person as an individual. Effective communication at the psychological level requires that we adapt our messages to the individual and interpret that individual's messages based on her or his uniqueness. Although we have two good friends, both of whom are American students at the same school, our communication with each friend at the psychological level will be adapted to each one as a unique individual, despite their affiliations and national origin. It is at this level, and this level only, that intimate communication occurs. Intimate communication involves *knowing* each other through *revealing* to each other private and personal information about ourselves. However, note that reaching the psychological level is often possible only after we have recognized and shared with each other our cultural and social commonalities. For this reason, not all interpersonal communication is intimate. Intimate communication comes about only after we have shared through other levels of interpersonal communication our broader and more basic common characteristics, beliefs, attitudes, and values, which is why most of us communicate intimately with very, very few people.

10. Communication Competence = Communication Effectiveness

We use the term *effectiveness* several times in this chapter.[2] Many people may speak, write, hear, and/or read the word *effectiveness* with little thought given to what it may mean. That is, *effectiveness* is one of those words people take for granted, and for which they believe that everyone has pretty much the same meaning. Like most words, effectiveness means different things to different people. This variety of meanings manifests itself in another misconception about communication, namely, that communication competence is the same as communication effectiveness. We want to dispel this myth.

Larson, Backlund, Redmond, and Barbour (1978) define communication competence as "the ability of an individual to demonstrate knowledge of the appropriate communicative behavior in a given situation" (p. 16). Other definitions have been offered

(Wiemann, 1977; Allen & Brown, 1976), but we favor this definition because it is more useful than others. Its superior usefulness will, we hope, become apparent in the following discussion. Wiemann's (1977) definition of communication competence stresses that the competent communicator is one who has the ability to successfully accomplish her or his communicative goals (p. 198). It is our opinion that successful accomplishment of one's goal is "effectiveness." Thus, effective communicators are those who can stimulate in the mind of another person a meaning they intend to or want to stimulate. If the receiver gets a different meaning from that intended by the source, we can say that the source has ineffectively communicated but he or she *still has communicated*. The distinction between effectiveness and competence is that a communicator may be effective without being competent (they get lucky, so to speak). Or he or she may be competent without being effective (even the best shot misses now and then). Besides the definition of Larson and colleagues (1978), just what do we mean by communication competence? An example may help clarify the matter.

Imagine two hopelessly *incompetent* communicators who purchase a bucket of fried chicken at a fast-food restaurant. After a few minutes of munching, the two find that the bucket has one piece of chicken left. Both individuals want the last piece. Words are exchanged; one person gets the piece of chicken, and the other person does not. We could now characterize the one who got the last piece of chicken as competent—he or she was "effective." Now imagine the same situation, only this time involving two extremely *competent* communicators. There is one piece of chicken in the bucket, and both individuals want it. They talk for a moment. One gets the piece of chicken, and the other does not. We could now characterize the person who missed getting the last piece of chicken as incompetent—he or she was "ineffective."

In the former situation, both individuals are incompetent communicators. We can, however, label the one who got the last piece of chicken as now being competent. He or she *displayed* knowledge of the communicative behavior *appropriate* for that given situation. This individual's knowledge was shown by the person's effectiveness in getting the last piece of chicken—the goal. The appropriate behavior was whatever the individual said or did that enabled her or him to get the chicken. In the latter situation, both individuals are very competent communicators. However, we can label the one who did not get the last piece of chicken as now being incompetent. He or she failed to display knowledge of the communicative behavior appropriate for that situation. This person's failure to get the piece of chicken (the goal) suggests ineffectiveness. The individual did not know how to communicate effectively her or his desire for the piece of chicken, thus becoming incompetent in that situation.

The point made here is that communication effectiveness is neither a necessary nor sufficient condition for communication competence. Just as a very incompetent communicator may be effective in a given situation, an extremely competent communicator may be ineffective in a given situation. It's a condition, again, much like golf. Even the most competent golfer can be ineffective on a given day at a given course. Oddly enough, it often happens that the most profoundly incompetent golfer is the one who makes the hole in one on the 200-yard fairway. In communication, just as in sports, communication competence does not equal communication effectiveness. *Competence has to do with understanding the way communication works. Effectiveness has to do with communicating successfully*.

KEY TERMS

accidental communication 4
channel 10
codes 8
communication 3
communications 3
compliance gaining 12
context 13
cultural level 25
decoding 9
decoding process 17
encoding 8
encoding process 8

expressive communication 5
external noise 17
feedback 11
gain understanding 12
internal noise 17
investigation process 16
language 8
message 10
noise 17
nonverbal messages 7
norms 13
persuasion 7

physiological noise 17
psychological noise 17
psychological level 26
receiver 9
relationship development 12
rhetorical communication 6
roles 13
rules 13
sociological level 25
source 8
uncertainty reduction 12
verbal messages 7

 REFERENCES

Allen, R. R., & Brown, K. L. (1976). *Developing communication competence in children*. Skokie, IL: National Textbook Company.

Berger, C. R., & Calabrese, R. J. (1975). Some explorations in initial interaction and beyond: Toward a developmental theory of interpersonal communication. *Human Communication Research, 1*, 99–112.

Berlo, D. K. (1960). *The process of communication*. New York: Holt, Rinehart & Winston.

Hall, E. T. (1959). *The silent language*. Greenwich, CT: Fawcett.

Knapp, M. L. (1978). *Social intercourse: From greeting to goodbye*. Boston: Allyn & Bacon.

Larson, C. E., Backlund, P. M., Redmond, M. K., & Barbour, A. (1978). *Assessing communicative competence*. Falls Church, VA: Speech Communication Association and ERIC.

McCroskey, J. C. (1982a). Communication competence and performance: A research and pedagogical perspective. *Communication Education, 31*, 1–8.

McCroskey, J. C. (1982b). *An introduction to rhetorical communication* (4th ed.). Englewood Cliffs, NJ: Prentice-Hall.

McCroskey, J. C. (2006). *An introduction to rhetorical communication* (9th ed.). Boston: Allyn & Bacon.

McCroskey, J. C., Larson, C. E., & Knapp, M. L. (1971). *An introduction to interpersonal communication*. Englewood Cliffs, NJ: Prentice-Hall.

McCroskey, J. C., & Wheeless, L. R. (1976). *Introduction to human communication*. Boston: Allyn & Bacon.

Watzlawick, P., Beavin, J., & Jackson, D. D. (1967). *Pragmatics of human communication*. New York: W. W. Norton.

Wiemann, J. M. (1977). Explication and test of a model of communication competence. *Human Communication Research, 3*, 195–213.

 DISCUSSION QUESTIONS

1. How would you describe the rhetorical situation of a campaign speech during a presidential election?

2. Describe a time when you were affected by internal or external noise, which prevented you from listening to a source's message.

3. Why do you think it's important for people to reduce uncertainty when they meet a new person?

4. Is it true that you cannot *not* communicate?

5. Describe a time when someone "told" you something, but you clearly did not receive the message.

NOTES

1. Many ideas in this section are based on similar ideas presented in J. C. McCroskey and L. R. Wheeless, *Introduction to Human Communication* (Boston: Allyn & Bacon, 1976), 3–10; and in J. C. McCroskey, *An Introduction to Rhetorical Communication*, 4th ed. (Englewood Cliffs, N.J.: Prentice-Hall, 1982), 17–21.

2. Much of the material in this section is taken from the discussion presented in J. C. McCroskey, "Communication Competence and Performance: A Research and Pedagogical Perspective," *Communication Education* 31 (1982):1–8.

2

Interpersonal Perceptions and Realities

OBJECTIVES

- Understand why receiver perceptions influence human communication.

- Be able to explain the three factors of source credibility.

- Identify and explain the three types of attraction.

- Explain the three types of homophily, and know what is meant by the *principle of homophily*.

- Explain how a source's extraversion may affect a receiver.

- Explain how a source's neuroticism may affect a receiver.

- Explain how a source's psychoticism may affect a receiver.

- Be able to differentiate between temperament and personality.

- Explain the two important features that help clarify what personality is.

- Understand the four different ways that personality characteristics can be exhibited by specific individuals.

- Understand the role of human biology in human communication.

- Explain the following personality traits: adventurousness, authoritarianism, dogmatism, emotional maturity, general anxiety, locus of control, Machiavellianism, self-control, self-esteem, tolerance for ambiguity, argumentativeness, verbal aggression, and exhilaratability.

Receivers' perceptions of sources are critically important in the human communication process. The reason is this: *messages are interpreted through their perceived source.* Perceptions of the source, therefore, determine perceptions of the message. For example, take the message "I love you." Would this message be perceived any differently if it were stated by your mother rather than by your lover? Would it make a difference if the message were sent by a stranger as opposed to a close friend, or if it were sent by a same-sex friend as opposed to an opposite-sex friend? Consider the statement "Eating broccoli is very dangerous to your health." What would you think if a friend of yours said this to you? A stranger? The surgeon general of the United States? Chances are that you would perceive and interpret the same message differently for each person who sends the message. This is because we perceive a message according to the way we perceive its source. If you know your friend hates broccoli, you might interpret the statement as a humorous one. If you like broccoli, you may reject the stranger's view because you may doubt he or she has any expertise on that subject. If the surgeon general says it, however, you might be hesitant to eat broccoli in the future.

No message is interpreted by a receiver apart from its source. The source–message relationship is so strong it has been found that receivers will create a source in their minds if the real source is unknown (McCroskey & Dunham, 1966). There is an inherent realization in people that to understand and evaluate a message, we need to know who the source of the message is. Almost 2,500 years ago, the great philosophers and rhetoricians of the day were well aware that the image or *ethos* of a speaker has a major influence on the impact of the speaker's message. Aristotle, Cicero, Plato, and Quintilian all stressed this source–message relationship in their speaking and writing.

People will grasp at almost anything to create the needed image of the unknown source. It has been found, for example, that when an unknown source is introduced by someone we know, we transfer much of the introducer's image to that unknown person. This has been called the "sponsorship effect" (Holtzman, 1966; McCroskey & Dunham, 1966). One place where use of this sponsorship effect is most obvious is in political campaigns, where unknown candidates make sure to have prominent local people introduce them to the audience. On the everyday level, most of us have asked someone, or been asked by someone, to introduce us to someone we would like to know. We intuitively recognize that the introducer's "sponsorship" will create a positive initial image. This is also why we ask important and/or well-respected people to write letters of recommendation for us.

In this chapter, we are going to explore how receiver perceptions of sources impact the communication process. First, we are going to look at a variety of perceptions a receiver may have about a source. Second, we will discuss the nature of personality and temperament in human communication, which will be followed by a discussion of the role of biology in human communication. Lastly, we will examine a number of personality variables that impact human communication.

▣ PERCEIVING SOURCES

The "image of the source" or "attitude toward the source" is a product of interpersonal perceptions. Three main categories of interpersonal perceptions have occupied the attention of communication scholars. These are source credibility, interpersonal attraction, and homophily (similarity). Other types of interpersonal perceptions that influence communication, but do not fit within the three main categories, will also be considered. For most of these types of interpersonal perceptions, we will give you an example of an instrument that researchers have used to measure that perception. These should help you see how this applies in your everyday life.

Source Credibility

The effects of credibility have received more research interest than any other interpersonal perception variable. Credibility refers to how *believable* we perceive a source to be. It is a multidimensional construct, meaning that there are different dimensions or ways in which credibility is perceived by a receiver. The three dimensions of source credibility are competence, trustworthiness, and caring/goodwill (McCroskey, 1966;

Physical attraction is extremely important in initial interactions.

McCroskey & Teven, 1999). An example of an instrument used to measure these perceptions is presented in Scales 1–3 in the appendix. The initial measure was developed by McCroskey (1966) to measure competence and trustworthiness. Caring/goodwill was added by McCroskey and Teven (1999).

Competence (Scale 1).   This dimension of credibility refers to the degree to which a source is perceived to be knowledgeable or expert in a given subject. This perception exists along a continuum ranging from completely incompetent to extremely competent. The perception is mediated, however, by how competent receivers perceive themselves to be. On a scale of 6 to 42, if Lisa perceived Linda's competence in matters related to automobiles to be 38, and her own competence to be 24, then Linda is probably quite competent in Lisa's mind. On the other hand, if Lisa perceives her own competence to be 24, and that of Linda to be 18, then in Lisa's mind Linda is probably not very competent.

Our perception of a source's competence has an impact on our response to that source. If we perceive sources to be more competent than we are, we are likely to accept their opinions and to follow their advice. Of course, if we perceive a source to be less competent than ourselves on a subject, our opinions on the subject are unlikely to be influenced by that source. Competence is usually the first judgment we make about a source's credibility. An equally important judgment follows—our perceptions of the source's trustworthiness.

Trustworthiness (Scale 2).   We may perceive a source to be competent on a subject. However, if we feel that we cannot trust that person to be honest about what he or she knows, we are likely to perceive that person as having little credibility. For example, you may perceive an automobile salesperson to be very knowledgeable (a 42 on our scale) with regard to a particular car. If, however, you believe that salesperson to be dishonest and untrustworthy in dealing with you, the salesperson probably has low credibility in your mind.

Perceptions of trustworthiness exist along a continuum similar to that of competence; our judgments of a source range from being completely untrustworthy to totally trustworthy. This perception, however, is not mediated by our perception of our own trustworthiness. That is, how trustworthy we perceive ourselves to be likely has little impact on how trustworthy we perceive a source to be. Even a person who is totally dishonest will assign very little credibility to a source perceived to be dishonest also. Perceptions of a source's character are important in communication, for we discount the validity and honesty of messages from a source we perceive to be untrustworthy. Moreover, we find little motivation to communicate with a source we perceive as untrustworthy because we cannot predict whether the person will be cooperative and straightforward with us. This occurs even when we perceive the source to be competent in a subject.

Caring/Goodwill (Scale 3).   The final component of credibility, goodwill, is defined as the perceived caring that a receiver sees in a source. If a receiver does not believe that a source has the best intentions in mind for the receiver, the receiver will not see the source as credible. Simply put, we are going to listen to people whom we think truly care for us and are looking out for our welfare. At the same time, if we suspect that someone may be trying to pull a fast one on us, we're going to be a lot more skeptical of anything he or she says. This does not mean that the opposite of caring is someone wanting to kill us (although that would certainly make us believe they do not have our best interests at heart!), but rather the source may just appear indifferent toward us, which makes us hesitant to believe her or him. With someone who is indifferent, it is a lot more difficult to determine her or his true intent. Ultimately, when a sender demonstrates that he or she cares about her or his receiver, it opens the path for better communication through understanding, empathy, and responsiveness.

Perceptions of source credibility are critical in the human communication process. If we perceive a source as having low credibility, we are likely to misperceive the messages (from the source's vantage point) that the person gives us. The messages may "sound good," but because we question the source's credibility we also question the validity of the messages. Furthermore, we are less likely to expose ourselves to, learn from, or be influenced by a source who is not credible than by a source who is credible.

Credibility perceptions are but one set of perceptions that influence our responses to and attitudes about a source. Another equally important set of perceptions relates to the source's attractiveness.

Interpersonal Attraction

When people first think of interpersonal attractiveness, they usually think of physical attractiveness. However, physical attractiveness is not the only form of attraction that affects our reactions to another person. Like credibility, attraction is a multidimensional construct. Besides physical attractiveness, we also judge sources on their social attractiveness and task attractiveness. Instruments designed to measure each of these three dimensions of perceived interpersonal attractiveness are provided in Scales 4–6 in the appendix. These measures were developed by L. McCroskey, J. McCroskey, and Richmond (2005).

Physical Attractiveness (Scale 4). A person's physical attractiveness is a perception—a perception that may not be shared by two people with different backgrounds or experiences, or who come from different cultures. This is why one person can think someone is very handsome or pretty and a second person thinks that same person is quite homely. Physical attractiveness relates directly to physical appearance. Thus, although the appearance of a given source may be attractive to one person, it may be unattractive to another person. Research says that this perception is especially important in initial encounters with a source. Our earliest perceptions of a source's physical attractiveness will, to some extent, decide our affinity (liking) for that source. Therefore, negative physical attraction means there is little likelihood that we will develop much affinity for the person. Physical attractiveness, thus, often is *the* critical perception. Often, there will be no communication at all if we do not perceive physical attractiveness in the other person. Just consider the last social affair you attended where there were many people with whom you were unacquainted. In making acquaintances with these people, who were you more likely to approach first or be receptive to—those you perceived as physically attractive, or those you perceived as physically unattractive? Beauty may be only skin deep, but sometimes we decide not to try to go any deeper if we don't like the skin!

Fortunately (from our vantage point, at least), the physical dimension of attractiveness becomes less important over time as we become more familiar with another person. In short, as the relationship progresses, physical attractiveness loses much—but probably not all—of its impact. The other dimensions of attraction become more important the more we get to know another person (and get below the "skin" level). Nevertheless, our earliest encounters with that person are impacted most by how attractive we perceive her or his physical appearance to be. This is because in our initial interactions with the individual, the only information we have about that person is what we can see. Essentially, until we know the person better, our thinking is that "what we see is what we get." We are more likely to initiate communication with a person whom we find physically attractive. Moreover, research suggests that, at least early on in a relationship, we are more likely to expose ourselves to and be influenced by a source we perceive as physically attractive. Sometimes, particularly when we have little other information about the person, we are even likely to attribute more credibility to a physically attractive person.

Social Attractiveness (Scale 5).　This dimension of attraction, social attraction, refers to the degree to which we perceive a source to be someone with whom we would like to spend time on a social level. It is not based solely on the physical appearance of the source (although that aspect is *not* irrelevant). It is primarily based on how friendly and likable the source is perceived to be. Social attraction is particularly important when the potential outcome of communication with the person is affinity. Typically, no matter how physically attractive we perceive someone to be, over time our attraction and liking for that individual rely more on how friendly and likable we perceive the other person to be. If you have ever been dissatisfied with a "gorgeous" or "handsome" date, it is probably because you found the person's communication to be uninteresting, unamusing, or boring—you found it hard to develop affinity for the individual. He or she may have looked nice but have been as socially stimulating as an attractive houseplant! One of the authors of this textbook remembers a female student who was absolutely infatuated with a guy who was "built like a Greek god." The female student went so far as to change her schedule to have class with this "Greek god." Unfortunately, the female student quickly realized that the "Greek god" was lacking a little upstairs. After about a week of class, the teacher of the class asked the female student if she was still infatuated with the guy, to which the female student said, "He's still pretty, but he really shouldn't open his mouth." Clearly, this is a case where physical attraction from afar got diminished as a result of social attraction.

Social attractiveness of a source is more important after initial encounters. If we perceive the person to be attractive on a social level, we are likely to want future interactions with the individual. Conversely, if we perceive the source to be lacking in social attractiveness, we are inclined to expend our communicative energies on other acquaintances and friendships.

Task Attractiveness (Scale 6).   The third dimension of interpersonal attractiveness refers to the degree to which we perceive the person to be a desirable one with whom to establish a work relationship. We perceive a source to be task attractive when he or she is viewed as one with whom it would be easy to work. We view her or him as one who probably would be productive in that work, and is motivated to achieve communication outcomes similar to the outcomes we want to achieve. Task attraction, therefore, is based on communication between source and receiver that is goal directed and effective for achieving those goals. This dimension of attractiveness is also related to the competence dimension of credibility. When we perceive a source as competent in a given task-related area, we will likely find that person to be an attractive one with whom to work in that area. An example of task attraction may be found in campus study groups. When cramming for a final exam in physics, if you desire to study with someone else, your choice of a study partner will be determined in large part by how competent you perceive that person to be in physics. If you know that person makes A's in the subject, he or she will be more task attractive to you than will be a classmate who is doing poorly in the course.

It is important to realize that the three dimensions of source attractiveness are *independent* of one another. In other words, a source can be perceived as having high task attractiveness but little or no physical or social attractiveness, and vice versa. Take, for example, the stereotypical fair-haired model. Most people find her highly physically attractive but also socially boring and an incompetent dope. Another example is the stereotypical computer "nerd." This person is perceived by many to be a very task-attractive individual when they need information about computers, but not as attractive on a physical and social level. Examples like these illustrate that source attractiveness is merely a matter of perception and not necessarily of reality. Blonde models can be very friendly and competent individuals, just as computer science majors can be likable and physically attractive. Simply put, a source is attractive only to the extent he or she is *perceived* as attractive. When sources are perceived as attractive, we are much more apt to attempt to communicate with them, to learn from them, and to be influenced by them.

Homophily

Another set of perceptions that affect our attitudes about and responses to a source are based on our *similarity* to the source, more technically known as *homophily*. This loosely translates as "coming from the same category." There is a *principle of homophily* that holds that the more similar two communicators are, the more likely they are to interact with one another, the more likely their communication will be successful, and the more similar they are likely to become. The more similar we perceive a source to be, the more attracted to that person we are apt to be, the more influence he or she is likely to have over us, and the more we are likely to learn from that individual. Three dimensions of similarity are particularly important to our perceptions of sources: demographic, background, and attitude. Measures of background and attitude homophily perceptions are presented in Scales 4 and 5 in the appendix. They were developed by L. McCroskey, J. McCroskey, and Richmond (2005).

Demographic Similarity.   Demographics are physical or social characteristics of an individual that are real and objectively identifiable: age, sex, height, socioeconomic status, educational level, religion, culture, and ethnicity. These are considered *real* characteristics because they are observable and knowable. They exist beyond the limitations of individual people's perceptions. Thus, demographic similarity refers to people's similarity on attributes such as those listed above. This type of similarity is more actual than perceived. In other words, if both you and the person sitting next to you are 20 years old, female, Hispanic, college sophomores, and Protestant, your demographic similarity is factual rather than perceptual. You may, of course, perceive yourselves to be similar (or dissimilar) on other dimensions. You also may over- or underestimate your similarity.

We can make certain predictions about the probable outcomes of communication between a source and receiver who have demographic similarities. For example, we can predict that a Native American who was raised on a reservation in South Dakota probably can return to that reservation after having obtained a teaching degree and be more successful in the reservation's school than a Caucasian teacher coming from Birmingham, Alabama. The reason is because, simply put, the Sioux teacher can better relate to Sioux children. Her or his basic demographic characteristics are more similar to those of the children than are the Alabamian's. As a result, they can understand each other's messages better than they can an "outsider's" messages.

Although demographic similarity is based primarily on actual characteristics, the other two dimensions of similarity are based on perceptions. Thus, they are akin to perceptions of credibility and attractiveness. We consider each below.

Background Similarity (Scale 7).   As a college student, do you feel more similar to one of your classmates than you do to a Marine cadet? As an American, do you feel you have more in common with other Americans than you do with Japanese? If you are from a large city, do you consider yourself more similar to someone from a large city than to someone from a Midwestern dairy farm? Chances are, if these questions are applicable to you, that you answer yes to each one. We perceive people who have backgrounds similar to our own as more similar to us than people with different backgrounds. Perceptions of background similarity are different from demographic similarity, however, because the similarity in background need not be real. For instance, when a student from New Mexico began study in West Virginia, he met another student from Idaho. The student immediately perceived some background similarity between himself and his counterpart. Both were from "the West." However, Pocatello, Idaho, is nearly the same distance from Grants, New Mexico, as is Morgantown, West Virginia. Nevertheless, the fact that both individuals were from "the West" and had come together in "the East" led one of them to perceive they had some degree of similarity. That they were not the same age, were of different religions, and had lived most of their lives in very different kinds of families indicated they were demographically not very similar, but being "Westerners" still produced the background similarity perception.

An important feature of background similarity is that it may be generated before any actual communication between the two people takes place. For example, a particular college student may perceive a similarity with *any* college student, although he or she could never know but a few such people. Another example can be drawn from the similarity we feel with certain television or movie personalities. Though we have never met and interacted with Matt Damon or Jessica Simpson, based on what information we do have about them, we may perceive that we have some background factors that are similar. Perceptions such as these lead to increases in *perceived* similarity. The greater the perceived similarity, the greater the likelihood for wanting to interact with the other person. The greater the perceived similarity, the more frequent interactions become. Subsequently, because of these shared background experiences, the more effective communication will be.

Attitude Similarity (Scale 8).   This type of similarity refers to the degree to which a receiver perceives her or his attitudes, beliefs, and values to be similar to those of a source. Like background similarity, it is based on perceived similarity in attitudes, not actual similarity. Unlike background similarity, however, perceptions of attitude similarity typically develop after the two people have become acquainted and have interacted with one another. Moreover, attitude similarity fluctuates over the span of a relationship. After interacting with a new acquaintance, for example, you may perceive that many of your attitudes are quite similar and thus develop perceptions of similarity with the person. Something may arise that causes you to discover that you and the other person differ greatly on an important issue. As a result, your perceptions of attitude similarity with that person may decrease or change sharply. This concept points out a critical restriction related to the principle of homophily described earlier.

Recall that the principle of homophily suggests that the more similar two individuals perceive themselves to be, the more likely they are to engage in communication, the more likely their communication will be effective, and the more likely they actually will become similar. However, exceptions to this principle exist. Take the case of divorce (or any process that terminates a relationship, for that matter). Divorce appears to suggest a major flaw in the principle of similarity. Two people meet, develop similarity and affinity with each other, grow to love each other, then discover that what they once thought were similarities are big differences, or at least they are perceived to be. Over time, therefore, the perception of similarity can change to the point where two people no longer perceive themselves to be similar. Knapp (1978) refers to this process as "differentiation." At the point of differentiation, we expect the relationship to begin deteriorating and eventually terminate. It is important to realize, therefore, that the principle of homophily applies only if *real* similarity exists, or when perceived similarity is not thwarted by reality.

OTHER PERCEPTIONS OF SOURCES

Our attitudes toward and responses to a source are affected by perceptions of that source's extraversion, composure, and sociability. These perceptions are pertinent to the perceptions of credibility, attraction, and homophily, and also are important perceptions in their own right. These perceptions, when first recognized, were labeled *dynamism*, *composure,* and *sociability* (McCroskey & Young, 1981). Subsequently, it has been learned that these perceptions are manifestations of three components of temperament. We will include both the original and new terms for these perceptions in the following sections.

Extraversion (Dynamism)

The term *extraversion* refers to the degree to which we perceive a source to be talkative, bold, dynamic, and outgoing. The opposite of extraversion is introversion. People in the general U.S. culture tend to have negative evaluations of people who are very introverted. In fact, generally, the more extraverted people are, the more positively they are perceived in important ways such as leadership ability, intelligence, friendliness, and attractiveness.

Composure (Neuroticism)

Perceptions of composure relate to the amount of emotional control we perceive a source to have. Composure perceptions are based on whether the source is poised, relaxed, and confident as opposed to nervous, tense, and uptight. People who are highly neurotic are likely to be hard to deal with, hence increasing the difficulty in communicating with them. People who are in control of their emotions are more likely to be easy to communicate with than those whose emotions may result in unpleasant interactions.

Sociability (Psychoticism)

Most of us seek to interact with people who we perceive to be likable, friendly, and pleasant. Perceptions of a source's sociability relate to how likable and friendly we perceive the person to be. Typically, if we perceive a person to be unsociable, we will avoid contact with that person. This perception is important to affinity and credibility. We are more inclined to like a sociable person. We are more likely to turn to that source for information. However, we are apt not to interact with people if we do not perceive them to be friendly. This is because the perceived lack of friendliness carries with it expectations of an unpleasant interaction.

So far, this chapter has discussed a most critical aspect of the human communication process: how the source is perceived by the receiver. Source perceptions are important to the communication process because of their ability to affect the receiver's attitudes toward both the source and the source's message. Moreover, these attitudes, in conjunction with perceptions of the source, affect the extent to which receivers will *expose* themselves to the source, *pay attention* to the source, *retain* and *learn from* the source's messages, and be *influenced by* the source. Perceptions of source credibility, attractiveness, homophily, and a positive temperament (high extraversion, low neuroticism, and low psychoticism) seem to have the greatest influence on a receiver's responsiveness to a source. Generally, the more credible the receiver perceives the source to be, the more attractive and similar he or she is to the receiver, and the more positive temperament he or she possesses, the more likely it is that the receiver will turn to, learn from, and be influenced by the source.

These sections have been intended to make you aware of just how complex the role of source is during human communication. Not only must receivers adapt their behavior according to how they perceive the source, but the source must also adapt to receivers' responses. It is this reciprocation of each other's behavior between source and receiver that makes interpersonal communication an interactional and transactional process. To the extent that people accurately perceive and appropriately respond to each other's behavior, their communication will be increasingly effective.

Now we turn to an examination of how people really differ from one another, not just the way they are perceived. Our perceptions of others are in part a function of their actual behaviors and, most importantly, their communication behaviors.

PERSONALITY AND TEMPERAMENT IN COMMUNICATION

No two people communicate in exactly the same way, with the possible exception of identical twins. This is true whether their primary role in an interaction is that of source or receiver. The effectiveness of a source's message is ultimately determined by the receiver's interpretation and understanding of that message. It is with the receiving process that individual differences among people may have their greatest impact on communication. For example, Kruvilla may state the same message to Tom that he states to Lucinda, but Tom responds much differently to Kruvilla's message than does Lucinda. Much of the reason for their different responses rests with the possible differences among their attitudes, beliefs, and values. Moreover, Tom may respond in one way to Kruvilla's message because Tom is a middle-aged male from Oregon, whereas Lucinda responds in another way because she is a teenage female from Mexico.

Personal orientations and general characteristics such as age, gender, and culture impact human communication. Also important are the specific characteristics of the individual that make her or him unique from other individuals. These are the focus of this section of the chapter. These characteristics are called *personality variables*.

Personality is the total psychological makeup of an individual, which is a reflection of her or his experiences, motivations, attitudes, beliefs, values, and behaviors. Moreover, a person's personality is derived from the interaction of these elements with the environment external to the individual. Thus, personality can be defined as *the sum of an individual's characteristics that make her or him unique* (Hollander, 1976). If all people had the same personality, they would all communicate the same way in any given context and in similar situations across contexts. Obviously, people do not have the same personalities. More than 2,000 personality variables have been isolated by personality psychologists, but most of these have not been studied with regard to determining how these variables relate to communication behavior. Thus, it is not fully known how certain personality variables affect human communication.

Personality Traits and Communication Behavior

Hollander (1976) discusses two important features that help clarify what personality is. The first feature distinguishes the *external* level of personality from the *internal* level. The external level consists of observable characteristics of an individual and is represented primarily by her or his typical behavior. The internal level includes the individual's attitudes, values, beliefs, interests and aspirations, and motivations. In interpersonal encounters, we tend to infer a person's internal level of personality from her or his external behavior. For example, we might observe Ron behaving in a loud, animated way in several situations. From Ron's behavior, we might infer that he is a fun-loving fellow who needs much attention from others.

The second feature of personality distinguishes its *dynamic* aspects from its *consistent* aspects. By dynamic, we mean that personality undergoes some degree of change as an individual learns from new experiences. Getting married, moving to another part of the country, living through some tragedy, losing a job, and even becoming involved in a new relationship are just some experiences that can change how a person looks at life (internal level) and how he or she behaves (external level). There are, however, many aspects of personality that remain consistent. Elements of the internal level of personality that are least likely to undergo change—such as values—are those that comprise the consistent aspect of personality. It is also these elements that account for consistency in an individual's behavior. The consistency seen in the behavior of someone who never misses a class, for example, could be attributed to that individual's belief that the best way to get the most out of a course is to always be present. It is this sense of consistency in our personality, then, that causes others to remark to us, "You haven't changed one bit, even after all this time."

We generally expect that the internal and external levels of personality will operate in unison with one another. That is, we expect people to behave according to the way they think and feel. In reality, however, this state of unison typically doesn't exist. An example can be taken from the many communication studies that have examined public speaking anxiety (more on this topic is in Chapter 3). These studies hypothesized that people with above-average public speaking anxiety would have certain physiological behaviors. It is thought that a person reporting a high level of public speaking anxiety would show, among other responses, a faster heart rate than would someone reporting a low level of apprehension. The research does not consistently support this assumption. The heart rates of many people with above-average public speaking anxiety are no greater than those of people with average and below-average public speaking anxiety.

Similarly, in our daily interactions with others we infer that, because an individual is exhibiting a particular behavior, he or she is "that kind of person." Such inferences are attributable to the expectations we have about another person's consistent behavior, expectations that are established through interactions with that person over time. Experience with your significant other, for example, may lead you to expect that if you don't say "I love you" once in a while, he or she will become despondent. Eventually you tend to regard the behavior from which this expectancy develops as characteristic of that person's personality. Then we say things like "Oh, she always gets upset about that" or "That is just his nature." As Hollander (1976) notes, it's only a short time until you begin to view this characteristic of others as a *trait*, or the way he or she "typically" behaves. In reality, there are four different ways that personality characteristics can be exhibited by specific individuals: traits, contexts, audience, and situational.

Trait. In the psychology of personality, *traits* refer to individual characteristics that are not found in all people, but only in relatively few. Traits are an individual's *predispositions* for responding in a certain way to various situations. That is, a given trait will exhibit itself in almost any situation responded to by the individual.

Context. The second way that personality characteristics can be demonstrated by individuals is within specific contexts. The basic contexts that communication scholars examine are interpersonal, group, meeting, public, and mediated. Contextual behavior occurs when people act in one context one way and in a different context in a way different from the first context. For example, one person may show a specific personality characteristic while speaking, but not when interacting with people one-on-one (interpersonal).

Audience. The third way that personality characteristics surface is dependent on the audience with whom an individual is communicating. We often act very different based on the audience with whom we are communicating. Most of us are not nearly as likely to crack jokes when talking with our boss one-on-one as we are when talking with our romantic partner. Different audiences have differing perspectives of how interactions should occur, so we tend to act differently based on the type of audience we are interacting with.

Situational. The fourth way that personality characteristics surface is dependent on the circumstances. There are times when, because of the situation, we just naturally start communicating in a pattern that is not normal for us. We refer to this behavior as "situational" because it is not generally replicated again. The authors of this book have a colleague who has spent many years public speaking. One day, while giving a presentation, he looked down to find his hand shaking from nerves. This person has not experienced anxiety while speaking ever, but for some reason during that specific situation nerves just grabbed a hold of him and took over, causing his hands to shake.

In short, differences in personality manifest themselves in variations in the communication behavior among people. These variations can occur within any component of the interpersonal communication process but particularly within those aspects that comprise the receiver's function—perceiving, decoding, processing, and responding. Before we examine a handful of specific personality traits, we need to discuss the role of human temperament and biology in communication.

THE ROLE OF BIOLOGY IN HUMAN COMMUNICATION

In the area of human communication, there are two prominent beliefs on how humans develop personality characteristics. On one hand, you have people who believe that humans are born tabula rosa, or as blank slates. Scientists who believe in the blank-slate conceptualization of human temperament believe that humans are born with no personality characteristics at all. Instead, blank-slate scientists believe that humans adopt behaviors because of their interaction with other people and their environment. Humans function as blank pieces of paper, and through their interactions with others and their environment, they are magically written on and this writing then turns into human behavior. This perspective is also referred to as *learning theory* because researchers believe that humans *learn* how they behave.

In research conducted using the learning theory model, researchers have found that learning does not explain what is happening most of the time in human behavior. If someone owed you $100 and gave you $15 instead, would you be satisfied? Yet for most behavioral sciences stuck in the learning theory model of research, understanding what causes 15 percent of human behavior is fine. Although learning theory was great during the nineteenth century and much of the twentieth century, we now know too much about how humans are impacted by their biology to still promote this perspective.

The opposite view of the blank slate is behavioral biology. Behavioral biology is defined as *the attempt to understand both the genetic and environmental contributions to individual variations in human behavior.* In other words, behavioral biologists believe that human behavior is not entirely caused through our interactions with our environment, but rather it is a combination of both environmental influences and our basic biological/genetic makeup. Behavioral biology primarily stems from two physical science pursuits: neuroscience (study of the brain and how it affects behavior) and behavioral genetics (study of how human genetics influences human behavior). If you would like to learn more about the scientific aspects of neuroscience, we strongly recommend that you read Simon LeVay's *The Sexual Brain.* And if you want to understand behavioral genetics, you should read Dean Hamer and Peter Copeland's (1998) *Living with Our Genes: Why They Matter More than You Think.* In the field of behavioral biology, there are a number of social scientists who examine how human biology impacts their specific area of knowledge. In psychology, you have psychobiologists who study how human genetics affect psychological traits. In sociology, you have sociobiologists who examine how human genetics affect sociological traits. And in communication, we have communibiologists who examine how human genetics affect communication traits.

By this point, we hope that you're wondering what the difference between personality and temperament is. Often, people from the blank-slate scientific community will use these two words interchangeably when they really are not intended to be. Personality and temperament are not the same thing. Temperament refers to an individual's genotype, characteristics present early in life caused by human biology. Personality, on the other hand, relates to a person's phenotype, or the interaction between an individual's genotype and her or his environment (nurture, diet, socialization, etc.).

It's one thing to know that behavior is impacted largely by human biology; it's another thing completely to know exactly how this occurs. A psychobiologist by the name of Hans Eysenck (1998) has helped us greatly in our efforts to measure and understand the impact of biology and human behavior. Eysenck originally posed in the 1940s that most of human behavior was determined by what he called two "supertraits": extraversion and neuroticism. Eysenck later added a third supertrait that he called psychoticism.

Extraversion, as previously mentioned in this chapter, exists along a continuum from *extravert* to *introvert.* People can exist at any point along the continuum. Extraverts are characterized by their desire to be sociable and have stimulation around them, and by their easygoing nature. Extraverts tend to be highly outgoing individuals who talk a lot and have plenty of friends and excitement in their lives. At the opposite end of the continuum, you have introverts. Introverts are quiet, asocial (or not social), serious, reliable, and controlled individuals. Walk into any room with as few as twenty people present, and almost always you will see people at both ends of the continuum.

Neuroticism also exists along a continuum ranging from highly neurotic to low neurotic. Some people believe we are all neurotic to an extent. Neuroticism is defined as an individual's tendency toward mania (being really happy) and depression (being really sad). In other words, neuroticism refers to the individual emotional stability that a person either does not have (high neurotic) or does have (low neurotic). People who are highly neurotic are prone to high levels of anxiety, depression, and panic attacks. Often, the highly neurotic individual will actually have serious medical problems that stem out of her or his neuroticism (high blood pressure, ulcers, acid-reflux, and possibly even heart attacks and strokes). People on the low side of neuroticism are not likely to be anxious, be depressed, or suffer from panic attacks; thus, they are able to alleviate some of the risk of having many serious medical problems.

Psychoticism is a word that most people don't tend to like because of its tendency to be associated with people who have serious psychological problems like schizophrenia and multiple personality disorder. In reality, psychoticism is a supertrait that all of us have in us to varying degrees. The definition of *psychoticism* is the extent to which an individual believes that society's norms and rules do or do not pertain to her or him. People who are highly psychotic tend to be loners, not empathetic (don't care about other people's emotions), and antisocial (violating social rules and norms). Highly psychotic individuals are also more likely to big risks. People at the opposite end of the psychoticism spectrum are high self-monitors. These individuals are very concerned with following social rules and norms, and take special effort to understand how those around them are feeling.

So what do supertraits have to do with human behavior and personality? In Figure 2.1, we see a pictorial representation of Eysenck's perspective on human behavior. In this chart, we see that Eysenck believed that human genetics actually influenced the extent to which any individual was extraverted, neurotic, and psychotic. In turn, our levels of extraversion, neuroticism, and psychoticism would impact human behavior. This does not mean that extraversion, neuroticism, and psychoticism impact *every*

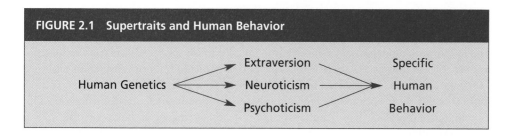

FIGURE 2.1 Supertraits and Human Behavior

human behavior the same. It is also possible that only one of the supertraits will actually impact an individual's behavior, and the other two supertraits will have nothing to do with that specific behavior at all.

 ## PERSONALITY VARIABLES IN COMMUNICATION

No two human beings are exactly alike, with the exception of identical twins who still may have minor variations. The number of ways people can differ from one another is probably infinite. However, one of the more meaningful ways, if not the *most* meaningful, involves our typical patterns of communication behavior. Many everyday references we make to people in our environment show our general awareness of such differences. Perhaps you've heard or even used comments such as these: "She never says much," "He surely has a strange way of dealing with people," or "She's the most abrasive person I've ever met." All of these comments share something in common; they refer to presumed habitual communication patterns of individuals and mark them as different from some (or many) other individuals. The comments also differ; they refer to various kinds of individual differences. That is, because of certain communication patterns and behaviors engaged in by an individual, we infer that he or she has a particular kind of personality. Although such inferences are sometimes incorrect, very often they are accurate. Some of these personality traits and how they affect communication behavior are the focus of this section.

Adventurousness

The person whose personality is characterized by a high level of *adventurousness* is always ready to try new things. He or she is sociable (high extraversion), tends to show an abundance of emotional responses like excitability (high neuroticism), and takes a lot of risks (high psychoticism). The person with a low level of adventurousness, however, tends to be cautious and withdrawn, and have feelings of inferiority. Highly adventurous people tend to show more interest in their communication with other people. They engage in discussions more openly and with more relevant contributions to the topic, and have a fairly high task orientation. In many circumstances, adventurous people tend to be more talkative than people who are less adventurous.

Authoritarianism

Authoritarianism refers to having an orientation toward power in social relationships. The authoritarian person seeks to be dominant over those seen as weaker and to be submissive toward those seen as stronger. This person tends to be more suspicious and less trusting than a nonauthoritarian individual. The person with a low authoritarian trait is more trusting of others and less inclined to strive for dominance in social situations. On a communication level, highly authoritarian individuals engage in behaviors that place them in positions of dominance over weaker persons. Or when the situation is such that a more dominant person is in control, they will take the submissive role. Because they are suspicious of others, they tend to confide in or seek important information from others more than nonauthoritarian people do. Authoritarianism has been linked to high levels of psychoticism but not to extraversion and neuroticism.

Dogmatism

Dogmatic individuals are rigid in their thinking and can best be described as "close-minded." Individuals with highly dogmatic personalities are sometimes equated with authoritarian personalities because they hold an unusually high respect for persons in authority. Such people are also characterized by a high degree of anxiety and insecurity (high neuroticism). They feel threatened by people with views opposing their own. Moreover, the dogmatic personality tends to conform to group influence more than to individual influence (low psychoticism), unless the other individual is an authority figure. Dogmatic people are very inflexible in their communication behavior and are intolerant of others who hold contrary views. Moreover, the dogmatic person's communication is more likely to be irrelevant to the topic of discussion and based more on emotions than on rational thinking. Two television characters who epitomize this personality trait are Archie and Meathead of the *All in the Family* series. Even the Irish father on the short-run sitcom *It's All Relative* is an example of a highly dogmatic individual.

Emotional Maturity

Emotional maturity distinguishes between people who are changeable, dissatisfied, and easily annoyed and those who are stable, calm, and well-balanced (low neuroticism). People who are more emotionally mature exhibit much greater flexibility in their communication behavior and less behavior oriented toward irrelevant social information and issues. Those who are less mature tend to be more likely to get into conflict with others and to engage in very hostile communicative behaviors.

General Anxiety

This personality trait distinguishes between those who tend to be tense, restless, and impatient most of the time, and those who generally tend to be calm, relaxed, and composed. It is important that *general anxiety* as a trait not be confused with communication apprehension. Although the person with high general anxiety is more likely to be communication apprehensive (see Chapter 3) than the person who is low in general anxiety, there is not a high correlation between these two characteristics. People with high general anxiety are likely to show more tension in communication with others. They are less likely to talk, and appear less interested in most topics of discussion when compared to people with low general anxiety. Those with general anxiety are likely to express their fears about all manner of potential problems that could occur, but are not likely to. Anxiety is almost purely a trait seen in people with high levels of neuroticism.

Locus of Control

The concept of *locus of control* refers to an individual's orientation toward the source of rewards for her or his actions. Two orientations are considered by this concept. Individuals who perceive that reward for actions follows from their own behavior are said to have an *internal* locus of control. They believe that they are the primary source of control for their behavior, and they take full responsibility for the outcomes of their behavior. Individuals who perceive that reward for actions stems from outside forces are said to have an *external* locus of control. These people believe that luck, chance, or other people have the primary control over their behavior and that there is little they can do to affect their lives. At the communication level, people with an internal orientation differ in important ways from those with an external orientation. Internals are more independent and more resistant to influence attempts than are externals. In competitive situations, internals rely more on their own knowledge and less on others' information. In contrast, externals look to good luck or help from others to succeed in a competition. Although externals are not consistently given to being influenced more than internals, they are less resistant but not more influenced. Externals are more likely to be influenced by a highly credible source than are internals. Finally, when attempting to influence others, externals tend to use more aggressive and impersonal messages; internals use more passive and personal messages. Research has shown that external locus of control is positively related to neuroticism but negatively related to psychoticism, whereas internal locus of control is negatively related to neuroticism and psychoticism.

Machiavellianism

A person with a *Machiavellian* personality views other people as objects to be manipulated for her or his own purposes. A person with a highly Machiavellian personality (or "high Mach") tends to show little concern for conventional morality and has little emotional involvement in the communication encounters in which he or she is engaged. High Machs tend to distrust everyone, so much so that they seem not to form perceptions of other people on the criterion of character. High Machs not only are willing to manipulate other people but also tend to be very successful at such manipulation and seem even to enjoy such attempts. In communication with others, the high Mach uses willful intent to influence people and does so with glee. Conversely, the high Mach is less likely to be influenced by others. Generally, in interpersonal communication, the Machiavellian personality displays a low regard for others, treats them as objects, and is unconcerned with the humanness of other people. Machiavellianism has been shown to

Santi di Tito (1536–1603), "Portrait of Niccolo Machiavelli (1469–1527)." Italian philosopher and writer of *The Prince*.

be related positively to both psychoticism and extraversion. To be a high Machiavellian, one has to rely on the ability to successfully communicate and appear sociable (extraversion), but has to have the antisocial mindset to pull it off (psychoticism).

Self-Control

Self-control is a personality variable that separates people who have much control over their emotions from those who have little control over their emotions. People who are high in self-control tend to be calmer, more composed, and more in control, and have less fear of communicating (low neuroticism). People low in self-control are more likely to experience anxiety while communicating. Their feelings of insecurity and lack of control lead them to be afraid of talking; they may withdraw from communication so that they do not lose control over their emotions and say things they do not mean. The opposite of self-control is psychoticism, so self-control and psychoticism are negatively related to each other.

Self-Esteem

Self-esteem refers to the view people have of themselves in terms of total worth. People with low self-esteem tend to lack confidence in their own ability and to evaluate their own competence negatively in almost any area. They expect failure in whatever they attempt to accomplish, including their interactions with others. As you might guess, low self-esteem is positively related to external locus of control and low self-control, so self-esteem is positively related to extraversion and negatively related to neuroticism. Therefore, those with low self-esteem tend to be followers in most interpersonal encounters; they are likely to accept other people's views because they consider their own views to be of less value. People with high self-esteem, on the other hand, are generally leaders in communication interactions. They are confident, expect to succeed, and expect to communicate well. If we place a person with high self-esteem in a dyad with a person with low self-esteem, the person with high self-esteem is most likely to dominate the interaction, whereas people with low self-esteem tend to see themselves as inadequate and believe others see them that way also. Innocuous comments of others are often taken as criticism by people with low self-esteem, and they tend to respond very defensively.

Tolerance for Ambiguity

Much communication is aimed at reducing uncertainty. *Tolerance for ambiguity* is a personality variable that distinguishes people who can operate effectively in communication situations in which there is a great deal of uncertainty from those who cannot operate effectively in such situations. People with low tolerance for ambiguity have a need to identify all questions or issues as either good or bad, or right or wrong. They are in constant search for correctness and closure. Thus, this type of person would rather make a decision today than seek information for a better decision tomorrow. Conversely, the person with high tolerance for ambiguity has less need for having things resolved. This person can continue communication over an extended period without needing to reach a resolution. People with a low tolerance for ambiguity are likely to become impatient in group meetings when decisions are not reached quickly. The result may be intemperate criticism of the group or individual members, which can lead to very bad interpersonal relationships.

Argumentativeness

Infante and Rancer (1982) defined argumentativeness as "a general stable trait which predisposes individuals in communication situations to advocate positions on controversial issues and to attack verbally the positions which other people hold on these issues" (p. 72). In essence, Infante and Rancer believe that there are people who actively approach arguments and other people who actively avoid arguments. However, approaching and avoiding arguments are not mutually exclusive concepts. Everyone has approach and avoidance needs when it comes to arguing. As long as your need to approach an argument is stronger than your need to avoid an argument, you will engage in the argument. If, however, your need to avoid an argument is stronger than your need to approach an argument, you will not engage in the argument. Let's look at a real-world example.

Imagine you are ten minutes late to work one morning and your boss decides to dock you an hour's pay for being late. You may have many arguments for why this isn't fair at all. Maybe other people are always late and never docked pay; maybe you stayed an hour later the night before. Although you may have arguments inside your head, you may or may not vocalize them to your boss. If you are scared of your boss, your desire to avoid an argument with your boss may outweigh your feelings of injustice. However, you may believe that your arguments for not being docked pay are strong and your boss should clearly listen to you, so you may approach the argument despite the voices in your head telling you to avoid the argument. Although weighing the approach and avoidant needs for engaging in an argument is the balancing act that most people go through when weighing whether or not to engage in an argument, there are some people who enjoy arguments and actively seek them out on purpose. People who are highly argumentative love to argue and will argue with anyone about almost anything at any time. The flip side is also true. There are some people who actively avoid arguing at all costs. People who actively avoid arguments generally do so because they do not feel comfortable in their own arguments or they perceive arguing as very similar to conflict. And because most people like to avoid conflict when possible, people who view arguments as conflicts will avoid arguments when possible as well. Some people, in order to avoid arguments, may also become verbally aggressive (Rancer, 1998).

Verbal Aggression

Verbal aggression has been commonly defined as message behavior that attacks a person's self-concept in order to deliver psychological pain (Infante & Wigley, 1986). Statements that purposefully are used to hurt another person are considered verbally aggressive. Maybe you've known someone who is constantly belittling those around her or him, or maybe just flies off the handle when talking with people. If so, then you probably have had contact with someone who is verbally aggressive. One reason people become verbally aggressive is when another person attacks her or his ideas. When people discuss ideas, some people feel that they are being attacked when others disagree with their ideas and will become defensive. When people become defensive, most people will attempt to build better arguments. Unfortunately, some people will run out of arguments and will instead result to name calling and verbal intimidation. Overall, verbal aggression in interpersonal relationships has been shown by researchers to be very negative (Wigley, 1998; Wrench, 2002).

Exhilaratability

Ruch (1993) defined exhilaration as "an emotion construct denoting a temporary increase in cheerful state that is observable in behavior, physiology, and emotional experience, and that occurs in response to humor but also to other stimuli" (p. 605). The word *exhilaration* comes from the Latin word *hilaris*, which means cheerful. One major way that causes individuals to be cheerful is through exposure to humor. We all feel more cheerful after watching a good comedian. In fact, the buzz we feel after watching a good comedian is real. After prolonged exposure to humor, our endorphin levels get elevated, making us feel good. Ruch defined exhilaratability as having three major components, cheerfulness, seriousness, and bad mood. Cheerfulness is the tendency to be happy and have a low threshold for smiling and laughter, a composed view of adverse life circumstances, a broad range of active factors that make us cheerful and smile, and a generally cheerful interaction style. The second component of exhilaratability, trait seriousness, is composed of a tendency for serious states; a perception that even everyday happenings are important and deserving of thorough and intensive consideration; the tendency to plan ahead and set long-range goals; the tendency to prefer activities for which concrete, rational reasons can be produced; the preference for a sober, object-oriented communication style; and a humorless or dull attitude about cheerfulness-related matters. The final component of Ruch's (1993) exhilaratability was bad mood.

Bad mood refers to individuals who are generally in a bad mood, sad (despondent and distressed), showing ill-humoredness (sullen and grumpy or grouchy feelings), and showing displeasure related to cheerfulness-evoking situations.

In a study conducted by Wrench and McCroskey (2001), the two authors examined the relationship between exhilaratability and Eysenck's supertraits. The results from this study along with results previously discussed in this chapter can be seen in Figure 2.2.

Even in almost identical circumstances, no two people can be expected to communicate in the same way. Although this is due in part to the fact that people's attitudes, beliefs, and values are different, it relates primarily to their differing personalities. Personality is the sum of characteristics that make an individual unique. Dozens of different personality variations have been studied by psychologists. However, only a few have been studied to figure out their impact on communication. Those personality variations that are important include adventurousness, authoritarianism, dogmatism, emotional maturity, extraversion and introversion, general anxiety, locus of control, Machiavellianism, self-control, self-esteem, tolerance for ambiguity, argumentativeness, verbal aggression, and exhilaratability. By understanding another person's level of each of these personality characteristics, you will be better able to adapt your communication to the person during communication. The next chapter is going to focus on specific communication personality characteristics that have been shown to be extremely important.

FIGURE 2.2   Communication Traits with Eysenck's Supertraits

Variable	Relationship to Extraversion	Relationship to Neuroticism	Relationship to Psychoticism
Adventurousness	+	+	+
Authoritarianism	NR*	NR	+
Dogmatism	NR	+	−
Emotional maturity	NR	−	NR
General anxiety	NR	+	NR
External locus of control	NR	+	−
Internal locus of control	NR	−	−
Machiavellianism	+	NR	+
Self-control	NR	−	+
Self-esteem	+	−	NR
Tolerance for ambiguity	−	−	NR
Argumentativeness	+	NR	+
Verbal aggression	NR	NR	+
Cheerfulness	+	−	−
Seriousness	NR	+	−
Bad mood	−	+	+

* NR = no relationship.
+ = positive relationship
− = negative relationship

KEY TERMS

adventurousness 45
argumentativeness 49
attitude homophily 36
authoritarianism 46
background homophily 36
bad mood 51
behavioral biology 43
caring/goodwill 33
cheerfulness 50
communibiology 43
competence 33
composure 39
consistency 41
contextual behavior 42
demographic homophily 36

dogmatism 46
emotional maturity 46
exhilaratability 50
external locus of control 47
extraversion 39
general anxiety 46
homophily 36
internal locus of control 47
learning theory 43
Machiavellianism 47
neuroticism 39
personality 40
personality traits 41
personality variables 40
physical attraction 34

principle of homophily 36
psychoticism 39
self-control 48
self-esteem 48
seriousness 50
situational behavior 42
sociability 39
social attraction 35
sponsorship effect 31
task attraction 36
temperament 40
tolerance for ambiguity 49
trustworthiness 33
verbal aggression 50

REFERENCES

Eysenck, H. J. (1998). *Dimensions of personality.* New Brunswick, NJ: Transaction.

Hamer, D., & Copeland, P. (1998). *Living with our genes: Why they matter more than you think.* New York: Doubleday.

Hollander, E. P. (1976). *Principles and methods of social psychology* (3rd ed.). New York: Oxford University Press.

Holtzman, P. D. (1966). Confirmation of ethos as a confounding element in communication research. *Speech Monographs, 33,* 464–466.

Infante, D. A., & Rancer, A. S. (1982). A conceptualization and measure of argumentativeness. *Journal of Personality Assessment, 46,* 72–80.

Infante, D. A., & Wigley, C. J., III. (1986). Verbal aggressiveness: An interpersonal model and measure. *Communication Monographs, 53,* 21–29.

Knapp, M. L. (1978). *Social intercourse: From greeting to goodbye.* Boston: Allyn & Bacon.

LeVay, S. (1993). *The sexual brain.* Cambridge, MA: MIT Press.

McCroskey, J. C. (1966). Scales for the measurement of ethos. *Speech Monographs, 33,* 65–72.

McCroskey, J. C., & Dunham, R. E. (1966). Ethos: A confounding element in communication research. *Speech Monographs, 33,* 456–463.

McCroskey, J. C., & Teven, J. J. (1999). Goodwill: A reexamination of the construct and its measurement. *Communication Monographs, 66,* 90–103.

McCroskey, J. C., & Young, T. J. (1981). Ethos and credibility: The construct and its' measurement after three decades. *The Central States Speech Journal, 32,* 24-34.

McCroskey, L. L., McCroskey, J. C., & Richmond, V. P. (2005). Analysis and improvement of the measurement of interpersonal attraction and homophily. *Communication Quarterly, 54,* 1-31.

Rancer, A. S. (1998). Argumentativeness. In J. C. McCroskey, J. A. Daly, M. M. Martin, & M. J. Beatty (Eds.), *Communication and personality: Trait perspectives* (pp. 149–170). Cresskill, NJ: Hampton Press.

Ruch, W. (1993). Exhilaration and humor. In M. Lewis & J. M. Haviland (Eds.), *The handbook of emotion* (pp. 605–616). New York: Guilford.

Wigley, C. J. (1998). Verbal aggressiveness. In J. C. McCroskey, J. A. Daly, M. M. Martin, & M. J. Beatty (Eds.), *Communication and personality: Trait perspectives* (pp. 191–214). Cresskill, NJ: Hampton Press.

Wrench, J. S. (2002). The impact of sexual orientation and temperament on physical and verbal aggression.

Journal of Intercultural Communication Research, 31, 85–106.

Wrench, J. S., & McCroskey, J. C. (2001). A temperamental understanding of humor communication and exhilaratability. *Communication Quarterly, 49*, 142–159.

▣ DISCUSSION QUESTIONS

1. How can the sponsorship effect explain the use of celebrities to endorse products in television?

2. Which factor of source credibility do you think is the most important when listening to political candidates? Why?

3. In classrooms, which form of attraction do you think is the most important for students? Why?

4. What is behavioral biology, and why is it important to human communication?

5. Explain the relationship between Eysenck's supertraits and tolerance for ambiguity.

3

Communication Approach and Avoidance Traits

OBJECTIVES

- Define and explain *shyness*.

- Define and explain *willingness to communicate*.

- Define and explain *communication apprehension*.

- Differentiate between shyness, willingness to communicate, and communication apprehension.

- Understand how shyness, willingness to communicate, and communication apprehension affect people in their everyday lives.

- Define and explain *talkaholism* (compulsive communication).

- Define and explain *self-perceived communication competence*.

- Define and explain *assertiveness*.

- Define and explain *responsiveness*.

- Understand the relationship between communication competence and androgyny.

Mary is the type of person who seldom has anything to say. When she's with other people, she seems to just go along with the crowd, seldom making any suggestions or having any complaints about what the group does. Her eyes tend to look everywhere but directly at the person with whom she is speaking. She usually sits or stands with her arms crossed, head facing downward, and shoulders and back slumped over. At school, Mary always selects a seat in the back or along the side of the room when she can. She never seems to get involved in class or school activities, and she is by herself most of the time.

Does the description of Mary remind you of anyone you know? A friend? A relative? Yourself? Chances are that you know many people who fit such a description. If you could think of one word to sum up Mary, what would it be? If *shy* is the word that comes to mind, it is probably because the term is the one most commonly used for describing the behavior of people like Mary. If someone close to you is a shy person, you know how difficult it can be to try to communicate with someone who is not willing to communicate with you. When a person is not willing to initiate communication, it is virtually impossible to communicate with that person effectively. All else being equal, the tendency to avoid and be unwilling to initiate communication and/or respond to the initiatives of others may be the most important factor leading to ineffective communication between people.

Martha is the type of person who always has something to say, regardless of the situation. When she is with other people, she seems to be the focus of the conversation. She always has an opinion or a suggestion, and doesn't hesitate to communicate her thoughts. She maintains eye contact with virtually everyone around her, and specifically with anyone to whom she is communicating directly. She pays close attention to what others have to say. At school, Martha usually sits near the front of the class and focuses her attention on the teacher. She is involved in many school activities and always seems to have a group of people around her, looking at her and interacting with her.

Does the description of Martha remind you of anyone you know? A friend? A relative? Yourself? Chances are that you know many people who fit such a description. If you could think of one word to sum up Martha, what would it be? *Outgoing* may be the word that comes to mind, or it could be numerous other words such as *extraverted, talkative, friendly,* and *leader.* If someone close to you is an outgoing person, you know how easy it usually is to communicate with someone who always seems to be willing to talk to you. Being willing to initiate communication with others and respond to their communication may be the most important factors leading to effective communication between people.

In this chapter, we are going to examine a number of communication approach and avoidance traits. Although these traits are related to one another, they each have a unique impact on how individuals communicate in everyday life. The traits that we will consider are shyness (Scale 9), willingness to communicate (Scale 10), communication apprehension (CA; Scale 11), compulsive communication (Scale 12), self-perceived communication competence (Scale 13), and sociocommunicative orientation (Scale 14). Before we examine these traits individually, you should complete the scales that have been used by researchers to measure them in the appendix. After you have completed the various scales based on your feelings about communication and your communication behavior and scored those scales, you will be in a better position to understand the nature of these traits and how they may be impacting communication in your everyday life—both your own and that of others around you.

DEFINING AND DISTINGUISHING AMONG COMMUNICATION TRAITS

Before we begin to discuss each of the communication traits, it is important that we define each trait and how it is similar to and/or different than the others.

Shyness

Shyness is *the behavior of not talking* (McCroskey & Richmond, 1982; Richmond, Beatty, & Dyba, 1985; Richmond & McCroskey, 1985, 1995). People who have a low willingness to communicate are very likely to behave in a shy manner. Compulsive communicators are unlikely to behave in a shy manner. Shy people exhibit a tendency to be timid or reserved, and to talk less than other people (Phillips, 1981). Shy people may or may not be apprehensive or see themselves as less communicatively competent.

Willingness to Communicate

Willingness to communicate is *an individual's predisposition to initiate communication with others* (McCroskey, 1992). The key here is "initiation" of communication. People who are highly willing to communicate will readily initiate communication with others, whereas those who have a low willingness to communicate will avoid communication by avoiding initiation of communication. Although communication apprehension (CA) and self-perceived communication competence are negatively correlated with willingness to communicate, many people who are not willing to communicate neither are apprehensive about communication nor see themselves as communicatively incompetent. Most compulsive communicators are highly willing to communicate.

Communication Apprehension

Communication apprehension is *an individual's level of fear or anxiety associated with either real or anticipated communication with another person or persons* (McCroskey, 1970, 1972, 1977, 1997, 2001, 2006; Richmond & McCroskey, 1985, 1995). People who are highly apprehensive about communication are likely to avoid communication with others and see themselves as being less competent communicators. They are likely to behave in a shy manner.

Self-Perceived Communication Competence

Self-perceived communication competence is *an individual's perception of her or his own competence in communication across a variety of contexts* (McCroskey, 1984, 1997). This should not be confused with actual communication competence. It is quite possible for individuals to think of themselves as much less, or much more, competent communicators than others would see them to be. However, communication choices of individuals are based on the individual's perceptions, not some external reality. Generally, we would expect people who see themselves as more competent communicators to be more willing to initiate communication, even to be a compulsive communicator, but less likely to suffer from CA and unlikely to behave in a shy manner.

Compulsive Communication

Compulsive communicators, commonly called *talkaholics*, are driven to communicate. Alcoholics crave alcohol, workaholics crave work, and talkaholics crave communication. Obviously, compulsive communicators are highly willing to communicate and very unlikely to behave in a shy manner. These talkaholics may be either higher or lower on CA and self-perceived communication competence than others; however, on average, they see themselves as somewhat more communicatively competent.

Now that you have a basic understanding of these communication traits, we will examine each of these traits in more detail. Some of these have been researched much more than others.

 # SHYNESS

Please answer two questions: (1) Do you presently consider yourself to be a shy person? And (2) if you answered "no" to the first question, was there ever a period in your life during which you considered yourself a shy person?

Zimbardo (1977) posed these same two questions to over 5,000 people in the western United States. His results were remarkable. More than 40 percent (2,000) of the people who responded answered "yes" to the first question, and over 80 percent (4,000) answered "yes" to one of the two questions. Generalizing these findings to the population as a whole, one can estimate that two out of every five people you meet consider themselves to be shy. And two more believe that they were shy at one time. Thus, only one person in five reports that they are not and never have been shy. To bring it a bit closer to home, if there are twenty-five people in your class, at least ten of them think of themselves as shy people now, and only five think they are not and never have been shy.

The authors of this book replicated Zimbardo's study with twice as many respondents as he had. Our results were virtually identical to his, although our data were collected in over fifty universities across the United States (Berger, Baldwin, McCroskey, & Richmond, 1983). We also found the same results with a sample of approximately 2,500 adult nonstudents in a national study (Allen, Richmond, & McCroskey, 1984). Clearly, many people think they are, or used to be, shy.

Defining shyness has been a difficult task for scholars. Zimbardo said, "Shyness is a fuzzy concept," meaning that shyness as a concept is too vague to explain with a single definition. Pilkonis, another shyness researcher and a former student of Zimbardo, has offered a behavioral description of shy people. Pilkonis, Heape, and Klein (1980) suggest that shy people "are characterized by avoidance of social interaction, and when this is impossible, by inhibition and an inability to respond in an engaging way; they are reluctant to talk, to make eye contact, to gesture, and to smile" (Pilkonis et al., 1980). We, like Pilkonis, find it useful to refer to shyness as *the behavioral tendency to not initiate communication and/or respond to the initiatives of others*. Presumably, this behavior stems from a preference for not communicating by the individual—a reduced willingness to communicate.

Zimbardo, in terms less specific than those used by Pilkonis, thinks of shyness as simply a *discomfort* associated with many different communication situations. In other words, a shy person is one who is likely to feel uncomfortable when communicating one-on-one with another person, when interacting within a group of people, when called on in class, when giving a talk, and when being introduced to a new acquaintance by a friend. This notion of shyness is very similar to CA, which also refers to discomfort associated with communication. As mentioned earlier in this chapter, communication apprehension is *the fear or anxiety associated with either real or anticipated communication with another person or persons*. Later in this chapter, we will deal

People with High CA love to hide behind their notes while giving a speech.

solely with CA. It is important to note that CA is but one factor that is associated with shy behavior.

Scale 9 in the appendix is a more direct and reliable method of measuring behavioral shyness. You will notice that no items on this measure have anything to do with fear or anxiety; hence, it is not "contaminated" by elements associated with these concerns. This enables researchers to have distinct measures of shyness and CA. This is important because many other things can cause a person to behave in a shy manner. We now have excellent research results indicating that shyness and introversion are highly and positively related. Hence, people can behave in a shy way without being either fearful or anxious. Because introversion (the opposite of extraversion) is one of the key factors of temperament, and it has been found to have a strong genetic base, this is the most likely causal factor in behavioral shyness.

Andrea Jung, Chairman and CEO of Avon Products, clearly appears more confident and less anxious speaking than the speaker on the previous page.

◫ WILLINGNESS TO COMMUNICATE (WTC)

Although shyness is a pattern of behavior, willingness to communicate (WTC) is a predisposition toward communication behavior, not a behavior itself. The amount of communication in which people engage differs greatly from person to person. There are people who talk constantly no matter what the situation or with whom they are interacting (we will consider these compulsive communicators, or talkaholics, later in this chapter). There are people who are constantly quiet from situation to situation, interaction to interaction. These are the people who are usually labeled shy. Although these people are much alike behaviorally in that they are low talkers, their reasons for being so may not be the same. There are at least six reasons that researchers have advanced to explain why people may prefer to communicate less: (1) genetic factors, (2) childhood reinforcement, (3) skill deficiencies, (4) social introversion, (5) social alienation, and (6) ethnic or cultural divergence.

Genetic Factors

You know that you have certain physical and emotional characteristics that you inherited from one or both of your natural parents. Perhaps you have your "mother's nose and your father's eyes." Maybe you share many of your father's physical traits, but have a personality more similar to your mother's. That we do inherit certain personality traits from our parents is crucial to the notion that a predisposition for low talk can be hereditary. Although early researchers (including the authors of this book!) believed that genetics played little if any role in the development of communication behavior, contemporary studies of genetics involving twins have accumulated findings that suggest that a trait known as *sociability* probably is genetic.

Sociability can be defined loosely as the degree to which people desire social contact with others. A person's level of sociability at a very early age appears to be associated with her or his sociability later in life. Much research in this area has compared the sociability levels of fraternal twins with those of identical twins (biologically identical). The general findings of this research show that identical twins are very similar in their sociability, but fraternal twins are not as similar. These findings have important implications for the genetic notion because of how some studies were conducted. Some of the research was conducted on adult twins who had varied social experiences different from those of their siblings. As adults, the twins had taken different life paths and developed relationships with different people in different environments. Although the identical twins had different social experiences, their predispositions for sociability remained similar. This suggests that environmental influences played less of a role in their sociability than did some genetic trait. It should also be noted that an individual's willingness to communicate has been shown to be positively related to Eysenck's supertrait extraversion and negatively related to neuroticism.

This does not mean that genetics is the sole cause of sociability, much less of one's level of WTC. It can be concluded, however, that genetic predisposition probably is *one* contributing cause of individuals' general level of willingness to communicate. Research in this area is not yet extensive. Many questions remain to be answered before we have the full picture of exactly how genetic factors influence this aspect of one's personality.

Childhood Reinforcement

You may be able to recall from your childhood instances when your parents praised you for talking in certain situations. You may recall when they ignored you or otherwise refused reinforcement for talking in other situations. What happened because of either of these instances? Chances are that if you were reinforced for talking, you talked more; if you were not reinforced for talking, you quit talking in some situations, or at least talked less. The latter may very well represent the experiences of many quiet adults when they were growing up. When you notice someone "acting shy" in a certain situation, it could be that as a child that individual received little or no reinforcement for talking in similar situations, or was punished for doing so. Moreover, it is even possible that the individual *was* reinforced for *not* talking. This occurs, for instance, when a parent buys a child an ice cream cone for not talking during a movie.

Another type of reinforcement that might explain the development of shyness is *modeling*. The theory of modeling suggests that people observe the behavior of other people and then try to engage in that same behavior if they see the other person rewarded for the behavior. Many children observe their parents or other significant relatives engaging in low talk in certain situations, such as in church. The children too become low talkers in those situations, especially when the low talk is reinforced. Looking at it a different way, some children will model the talkative behavior of others, receive no reinforcement for such behavior, and because of that become less talkative.

Reinforcement offers a viable explanation for why many people are low talkers. Reinforcement and modeling theories are very predictive of some kinds of communication behavior. For example, children learn their language(s) by listening to the people around them and modeling what they say and the way they say it. They then are rewarded when they use the language well by the people around them. To go from language learning to WTC, however, is quite a leap in generalization. There is no research available that provides support for this speculation. We suggest, then, that reinforcement patterns in childhood may contribute to one's level of WTC, but it probably is not a major causal factor.

Skill Deficiencies

An interesting informal study was conducted at the University of Texas. In hypothetical situations, male college students were asked to act out the process they go through in telephoning a woman for a first date. Many men very easily picked up the phone, dialed a number, and portrayed the typical conversation they would likely engage in. Others, however, had a very difficult time completing the task. Some could not even finish dialing the number before they gave up in total frustration. They were actually frightened of making the call. Their fright was not due to a lack of knowing the other party well, for there was no other party. Nor was it due to a fright of telephones, for the telephone used was a toy one. For the most part, the frustration and the fear experienced by these young men were due to a skill deficiency. They did not know how to ask a woman for a date!

Most of us have an inability to engage in certain activities. Some of us are poor singers, some of us are unable to swim, some of us could not dance if our lives depended on it, and most of us have no idea at all about how to drive a large truck or fly an airplane. Whenever we lack sufficient skills for performing a particular activity, we usually avoid situations that would require us to use those skills. Communicating is no different. As we noted earlier, communication is a learned process, a skill that is acquired through much practice and experience. Without that skill, people may become less willing to communicate and may be labeled "shy" by others with whom they come in contact.

Many problems of oral communication are considered skill deficiencies. Articulation problems, stuttering, voice impairments, and the like are just a few. In the United States, people who speak English as their first language often find communicating with Spanish-speaking people to be problematic. Whether the communication skills a person lacks are physical or linguistic, very often that individual is apt to be less willing to communicate in situations that demand use of those skills. Imagine taking a first course in conversational Cantonese (a Chinese dialect) in which the instructor presents all of the content to you in that language. Chances are quite high that you would withdraw from that course to avoid failing it miserably. In short, some people may become less willing to communicate not because they have no desire to communicate, but because they are inept in certain communication skills. If they can improve their skills, they would likely increase their attempts at communicating.

Social Introversion

Extraversion/introversion is a heavily researched area in the field of personality as we discussed in the previous chapter. It concerns the degree to which people desire to interact with others. Some people have a very strong need or desire to interact with others (social extraverts), and others prefer to be alone most of the time (social introverts). The people in the former group need frequent contact and communication with other people. Those in the latter group prefer their own company, and are most likely to be less willing to communicate. This is not because they lack appropriate communication skills, but because they perceive little need for interacting with others. People like this are quite apt to be labeled shy, but they usually are neither unskilled in communication nor apprehensive about it. They just do not have as much need for it as others do.

Social Alienation

Most of us try to conform to the norms and values of our society. We complete some level of education because it is a norm in our society to do so. We make plans to be successful at our chosen careers, to raise a family, and to retire leisurely because these are high values for members of our society. People who conform to society's norms, whatever they may be, are said to be "well-adjusted"—they do what society expects of them. People who do not conform to the norms and values of society, however, are said to be "alienated" from the society. They reject what society values and make few or no attempts to follow those values. Subsequently, they become *socially alienated*. Social alienation is related to the temperament variable called *psychoticism*, another genetically based element.

A norm of most societies, and especially of the general American society, is that of engaging in a moderate to high amount of communication with others. Although the society values communication in its own right, it also deems communication necessary for the achievement of goals and other values. The socially alienated individual may reject the value of communication and become a low talker. This person simply does not see the value in communication to the extent that most of the rest of the people in the society do. The individual's rejection of this value may be due to a lack of interest in attaining the goals and values that are sought by other members of society. Perhaps the individual dismisses the value of communication because he or she sees others using it in ways that are negative and inappropriate to the individual. When someone views communication in these ways, that person may become much less willing to communicate.

Ethnic or Cultural Divergence

If someone were to ask you if people are the same in all parts of the country, how would you reply? Think about it just a moment. Are natives of southern California any different from those born and raised in Indiana? Are the behaviors, customs, and values of Cornhuskers in Nebraska like those of people from Massachusetts? You probably don't have to think long to answer "no" to these questions. Within almost any large, well-developed culture, like the general American culture, are many co-cultures and ethnic groups. Within the United States, we see cultural and ethnic divergence not only from one state to another but also among different regions of a given state, and even among different neighborhoods within a given city. Communication norms in these various groupings are not alike; dialects are different, conversational rules are different, and some tend to value silence more than talk.

Even when people share a common language, sometimes it is difficult to adapt one's communicative behavior to the norms of a group with which one is unfamiliar. We may find that others use a common word to refer to something else, or that a familiar gesture we use has no apparent meaning for others. The problem can arise whether it involves a person from a majority group entering a minority environment (a young white female from Kansas beginning classes at the University of Hawaii) or a person from a minority group entering a majority environment (a young Hispanic male from East Los Angeles moving to a rural community in predominantly white West Virginia). Whether one is moving across the country, to a different county in the same state, or just to a new neighborhood can present people with a certain amount of anxiety. In each situation, the outsider moving in may be unable to cope with the heavy demands of trying to communicate in a new environment, and thus, the outsider may become less willing to communicate. Consider a foreign student whom you know. You might think of the person as shy, but when that person is back home or with friends from her or his native culture, he or she might be very talkative.

Clearly, being in a cultural context where one's communication traits tend to be stifled does not necessarily mean that this actually changes one's traits. The traits are still there, but the individual may learn to adapt her or his behavior to that which is expected in that context. Such apparent changes are likely to disappear quickly when the person is back in a familiar culture. Hence, this is not likely to be a cause of one's communication traits even though one's behavior undergoes a temporary modification.

▣ COMMUNICATION APPREHENSION (CA)

Interpreting Personal Report of Communication Apprehension–24 (PRCA) Scores

Your score on the Personal Report of Communication Apprehension–24 (PRCA) Scale (Scale 11 in the appendix) should range between 24 and 120 (if it is below 24 or over 120, you have made a computational error). The PRCA Scale is designed to measure a general trait of CA, how a person typically reacts to oral communication with others. The higher your score, the more apprehension you generally feel about communicating.

Between 60 percent and 70 percent of the people who have completed the PRCA Scale have scores ranging from 50 to 80. This is called the "normal" range. If your score falls anywhere outside this range, the idea of CA may be especially relevant to you personally. If your score is between 24 and 50, you are among those in our society who experience the least CA. You are apt to be a higher talker and may actively seek out opportunities to interact with others. Very few, if any, communication situations cause you to be fearful or anxious. If your score is somewhere between 50 and 60, you experience less CA than most people. However, you are likely to feel some fear or anxiety about some context(s). If your score falls between 60 and 70, your level of CA is similar to that of most people. There are some communication situations that may cause you to feel anxious or tense; in others, you will feel quite comfortable. If your score is between 70 and 80, you experience more CA than most people. Probably many communication situations cause you to be fearful and tense, but some do not bother you. If your score falls between 80 and 120, you are among those who experience the most CA. You likely are a low talker, one who actively avoids many communication situations because you feel much anxiety and tension in those situations.

Let us examine a little more closely those who fall within the various score ranges on the PRCA Scale. People in the "normal" range (50 to 80) tend to respond quite differently in different situations. They may be very tense in one situation (when giving a speech) but quite comfortable in another (when out on a date). Those who score in the "low" (below 50) and "high" (above 80) ranges tend to respond to most communication situations in the same way. Researchers consider both extremes to be abnormal. The "low" communication-apprehensive person is considered abnormal because this person is unlikely to feel any fear or anxiety about communicating even in situations in which he or she *should* be anxious (for example, when entering her or his very first job interview). Such people just aren't bothered by oral communication.

Although this is often an advantage, it *is* normal to feel some fear in response to a threatening situation. The person who experiences no fear in such situations usually makes poor decisions about when to communicate and when not to (therefore the expression "Insert foot in mouth"). The "high" communication-apprehensive person is considered abnormal because this person usually experiences fear and anxiety about communicating. They even experience apprehension in situations where they probably should not be anxious (for example, when calling a friend on the phone). Such people are likely to avoid communication in most situations. This avoidance can be quite costly when communicating would be to the person's advantage. A common example is the student who never participates in class discussion even when participation is a criterion for a higher grade.

Although some people desire to communicate with others and see the importance of doing so, they may be impeded by their fear or anxiety. People who lack appropriate communication skills or whose communication is ethnically or culturally divergent may also experience CA. Most people who are communication apprehensive, however, are neither skill deficient nor different from others in the general culture. Typically, they are normal people who are simply afraid to communicate. Because it is natural for people to avoid things they fear, communication-apprehensive people tend to be less willing to communicate. Therefore, they may be labeled shy by others around them. It is important to note, also, that many communication-apprehensive people do not feel restricted by their feelings about communicating—they can be as happy and as productive as nonapprehensive communicators. Most of the social problems experienced by these individuals stem from how they are perceived by others and how others respond to them.

Communication Apprehension as a Trait

It is most useful to think of CA as existing along a four-point continuum (see Figure 3.1). Starting at one extreme end of the continuum and moving to the other extreme, the four points are CA (1) as a trait, (2) in a generalized context, (3) with a given individual or group across contexts, and (4) with a given individual or group in a given situation. Each type of CA is examined below.

When we say "as a trait," we mean CA is a part of an individual's personality. Such a trait is most important for those people who have either very high or very low levels of CA. It is this trait that the total score on the PRCA Scale was designed to measure. An extreme score on this measure suggests that your behavior is influenced as much, if not more, by your general fear or anxiety about communication as by any specifics of a communication situation in which you find yourself. At the extremes of the trait, either you

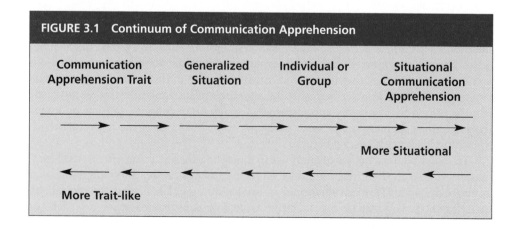

FIGURE 3.1   Continuum of Communication Apprehension

Communication Apprehension Trait	Generalized Situation	Individual or Group	Situational Communication Apprehension

More Situational

More Trait-like

experience high degrees of anxiety in most communication situations, or you experience very little anxiety in most communication situations.

We should note at this point that from 15 to 20 percent of the population falls within each extreme category. Thus, if you score very low, or very high, on the PRCA scale, you are outside the normal range of scores where about two-thirds of the population score. At one end we have the people we call *high CAs,* and at the other we have the *low CAs.* Whenever we use these terms, or reference *moderate CA* (the normal range), we are referencing trait CA.

Communication Apprehension in Generalized Contexts

This view of CA recognizes those individuals who experience high levels of anxiety about communicating in a particular context or situation but who have much less or even no anxiety about communicating in other contexts. The PRCA Scale, besides giving a measure of trait CA, can be broken down to yield measures of CA in four generalized contexts: talking within small groups, speaking in meetings or classroom situations, talking in dyadic interpersonal encounters, and presenting public speeches.

For these scales, a score above 18 is high, and a score above 23 shows an extremely high level of CA about that generalized context. It is quite possible for you to score very high in one context but relatively low in another, or even all of the others. If this is the case, it indicates you are highly apprehensive about some but not all generalized contexts.

Perhaps you scored high on the measure for group communication but low on the others. Here, you feel apprehensive about communicating in situations in which you find yourself involved in a small group. Two types of groups are important here. One type is the task-oriented group. This type of group is one in which the participants get together for solving one or more problems (for example, a group of students who meet to study for an exam). The other type of small group is the social group, the type that is formed for enjoyment, amusement, and/or sharing friendship.

A person could feel apprehensive about communicating in either type of group for many reasons. Perhaps the person feels that other group members are too critical of her or his ideas or suggestions. Perhaps the person feels that her or his own contributions aren't important to the other members. Or the person's attitude is as follows: more than two people can't carry on a meaningful and effective oral exchange, so why get involved? For the person who is highly apprehensive in small-group contexts, but not in others, there is simply some aspect of small-group situations that causes the individual much discomfort when participating in them.

You might have a higher level of CA in a meeting than in other situations. Meetings are similar to the group situation. Here the group is larger and communication among participants is relatively formal and stylized. A good analogy is the typical college classroom. You may be very talkative when with your friends, when on a date, or even when meeting a new acquaintance. The formal structure of the classroom, along with the added pressure of anticipating having to display your knowledge orally, may cause you much anxiety in that context. Most people can communicate quite openly and easily when they have much freedom in what to say and when to say it; however, when they confront a context, such as in a classroom or committee meeting, where communication is restricted by explicit rules, they can become very apprehensive.

If your level of CA is higher for dyadic interpersonal contexts than for the others, you experience anxiety when interacting with others on a one-on-one basis. There are several interpersonal contexts in which one might feel highly apprehensive about communicating. One context is when someone is interacting with a peer. The person may be so concerned with trying to make a good impression that it leads to much tension and anxiety. Another interpersonal context in which many people feel anxious is in interacting with a teacher. The individual may be very talkative in class. However, when facing a teacher one-on-one, the person experiences anxiety because of uncertainty about how to react to the teacher or about how the teacher might respond. A third anxiety-producing dyadic context is that involving romantic or possibly romantic encounters. Some people approach communication with potential romantic partners with confidence. Others, however, because of past negative experiences or anticipated negative consequences, find communicating with potential romantic partners to be quite traumatic. This is precisely the feeling experienced by the male college students in the telephone experiment mentioned earlier in this chapter. Their lack of appropriate communicative skills had resulted in enough "failures" for them that even pretending to call a female for a date caused them much apprehension.

Have you ever interviewed for a job? How did you feel about it as the time grew nearer? If you have never had an interview, how does anticipating that time make you feel? Feeling some anxiety about such interpersonal situations puts you in the majority. A job interview, particularly the first one, is a very strange and novel experience, and few people really know how to deal with it. Communication is the key to a successful interview. Specifically, what kind of communication? Being uncertain and fearful about what to say in a job interview and how to respond to the interviewer can result in high levels of CA in those contexts. Many people feel apprehensive when communicating with their supervisors at work. This feeling may stem from a need to make a good impression on the supervisor. Perhaps it stems from a fear of having the ideas one puts forth to the supervisor explicitly rejected. Conversely, many supervisors have a high level of anxiety about communicating with subordinates. Their apprehension could stem from anticipating complaints about how matters involving subordinates are being handled. Their apprehension could stem from not having the information subordinates want or need to carry out their jobs in an effective way. Whether the situation is formal or informal, and whether it involves friends or strangers or people of equal or different status, many individuals find dyadic interpersonal contexts to be very anxiety producing.

Public speaking is the generalized context that causes the most problems for the most people. In fact, several national studies have indicated that the fear of public speaking is the number one fear of Americans (above snakes, drowning, heights, and death). Public speaking places one in a conspicuous position in front of others who will be evaluating you and critically evaluating what you have to say. Most people have little experience and little to no training in effective speech making, so it is not surprising that many people find this context threatening.

Communication Apprehension with a Given Individual or Group across Contexts

Let us now examine CA experienced because of interacting with a specific individual or group in *any* context. Nearly 95 percent of the population reports having felt apprehension at least once in their lives when communicating with some specific person or group. It is not the communication context that triggers the problem; it is the other people!

Some people simply cause us to be apprehensive. It may be a parent, a teacher, a certain salesperson, the IRS agent, the principal, or the boss. This anxiety may be a function of how others behave toward us (for example, "Bring home an F, and you're on your own!"), or perhaps the role they play in our life ("Hello. I'm here to audit your tax returns for the past five years"). For most of us, there is someone we know who makes us feel totally relaxed when interacting with her or him. It also is quite normal for us to find talking with some specific person or group to be anxiety producing. Have you talked with your priest, rabbi, or minister lately? Try talking to someone you find to be very sexually attractive in the town where you live.

Communication Apprehension with a Given Individual or Group in a Given Situation

Virtually 100 percent of us experience CA with a given individual or group in a given situation. Most of the examples we can think of seem extreme. For example, you have to apologize to a friend for offending that person, a police officer you know pulls you over and informs you that your license plate is missing, you arrive home to find a message that tells you your date has had a last-minute change of heart, a teacher confronts you after class with the accusation that you have been cheating, or you have to tell your parents something that you know they won't like. What separates CA in these situations from the other forms of CA is that these situations are unique encounters with the other individuals. These are not situations you have chosen; they are situations that have been thrust on you. Thus, although we generally would not be apprehensive about communicating with the other persons, the specific situation arouses anxiety. Most of us can communicate quite easily with our mothers, but forgetting Mom's birthday can lead to quite a hair-raising communicative event.

CA, therefore, is a fear or anxiety about communicating that can stem from one's basic personality or temperament, the type of communication expected, the person or persons with whom we anticipate communicating, or the unique circumstances surrounding a given interaction. No matter its source, CA causes us discomfort, may result in our avoiding communication, and can result in our being ineffective in our communication with others.

Causes of Trait Communication Apprehension

In research looking at Eysenck's supertraits and CA (Beatty, McCroskey, & Heisel, 1998; Heisel, McCroskey, & Richmond, 1999; McCroskey, Heisel, & Richmond, 2001), research found that CA was negatively related to extraversion and positively related to neuroticism. Essentially, high communication apprehensives are "emotionally unstable introverts," and low communication apprehensives are "emotionally stable extraverts." Trait CA is associated with personality and temperament (Beatty, McCroskey, & Valencic, 2001). Thus, the causes of this type of communicative anxiety are much like those of many personality variables, namely, it is primarily a function of genetic factors, but sometimes is also impacted by cultural and/or experience.

Causes of Situational Communication Apprehension

The causes of situational CA *appear* to be clear. Buss (1980) has provided a useful exposition of the major elements in a situation that he believes can lead to CA. They are novelty, formality, subordinate status, conspicuousness, unfamiliarity, dissimilarity, excessive attention, evaluation, and prior failure. Additionally, Daly and Hailey (1983) suggest that high evaluation and previous failure can cause situational CA. Each of these elements is discussed in the following paragraphs.

Novelty. Recall your first day alone at college. Did you find it a difficult situation to deal with initially? If so, it was probably because college was a *novel,* or new, experience for you. Novel situations present us with increased uncertainty about how we should behave: the first date, a new job, meeting a dating partner's parents. Each is a novel situation, and approaching them is very likely to increase CA.

Formality. We behave much differently than normal when we dress in formal attire and attend some auspicious occasion. *Formal situations* are associated with highly prescribed behaviors. In these situations, the prescribed behaviors are deemed "appropriate," and there is little latitude for deviation from them. Because of the narrower restrictions placed on acceptable behavior in formal situations, CA is likely to increase in such situations. The same is true when we interact from a *subordinate position*. In these situations, the person holding higher status defines what is appropriate behavior. Examples are seen in teacher–student, employer–employee, and politician–constituent interactions, and the like.

Conspicuousness. You may have experienced the embarrassment of attending a family reunion. You probably experienced having all your aunts and uncles, many of whom you do not even know, gawk and fuss over you. Perhaps more than anything else, being *conspicuous* in one's environment sharply increases CA. This is precisely what causes your fear when you rise to give a speech or accept an award, or stand to make a comment in a meeting or crowded classroom, or when you are introduced for the first time to a long line of distant relatives.

Unfamiliarity.   How do you feel when you attend a large party where you know perhaps only one or two people? Do you find yourself standing alone in a corner just waiting for someone to come over and begin a conversation? Many people feel much more comfortable when communicating with people they know than when communicating with people they do not know. Generally, the more *unfamiliar* the people around us, the more likely our CA will rise.

Dissimilarity.   In much the same way as unfamiliarity, *dissimilarity* of those around us causes CA to increase. For most of us, talking to people who are similar to us is easier than talking to people who are greatly different. If you are a social sciences major, try carrying on a conversation with a diehard engineering major. If you are a science major, try talking to an English major. You may find the conversation very difficult to maintain. There are exceptions, of course. Some people are less comfortable when talking to people like themselves than when talking to people who are very different, or even strangers. This is because the former is more likely to make evaluations about us that may prove threatening.

Excessive Attention.   Most of us do not like to be stared at (depending on the attractiveness and intent of the one doing the staring, that is). Neither do we care to be ignored by others. A moderate degree of attention from others is usually the most comfortable situation. *Excessive attention,* such as staring or having someone probe into our private thoughts, can cause our level of CA to rise sharply.

Evaluation.   Many students have little trouble in talking with their teachers until the teacher begins *evaluating* the student's classroom performance. The same holds true for workers in relation to their supervisors. When we are evaluated, we tend to become more anxious than we would otherwise. As the intensity of the evaluation increases, so might the level of apprehension. Research done on apprehension associated with writing suggests an exception to this possibility, however. Daly and Hailey (1983) have found that high evaluation improves the performance of good writers but worsens the performance of poor writers. We can speculate that the same holds true for oral communication, but no research has substantiated that speculation yet.

Prior Failure.   Finally, of all the causal elements of CA discussed, the most important of all may be previous failure. When we fail at something once, it is increasingly likely that we will develop a fear of failing again. It is a case of expectations. If we expect to fail and do so, but are unable to decide the successful behavior to engage in, we are quite apt to develop apprehension. Of course, success causes both success and confidence, and thus reduces apprehension.

To summarize, many elements that are tied to the communication situation appear to increase CA. It is important to note, however, that the absence of these elements is presumed to *decrease* CA. Few if any of these elements are under our direct control. Situational CA, then, would appear to be produced and, to a large extent, controlled by others in our environment. Thus, the only way to deter the unpleasant aspects of this form of CA is to avoid or withdraw from anxiety-producing communication situations. As we will see in the next section, avoidance and withdrawal from interaction are two of the many effects of CA.

Although all of the above seems obvious and straightforward, more recent research has raised serious questions about how much impact these variables in the situation really have. Research by Beatty (1988) and others (Beatty & Friedland, 1989) has shown that people's presumed responses to situations actually are more trait-like than situation produced. People who tend to be sensitive to evaluation, for example, see all situations as more evaluative than do people who do not have this trait. People who tend to be sensitive to conspicuousness report feeling more conspicuous than do other people, no matter how conspicuous they really are.

What is making these "obvious" causes of situational CA appear obvious is that both experts and normal people are susceptible to what is known as *basic attribution error*. It has been demonstrated that people prefer to attribute their own negative feelings and behaviors to situational matters beyond their control than to their own traits and emotions. It is, therefore, not surprising that when we try to explain why we are fearful or anxious, we seek "obvious" and apparently reasonable external factors to blame rather than admit to a failing of our own, small though it may be.

In reality, situations cannot cause anything. They are stable. (When was the last time you saw a situation chasing someone down the street?) People choose situations, not the other way around. When we fear or are anxious about a situation, we usually avoid it, and, hence, we experience no negative effects of that situation. "I'm afraid of roller coasters, so I don't ride them." "I can't swim, so I don't jump into pools of water." However, when we are forced into a situation that we don't want to encounter, there may be a problem. "I have never given a speech, and never plan to." "That class requires me to give speeches, so I won't take it." "It is required for graduation? Oh NO!!" It is not the situation that is causing the problem; it is when people force others into situations, which they normally would avoid, which causes the problem.

Effects of Communication Apprehension

The most obvious effects of CA are internal discomfort, avoidance or withdrawal from communication situations, and communication disruption. People experience CA internally. That is, the experience of CA is a mental one—it is felt psychologically. Thus, although some individuals may experience CA to greater or lesser degrees than other individuals, or only when with certain people or in certain situations, the one thing people all share in common when anxious about communicating is an internally experienced feeling of discomfort. Typically, the lower our CA, the lower our discomfort communicating.

People tend to differ in their individual responses to CA. Some handle it well and can communicate effectively despite their internal discomfort. For most people who experience CA, however, particularly high levels of it, communication is a problem. Three typical response patterns emerge when CA is experienced: communication avoidance, communication withdrawal, and communication disruption.

When people are confronted with a situation that they expect will make them uncomfortable and they have a choice of whether to enter the situation, they can decide to either confront the situation and make the best of it or avoid it and thus avoid the discomfort. An analogy is the student who receives poor midterm grades and decides not to go home for spring break: by not going home, the student avoids the discomfort of having to face Mom and Dad's wrath about the grades (this assumes, of course, that the student has a choice of whether to go home). Frequently, people with high CA will avoid situations that require them to communicate orally with others.

It is not always possible for a person to avoid communication. Sometimes there is no reason to expect a situation to cause discomfort, so a person may enter it with her or his psychological guard down. When situations such as these arise, withdrawal is the typical response for the person experiencing CA. The withdrawal may be total (such as absolute silence) or partial (such as talking only when absolutely necessary). An example of possible withdrawal is the student who speaks in class only when directly called on by the teacher. Another is when a person in a one-on-one interaction only answers questions and gives responses but never initiates conversation. When unable to avoid a communication situation, the high CA usually will withdraw from interaction, if possible.

A third typical response to CA is communication disruption. This disruption can take two forms. One form is disturbed or nonfluent communication. Examples are stuttering, stammering, speaking too softly, increased pauses, use of inappropriate gestures and expressions, and poor choices of words and phrases. The other form of disruption is overcommunication. This is an overcompensation reflected in one's attempt to succeed in the situation despite the internal discomfort it causes. An example is a person who takes a public-speaking course despite her or his extreme stage fright. Thus, the high CA is likely to use inappropriate behaviors in a discomforting communication situation. It is important to note, however, that disruption is also characteristic of people with inadequate communication skills and that overcommunication is often mistaken for low apprehension.

EFFECTS OF SHYNESS AND WTC

WTC produces important effects only if the person's WTC impacts their behavior. People who have a high WTC are not likely to engage in shy behavior. People who have a low level of WTC are most likely to exhibit shy behavior. That is, they initiate fewer communicative interactions and respond less positively to others who attempt to initiate interaction with them. Lower WTC leads to shyness, and the shy behavior causes problems. The effects of shyness, then, can be considered from two viewpoints: the person's own behavior in different social contexts, and the perceptions other people have of the person who is shy.

We turn first to the quiet person's behavior in the classroom, in small groups, in dyads, in social situations, and in occupational choice. Again, when we refer to quiet people we are thinking of low talkers, people who exhibit shy behavior. Thus, the behaviors and perceptions discussed below apply equally well to people who are shy because they have high CA, and to others who are simply low in WTC for other reasons.

The typical U.S. classroom environment demands a high level of communication. Thus, the classroom behavior of low talkers can be expected to differ from that of high talkers. Much research has focused on how low and high talkers differ in their classroom behavior. There are many differences in how low talkers, particularly high CAs, will avoid small classes in which there are many opportunities for student–student and student–instructor interaction. They prefer large lecture-type classes in which most communication is the instructor talking to students and the students remaining quiet and listening. Low talkers avoid classes that require oral reports or speeches and in which part of the grade is based on "class participation." When they must be in such a class, they almost never volunteer to participate, choosing to wait until they are called on by the teacher. Low talkers often will drop a class that has high communication demands, even if it is a required course. Finally, low talkers differ from high talkers in their preference for seating in the classroom. When given a choice of where to sit, low talkers will choose to sit along the sides or in the rear of the classroom. This is because most interaction takes place in the front and down the middle of the room.

Although a small-group setting is not as threatening to most people as, say, a public-speaking setting, it still places great communication demands on the participants. Thus, differences abound between low and high talkers in group settings. Typically, the low talker will avoid small-group interactions. When avoidance is not possible, withdrawal occurs in several forms. The low talker may withdraw from group discussion by remaining quiet. If required to speak, low talkers will often make irrelevant comments, apparently in hope that this will get other group members to stop asking them questions. When questioned in a group setting, the favored response of many low talkers is a simple "I don't know." Finally, as in the classroom, low talkers will choose seats in a group setting that inhibit their interaction with other members. They will avoid seats at the head or foot of the table and choose inconspicuous seats along the side.

As in other settings, communication in dyads (one-on-one interactions) differs sharply for low and high talkers. In general, low talkers take on a submissive, follower role in dyadic encounters. They refrain from saying much about themselves to their partner, but they have a high concern that their partner understands or agrees with what they have to say. The latter is evidenced in the low talker's heavy use of "trailers" such as "You know?" "OK?" and "You see?"

High talkers tend to involve themselves in more social activities and situations than do low talkers. Some of the most striking differences between low and high talkers in their social behaviors relate to dating and marriage. Low and high talkers have equally normal desires for heterosocial (opposite-sex) relationships (presuming that is their sexual orientation). Low talkers tend to engage in much more steady dating than do high talkers. That is, low talkers are more likely to have an exclusive heterosocial relationship than are high talkers. This tendency toward exclusive relationships is also seen in the marital behavior of low talkers. In one study, over 50 percent of the low talkers (here, communication apprehensives) married within one year after completing their under-graduate degrees. No similar pattern was found for high talkers. What these behavioral tendencies suggest is that low talkers find it difficult to establish social relationships, so they make very strong efforts to maintain ones they can establish. High talkers appar-ently find the establishment of relationships to be not so difficult. Thus, they are more apt to allow established ones to end and look forward to beginning new ones.

Finally, it is important to consider the differences between low talkers and high talk-ers in their choices of occupations. The choice of an occupation is one of the most signif-icant decisions one can make. It determines whether the person will be successful, what the person's social and economic standing will be, and, to a large extent, whether the per-son will be happy in later life. Many factors influence one's selection of an occupation, but one important factor is the person's willingness to communicate. Low talkers tend to choose occupations with lower communication demands than those chosen by high talk-ers. Thus, low talkers are more likely to select occupations such as forest ranger, auto mechanic, accountant, and lab technician. High talkers may lean more toward salesper-son, trial lawyer, telephone operator, and broadcast journalist. What about teaching as an occupation? Interestingly, research has found that teachers who are low talkers prefer the lower elementary grades and preschool to secondary and college teaching. This may be because teaching young children is less likely to garner direct social and professional evaluation from students than does teaching older children and adults.

In summary, the effects of WTC on communicative behavior are most apparent in the differences in the behaviors of low talkers compared with high talkers. Generally, low talk-ers will avoid any communication situation that they anticipate will result in discomfort. They will avoid taking classes that place high demands on communication. They will avoid small-group interactions whenever possible. They will avoid self-disclosure and disagree-ment in dyadic situations, they will avoid ending established heterosocial relationships, and they will avoid occupations that require a high level of communication. When avoidance is impossible, low talkers typically will withdraw from the communication situation.

It is important to realize these are typical response tendencies of people with low willingness to communicate and particularly highly communication-apprehensive per-sons. However, some people who are highly willing to communicate will also engage in these behaviors on occasion. Nor do all people who have low levels of willingness to communicate engage in the same avoidance behaviors. Recall, as we noted above, that some will choose to confront rather than avoid the demands of a discomforting situation and try to overcome it. Therefore, we should exercise caution when observing the behavior of others. For instance, just because an individual is quiet in the classroom does not mean that person is highly apprehensive; he or she may be a heavy daydreamer or an uninterested student.

This brings us directly to a consideration of some perceptions others have of shy and high CAs. We first look at people's general perceptions of low talkers in terms of their attractiveness, competence, anxiety, and leadership. Next we look at how low talk-ers are perceived in three specific settings—school, social, and work.

PERCEPTIONS OF QUIET PEOPLE

As we noted earlier, our society places a great deal of importance on communication. It is no surprise, then, that low talkers are usually perceived as unfriendly. Therefore, low talkers are viewed as less attractive than are talkative people. Moreover, even low talkers perceive other low talkers to be less attractive than talkative persons.

Low talkers are perceived as less competent than talkative people. Research has found people to have a stereotype of a quiet person as less competent and less intelligent. Fortunately, this is only a stereotype. We say this is fortunate because stereotypes do not hold true for all members of a group. There are just as many intelligent low talkers as there are stupid low talkers. Similarly, there are as many stupid talkative people as there are intelligent talkative people. Nevertheless, the general perception of low talkers is that they are less competent and less intelligent.

A frequently accurate perception of low talkers is that they are generally more anxious than talkative people. Although not all low talkers are apprehensive about communication, many are, and their tendency for apprehension is generalized to other low talkers. This leads to another stereotype: that low talkers are anxious people.

The role of leader in most situations requires at least a moderate degree of communication with other people. Thus, low talkers are perceived to be poor leaders. This perception is very often correct. There are, of course, instances in which quiet people function as leaders, for example, by providing some very needed information that helps a group reach a decision. However, even in these situations the low talker is unlikely to be perceived as a leader.

Perceptions such as the ones just presented are important for several reasons. For one, it is how we perceive people that will determine the nature of our relationship with them. For another, how we perceive people will have a significant impact on our interactions with them in certain settings. Three of these settings will be explored in greater detail in the interpersonal, organizational, and instructional chapters later in this book.

Overall, people have perceptions of low talkers that characterize them as being in a highly undesirable condition, and that make them appear incompetent. Is this necessarily true? Fortunately, it is not. As noted previously, many quiet people are most happy and content with their lives. Many are successful at what they do. When offered help to overcome CA, many quiet people decline. Many have adjusted well to their lifestyle and have no desire to change. Nevertheless, people who are highly willing to communicate, and happily engage in communication with others, generally have a major advantage in this culture over those less willing to communicate.

COMPULSIVE COMMUNICATION (TALKAHOLICS)

Up to this point in this chapter, we have focused primary attention on one end of the willingness to communicate continuum. We may have created a dichotomy in your mind—an image of two kinds of people in the world—those who are "normal" and those who are "quiet." We do not want to go to the next chapter without modifying that image. Not all nonquiet people are "normal."

Have you ever known someone who talked too much? When we ask this question of groups to whom we talk, we find almost everyone will answer "yes" to this question. Our research, and that of others, which stretches back for over a half-century suggests that increased talking, up to a very high level, has nothing but positive outcomes. Thus, perceptions that someone talks too much must indicate a response to the quality of the talk of that person, not the quantity.

Does this mean there are no really extremely high talkers out there? Of course not. We all know people who "never shut up." Someone in your family may fall into that category. We refer to these extremely high willing to communicate people as *talkaholics,* or compulsive communicators. If you scored above 40 on the Talkaholic Scale (Scale 12 in the appendix), welcome to the group! Our research suggests that about one person in twenty can be placed in this category.

Talkaholics generally recognize that they are compulsive communicators. They can't change, even if they want to—and very few, we have found, want to. In the general American culture, one is rewarded for being a talkaholic much more often than one is punished. Talkaholics have told us repeatedly that their talking has gotten them in trouble. However, their solution to the problem has been to just keep on talking and get themselves out of that trouble!

Being a talkaholic can be detrimental for a person, as criminal talkaholics have found when they have been unable to keep quiet about their activities! It can also be an advantage to people in cultures that value communication highly (as the general American culture does). It can be particularly advantageous in occupations that require a great deal of contact with the public. Being able to maintain a constant stream of chatter can be highly profitable and rewarding in many occupations. We have found, for example, that the proportion of talkaholics in an audience of communication professors and graduate students at a national convention was almost five times as high as we have found in the general public! Could this be the reason they were drawn to that profession?

Are these talkaholics the people we all recognize as the "people who talk too much"? The research in this area indicates they are not. Many talkaholics are not seen as excessive communicators, but some are. Some talkaholics are not skilled communicators, so they are more likely to engage in low-quality communication behavior that would lead to negative perceptions. Also, to our surprise, we found that there was almost the same proportion of talkaholics who are high communication apprehensives as there was of those who are low communication apprehensives. These apprehensive-but-compulsive communicators are trying to defeat their fear of communication by doing more of it. It is likely that many of them do not communicate all that well. From a supertrait perspective, talkaholism relates positively to Eysenck's supertrait extraversion and not at all to neuroticism or psychoticism. Research has also shown us that talkaholics and people with a high willingness to communicate tend to also be fairly competent communicators, so the next section in this chapter is going to examine communicator competence.

COMMUNICATION COMPETENCE AND SELF-PERCEIVED COMMUNICATION COMPETENCE (SPCC)

As discussed in Chapter 1, when we refer to someone as "communicatively competent," we are suggesting that the person has "adequate ability to make ideas known to others by talking or writing" (McCroskey, 1984, p. 263). This is communication competence at its most basic level. It ignores feelings, attitudes, and behavior, focusing simply on being understood. Basic communication competence depends on at least three elements: (1) a cognitive understanding of the communication process, (2) the psychomotor capacity to produce necessary communication behaviors, and (3) a positive affective orientation toward communication. To put it more simply, to achieve basic communication competence, you must develop an understanding of what you need to do, develop the physical behaviors required to do it (learn to write, articulate words, and so forth), and want to do it.

If you are reading this book, you most likely have developed a sufficient set of psychomotor (behavioral) skills for many kinds of oral communication, though you may lack skills for certain types of communication. You may or may not have a positive attitude toward communication. Thus, the greatest need you probably had when you began this book was the development of a greater cognitive understanding of the communication process.

So, how does one tell if he or she is a competent communicator? Well, this question is unfortunately too simplistic and requires a rather extensive answer. The Self-Perceived Communication Competence (SPCC) measure (Scale 13 in the appendix) examines your perceived level of communication competence in relation to different communication contexts (public, meeting, group, and dyadic) and your perceived level of competence when communicating with a variety of different receivers (strangers, acquaintances, and friends). It is possible to be completely competent when communicating with your friends but not be competent at all in your communication with strangers; this is why this measure looks at your competence across a variety of situations and groups of people.

Unfortunately, basic communication competence is not enough. Most of us do not simply want to be understood by others. We also want them to like us, we want to build relationships with them, and frequently we want to influence them. In short, we want to be *interpersonally* communicatively competent. Interpersonal communication competence rests on a foundation of general communication competence. The interpersonally competent communicator exhibits three critical elements in her or his communication: assertiveness, responsiveness, and versatility.

Interpersonal communication competence begins with an individual's sociocommunicative orientation (SCO). The assertiveness-responsiveness measure that you completed for yourself measures the two dimensions of SCO (Scale 14 in the appendix). Your score on each dimension of SCO can range from 10 to 50. The higher your score on each dimension, the more assertive or responsive you see yourself. These scores represent the primary components of your sociocommunicative orientation.

If you would duplicate this measure and give it to a half-dozen people who know you well—not necessarily people who are good friends, just people who know you well—you can get a picture of how others see your communication. You will notice that this instrument is very much like the SCO. However, it represents the perception of you by someone else rather than your perception of yourself. We call this a measure of sociocommunicative style (SCS). SCS is the way others see you, whereas SCO is the way you see yourself. If you have a clear and undistorted self-perception, and you behave the way you report on the measure of your SCO, the scores you get on the SCS measure (on *average,* not every individual person's score) should be very similar. Richmond and McCroskey (1990) developed these measures of assertiveness and responsiveness to help people gain insight into their probable level of communication competence.

Implicit in the concept of communication competence, as we are using it here, is the idea that a person's level of competence is very similar across many contexts. That is, an individual's level of communication competence is "trait-like." It is rooted firmly in the person's personality and temperament. The impact of personality on communication behavior has been clearly demonstrated for decades (McCroskey & Daly, 1987). Similarly, it has been established that individuals exhibit trait-like differences in their basic communication styles (Norton, 1983). These styles also have been examined under such labels as "personal style" (Merrill & Reid, 1981), "social style" (Lashbrook, 1974), and "psychological androgyny" (Bem, 1974; Wheeless & Dierks-Stewart, 1981). These approaches are rooted in Jungian psychology and are represented in the very popular Myers-Briggs personality inventory, which often is used when counselors are helping people make decisions with regard to occupational choices.

These style-based approaches characteristically suggest two or more dimensions to the individual's style, which are assumed to result in differential communication behaviors. These behaviors are presumed to communicate distinctive impressions of the individual to others. This set of behaviors is what we have chosen to refer to as the person's *sociocommunicative style.* It is presumed that observers can gain insight into the personality of individuals by taking note of their characteristic communication behaviors (Thomas, Richmond, & McCroskey, 1994). The two most commonly referenced dimensions of sociocommunicative style are assertiveness and responsiveness. Assertiveness is characterized by descriptors such as independent, dominant, aggressive, competitive, and forceful. Conversely, responsiveness is characterized by describers such as helpful, sympathetic, compassionate, sincere, and friendly. McCroskey, Richmond, and Stewart (1986) note that a third component, versatility, is characterized by being able to adapt one's communicative style to the needs of the rhetorical situation. We will consider all three of those components.

Assertiveness

Assertiveness is the capacity to make requests; actively disagree; express positive or negative personal rights and feelings; initiate, maintain, or disengage from conversations; and stand up for oneself without attacking another. Previously, Bem (1974) and Wheeless and Dierks-Stewart (1981) researched communicative assertiveness, but they called the term "masculinity." This, of course, does not suggest that only males are likely to exhibit this element of communication. However, in many societies the stereotype of appropriate male communication behavior is closely associated with this characteristic.

Terms that are commonly used to describe a person who engages in assertive communication behaviors include *willing to defend own beliefs, independent, forceful, strong personality, dominant, willing to take a stand and act as a leader,* and (of course) *assertive.* You will recognize these as items on the SCO and SCS scales. Such terms do describe the stereotypical male image in American society, but more importantly, they describe a person who is in control both of self and of the communication process.

It is important that we distinguish between assertiveness and something with which it often is confused—aggressiveness. Aggressiveness essentially is assertiveness *plus.* That is, the aggressive person not only stands up for her or his rights, but also demands that others yield their rights. An assertive person, for example, makes *requests;* an aggressive person makes *demands.* Assertive individuals insist that others respect their rights; aggressive people do the same thing while ignoring the rights of others.

The effects of assertiveness and aggressiveness can be similar, yet essentially they are different. To clarify, either approach is likely to help people get their way. In the process, however, the assertive individual is likely to maintain good relationships with others, but the aggressive individual is likely to alienate others. The interpersonally competent communicator, of course, can influence others while maintaining good relationships with those others.

Our research indicates a major factor that inhibits individuals from behaving in an appropriate assertive manner in communication is shyness brought on by communication apprehension. Engaging in assertive behavior usually prompts others in an interaction to communicate more. Highly communication-apprehensive individuals, of course, tend to avoid communication. Thus, often high apprehensives may simply yield their rights rather than assertively defend them and thus have to communicate more. Highly apprehensive individuals, therefore, are frequently not interpersonally competent communicators.

Responsiveness

Responsiveness is the capacity to be sensitive to the communication of others, to be a good listener, to make others comfortable in communicating, and to recognize the needs and desires of others. Previously, Bem (1974) and Wheeless and Dierks-Stewart (1981) referred to this aspect of communication as "femininity." This label does not suggest that only females can be responsive to others, but suggests that this is the American stereotype of appropriate female communication behavior.

Terms that are commonly used to describe a person who engages in responsive communication behaviors include *helpful, sympathetic, compassionate, sensitive to needs of others, sincere, gentle, warm, tender, friendly, understanding,* and (of course) *responsive to others.* Again, you will recognize these as items from the SCO and SCS scales. Although such terms do describe the stereotypical female image in American society, in a broader sense they describe any person who is open to the communication of others and empathic with those others.

Empathy is the capacity of an individual to put her or himself into the shoes of another; to see things from the other person's vantage point. This is communicated to the other person both verbally and nonverbally. When we state the other person's view correctly (in their mind) or say things like "I see your point," "I understand what you mean," or "I have had that experience too," we communicate empathy and responsiveness. We also communicate responsiveness when we look at other people when they are talking, and when we smile at them, lean toward them, touch them, and so forth. In other words, we communicate responsively when we are immediate with others.

It is important to distinguish between responsiveness and submissiveness. The two are confused with each other. *Submissiveness* is the yielding of one's rights to another. Responsiveness is recognizing the needs and rights of another *without* yielding one's own rights. The responsive individual understands and acknowledges the feelings of the other person. The submissive individual does that, but also goes on to yield to the requests of the other person even when that requires that the submissive person go against her or his own feelings, rights, or needs.

As with assertiveness and aggressiveness, the effects of responsiveness and submissiveness are similar yet essentially different. Either approach is likely to get at least momentary liking from the other person. That liking is produced at the cost of one's own well-being for submissiveness, but not for responsiveness. The interpersonally competent communicator, of course, can generate good relationships with others while maintaining a position of influence with them.

As we stated earlier, shyness brought on by communication apprehension is a major factor that inhibits individuals from behaving in an appropriately responsive manner in communication. Being responsive in interpersonal communication presents an invitation to others to talk more. As we have repeatedly noted, high communication apprehensives typically do not want to increase their communication with others. Thus, high apprehensives may be unresponsive to others' communication to avoid more communication. As a result, these individuals are likely to be seen as cold and unfriendly. Highly apprehensive individuals, therefore, are frequently not interpersonally competent communicators.

Versatility

The critical element in interpersonal communication competence is versatility, the capacity to be *appropriately* assertive and *appropriately* responsive depending on the context. Terms that are used to describe individuals who are versatile communicators include *accommodating, adaptable, flexible, informal, compatible with others,* and *versatile*. Terms for individuals who lack this capacity include *rigid, inflexible, disliking of change, uncompromising,* and *unyielding*. As you can see, versatility appears to be related to how dogmatic, as opposed to open-minded, a person tends to be. Although it is true that versatility is rooted in an individual's temperament (Cole & McCroskey, 2000), we do not suggest that even a highly dogmatic individual cannot learn to *communicate* in a versatile manner.

Individuals who are versatile in their interpersonal communication behavior are those whose basic personality permits them to be adaptable rather than rigidly consistent in communicating with different people or communicating with the same person at different times. In other words, versatile individuals adapt their style of communication to the individuals with whom they are communicating and to the demands of the situation. Although this is much more difficult for people with rigid personalities, it need not be impossible.

Consider, for example, a situation in which you are communicating with a highly aggressive individual. Should you be highly assertive in response? Should you be highly responsive? The former choice might lead to confrontation and conflict, and the latter to submission. Neither would be seen as the "best" way to behave. The competent interpersonal communicator will be assertive when it was necessary to defend her or his own rights and he or she would remain responsive to the other's communication without submitting to unreasonable requests or demands. An outside observer would see the competent individual behaving differently at different points in the interaction.

For a very crude self-measure of your own versatility, see Figure 3.2. Where would you put yourself generally? Where would you classify yourself when on a date? At work? Talking to your mother? Talking to a teacher? Returning an appliance you bought that does not work? Getting rid of a door-to-door salesperson? Talking to someone you know stole your book?

If you can easily classify yourself, and you place yourself in the same classification in most of the other contexts cited, you probably are not very versatile. On the other hand, if you had difficulty locating where you should be placed or found you moved all over the place depending on the other contexts, you may be quite versatile.

Not a great deal is yet known about why some people are highly versatile and others are not. There is a strong indication that versatility is associated with an individual's personality, as we noted previously. High CAs, for example, tend to be less versatile. In contrast, highly manipulative individuals, or high Machiavellians, tend to talk in groups no more than the average but to participate at the time it counts most. These highly effective individuals clearly exhibit versatility. Versatility clearly is more than just open-mindedness.

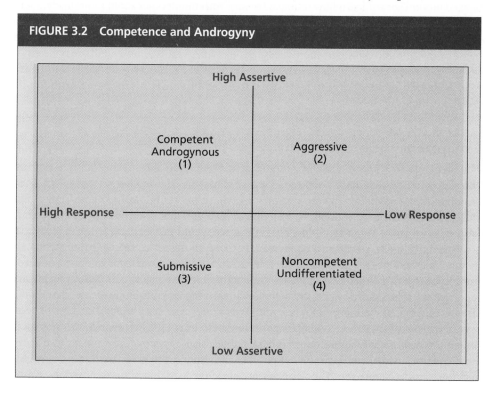

FIGURE 3.2 Competence and Androgyny

High Assertive

Competent
Androgynous
(1)

Aggressive
(2)

High Response — Low Response

Submissive
(3)

Noncompetent
Undifferentiated
(4)

Low Assertive

Another construct has appeared in the communication literature that is very similar to the construct of versatility. This is a personality-type trait that is called "rhetorical sensitivity" (Hart, Carlson, & Eadie, 1980). The rhetorically sensitive person falls midway between two extremes on a continuum. At one extreme are persons who Darnell and Brockriede (1976) describe as seeing "any variation from their personal norms as hypocritical, as a denial of integrity, as a cardinal sin." These individuals are the stereotypical bullheaded, rigid dogmatics. At the other extreme are those persons who Darnell and Brockriede describe as having "no Self to call their own. For each person and for each situation they present a new self" (Darnell & Brockriede, 1976). Such people are the "chameleons" of the world. They change their attitudes and feelings at a mere suggestion from another.

The rhetorical-sensitivity construct is both personality based and attitudinal in nature. However, it is one good explanation for why some people communicate in a versatile manner and others do not. Nevertheless, personality is not the only factor contributing to a person's versatility. Training programs in both assertiveness and in nonverbal sensitivity (responsiveness) have been proven effective in altering people's basic communication behavior. For some people who were deficient in either assertiveness or responsiveness skills, these programs have produced remarkable positive change; people have become more versatile communicators. For others, however, these programs produce behaviors better characterized as "obnoxiously aggressive" or "wimp-like." The key is the motivation of the individual who enters such training. If one's goal is to become more versatile, it appears that is the likely outcome. However, if one's goal is to "learn how to stop being pushed around" or to "learn how to make friends," other outcomes seem more likely.

Becoming a competent interpersonal communicator is more than simply wanting to do so. One must develop both an understanding of the nature of effective interpersonal communication and the necessary behavioral skills. These skills may be sufficient to make a person both assertive and responsive. To become versatile and truly interpersonally competent, the motivation to be an effective interpersonal communicator is critical.

Competence and Androgyny

The elements of assertiveness and responsiveness generally have been found to not be correlated to any meaningful degree. That is, a person who is high on one SCO/SCS dimension may be either high or low, or somewhere between, on the other. Figure 3.2 shows categories that may exist as a function of high and low assertiveness and high and low responsiveness. As indicated in Figure 3.2, we would expect a person who is highly assertive and highly responsive (quadrant 1) to be the most competent interpersonal communicator. On the other hand, the person who is characteristically neither assertive nor responsive (quadrant 4) is the least likely to be interpersonally competent. Interestingly, research has shown that most people who are highly communicatively apprehensive fall in this latter category.

In the Bem (1974) and Wheeless and Dierks-Stewart (1981) research, those whom we consider most likely to be competent are called "androgynous." This means that they characteristically display communication behaviors that are both masculine (assertive) and feminine (responsive). Those whom we consider least likely to be competent are referred to in the Bem (1974) and Wheeless and Dierks-Stewart (1981) research as "undifferentiated." This means that they characteristically display neither masculine (assertive) nor feminine (responsive) behaviors.

In the other two quadrants in Figure 3.2, we point to communicators who characteristically are either assertive or responsive but not both. We might refer to these individuals as *partially competent*. In quadrant 2, we find those individuals we label "aggressive" or "masculine" from the Bem (1974) and Wheeless and Dierks-Stewart (1981) perspective. These are the people who are highly assertive but lack responsiveness. They are quite willing to stand up for themselves, but they do not exhibit a concern for others.

In quadrant 3, by contrast, we see communicators whom we label "submissive" or "feminine" from the Bem (1974) and Wheeless and Dierks-Stewart (1981) perspective. These people are highly responsive but lack assertiveness. They are quite willing to respond to the needs and desires of others but are unwilling to stand up for themselves.

Competence and Context

The view of interpersonal communication competence advanced to this point has focused on the characteristic communication behavior of an individual. In other words, we have focused on trait-like communication behaviors that are likely to be exhibited by an individual no matter what the context of communication. This static view of competence, although useful, may be very misleading.

All communication occurs in a context. No single communication behavior is appropriate in all contexts. There are few communication behaviors that are never appropriate (even belching at the dinner table is appropriate in some contexts in some cultures). The competent interpersonal communicator, then, can do more than just always be assertive and responsive. Sometimes being assertive might cost a person her or his job. Sometimes being responsive might encourage a repulsive person to communicate with us even more. Although the people we have labeled *androgynous* may have the best chance to be interpersonally competent, there is no guarantee that they will be so in any given context. In fact, the "undifferentiated" person may behave more appropriately in some contexts.

CONCLUSION

In this chapter, we have explored a number of communication variables that are extremely important to explain how and why people communicate (shyness, willingness to communicate, communication apprehension, compulsive communication, perceived communication competence, and sociocommunicative orientation style). The range of willingness to communicate crosses a broad spectrum. It ranges from the excruciatingly quiet person to the talkaholic, with most people being in the normal range in between. The level of an individual's willingness to communicate can have a major influence on that person's life. In the next chapter, we are going to focus on messages and meanings.

 **KEY TERMS**

assertiveness 77
basic attribution error 71
communication
    apprehension 55

communication competence 56
empathy 79
responsiveness 77
shyness 55

talkaholic (compulsive communi-
    cator) 57
versatility 77
willingness to communicate 56

REFERENCES

Allen, J., Richmond, V. P., & McCroskey, J. C. (1984, November). Communication and the chiropractic profession III. *Journal of Chiropractic, 21,* 36–39.

Beatty, M. J. (1988). Situational and predispositional correlates of public speaking anxiety. *Communication Education, 37,* 29–39.

Beatty, M. J., & Friedland, M. H. (1989). Public speaking state anxiety as a function of selected situational and predispositional variables. *Communication Education, 38,* 142–147.

Beatty, M. J., McCroskey, J. C., & Heisel, A. D. (1998). Communication apprehension as temperamental expression: A communibiological paradigm. *Communication Monographs, 65,* 197–219.

Beatty, M. J., & McCroskey, J. C., & Valencic, K. M. (2001). *The biology of communication: A communibiological perspective.* Cresskill, NJ: Hampton Press.

Bem, S. L. (1974). The measurement of psychological androgyny. *Journal of Consulting and Clinical Psychology, 42,* 155–162.

Berger, B. A., Baldwin, H. J., McCroskey, J. C., & Richmond, V. P. (1983, Summer). Communication apprehension in pharmacy students: A national study. *American Journal of Pharmaceutical Education, 47,* 95–102.

Buss, A. H. (1980). *Self-consciousness and social anxiety.* San Francisco: W. H. Freeman.

Cole, J. G., & McCroskey, J. C. (2000). Temperament and sociocommunicative orientation. *Communication Research Reports, 17,* 105–114.

Daly, J. A., & Hailey, J. L. (1983). Putting the situation into writing research: Situational parameters of writing apprehension as disposition and state. In R. E. Beach and L. Bidwell (Eds.), *New directions in composition research.* New York: Guilford.

Darnell, D., & Brockriede, W. (1976). *Persons communicating.* Englewood Cliffs, NJ: Prentice-Hall.

Hart, R. P., Carlson, R. E., & Eadie, W. F. (1980). Attitudes toward communication and the assessment of rhetorical sensitivity. *Communication Monographs, 47,* 1–22.

Heisel, A. D., McCroskey, J. C., & Richmond, V. P. (1999). Testing theoretical relationships and non-relationships of genetically-based predictors: Getting started with communibiology. *Communication Research Reports, 16,* 1–9.

Lashbrook, W. B. (1974). *Toward the measurement and processing of the social style profile.* Eden Prairie, MN: Wilson Learning.

McCroskey, J. C. (1970). Measures of communication-bound anxiety. *Speech Monographs, 37,* 269–277.

McCroskey, J. C. (1972). The implementation of a large-scale program of systematic desensitization for CA. *Speech Teacher, 21,* 255–264.

McCroskey, J. C. (1977). Oral communication apprehension: A summary of recent theory and research. *Human Communication Research, 4,* 78–96.

McCroskey, J. C. (1984). Communication competence: The elusive construct. In R. N. Bostrom (Ed.), *Competence in communication.* Beverly Hills, CA: Sage.

McCroskey, J. C. (1992). Reliability and validity of the willingness to communicate scale. *Communication Quarterly, 40,* 16–25.

McCroskey, J. C. (1997). Willingness to communicate, communication apprehension, and self-perceived communication competence: Conceptualizations and perspectives. In J. A. Daly, J. C. McCroskey, J. Ayres, T. Hopf, & D. M Ayres (Eds.), *Avoiding communication: Shyness, reticence, and communication apprehension* (pp. 75–108). Cresskill, NJ: Hampton Press.

McCroskey, J. C. (2001). *An introduction to rhetorical communication* (8th ed.). Boston: Allyn & Bacon.

McCroskey, J. C. (2006). *An introduction to rhetorical communication* (9th ed.). Boston: Allyn & Bacon.

McCroskey, J. C., & Daly, J. A. (Eds.). (1987). *Personality and interpersonal communication*. Newbury Park, CA: Sage.

McCroskey, J. C., Heisel, A. D., & Richmond, V. P. (2001). Eysenck's BIG THREE and communication traits: Three correlational studies. *Communication Monographs, 68*, 360–366.

McCroskey, J. C., & Richmond, V. P. (1982). Communication apprehension and shyness: Conceptual and operational distinctions. *Central States Speech Journal, 33*, 458–468.

McCroskey, J. C., Richmond, V. P., & Stewart, R. A. (1986). *One on one: The foundations of interpersonal communication*. Englewood Cliffs, NJ: Prentice-Hall.

Merrill, D. W., & Reid, R. (1981). *Personal styles and effective performance: Make your style work for you*. Radnor, PA: Chilton Book.

Norton, R. (1983). *Communicator style: Theory, applications, and measures*. Beverly Hills, CA: Sage.

Phillips, G. M. (1981). *Help for shy people*. Englewood Cliffs, NJ: Prentice-Hall.

Pilkonis, P., Heape, C., & Klein, R. H. (1980). Treating shyness and other relationship difficulties in psychiatric outpatients. *Communication Education, 29*, 250–255.

Richmond, V. P., Beatty, M. J., & Dyba, P. (1985). Shyness and popularity: Children's views. *Western Journal of Speech Communication, 49*, 116–125.

Richmond, V. P., & McCroskey, J. C. (1985). *Communication: Apprehension, avoidance, and effectiveness*. Scottsdale, AZ: Gorsuch Scarisbrick.

Richmond, V. P., & McCroskey, J. C. (1990). Reliability and separation of factors on the assertiveness-responsiveness measure. *Psychological Reports, 67*, 449–450.

Richmond, V. P., & McCroskey, J. C. (1995). *Communication: Apprehension, avoidance and effectiveness* (3rd ed.). Scottsdale, AZ: Gorsuch-Scarisbrick.

Thomas, C. E., Richmond, V. P., & McCroskey, J. C. (1994). Is immediacy anything more than just being nice? The association between immediacy and socio-communicative style. *Communication Research Reports, 11*, 107–115.

Wheeless, V. E., & Dierks-Stewart, K. (1981). The psychometric properties of the Bem sex-role inventory: Questions concerning reliability and validity. *Communication Quarterly, 29*, 173–186.

Zimbardo, P. G. (1977). *Shyness: What it is, what to do about it*. Reading, MA: Addison-Wesley.

DISCUSSION QUESTIONS

1. Describe a time when you've interacted with another person who exhibited a high willingness to communicate.

2. How is shyness exhibited in people's day-to-day lives?

3. If you are interacting with someone who is high CA, how should you alter your communicative behaviors?

4. Are you competent/androgynous, aggressive/masculine, submissive/feminine, or noncompetent/undifferentiated? How does this affect your communication with other people?

5. Why do you think androgynous people are more communicatively competent?

4

Distinctions between Verbal and Nonverbal Messages

Relationships between Verbal and Nonverbal Messages

Functions of Nonverbal Messages

Accenting • Complementing • Contradicting • Repeating • Regulating • Substituting

Nonverbal Messages

Body Movements and Gestures • Physical Appearance and Attractiveness • Dress and Artifacts • Facial Expressions and Eye Behavior • Use of the Voice • Territory and Personal Space • Touch • Environmental Factors • Smell • Time

Messages and Meanings

OBJECTIVES

- Distinguish between verbal and nonverbal messages.

- Explain the six functions of nonverbal messages.

- Be able to explain the fifteen different categories of nonverbal messages.

Meanings are in people, not in words. When we want to get others to share our thoughts or feelings, we usually use words. When we are concerned with verbal messages, our primary focus must be on words. However, verbal messages are not always words.

Verbal messages involve coded language. English, Spanish, French, Chinese, and Russian are but a few of the thousands of languages from which people create verbal messages. It is important to realize that there are other forms of coded language as well. The smoke signals of Native American tribes, a whistling system in the Canary Islands, drumbeats in parts of Africa, and gestures used by the deaf in North America (American Sign Language) all represent languages used to create verbal messages.

In this picture, two people are using sign language, which is considered a form of verbal messages.

The critical element in language—therefore, in verbal messages—is the sharing of a common code between two communicators. When people are lacking a shared language, communication by means of verbal messages is literally impossible. In such circumstances, communication must be achieved entirely through nonverbal messages (Andersen, Garrison, & Andersen, 1976; Hall, 1959, 1966; Harrison, 1974; Donaghy, 1980). It is important that we distinguish at the outset between these two primary forms of messages.

◼ DISTINCTIONS BETWEEN VERBAL AND NONVERBAL MESSAGES

Distinguishing between verbal and nonverbal messages is no simple task, although the differences seem obvious on the surface. People think of communicating "with words" as verbal and communicating "without words" as nonverbal. *Words* suggests a linguistic code (Richmond, 1992; Richmond & McCroskey, 2004). As we noted above, some languages do not have words as we commonly use that term. In addition, some nonverbal gestures (called *emblems*) are word-substitutes. Examples of these include head shaking to show yes or no, the OK gesture, the peace gesture, counting gestures, and "throwing another a kiss." Clearly, there is a gray area between verbal and nonverbal messages that permits reasonable people to disagree about how a particular message should be classified. However, that gray area is restricted.

Compared to nonverbal messages, verbal messages are more *explicit* and *precise*, and are framed in a *linguistic* code (Hickson & Stacks, 1993; Knapp & Hall, 2001; Richmond, 1992; Richmond & McCroskey, 2004). Verbal messages primarily convey information or content in communication. In other words, verbal messages are the *cognitive* component of the communication process. When a mother tells a young child to "sit," she is attempting to convey the information to the child that he or she is to be seated. The content may be clear in verbal messages, or it may be ambiguous. For example, if the mother were to say to the child, "Repose [act of resting] on a seat," the child might not understand the language. Therefore, the child could not understand the message that presumably tells her or him what to do.

The verbal message component of the communication process is the provider of content and information, and it generally is used to clarify. However, we must be careful in assuming that the verbal message always is clear. For example, when a young child doesn't understand a particular word, someone may tell the child to "look up the word" in the dictionary. Of course, often children cannot spell words, so they cannot possibly "look up the word." If they are lucky enough to spell the word, they might find several definitions for the word. All the definitions have different connotations based on the context in which the word is used. For example, the word *bag* has several different common definitions. It can be used to refer to a sack, a valise, a purse, a brown sack, a poke, or a receptacle of leather or cloth. As we can see, the verbal component of communication can convey the content or cognitive aspect of the message; however, we still need to understand the context in which the verbal message is being used to understand the content satisfactorily.

Compared to verbal messages, nonverbal messages tend to be more *implicit,* often *imprecise,* and usually *nonlinguistic* by nature (Hickson & Stacks, 1993; Knapp & Hall, 2001; Richmond, 1992; Richmond & McCroskey, 2004). They represent such things as the attitudes and emotions of the source. In other words, the nonverbal message component of the human communication process is the *affective* component. Based on such things as the source's body movements, vocal qualities, and facial expressions, the receiver can get an idea about how the source feels. Nonverbal messages can help clarify the verbal message and often can even be used in place of the verbal. However, we must be as cautious in interpreting nonverbal messages as we are when interpreting verbal ones. Much of our accidental and expressive communication is produced by nonverbal messages. A nonverbal message in one culture (particularly an emblem) might not mean the same thing in another culture. For example, the OK sign in American society is perceived as an obscene gesture in South America. Similarly, shaking one's head from side to side conveys "no" in many cultures, but it conveys "yes" in Bulgaria. Touching someone in one context may be taken as an indication of warmth and intimacy. In another context, the same touch may lead to a charge of attempted assault or sexual harassment.

In sum, verbal messages typically represent the *cognitive component context* in communication, whereas nonverbal messages represent the *affective* component. Communicating one component without the other is virtually impossible, for they usually accompany one another. Meanings are produced in the minds of others by both verbal and nonverbal messages individually. But most meaning is produced by verbal and nonverbal messages together. As important as it is to distinguish between verbal and nonverbal messages, it is at least as important to understand how they function together.

RELATIONSHIPS BETWEEN VERBAL AND NONVERBAL MESSAGES

Several years ago, researchers tried to figure out how much of the meaning in communication is stimulated by nonverbal messages as compared to verbal messages. Estimates of the portion attributable to the nonverbal messages ran from 65 to 93 percent in the various studies. Such figures are often used to illustrate how important it is to study nonverbal communication. However, these findings are completely meaningless in terms of their generalizability to everyday communication situations. These estimates are artifacts of contrived experiments in artificial laboratory settings and have no necessary relationship to the way real human beings communicate.

Consider the following examples. (1) Someone walks by your room and sees you intently reading a textbook. That person concludes you are studying and goes on without interrupting you. (2) You type a letter to your friend describing what you did during spring break. Your friend reads your letter and decides that you had a good time. In the first example, we believe that 100 percent of the meaning was stimulated nonverbally—you did not speak or write at all. In the second example, we believe that virtually 100 percent of the meaning was stimulated verbally—although if you spilled coffee on the letter before you sent it, the resulting spot might have generated a conclusion that you were sloppy! What is the point? The relative importance of verbal and nonverbal messages depends entirely on the context of a given communicative event. Often, unlike the above examples, both types of messages are present, and they work together to produce meaning in the receiver's mind. To understand this relationship better, let us consider the six major functions of nonverbal messages in relationship to verbal messages.

FUNCTIONS OF NONVERBAL MESSAGES

Accenting

In this function, the primary role of nonverbal messages is to *accentuate* or emphasize a particular point in the verbal message. For example, a skilled speaker knows when to raise or lower the voice when making a dramatic point. Although nonverbal messages are important in accenting or emphasizing a verbal point, the timing needs to be precise or the messages will seem "out of sync" with the verbal. For example, the public speaker who says, "I want to make three major points," and then raises three fingers after having completed that phrase is "out of sync."

Nonverbal accenting can use many areas of nonverbal communication, such as gestures, touch, vocal cues, and so on. This is the way people indicate which of their verbal messages are most important (in their own mind, at least) and which are of lesser concern. Teachers, for example, need to be very effective in using nonverbal messages in this way. If teachers are not effective, their students are very likely not to know what to put into their notes, study, and remember for tests later. Teachers who are ineffective in accenting, either with nonverbal behaviors or with other methods (such as providing written objectives), often are criticized for playing the game students hate most: guess what's in my mind! Injunctions such as "Study everything!" are most likely to result in students studying things that are unimportant and complaining, "The test is unfair."

Complementing

The function of *complementing* is to reinforce or enhance the verbal message. For example, when telling someone you love them, you may be hugging and holding that person. This is different from accenting. Here, nonverbal complementing has to accompany the verbal message in order for the meaning of the verbal to be stimulated the way it should be. As we noted above, nonverbal messages are best at stimulating *affective* meaning. Therefore, when verbal messages address affective matters (e.g., feelings, emotions, liking, and disliking), it is particularly important that appropriate nonverbal messages complement those verbal messages.

Contradicting

Sometimes nonverbal messages *contradict* the verbal. For example, when we tell someone in a sarcastic tone that he or she is "wearing a lovely outfit," our nonverbal message has contradicted the verbal message. Sometimes we mean to contradict; at other times, we don't.

Generally, when verbal and nonverbal messages are in conflict, people tend to lean most heavily on the nonverbal to make sense of what is happening. That is, we tend to believe the nonverbal more than the verbal. This may be because most people think it is easier to lie verbally than it is nonverbally, although this generally held belief is not always true. We must be particularly careful in this regard when we are communicating with children. Most children understand and adopt the adult norms by the time they reach their teenage years, and many do so several years earlier. However, all young children, many older children, and even some adults are not sensitive to the importance of nonverbal messages that are inconsistent with verbal messages. Therefore, these individuals respond to the verbal message. Sarcasm and satire are lost on them. These people are particularly unresponsive to humor in which the nonverbal messages suggest that one should discount the serious tone of the verbal message.

Repeating

A repetition of the verbal message in a nonverbal manner is termed *repeating*. For example, after shouting over a crowd that things are OK, we might also give a "thumbs up" sign, and our meaning will be more likely to be understood.

Redundancy is a critical factor in facilitating communication of information and understanding. Redundancy can be created by presenting more than one verbal message designed to stimulate the same meaning (a very good method). However, the use of nonverbal messages often is much simpler and frequently is more effective.

Regulating

The *regulation* function serves to coordinate the flow of speech. This can be done by the vocal inflection, the movement of the body, the facial expressions, eye behavior, or several nonverbal cues in combination. In other words, the regulation function lets one person know when it is her or his time to speak in a conversation.

Conversations involve different individuals taking turns speaking. The rules for these interchanges are complex and usually learned through trial and error; therefore, many people do not learn them well. We can indicate verbally to someone that it is her or his turn to talk (such as a teacher might do in a class discussion). However, many conventional interactions are regulated by nonverbal messages. These messages operate at a barely conscious level, and if they are working well, the interaction flows smoothly without awkward silences or "talk-overs."

Substituting

When the nonverbal behavior is used in place of the verbal, this is termed *substituting*. For example, when you dislike something that someone says to you, all you may have to do is to stare hard at that person to get your meaning across.

Substitution is used often when barriers to verbal communication exist. When you are trying to say goodbye to someone at a crowded airport, you simply throw the person a kiss or wave goodbye. This is different from repeating. Substituting occurs when the nonverbal is used for the verbal, whereas repeating is when the nonverbal is used right after the verbal.

In summary, both verbal and nonverbal messages have the potential to stimulate meaning in the minds of others. In ongoing interpersonal communication, however, most meaning is stimulated by a combination of the verbal and nonverbal. Although words and the sequencing of words account for the bulk of what we refer to as *verbal* messages, the variety of *nonverbal* messages in interpersonal communication is much greater. It is the interplay of these two types of messages that makes human communication the vital and fascinating process it is.

■ NONVERBAL MESSAGES

We have chosen to break nonverbal messages into ten categories. We will begin with the category that many people call *body language* (Fast, 1970). Although that label is not appropriate, because these behaviors do not form a language, the category does include all those elements that encompass body movements and gestures.

Body Movements and Gestures

Body movements and gestures are commonly referred to as *kinesics* (Birdwhistell, 1970). Kinesics refers to any movement of the head, arms, legs, hands, and so on (Richmond & McCroskey, 2004). Some authors have suggested that there are approximately 700,000 possible physical signs that can be transmitted by body movements. One author has suggested that there are twenty-three distinct eyebrow movements, and that each communicates different meanings to receivers. Like most nonverbal messages, body movements and gestures are both learned and innate. However, we adopt the movements that are acceptable in our culture for communication. For the purpose of clarification, we will examine the six main areas of kinesics: emblems, illustrators, regulators, affect displays, adaptors, and courtship-readiness cues.

Emblems.   This type of gesture has a specific meaning for those sending and receiving the message. Emblems, as we noted earlier in this chapter, have a direct verbal translation and the gesture(s) can be used in place of a verbal message. Emblems are behaviors that could be considered equivalent to verbal messages because of the coded, linguistic translation that is typical of such messages. Common emblems are the OK sign, nodding your head in agreement or disagreement, the hitchhiking sign, the wave for greeting, and so on. All these emblems are common in the North American culture. They can be used for verbal messages, and the meaning stimulated will probably be the same. Like many of our verbal messages, emblems represent very precise meanings. Emblems are excellent sources of nonverbal communication in interpersonal relationships. Emblems often express much more of what we mean than do verbal messages. For example, if you are caught in a traffic jam and someone behind you keeps honking the horn, you can always give them a gesture allowing that person to know exactly what you are saying. But others may not take too kindly to this emblem and will return an emblem of their own. For example, they might raise their arm, clench their fist, and touch their other hand to the upper arm of their raised hand. You will know exactly what they are saying to you. Emblems are a very effective nonverbal means of communicating, without ever saying a word. Most emblems are not as offensive as these driving-related ones!

Illustrators. In this instance, the body movement and gestures are used to illustrate or add meaning to the verbal message. Illustrators help to clarify the verbal message. Illustrators are primarily made by using our hands, but not exclusively.

Small children will learn what illustrators to use with their words, and as they get older their gestures become more refined but fewer. The young child, for example, cannot say "water." However, the child probably can say something like *wawa* while pointing to a faucet, thus communicating her or his desire to a parent. As the child's language skills expand, such gestures will disappear because they are no longer needed. Small children, until about the age of 7, rely heavily on illustrators to convey meaning, but after 7 they start adopting the adult verbal norms. They use less illustration, and it is more refined and adapted to the verbal dialogue.

Illustrators are also used to help in the synchronization of verbal and nonverbal message flow. The use of illustrators in interpersonal communication will help punctuate or synchronize the communication. For example, when we are excited, we use gestures that exhibit enthusiasm.

Regulators. These nonverbal gestures help us figure out the beginning and ending of turns in interpersonal communication. They assist us in regulating spoken language. This has been described by some as the "turn-taking system" in conversation. There are four major turn-taking situations (turn-yielding, turn-maintaining, turn-requesting, and turn-denying) that can take place in interpersonal communication. All of the turn-taking cues help in the flow of interpersonal communication. Regulators tell us when it is time to talk, cease talking, and listen, and how to refuse our turn to talk.

Affect Displays. These are nonverbal behaviors that reflect one's emotional state (Mehrabian, 1971, 1972, 1981). Affect displays could be facial expressions, body posture, or a combination of these. Think of a person who always looks sad and tired, and has a slumped posture. What is your perception of that person? You probably think of that person as unhappy, sad, or maybe lazy. You may even avoid communication with such individuals because their affect displays are so depressing. You just know an interaction with them would be about some illness or problem that is bothering them. Therefore, how we display our feelings and emotions through our body movements and gestures will determine to a large extent whether others want to communicate with us and the type of communication that takes place.

Adaptors. Adaptors are movements that are usually exhibited unconsciously and are associated with tension or anxiety. As anxiety increases, the adaptors tend to increase. For example, in the initial acquaintance stage of a relationship, adaptor behaviors of each individual may be quite common. As the relationship becomes more secure, the adaptors will decrease. Typical adaptors include playing with hair, smoothing clothes, toying with an object, and scratching. Some adaptors can even be something as extreme as touching another's hair or removing lint from the other person's clothing.

Certain people use more adaptors than others. For example, the generally anxious personality types might bite their nails, scratch their heads, smooth their clothing, and pick at your clothing within one interaction. Anxious people often are not even aware of what they are doing or of the impact it has on interaction. Using lots of adaptors can make receivers nervous and uncomfortable, and they might even wish to end the conversation.

Courtship-Readiness Cues.   Another area of kinesics that has received extensive consideration is courtship (LaFrance & Mayo, 1978; McCroskey, Larson, & Knapp, 1971; Morris, 1971). Here we are concerned with the behaviors exhibited in the courtship situation. *Courtship readiness* is shown when someone tries to display muscle tone, sucks in the stomach, and stands straight to impress another. *Preening behavior* is revealed in such actions as stroking the hair, fixing the collar on a dress or shirt, touching up one's makeup, and adjusting clothing such as socks and ties. Such behavior usually accompanies courtship-readiness cues. *Positional cues* refer to how we arrange our bodies either to adapt to or to reject others. We sit with an open body position when we want to let others know we are willing to talk with them. On the other hand, we sit with a closed body position to show that we are not interested in conversation. *Actions of appeal or invitation* include flirtatious glances, batting one's eyelashes, seductive body movements, flexing the muscles, and thrusting out the chest. Both males and females engage in these behaviors when meeting or becoming acquainted with a person of the opposite sex whom they find attractive (Eakins & Eakins, 1978).

Research has unearthed some behaviors that are typical of both males and females who find someone of the opposite sex attractive. Females may lower their eyes, smile more, tilt their head, yield space to the male, cuddle, yield talking time to the male, bat their eyelashes, and generally exhibit less dominant nonverbal behaviors. In comparison, males when conversing with females will stare more, point, take more space, initiate touch, keep their head erect, have a straighter posture, and generally appear to be more dominant. One might ask, Isn't this a bit sexist? No, it is simply a fact of interpersonal communication between males and females in the general American culture. The above behaviors tend to be present in many female–male interactions. There are exceptions: in a work environment in which the boss is female and the subordinate is male, and in a student–teacher relationship in which the teacher is female and the student male. However, in most male–female interpersonal communication, when the participants like each other, some behaviors listed above tend to be present. In some other cultures, the presence of these behaviors is even more pronounced than in the United States, and in some it is less pronounced.

Our body movements and gestures help to control the flow of speech, coordinate interactions, define relationships, and establish meaning in the mind of the receiver. Our body movements and gestures also suggest our emotional state and the type of person we are.

Physical Appearance and Attractiveness

Our physical appearance and general attractiveness often will determine whether another person wants to interact with us (Argyle, 1975; Rosenfeld & Plax, 1977). This level of desire for contact will decide whether the person will initiate a conversation with us and/or respond positively if we try to initiate the conversation. Once the conversation is initiated, general physical attractiveness may not be of such vital concern, for people are then more concerned with social or task attraction. However, physically attractive people are given higher grades and receive more attention in school, and are perceived by others as more likable, more socially skilled, and more sociable. Evidence shows they are even given lighter prison sentences than their unattractive counterparts when convicted of a crime. Indeed, physical appearance is a powerful nonverbal message.

The type of body structure a person has will also influence how others react to them (Cortes & Gatti, 1965; Sheldon, 1940, 1942). The *endomorphic* body type is rounded or heavy, with a large abdomen. This person tends to be perceived by others as sociable, slow, lazy, calm, soft-hearted, and kind. The *mesomorphic* body type is the triangular or athletic body shape, which is muscular, firm, and has good posture. The person with this body type tends to be perceived as intelligent, outgoing, confident, energetic, dominant, and determined. The *ectomorphic* body type is very thin, fragile, and flat, and has poor muscle tone. Such types look much like a light pole. They tend to be perceived as tense, awkward, high-strung, detached, anxious, tactful, and withdrawn. As we can see from the above descriptions, the mesomorph is the preferred body type in terms of positive perceptions; however, not all of us are mesomorphs, so we should be aware of how others view us. Our body type will determine, to a major extent, how we will be perceived and reacted to in interpersonal interactions. The thin female is perceived as unstable, anxious and high-strung, and the thin male is perceived in a similar manner. The short, rounded heavy female is seen as unattractive in our society and is often avoided by males as a prospective date. However, the round, heavy male is more accepted, particularly if he is the class clown. The problem arises when people think they know how others should communicate based on their body type and then see their expectations violated. For example, a mesomorphic male who is extremely anxious, nervous, and quiet is counter to the stereotype of the mesomorph. Therefore, we should realize we cannot judge how to communicate with that person based solely on his physique.

Our physical appearance and general attractiveness determine both whether others will communicate with us and the type of interaction that takes place. Other physical factors might impinge on the above. Our skin tone, our hair, the amount of skin we expose, and our height and weight can determine how others will react to us. Generally, our society believes that having a tan is good, that hair should be clean and the length should fit the norm of the culture, and that tactful exposure of the skin is acceptable. We also believe that being tall is positive for men, average height is positive for women, and that neither sex should be overweight, although it is more acceptable for men than for women.

In summary, our general body appearance and attractiveness predict how others will respond to us and how we respond to others. We might say, "Beauty is in the eye of the beholder" or "Beauty is only skin deep," but we should remember that often people don't get past our general appearance to communicate with us and find what lies beneath. Our appearance sends a volley of nonverbal messages to others whenever we come anywhere near them. Maybe that is why most of us are so sensitive to making ourselves look better through our use of dress and artifacts.

Dress and Artifacts

Clothing communicates status, attitudes, values, professional goals, cultural background, occupation, sex, and age (Rosenfeld & Plax, 1977). The way we dress influences how others communicate with us on a daily basis.

We've all heard the expression "You are what you eat." Well, "You are what you wear," at least in the eyes of the receiver. If you dress as if you work for IBM, you will normally be treated accordingly. If you dress like a coal miner, you will probably be treated accordingly. Try dressing in a sloppy, careless, unclean manner, then go to your local bank and try to cash a check. The people there are likely to scrutinize your appearance, decide you look like a bad risk, ask for identification, check your account, and then cash your check. If you dressed in a neat, clean, businesslike manner and asked to have a check cashed, the people at the bank would probably comply with minimal hassle because your appearance says you are reliable. You can also repeat this exercise in department stores, and see how salespeople treat you differently based on what you are wearing.

Clothing has three main functions: *comfort and protection* (to keep ourselves warm and safe from objects in the environment), *modesty* (to keep from view those parts of our anatomy that our culture says shouldn't be visible), and *cultural display*. The cultural display we make with our clothing is a primary basis that others use to judge our attitudes, values, and background. Years ago, cultures would decide what attire one could wear based on one's social standing in that culture. Therefore, it was easy to distinguish one social class from another. Fortunately, that is not so today in North America. We are fairly free of restraints in terms of what we can or cannot wear. We do have to wear clothing to cover our private areas. However, how much or how little we wear beyond that is primarily up to us. We should realize that if we want to deviate from the general norm, we usually will be stereotyped in a *negative* manner. However, there are groups of people who are allowed idiosyncratic behaviors in dress. For example, celebrities can dress in a very bizarre manner and still be accepted. In addition, many entertainers can dress in unusual fashions and still be accepted. In fact, their attire is part of their celebrity status. Imagine RuPaul without the wig and dress, Marilyn Manson without the makeup and gothic clothing, or Elton John without the flashy clothing and unique sunglasses; it just wouldn't be the same. However, most of us must dress according to the culture in which we live and work. If we don't, we run the risk of being alienated from peers and not being able to establish effective interpersonal relationships with others.

Artifacts are items such as jewelry, glasses, makeup, and so on that contribute to how others judge us. Women, more than men, have made the contact lens market an enormous success. In fact, about three-fourths of all contact lens wearers are female. The obvious reason for this is the belief that glasses make women look less attractive, or as the old saying goes, "Men don't make passes at women who wear glasses." In recent years, however, some women have chosen to wear glasses, and other elements of less than attractive artifacts and clothing, because they do not *want* men to make passes at them.

Some research indicates that people who wear glasses are perceived as more intelligent, industrious, and dependable. Indeed, how a person uses her or his glasses often determines how that person is perceived. When someone in a meeting removes glasses, folds them, and relaxes, this is sometimes a signal that the meeting has ended. When someone throws glasses across the table, this usually signals extreme displeasure. When people remove their glasses and rub their eyes, they might be signaling they are tired, bored, or confused. People who wear tinted glasses indoors may be doing so because they wish to mask their feelings or are insecure. Of course, some people wear tinted glasses because their eyes are highly sensitive to light.

In summary, the type of clothing and the kinds of artifacts we use give others cues to our socioeconomic status, our attitudes, and even our jobs. These enhancements of physical appearance have a significant impact on interpersonal relationships.

Facial Expressions and Eye Behavior

Someone once observed, "Our face is our window to the world." Our facial appearance provides others with information about our race, gender, nationality, emotional state, and age, and even the type of person we are (Ekman & Friesen, 1975; Ekman & Rosenberg, 2005). Our face is the most expressive part of our body. From isolated pictures of only eyes and eyebrows, we can often predict the emotional state of an individual. We frequently can tell if a person is sad or happy, disgusted or pleased.

Research suggests that some of our facial expressions are innate. Blind children have facial expressions similar to those of sighted children. The fact they are blind shows they did not learn to behave the way others do by watching and then imitating. Many facial expressions are inborn. The smile is the universal facial expression of happiness or friendliness. It is a natural, easy response, and our parents enhance it by teaching us that we should smile to show friendship. This is one of only a very limited number of *pancultural nonverbal behaviors,* that is, one of only a few nonverbal behaviors that are used and responded to in the same way across many or all cultures.

Researchers suggest that we use four facial management techniques when controlling our facial expressions. We *intensify* or exaggerate our facial expressions (for example, our wedding day or birthday might cause us to intensify our positive facial expressions). We *deintensify* when we learn to control or subdue an expression (for example, we might be excited that we got an A on an exam, but if we find out our best friend got a D, we might suppress our elation at our own grade around our friend). We *neutralize* when we avoid showing any facial expression. For example, in the general American culture when a young man is being punished by a teacher, he must remain stoic. Lastly, we *mask* when we conceal our real emotions (for example, not letting our best friend know we cannot tolerate her or his boyfriend or girlfriend). We manipulate our facial expressions to fit the situation and to develop more effective interpersonal relationships with others. We learn to conceal or mask our real emotions and expressions according to the norms of our society. A classic example of this is people who serve as masters of ceremonies on television game shows. After introducing several thousand people, he or she probably could not care less about the contestants and their darling loved ones. However, the game show host has to mask the real emotions and carry on with the show. He or she keeps smiling, nodding, kissing, handshaking, hugging—and being employed.

Seven basic emotions can be identified fairly consistently by facial expression. Research indicates that people can readily, and with considerable accuracy, identify the following emotions based solely on facial and eye expression: sadness, anger, disgust or contempt, fear, interest, surprise, and happiness (or SAD FISH).

As with most of the nonverbal areas, oculesics (eye behavior) has several functions, in this case seven. The first, and some believe most important, function of eye behavior is to control the flow of interaction. It is the prime method we have of controlling turn-taking in conversations. The second function of eye behavior is to establish a relationship. We look more and longer at people we want to interact with. The third function of eye behavior is to help in maintaining a relationship. We maintain a person's eye contact if we like that person. The fourth function of eye behavior is to express our feelings about a person or a situation. The fifth function of eye behavior is to show respect to another (looking down or away when speaking to someone of higher status). The final function is to communicate our attention to and interest in what the other person is saying during a conversation.

Our face and eyes provide others with an impression of how we feel about them. As a result, these nonverbal messages are very important in the maintenance and development of relationships.

Use of the Voice

Vocalics refers to the use of, and the characteristics and qualities of, the human voice (Addington, 1968). This category of nonverbal messages is sometimes called *paralanguage*. Although it is not in any sense *language*, it most frequently occurs simultaneously with verbal messages. Vocalic inflections are potent nonverbal messages that aid in stimulating intended meaning in the mind of the receiver beyond those that could be stimulated by the verbal message alone. For example, the person who uses sarcasm is really intending to communicate a meaning the opposite of what her or his words are saying.

Vocalic cues affect how others see you (Davitz & Davitz, 1961). When you open your mouth, you have either confirmed the image your dress and body give to another, or you have negated that image. In addition, in oral communication at least, an old adage is true: "It's not what you say; it's how you say it." Oral verbal messages do not exist without vocalic messages, although some vocalic messages can exist without verbal messages (sighing, laughing, groaning, moaning, etc.).

The main failing of written verbal communication is the absence of vocalic cues to tell a reader how to interpret the verbal message. Written communication is a pitifully poor substitute for oral communication. Maybe this is why our schools spend years trying to teach us to read and write, and frequently ignore oral communication completely. In the world of Internet chatting, the use of *emoticons* (symbols used to express emotions) has been developed to help in how written messages should be interpreted. For example, the emoticon :) is a smile, which indicates happiness. The emoticon ;(is a frowny face, which indicates sadness. *lol* is a representation for laughing out loud. And *ROFL* is "rolling on the floor laughing." The purpose of emoticons is to give Internet chatters and text messengers a sense of nonverbal communication because it does not exist. This idea will be discussed in greater detail in Chapter 14.

The use of your voice serves six important functions: (1) it communicates an image of you to another, (2) it communicates your emotional state, (3) it indicates your socioeconomic level and status, (4) it can serve to indicate your background and culture, (5) it can be used to regulate the flow of conversation, and (6) it can be used to show interest or disinterest in another (Richmond & McCroskey, 2004).

Paralinguistic cues are usually divided into two major categories: (1) vocal quality, such as pitch range, articulation, rhythm control, and lip control; and (2) vocalizations, such as vocal characterizes (e.g., laughing, crying, and yawning), vocal qualifiers (e.g., pitch height, intensity, and loudness/softness), and vocal segregates (e.g., *Hum, Huh, Uhh,* and *Shh*). These qualities suggest to others what is the individual's emotional state.

Finally, vocalic cues, or lack of them—silence—can display someone's age, sex, socioeconomic status, background, weight, height, and educational level. In fact, research suggests that vocal cues help more in stimulating meaning for content than the actual words themselves. The type of voice one has also contributes to how that person will be perceived by others.

In summary, much meaning can be gleaned by listening not to what a person is saying, but to how the person is saying it. Vocalic cues are one of the best means of determining exactly what someone means by their verbal messages, but they are not infallible. If they were, we would never need to misunderstand one another again!

Territory and Personal Space

Proxemics refers to the way space is used in communication (Hall, 1983). Research suggests that the way a person uses space is determined by one's age, gender, status, and cultural orientation. The use of space, as with other nonverbal areas, differs dramatically from one culture to another.

Personal space is the movable, portable space that goes wherever we go. Personal space is like an "invisible bubble" we carry around with us. It expands and contracts based on our response to the person with whom we are communicating. For example, if we like someone, we are more likely to let that person into our bubble than a person we don't like.

Research has shown that the space needs of males and females vary, but the differences are dependent on the facial expression and eye behavior of the other person. For example, males will stand closer to someone who is not looking at them. Research also indicates that young children, up to the age of 7 or so, are much more likely to violate spatial norms of adults. After age 7, children start getting adult spatial norms.

People from some Latin American countries, Italians, people from the Middle East, and Puerto Ricans tend to have closer distances when talking to each other. On the other hand, Germans, Chinese, Japanese, and Americans generally prefer greater distance when communicating. However, these general patterns are subject to substantial variation within each of the major groups. For example, people with higher status in most cultural groups stand closer to, or even tower over, people with lower status.

One researcher identified four distinct categories of personal space that apply to the North American culture (Hall, 1983). *Intimate distance* is from zero to eighteen inches and generally is reserved for lovers and people who are very involved with one another. Occasionally, young children are allowed to enter the intimate zone even if they are barely known. *Personal distance* is from eighteen inches to four feet and is used for conversations between friends and relatives, and for casual business. The *social distance* is from four to eight feet and is reserved for formal, impersonal business relationships. Lastly, the *public distance* is from eight feet to the end of a person's vision or hearing. This distance is reserved for very formal, lecture-type situations (common in large lecture classes).

When the above norms are violated or your personal space is invaded, several options are available to you (Scheflen, 1972; Scheflen & Ashcraft, 1976; Sommer, 1969). First, you can *withdraw* from the situation. For example, if you don't like having your space invaded while in a public restroom, you can leave. Second, you can learn to *avoid* situations in which you know you are likely to have your space invaded. If you don't like being in large crowds, you can stay away from ball games and concerts where such crowding is likely to occur. Third, you can build boundaries or *insulate* yourself from others invading your personal space. For instance, you could pile your books and CDs and other items between yourself and your roommate to show where your side of the room begins and your roommate's ends. Several years ago in our department, we had a faculty member who drew a line down the center of his office to indicate to his office mate that she was not to cross that boundary. He then went on to install carpeting that helped identify the line. Finally, you can *fight* or defend your space. With this option, you challenge anyone who invades your space, and tell them to move away. Of course, you must be prepared to actually physically "back up your talk" if they persist. Otherwise, it is wise to avoid this option.

When a person has occupied a space or territory for such a long time that it becomes her or his or is associated with that person, this is known as *territoriality* (Scheflen & Ashcraft, 1976). That person becomes the owner of that space. Territoriality refers to the use of space that is permanently located or only semimovable (for instance, Archie Bunker's chair in *All in the Family* represented his space in the living room). People tend to claim territory even in public settings. For example, students often choose a favorite place to sit in class, and if they return to class the next time and someone is sitting in their territory, they are offended. We claim our territory in many ways: we designate it by use of markers (books, coats, umbrellas, and so forth), we get it by using it often enough that others grant it to us (this is called *tenure*), and we label our place with our name on our territory ("Don's Room," for example).

How we use our personal space and territory communicates nonverbal information about us to others. For example, the faculty member who drew the line down the center of his office may have been saying that he did not like his office mate and did not want any interaction with her. He may have just been highly territorial, very possessive of his space. He was perceived negatively by others as a result. We must learn how to use our space wisely and recognize when we are being driven by territorial impulses. Otherwise, we are likely to offend people without even knowing we have done so.

Touch

Haptics refers to the use of touch and how touch is used to communicate. Again, norms about this category of nonverbal behavior vary from culture to culture. For example, Northern Europeans and Americans tend to be nontactile, or non-touch-oriented, whereas Arabs and Latin Americans tend to be more touch-oriented. This is not to suggest that Americans don't like to touch or be touched; it is simply that they do not employ touch as a form of communication as much as some other cultures do.

There are five different types of touch. The first is *functional-professional* touch, which is very businesslike and tends to be cold and impersonal. A physical examination by a medical professional represents this type of touch. The *social-polite* type of touch is a way of recognizing another person according to the rules of the culture. A handshake is an example of this type of touch. The *friendship–warmth* touch is used to let people know you have a sense of their uniqueness as individuals. Hugging or putting an arm around someone is an example of this. The *love–intimacy* touch lets someone know you are committed to her or him. Stroking another's face would be an example. Lastly, *sexual-arousal* is the most intimate level of touch. This is associated with the physical attractiveness between two people. It is very stimulating, and an example of this would be sexual intercourse.

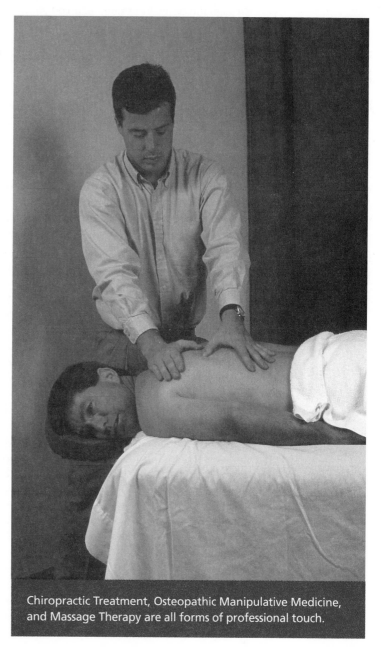

Chiropractic Treatment, Osteopathic Manipulative Medicine, and Massage Therapy are all forms of professional touch.

The type of touch we give another determines our communication with that person. In the dating relationship, if a young man touches a woman's intimate area before she wants him to, the relationship could be over. Morris (1971) lists the twelve steps that lead to sexual intimacy among heterosexuals in the American culture. According to Morris, a person is stereotyped by the rapidity or slowness through which he or she goes through the steps. For example, if you go from step one to step eight in ten minutes, you are fast (and possibly arrested!) The steps are dependent on the relationship and verbal communication between the two people involved. The steps are as follows: (1) eye to body, (2) eye to eye, (3) voice to voice, (4) hand to hand, (5) arm to shoulder, (6) arm to waist, (7) mouth to mouth, (8) hand to head, (9) hand to body, (10) mouth to breast, (11) hand to genitals, and (12) genitals to genitals.

The first six steps are generally considered to lead to *immediacy* (more on this in Chapter 5) in the relationship, whereas steps 7 through 12 are seen as reflecting increasing levels of *intimacy*. Immediacy, which is psychological or physical closeness, is a desired aspect of interpersonal relationships, including those in the work place. Intimacy is the desired outcome in a relationship in which the individuals have a strong consensual sexual feeling for each other. Clearly, the last six steps of Morris' steps are out-of-place in today's work place. Some consider steps 4 through 6 to be inappropriate as well. There are even extreme views that place step one out-of-bounds! Many Islamic cultures, in which women are required to wear burkas that cover them from head to toe with only their eyes showing, provide an example of a culture in which step 1 is out-of-bounds. Immediacy will be discussed in the next chapter, because it is the primary nonverbal means for developing healthy communicative relationships without being intimate.

As we stated earlier, American society tends to be nontactile. An estimated 15 percent of the population are "touch avoidants." These are people who do not like to be touched and generally avoid touching others (Andersen & Leibowitz, 1978). They are often perceived by others as cold and aloof. It is often quite damaging to a relationship when a very immediate person is dating a touch avoidant. Neither can cope with the touching behavior of the other, and the relationship is likely to breakup. This doesn't mean that touch avoidants won't or can't be intimate. It does mean that they are not likely to be as responsive to touch or to initiate touch as often as someone who is immediate.

Lastly, the lack of touch or touch deprivation can be devastating to infant growth and development. Infants who are not touched and held tend to be slower in developing psychomotor and cognitive skills; they read later than infants who receive touch; and they are less mature. From a very early age humans need to be held, loved, and touched. The type of touch we use with others will determine to a large extent the type of communication we receive. In general, if we are immediate, we will have a better quality of communication than if we are nonimmediate.

Environmental Factors

The environment plays a significant role in establishing communication norms in various settings (Maslow & Mintz, 1956; Mintz, 1956). The way the environment is arranged can determine the type and amount of communication which occurs. There are six perceptual frameworks by which we view our environment: formality, warmth, privacy, familiarity, constraint, and distance.

The *formal* environment is one in which people feel that they cannot communicate or that they should limit their communication. For example, many business establishments have very formal structures, (banks, funeral parlors). Sometimes, managers try to make the environment less formal so that people will be more relaxed and communicate more. Others may increase the formality to reduce the amount of social interaction and encourage less talking.

A *warm* environment is one that says, "Stay a while and talk. Do not hurry up and eat, or step aside." Most fast-food chains do not want to create a warm environment. They have seating arrangements designed to encourage you to leave, not linger.

An environment that is conducive to *privacy* elicits a different type of conversation from one that is not private. A private environment encourages a more personal type of conversation, whereas a public environment encourages a very impersonal conversation.

Familiarity breeds contempt? Not quite. In fact, most people like being in environments, with which they are familiar. They can predict who will be there and what is expected of them. The unfamiliar environment increases anxiety and makes many people uncomfortable.

Our perceptions of *constraint* depend on the duration of the restraint, its location, and the amount of privacy we have while being restrained. For example, we can all adjust to sitting in a three-hour lecture class, but not many of us could easily adjust to a jail sentence. We know we will eventually be allowed to leave class, and we have some control over the environment. However, in jail we cannot leave until the authorities say we can. In such a case, we have no control over our environment.

Lastly, the *distance* established by the environment determines the type of communication (Exline, 1971; Henley, 1977; Korda, 1975, 1977). The distance can be actual or psychologically perceived distance. For example, some bosses may be only ten feet from their subordinates; however, the boss can create a much greater sense of distance by being psychologically distant with employees by being nonimmediate.

Research shows that when placed in an ugly room, people become discontented, irritable, bored, fatigued, and generally "want out" of the environment. Conversely, people placed in attractive surroundings work harder, are less fatigued, communicate more, are less irritable, and do not mind remaining in the setting for a reasonable period.

What distinguishes an attractive setting from an unattractive setting? The answer is not simple. What is agreeable to one person may not be agreeable to another. However, environmental factors seem to have a predictable impact. The color of an item or of a room will determine how someone reacts. For example, green will sell vegetables but it is not likely to sell bread. Black is associated with darkness and power, red with excitement, blue with coolness. Room lighting should be moderate, not too bright or glaring or too dim. Either variation will lower the effectiveness of the environment. The sound should be compatible with the environment. If it is a western dance hall, then it should be playing country and western music. If it is a classroom, then it should have background music that won't interfere with the work by calling attention to itself. Finally, the optimal temperature for a work environment is around 68 degrees. Some would claim this is too cool; however, people are more stimulated in a cooler room than in a hot room.

The environment and its characteristics determine mostly the type and amount of communication that will take place between people. In most circumstances, we should try to manipulate our environment so that it is conducive to conversation and interaction. In other words, we should strive for a more immediate environment.

Smell

Our sense of smell (olfactics) helps us perceive the world around us and determines what communication is appropriate (Winter, 1976). For example, someone with bad breath starts talking to you, what is your initial response? It probably is to back away as fast as possible. However, if it happens to be your teacher or your boss, you cannot leave that easily. If it is a loved one, you probably can mention it to that person. He or she might even appreciate it. For years, researchers in nonverbal communication choose not to discuss smell, but more recently there has been considerable thought in the area. Scholars have concluded that our sense of smell affects our moods, attitudes about others, perceptions of others, and communication orientation toward others.

Our sense of smell is very personal, like our judgment of beauty. Some recent research has indicated that on a pleasantness/unpleasantness odor scale, the odors that were rated as unpleasant were associated with the undesirable characteristics of people such as ugliness, poor health, and obesity. Therefore, we will tend to judge others not only by their appearance but also by the odors we think or perceive that they emit. People tend to associate unpleasant odors with sick people and hospitals, when some hospital odors are quite pleasant. However, we have been taught from childhood that hospitals have undesirable odors and that people in hospitals smell bad. Babies don't always smell bad. When they have been lathered in baby lotion, they smell wonderful to most people. However, to many people, baby lotion is an offensive odor.

Practitioners in the medical field sometimes draw on their sense of smell to help diagnose ailments. For example, years ago physicians knew yellow fever by its butcher-shop odor, and scurvy and smallpox by their putrid odors. Typhoid fever smells like freshly baked bread, diphtheria has a very sweet odor, and the plague has the smell of apples. More recently, medical research into the area of smell has taken a more scientific turn. Some medical schools are encouraging medical students, interns, and residents to learn to identify odors associated with specific illnesses; the physician can then make a quicker diagnosis, perhaps saving precious seconds. Using their sense of smell, physicians can diagnose alcohol poisoning, diabetic coma, and general comas this way.

Our sense of smell affects how we perceive others from cultures different from our own. The general American culture is a very unnatural one in that we try to cover up or disguise our true body scents. The artificial components in perfumes, toilet paper, tissues, deodorants, toothpaste, and so on contribute to a higher rate of allergies in this country than in others. Have you ever tried to find any product that has its natural scent? These products usually say "unscented," which means that they still have probably been tampered with but not as much as the rose scented, the pine scented, or the bubble-gum scented. Scents usually have to be added to products even to make them *unscented*! Even our laundry detergents and our soaps are scented. Our culture has a phobia about the natural odor of the body. People in some Middle Eastern countries, on the other hand, are taught from childhood to breathe in each other's faces. Of course, to us this would be quite offensive, but to them it is a way of life.

In summary, it can be stated that our olfactory senses affect our perceptions of others and our communication with them. Our sense of smell is a very pervasive, unconscious determiner of how we feel about others.

Time

What is this thing we call time? We cherish our time; we love to spend it, save it, give it to others; we have no time; we have free time, time limits, time tests, Central time, Eastern time, formal time, informal time, a lifetime. Time is another nonverbal element that affects us in an unconscious manner. When someone is late for a business appointment, we make judgments about that person, usually negative ones. When a student is late for class, most teachers, either consciously or unconsciously, form a negative evaluation of that person. We think our time is important and we don't like someone *wasting* time. In fact, we become very offended when someone wastes our time, and we think of that person in a very negative light.

A person's use of time communicates much about that person to others. In communication, people often research chronemics, or the study of how we perceive, define, and react to this thing called *time*. Americans tend to be very time conscious and do not like waiting or having their time wasted. After all, "Time is money." Americans like to talk faster than people in some other countries because they can get more in; they do not like waiting and are offended when they travel where they have to wait. Americans tend to be *monochronic;* that is, they like to do one thing at a time. People in many other cultures, such as some in Latin America, tend to be *polychronic*—they do several things at one time. In computer lingo, we refer to this as multitasking. Some Latin Americans may hold several business meetings in the same room simultaneously, and it takes American business people a long time to adjust to this. Monochronic, time-oriented cultures try to do one thing *well* at a time. However, they seem inflexible and insensitive to the needs of others. Polychronic, time-oriented cultures tend to overload people by having too much going on at once, but they seem more sensitive to the needs of others and more flexible. Besides monochronic and polychronic time orientations of cultures, there are three common cultural time orientations: technical, formal, and informal.

Technical time is concerned with the scientific measurement of time. Technical time is very precise, logical, and "Spock-like." It has no real impact on interpersonal communication, but it has a great impact on mass communication. Technical time is the scientific time used by NASA and many mass-communication projects. Technical time is so important that the U.S. Department of Defense charges the U.S. Naval Observatory to oversee the "Master Clock" in Washington, D.C. Ultimately, technical time is extremely important because it is intricately linked to Global Positioning Systems used by the U.S. Military, Air Traffic Control, and nautical activities. Not only is the Master Clock of the utmost importance, it is a possible target of terrorism, so the United States has an alternative site located at Schriever Air Force Base near Colorado Springs.

Formal time is the traditional time orientation of a culture. For example, our traditional time is by days, months, years. We measure formal time by a calendar. Some cultures measure formal time by the seasons, tides, and so on. Formal time is also less associated with interpersonal communication. However, people need to be aware of the differences in formal time systems so they know how other cultures operate.

Informal time is the most difficult time orientation to understand. It is the orientation most relevant to interpersonal relationships. It is not precise and cannot be exactly measured. Informal time is the time orientation for a culture in a specific situation. Another way of defining informal time is to say it is the casual time of the culture. For example, when we say "*in a minute*" we probably really mean in a *few* minutes. Only the person using the expression can really be sure what he or she means. It is very difficult, if not impossible, to understand the informal time of a culture in which you have not lived for a long time. Often you have to experience it or have an expert explain the difference in informal time orientations to you. In most parts of the United States, when we say a party will start at 7:00 P.M., most people know to arrive between 7:00 and 7:30 P.M. However, in other cultures, arrival time could mean anywhere from 7:30 to 9:00 P.M. It is very difficult for most Americans to adjust to the informal times in other cultures because we are so time-bound to our own.

The next major time orientation is the *psychological* time orientation. People can be past, present, or future oriented. Past-oriented cultures dwell on the past and love reliving old times. These people have a deep respect for the elderly. The Chinese culture is an example of this orientation.

Present-oriented societies are concerned with the here and now. Their philosophy is "Eat, drink, and be merry, for tomorrow you might die." Latin Americans and Spanish Americans tend to be present oriented.

Lastly, a future-oriented society is concerned with what will take place tomorrow or in the future. American society is a prime example of this. For years we have studied the detrimental effects of the environment on the ozone layer. We have tried to adapt our culture to that future concern by putting proper exhaust systems on cars and eliminating spray cans. We are also currently concerned with the future of the world in the nuclear age. Many people in other parts of the world have difficulty understanding the American obsession with the future.

Psychological time orientation determines what a culture's communication will focus on—do we talk about what was, what is, or what will be? When people with different psychological time orientations try to communicate, there is a tendency for them to talk past one another and to think the other person is not interested in "what is important."

The last major time orientation is concerned with a person's *biological* time. Our body often decides how we think, feel, and react to others throughout the day. When our body is at its peak, we function well; when it is low we function poorly. In fact, airlines have started trying to determine the peak times and low times for their pilots so they do not assign them to fly during their low times. Another way to look at this is our natural rhythms. Most of us can be classified as "owls" or "sparrows." Owls are at their peak in late afternoon and evening and at their worst in early morning. Sparrows are at their best in the early morning and at their worst in the late evening. Consider the impact on the owl student who has early morning classes. This individual is barely awake and functioning, and will probably perform more poorly in the classroom in the early morning than her or his counterparts, those chirping little sparrows. However, the sparrows are dying in their late afternoon classes, whereas the owls are becoming lively and hooting like crazy. There are also some people who are "sprowls." They never seem to run down.

Besides cultural, psychological, and biological time orientations, there are personality types, or personality orientations, that determine time orientations. For example, people with Type A personalities are very time oriented. Everything is scheduled and time governs their lives. They tend to be very anxious people who are always clock-watching. In fact, they are compulsive in their time orientations and hate to have their routine disturbed. These people tend to have health problems because they don't take the time to rest, or when they do take a vacation they spend their time working or worrying about work. However, they get a lot accomplished and are very work oriented.

The Type B personality person is less time oriented and does not let time rule her or his lifestyle. These people are concerned with their jobs and will get the job done, but not at the expense of their happiness. They tend to be more relaxed and less time conscious. They also tend to have less health problems.

Clearly, we need to understand and identify with the time orientations of others to have better communication relationships. Time is pervasive; it is always there impacting what others think of us, and what we think of others.

In this chapter, we have looked at the various types of nonverbal messages in some detail. Our focus has been on the association between nonverbal messages and the meanings stimulated by those messages in the minds of people. In the following chapter, we will turn our attention to the role of messages in ongoing interpersonal relationships.

 KEY TERMS

REFERENCES

Addington, D. W. (1968). The relationship of selected vocal characteristics to personality perception. *Speech Monographs, 35,* 492–503.

Andersen, P. A., Garrison, J. P., & Andersen, J. F. (1976). Defining nonverbal communication: A neurophysio-

logical explanation of nonverbal information processing. *Human Communication Research, 6,* 74–89.

Andersen, P. A., & Leibowitz, K. (1978). The development and nature of touch avoidance. *Environmental Psychology and Nonverbal Behavior, 3,* 89–106.

Argyle, M. (1975). *Bodily communication*. New York: International Universities Press.

Birdwhistell, R. L. (1970). *Kinesics and context*. Philadelphia: University of Pennsylvania Press.

Cortes, J. B., & Gatti, F. M. (1965). Physique and self-description of temperament. *Journal of Consulting Psychology, 29*, 434.

Davitz, J. R., & Davitz, L. (1961). Nonverbal vocal communication of feeling. *Journal of Communication, 11*, 81–86.

Donaghy, W. C. (1980). *Our silent language: An introduction to nonverbal communication*. Dubuque, IA: Gorsuch Scarisbrick.

Eakins, B. W., & Eakins, R. G. (1978). *Sex differences in human communication*. Boston: Houghton Mifflin.

Ekman, P., & Friesen, W. V. (1975). *Unmasking the face*. Englewood Cliffs, NJ: Prentice-Hall.

Ekman, P., & Rosenberg, E. L. (Eds.). (2005). *What the face reveals: Basic and applied studies of spontaneous expression using the Facial Action Coding System (FACS)* (2nd ed.). New York: Oxford.

Exline, R. V. (1971). Visual interaction: The glance of power and performance. In James K. Cole (Ed.), *Nebraska Symposium on Motivation* (pp. 163–206). Lincoln: University of Nebraska Press.

Fast, J. (1970). *Body language*. New York: M. Evans.

Hall, E. T. (1959). *The silent language*. Garden City, NY: Anchor Press/Doubleday.

Hall, E. T. (1966). *The hidden dimension*. Garden City, NY: Anchor Press/Doubleday.

Hall, E. T. (1983). Proxemics. In A. M. Katz & V. T. Katz (Eds.), *Foundations of nonverbal communication: Readings, exercises, and commentary* (pp. 5-27). Carbondale: Southern Illinois University Press.

Harrison, R. P. (1974). *Beyond words: An introduction to nonverbal communication*. Englewood Cliffs, NJ: Prentice-Hall.

Henley, N. M. (1977). *Body politics: Power, sex, and nonverbal communication*. Englewood Cliffs, NJ: Prentice-Hall.

Hickson, M. L., III, & Stacks, D. W. (1993). *Nonverbal communication: Studies and applications*. Dubuque, IA: Brown & Benchmark.

Knapp, M. L., & Hall, J. A. (2001). *Nonverbal communication in human interaction* (5th ed.). Belmont, CA: Wadsworth.

Korda, M. (1975). *Power! How to get it, how to use it*. New York: Random House.

Korda, M. (1977). *Success: How every man and woman can achieve it*. New York: Random House.

LaFrance, M., & Mayo, C. (1978). *Moving bodies: Nonverbal communication in social relationships*. Monterey, CA: Brooks/Cole.

Maslow, A. H., & Mintz, N. L. (1956). Effects of esthetic surroundings: I. Initial effects of three esthetic conditions upon perceiving "energy" and "well being" in faces. *Journal of Psychology, 41*, 247–254.

McCroskey, J. C., Larson, C. E., & Knapp, M. L. (1971). *An introduction to interpersonal communication*. Englewood Cliffs, NJ: Prentice-Hall.

Mehrabian, A. (1971). *Silent messages*. Belmont, CA: Wadsworth.

Mehrabian, A. (1972). *Nonverbal communication*. Chicago: Aldine-Atherton.

Mehrabian, A. (1981). *Silent messages: Implicit communication of emotions and attitudes* (2nd ed.). Belmont, CA: Wadsworth.

Mintz, N. L. (1956). Effects of esthetic surroundings. II. Prolonged and repeated experience in the "beautiful" and "ugly" room. *Journal of Psychology, 41*, 459–466.

Morris, D. (1971). *Intimate behavior*. New York: Random House.

Richmond, V. P. (1992). *Nonverbal communication in the classroom*. Edina, MN: Burgess International Group.

Richmond, V. P., & McCroskey, J. C. (2004). *Nonverbal behavior in interpersonal relations* (5th ed.). Boston: Allyn & Bacon.

Rosenfeld, L. B., & Plax, T. G. (1977). Clothing as communication. *Journal of Communication, 27*, 23–31.

Scheflen, A. E. (1972). *Body language and the social order: Communication as behavioral control*. Englewood Cliffs, NJ: Prentice-Hall.

Scheflen, A. E., & Ashcraft, N. (1976). *Human territories: How we behave in space-time*. Englewood Cliffs, NJ: Prentice-Hall.

Sheldon, W. H. (1940). *The varieties of the human physique*. New York: Harper and Brothers.

Sheldon, W. H. (1942). *The varieties of temperament*. New York: Hafner.

Sommer, R. (1969). *Personal space: The behavioral basis of design*. Englewood Cliffs, NJ: Prentice-Hall.

Winter, R. (1976). *The smell book: Scents, sex, and society*. Philadelphia: J.B. Lippincott.

DISCUSSION QUESTIONS

1. Why is an individual's physical appearance so important during initial interactions?

2. What are the seven primary facial expressions? Why are these considered to be primary facial expressions? Do you agree or disagree? Why?

3. How do religious buildings communicate a sense of formality?

4. Do you consider yourself monochronic or polychronic? Why?

5. Explain the four quasi-courtship cues. How have you participated in these courtship cues in your own life?

5

Messages and Relationships

OBJECTIVES

- Define and explain *immediacy*.

- Differentiate between verbal immediacy and nonverbal immediacy.

- Understand how nonverbal immediacy can be enhanced in each of the fifteen different categories of nonverbal messages.

- Define and explain *intimacy*.

- Define and explain *self-disclosure*.

- Explain the difference between intimacy and sexual relations.

- Define and explain *status*.

- Understand how status gets communicated nonverbally.

Whenever two people engage in communication, they have an interpersonal relationship (McCroskey & Daly, 1986; McCroskey, Larson, & Knapp, 1971). We all have dozens of interpersonal relationships. Many people have hundreds. Not all relationships are alike. In fact, the *only* thing all relationships have in common is that they involve communication. Communication, then, is the foundation on which relationships are developed. Some people even go as far as to suggest that communication *is* the relationship.

If relationships are different from one another and communication defines the nature of the relationship, it follows that to understand relationships, we must understand the communication that goes on in those relationships. Relationships have three important dimensions: immediacy, intimacy, and status. The variability of these three dimensions accounts for much of the difference that we recognize in the relationships we have with others. Although these three dimensions are distinct from each other, they are also frequently related. We will consider each in more detail.

▣ IMMEDIACY

Immediacy refers to *the degree of perceived physical or psychological distance between people in a relationship* (Mehrabian, 1971, 1981). An immediate relationship is one in which the people in the relationship see themselves as close to one another. At the outset, almost all relationships are nonimmediate. Some become more immediate as communication continues, but most never do.

Our feelings about others with whom we come in contact are communicated to them through both our verbal and our nonverbal messages, just as their feelings are communicated to us. Thus, the verbal and nonverbal messages we send and receive in a relationship will define the level of immediacy that develops in that relationship.

Verbal Immediacy

What other people say can cause us to feel either closer to or more distant from them. Increased immediacy is produced by verbal messages that are responsive to the other person in the relationship, messages that suggest openness to the other, friendship for the other, or empathy with the other. Such simple things as the use of the pronoun *we* rather than *you*, or using *you and I* or *us*, will increase feelings of immediacy.

An important method of increasing immediacy in a relationship is sending verbal messages that encourage the other person to communicate. Such comments as "I see what you mean," "Tell me more," "That is a good point," and "I think so too" will create increased immediacy. Contrast these comments with the following: "Oh, shut up," "That is stupid," "I thought of that years ago," and "Frankly, I don't care what you think." If you were to hear any of the latter comments, would you want to communicate more? How close would you feel to the person who made such a comment? Clearly, a direct way to modify feelings of immediacy is through verbal messages. However, there are many nonverbal messages that can accomplish the same end, although they often are much less direct. Because directness often is seen as inappropriate behavior in a nonimmediate relationship, increasing immediacy usually is accomplished primarily via nonverbal messages. Fortunately, there are many types of nonverbal messages that tend to increase, or decrease if you wish, immediacy.

Nonverbal Immediacy

The second type of immediacy is nonverbal immediacy, the degree of perceived physical or psychological distance between people in a relationship as a result of nonverbal behaviors (Andersen, 1979; McCroskey & Richmond, 1992). Scales 15 and 16 are designed to measure nonverbal immediacy. Scale 15 is designed to measure an individual's perception of her or his personal nonverbal immediacy, whereas Scale 16 is designed to measure an individual's perception of someone else's nonverbal immediacy. Specifically Scale 16, as it is written here, is designed to measure an individual's perception of her or his supervisor's nonverbal immediacy. Nonverbal immediacy can be examined through each of the categories of nonverbal communication discussed in the previous chapter.

These two men are clearly sitting in a nonverbally immediate fashion.

Gestures, Body Movements, and Immediacy. The position of your body when communicating with another, your posture, and the type of gestures you employ all contribute to an immediate or nonimmediate perception. The person who seems relaxed, has an open body position, leans forward when communicating, and gestures in a positive manner is much more likely to be perceived as immediate than the person who seems closed and distant.

Nonimmediate body movements are exemplified by a closed body position (arms folded), very little gesturing, and a tense posture. This type of individual makes people feel uncomfortable; communication is very limited and often even is terminated. We are unlikely even to approach a person who has a nonimmediate posture. For example, the teacher who is always distant or nonresponsive to students in her or his nonverbal body movement is saying, "I don't want interaction with you." Students can subconsciously realize this based solely on the nonimmediate body positions and gestures.

Physical Appearance, Attractiveness, and Immediacy. Even if you are not the most attractive person alive, you can still present an appearance that says you are open to others. *Ectomorphs* tend to have body stances that say that they are tense and perhaps afraid of communication. This can be corrected by learning to relax and present a less tense body stance. *Endomorphs* tend to stand in a rather uncaring, perhaps even sloppy stance. This too can be corrected. The *mesomorph* has the most immediate body stance. Even if your shape or general appearance is not that of Miss America or Mister Universe, you can still present an immediate or responsive image of yourself by using a more positive body stance. In fact, this will improve people's perceptions of you and your appearance. If you have a positive, open, receptive body stance, despite your body type, people will respond to you more favorably.

Dress, Artifacts, and Immediacy. These factors depend on the communication context and the individuals involved. However, although your attire should match the context, you can still present an immediate image. For example, the teacher who dresses in casual rather than formal attire is more likely to put the class at ease than one who dresses in a very formal manner. By *casual*, we mean informal, not sloppy or carelessly dressed. The supervisor who dresses in a casual fashion is more likely to be able to communicate with employees on an informal basis than the supervisor who dresses in a nonimmediate way, the way that says, "I'm the boss, and you are obviously beneath me."

The effects of dress and artifacts are very important in developing an immediate relationship. We already know that how people dress predicts whether others will want to interact with them. Therefore, someone who dresses to make others feel that he or she is above them presents a nonimmediate image. This is not to say that teachers should dress like students or that supervisors should dress like their employees. It does suggest that less formal attire will let people feel as if they can approach you.

Facial Expression, Eye Behavior, and Immediacy. An old adage is true, particularly with nonverbal behaviors: "You catch more flies with honey than with vinegar." The person who has a positive facial expression is more likely to be approached by others, to be communicated with by others, and to be perceived in a positive fashion by others.

Do you know someone who has had a frown line between the eyes ever since you can remember? This person probably presents a very nonresponsive image to others. Your facial expressions and eye behavior are very important in establishing an immediate perception. The positive cues, such as smiling, nodding, eye contact, and an overall positive facial expression, all say to others that you like them and are interested in them and in what they are saying. Consider the teacher who always wears a scowl, never smiles, and has very little eye contact with students. This teacher will not be perceived as immediate and may even be perceived as unfriendly, cold, and uncaring.

Voice and Immediacy.   As suggested earlier, "It's not what you say, but how you say it." The words *I love you*, when said with the appropriate inflection, can even say you *dislike* someone. To present an immediate image through your voice, you need to have vocal variety. This shows that you are interested in the other person. The person who speaks in a monotone not only is boring but also may be perceived as not caring.

Vocal variety includes several vocal activities such as animated, dynamic, attentive, and using tones and inflections that suggest you like and care about what the other person says. For example, the person who has a flat voice and very little vocal variety in a conversation appears uninterested in what you have to say. It is particularly important when talking with young children to have positive vocal qualities. Much of what young children hear are the nonverbal tones, not the words, and often they will misinterpret. For example, young children (under 12) usually interpret sarcasm or satire literally. If you say to the 8 year old who just threw a ball through the neighbor's window, "Oh, Johnny, that was wonderful," Johnny may perceive that it *was* great and wonderful, and he might do it again.

Space and Immediacy.   How do you feel when you try to stand close to someone and the person keeps backing away? Probably very uncomfortable. There are several possible explanations for this behavior: (1) the person is from a culture different from yours and feels uncomfortable when being approached, (2) the person is a touch avoidant, (3) the person is generally nonimmediate and realizes that backing away and keeping a distance make it less likely that he or she must interact, or (4) the person is communication apprehensive and backs away, realizing that this will inhibit communication.

In order for people to be perceived as more immediate, they need to reduce the distance between themselves and receivers. As the distance is reduced, the likelihood of successful communication increases because there is more eye contact and immediacy.

In terms of territoriality, individuals need to arrange their space in a way that says, "Come in, you're welcome here." Often, we do the opposite because we do not want people to stay too long. For example, there are many professors who arrange their offices in a nonimmediate manner so that students will feel uncomfortable and not take up too much of their time. These professors will make sure that the student sits across the desk from them and probably in an uncomfortable chair.

A person's territory can tell a lot about how that individual wants to interact with others. A nonimmediate environment discourages communication; an immediate territory encourages it. Supervisors also are often very well aware of the arrangements of territory and its effects on their subordinates.

Touch and Immediacy.   This nonverbal area creates a more immediate relationship than does any other. However, a person must be cautious not to interpret touching behavior by another as an overture to an intimate relationship. As suggested earlier, touch is the most potent of nonverbal messages and is likely to stimulate very strong meanings. When a supervisor touches a subordinate on the arm or pats the subordinate on the back, the supervisor most likely is being immediate in an attempt to establish a more immediate relationship. However, some subordinates, particularly ones of the opposite sex, could misinterpret this. Therefore, we have to learn when touch is immediate or a sign of desired intimacy. The person who avoids touch or does not like to be touched may be perceived as very nonimmediate and very unfriendly.

When possible, we should touch others to show we like and respect them. The touch should be done so it is not likely to be interpreted as an overture to intimacy. With society's currently heightened sensitivity to sexual harassment, many people find it wiser to sacrifice a potentially improved communicative relationship to avoid being charged with inappropriate touching behavior. Although touch can substantially enhance a communicative relationship, it probably is best used when a very good relationship already exists. Particularly in the workplace and the school, touch probably should be avoided in the early stages of relationship development.

Environmental Factors and Immediacy. We should strive to create an environment that stimulates feelings of familiarity, warmth, and comfortableness in the receiver. In this type of environment, people are more relaxed and may communicate more freely. Business executives often have their offices arranged in one of two ways—one nonimmediate, and the other immediate. The immediate environment usually consists of subdued lighting, comfortable seating, fewer barriers between the executive and client or employee, and pleasant color tones. The nonimmediate environment has many barriers built between the executive and client or employee, bright lighting, uncomfortable seating, and colors that say, "Go away."

Some people in the business world have constructed their offices so that they can present either environment in the same room. They usually have a seating area away from the desk so that they can have the immediate atmosphere should they choose. However, they still like to maintain a nonimmediate environment so that they can encourage people not to stay a long time if they choose to do so.

Smell and Immediacy. Obviously, if we emit an unpleasant body odor, people will avoid us. Heavy, opulent odors can be offensive to others and discourage interaction. For example, think of the teenage male who didn't quite understand that he shouldn't bathe himself in cologne. We've all walked by someone and wanted to cough because the person was a little overly odious. Humans also produce natural scents, and we also have smell detectors called *pheromones*. These help us decide what odors attract and what odors repel us. Many commercial perfume companies have taken advantage of this by suggesting that their perfume will stimulate another's pheromones. We must be cautious about the scents we use and the impact these scents have on others. Remember, what attracts one person can repel another. We should not, however, underestimate the power of appropriate enhancement of an environment through smell. Many real estate agents know that having the odor of baking bread in a home, when potential buyers are shown through it, will substantially increase their liking of the house. This is an odor that increases the environmental immediacy for most (but not all!) people, and gets the communication about the house off to a very good start.

Time and Immediacy. One way to alienate almost anyone in this culture is to be consistently late. Our society demands that people be on time, and we do not tolerate lateness very often. If we wish to create an immediate atmosphere, or at least set the stage for creating one, we need to adapt to the time orientations of the culture. In our culture, this means that we should be on time and, if possible, a little early for appointments. Many executives will make their clients wait to establish their power and authority. This does not endear them to those clients. Many women still think they should keep their dates waiting. If they do that too often, they may have to find a new date. Few people like to be kept waiting. Time is one way we can create the atmosphere for immediacy to take place.

Outcomes of Immediacy

In this section, we have defined immediacy and discussed ways to be more immediate in each of the categories of nonverbal behavior. However, we have not explicitly stated the positive outcomes from establishing immediacy. There are several, and all are related to the establishment of a more effective interpersonal relationship.

First, immediacy will usually lead to an increase of communication between participants and interactants (McCroskey & Richmond, 1992). When people feel immediate with each other, they become more relaxed and open to communication. Second, immediacy will lead to increased attentiveness by the interactants. When we feel immediate with another person, we naturally tend to focus attention on that person. Third, immediacy will increase the likelihood that listening will improve between the interactants. Because immediacy increases openness and attentiveness, one is less likely to be defensive in response to what the other person is saying. Therefore, one's listening is directed more toward understanding what the other person is saying rather than preparing to respond to an attack. Fourth, immediacy will lead to liking between the interactants. Communication in such a positive environment is very pleasant for the individual, and these positive feelings become associated with the other person in the interaction. These four outcomes of immediacy, of course, lead to the fifth and most important outcome, more effective communication.

Considerable research on immediacy has focused on the learning environment. The results of that research strongly suggest that increased immediacy between teacher and student leads to a variety of positive outcomes. Immediacy will help the student and teacher establish a better interpersonal relationship. Immediacy will lead to students taking other courses from the teacher who is perceived as immediate. Immediacy will cause increased learning by the student because the student likes the teacher and will listen to her or him. Immediacy between teacher and student will mean fewer disciplinary problems. Finally, immediacy will lead to a more positive relationship between teacher and student, and thus increase communication. Of course, many teachers choose to be nonimmediate because they do not want increased interaction in their classroom, and many students refuse to be immediate and friendly with their instructors because they feel uncomfortable. If students and teachers can be more immediate, the classroom generally is a more positive environment for both.

There can be some disadvantages to immediacy. First, sometimes, behaviors intended to increase immediacy are misinterpreted as invitations to intimacy. Second, immediacy may reduce the privacy between individuals as a function of increasing the pressure for communication to increase. Third, immediacy can increase the anxiety of the touch-avoidant or communication-apprehensive individual. Because immediacy increases the feelings of closeness and need to communicate, these individuals may find immediate situations unpleasant. And fourth, immediacy can make people feel as if they have lost control of the situation. For example, some teachers are afraid that immediacy will lead to a loss of classroom control, when it usually has the opposite effect. Students are pleased to have an immediate, open teacher and usually behave better than in the traditional classroom. Nevertheless, people with high control needs may feel less comfortable in more immediate settings. To be open to communication with another is to relinquish some control over the relationship.

The use of a single nonverbal behavior is not going to create the perception that you are an immediate, responsive individual. A combination of immediate nonverbal behaviors leads one to be perceived as immediate. If you want to be perceived as immediate, you should consider using such immediate nonverbal behaviors as positive gestures, leaning forward, showing positive facial expressions, much vocal variety, touching others when appropriate, dressing casually but appropriately for the communication context, directing your body orientation toward the other person, using scents that are not overpowering, and being on time. Fortunately, you do not need to engage in all these behaviors all of the time. Rather, you should employ those that you can use comfortably and appropriately. Over time, you can develop an immediate attitude that will lead you to engage in these behaviors as a matter of course and without constant conscious attention.

If you are perceived as immediate, you will be seen in a more positive manner. You will be perceived as sociable, likable, and, most of all, responsive to others. And, as we discussed previously, responsiveness leads to more effective interpersonal relationships.

 INTIMACY

Intimacy refers to the perceived depth of a relationship between people (Richmond, 1992; Richmond & McCroskey, 2004). People in an intimate relationship see themselves as highly connected to each other. Often, an individual in such a relationship is reluctant to make even a relatively minor decision that might affect the other person without first communicating with that person. People in a highly intimate relationship see their partner as an extension of themselves, and vice versa.

Very few relationships reach a point of high intimacy. Most of us will be very fortunate to have more than one such relationship in a lifetime, and some of us will never have one. Intimate relationships demand much of the people who are in them. Few of us have either the capacity or the willingness to extend ourselves as far as would be necessary to develop many intimate relationships.

Highly intimate relationships in the American culture provide the most common context for two things: self-disclosure and sexual relations. However, both can and do occur in relationships that are less than intimate. One of these focuses primarily on verbal messages, and the other on nonverbal messages. Let us look at each.

Self-Disclosure

Messages of a self-disclosive nature reveal information that is private and personal to another. In general, people tend to self-disclose to those in whom they have much trust and confidence, and who they have known for a long time. However, there are exceptions to this rule. Some people will reveal anything, anytime, to anyone. These people are called *high self-disclosers*.

A coauthor of this text once had a female student who, on the first day of class, told the instructor how she had lost 350 pounds by having gastric bypass surgery. In the same breath, she told the instructor she had two abortions because of bad love affairs, and then revealed that she had the "hots for many of the men in class." This was all within the first five minutes of class. Not only was the instructor a bit taken aback, but the instructor also did not want or *need* to know this information to communicate with the student.

High self-disclosers often cannot tell when to stop disclosing or what not to disclose, and they tend to make others feel uncomfortable by telling too much personal information about themselves. They are sending messages that are appropriate for a highly intimate relationship within a nonintimate one.

Low self-disclosers are those people who do not reveal any information about themselves unless forced to do so. They also make people feel uncomfortable, but for different reasons. Low self-disclosers reveal so little about themselves that others have a difficult time learning how to communicate with them. There is no way to reduce any uncertainty. The communication might come to a halt because one does not know how to communicate with the other. Communication apprehensives tend to be low self-disclosers because of their fear of communication. They wish to avoid communication, and the most threatening communication of all is that about the self. Avoidance of self-disclosure tends to reduce other communication as well.

In general, if one constructs verbal messages that reveal personal information to another, then reduction of uncertainty can occur and people can start interacting more comfortably. You can self-disclose about attitudes and values and be secure in the fact that you are only opening the lines of communication. However, when you start revealing very intimate information about yourself to others, don't be surprised if they start to feel uncomfortable. Only in the 1960s did North Americans buy into "letting it all hang out." However, a certain amount of self-disclosure will lead to more open and honest communication between source and receiver. It may even increase the communication between the two by finding things in common.

Think of some relationships that you have at home, work, and school. Consider the following self-disclosure statements and decide in which relationships you might be willing to state them, presuming these were true: "I like bowling." "I attend Harvard University." "I have herpes." "My spouse and I are getting a divorce." "My lover and I had sex last night." "I was arrested for reckless driving yesterday." "I ran over a child when I was 16." "I went to the ball game last Saturday." "I have a 3.5 GPA." "I really do not like Bill." "My boss made a pass at me this morning." "My favorite meal is steak and baked potato." "I am an alcoholic." "I am a Democrat." "I lied to you about that."

All the above statements tell something personal about the speaker. However, they are not all appropriate for all relationships. Each statement could be damaging to a relationship. Each, believe it or not, could strengthen a relationship. It all depends on the relationship. Can you provide an example (hypothetical, of course) for each statement in which it would be appropriate and helpful to a relationship? If you can, you have a feeling for the intimacy dimension of relationships.

Sexual Relations

Having a sexual relationship with another person is generally considered one of the most intimate behaviors one person can share with another. Although talking is usually associated with sexual relations, sex is primarily a set of nonverbal behaviors. Engaging in sexual relations is a highly intimate behavior, but the presence of sexual relations does not guarantee that the participants actually have a highly intimate relationship. Sexual relations can be, and are, engaged in by people who have a very nonintimate relationship (LeVay, 1993). This is generally called *casual sex.*

In American society, there is a strong tendency to equate sexual relations with intimate relationships. Such an equation is misleading. An intimate relationship is one in which there is considerable depth and feeling by both people. Such feelings have no necessity of being associated with sexual desire or fulfillment. Many heterosexual females have intimate relationships with other females, but sex is not involved. Although this is not as common among heterosexual men, because such intimacy among men is viewed by many as nonmasculine, many heterosexual men do have healthy, intimate relationships with other men.

In contrast, many sexual relationships are far from intimate. One of our friends often tells us of his desire for "a short, intense, meaningless relationship." What he means is sex with no strings attached and no repercussions later. Such wants by both females and males lead to the phenomenon known as *instant intimacy* (Richmond & McCroskey, 2004), when you go from eye to body, to genital to genital, in a very short period of time. This was illustrated in a movie a few years ago with the following conversation in a singles bar:

Male: Hi there. I'm Bob.

Female: Hi. I'm Kim.

Bob: Come here often?

Kim: No, this is my first time.

Bob: I'm a Virgo. What is your sign?

Kim: I'm a Libra.

Bob: Great? Let's get out of here and go to my place.

Kim: O.K.

Although it would be easy to laugh at such a scene, or to raise serious moral questions about Bob and Kim, to do so would miss something very important. Bob and Kim may have wanted something more than sex; they may have wanted an intimate relationship, but were willing to accept sex as a substitute. This is not unlike a scene that often occurs on trains, planes, bars, and the Internet. Complete strangers strike up a conversation, and in minutes one or both will be revealing things that normally would be reserved for a highly intimate relationship. Humans seem to have a strong need to have an intimate relationship within which they can share some of their life with another. Not everyone has such a relationship. This leads some to engage in verbal (self-disclosures) and nonverbal (sexual relations) communication in other relationships in which the behavior may not be appropriate and may even be very harmful.

◉ STATUS

Status refers to a person's position in some hierarchy. Status itself is not usually of much consequence in a relationship. However, the difference between people's status in a relationship is very important. This *status differential*, as it is called, can have a major influence on the communication that is considered appropriate or inappropriate in a relationship (Richmond, McCroskey, & McCroskey, 2005). One should also realize that our discussion of status in the following section is culturally based, so how we talk about status in the U.S. culture may not be consistent with how status is exhibited and dealt with in other cultures.

A higher-status person in a relationship tends to control that relationship and the communication in it. The teacher in the classroom, the boss in the office, the coach on the field, and the sergeant in the barracks are all examples of this phenomenon.

People often use status markers, like large desks, to indicate their status while communicating with others.

Although some changes have taken place in recent years, in traditional female–male relationships the male usually has the higher status and exerts the most control. Typically, it is the male who is allowed to initiate a request for a date. He is also allowed to suggest where the couple should go, and it is he who is expected to initiate conversations with the female. There are, of course, many exceptions to this general pattern.

When any significant status differential exists in a relationship, it is the higher-status individual who has the freedom to initiate and terminate communication encounters. Their messages are characteristically dominant, whereas the lower-status person's messages are submissive. The higher-status individual has the choice of not only what topics can be discussed but also when and for how long they can be discussed. Higher status leads to verbal dominance, and lower status to verbal submission.

Status differential not only affects verbal communication in a relationship but also has a powerful impact on nonverbal communication. Status differential has an impact on eye contact, body position, posture, gestures, vocal activity, interpersonal distance, use of territory, touching, use of time, and physical appearance.

Eye Contact

People of lower status are expected to, and usually do, look more consistently at a person of higher status. However, if the status differential is very large (e.g., high school student and college president), the lower-status person is expected to lower the eyes as a sign of deference. The higher-status person not only is free to look or not look as he or she sees fit, but also is even allowed to stare at the lower-status person. Such a prolonged stare by a lower-status person, however, would normally be inappropriate.

Kinesic Behaviors

A lower-status individual in a relationship is expected to face the higher-status person directly when communicating with that person. However, the higher-status person can literally face any direction he or she wants. Similarly, the higher-status individual may have as relaxed a posture as desired, but the lower-status person should always exhibit at least somewhat more formal posture. Higher-status individuals often have much more expansive gestures than do lower-status people, although the higher-status person may choose not to gesture at all. The gestures of the lower-status person are expected to be in the direction of the higher-status person.

Vocal Behavior

Higher-status individuals are allowed to speak louder than their lower-status counterparts. Similarly, they are allowed to interrupt the lower-status person at will. Loud talking or interruptions by lower-status people generally are seen as inappropriate and may generate a hostile response.

Use of Space and Touch

Interpersonal distance and touch are almost completely controlled by the higher-status individual in a conversation. If the higher-status person does not touch the lower-status person, it usually is inappropriate for the lower-status person to initiate touch. Similarly, lower-status individuals are expected to "hold their position" so that the higher-status person can move closer or further away as he or she chooses. Generally, the higher the status differential in a relationship, the greater the interpersonal distance that will be maintained and the less likely that there will be touching between the interactants.

In general, the higher the status of an individual, the more territory that person will command. Lower-status individuals are expected to respect that territory and not enter it unless invited. On the other hand, higher-status people are presumed to have the right to enter the territory of lower-status individuals whether invited or not. For example, students who sit on the teacher's desk are asking for trouble, but teachers are presumed to have the right even to go through a student's desk if they choose.

Use of Time

Higher-status people control the time for communication with those of lower status. They decide not only when it will occur but also how long it will last and what shall be discussed. Further, the higher-status person is allowed to be late if he or she chooses, but the lower-status person is expected to be on time—or early. A lower-status person who is late for a meeting may arrive to find the meeting canceled.

Dress

People of higher status tend to be better dressed than those of lower status. The higher-status person also has the added flexibility to dress as he or she sees fit when interacting with a person of lower status. In male dyads, it is not uncommon to see the man with higher status remove his suit coat when talking to a lower-status person while the other man keeps his on.

We hope that you have been sensitive to the fact that in all of the descriptions outlined here, we have been considering status as a relative variable. Status differential emphasizes the *differences* in status between people. Thus, in two different relationships an individual may find vastly different status differentials present. In one case a person can be the higher-status individual, and in the other he or she may be the lower-status one. The college dean is an example. One hour, he or she may be meeting with a student. There is a sizable status differential, and the dean is the higher-status person. The next hour, the dean may be meeting with the university president. In that meeting, the dean's position is completely reversed. The people in the relationship define the status differential, and the status differential defines the kinds of messages that one can send in that relationship.

Levels of immediacy, intimacy, and status all place boundaries on the types of verbal and nonverbal messages that can be sent in a relationship. Each dimension of the relationship contributes to determining what communication is appropriate and what is inappropriate. In addition, the culture in which the relationship exists determines the rules for interaction within the various levels of immediacy, intimacy, and status. Messages, then, stimulate different meanings in different relationships within a given culture, but they also stimulate different meanings in very similar relationships in different cultures.

 KEY TERMS

immediacy 111   intimacy 117
status 120   self-disclosure 117

REFERENCES

Andersen, J. F. (1979). Teacher immediacy as a predictor of teaching effectiveness. In D. Nimmo (Ed.), *Communication Yearbook, 3.* New Brunswick, NJ: Transaction.

LeVay, S. (1993). *The sexual brain.* Cambridge, MA: MIT Press.

McCroskey, J. C., & Daly, J. A. (1986). *Personality and interpersonal communication.* Beverly Hills, CA: Sage.

McCroskey, J. C., Larson, C. E., & Knapp, M. L. (1971). *An introduction to interpersonal communication.* Englewood Cliffs, NJ: Prentice-Hall.

McCroskey, J. C., & Richmond, V. P. (1992). Increasing teacher influence through immediacy. In V. P. Richmond and J. C. McCroskey, *Power in the classroom: Communication, control, and concern* (pp. 101–119). Hillsdale, NJ: Lawrence Erlbaum.

Mehrabian, A. (1971). *Silent messages.* Belmont, CA: Wadsworth.

Mehrabian, A. (1981). *Silent messages: Implicit communication of emotions and attitudes* (2nd ed.). Belmont, CA: Wadsworth.

Richmond, V. P. (1992). *Nonverbal communication in the classroom.* Edina, MN: Burgess International Press.

Richmond, V. P., & McCroskey, J. C. (2004). *Nonverbal behavior in interpersonal relations* (5th ed.). Boston: Allyn & Bacon.

Richmond, V. P., McCroskey, J. C., & McCroskey, L. L. (2005). *Organizational communication for survival: Making work, work* (3rd ed.). Boston: Allyn & Bacon.

DISCUSSION QUESTIONS

1. Which do you think is more important to relationship development, verbal or nonverbal immediacy?

2. What are some simple behaviors a trainer can employ to help her or his trainees perceive her or him as being nonverbally immediate?

3. What are the positive outcomes of nonverbal immediacy?

4. Have you ever self-disclosed information you shouldn't have to someone? What were the ramifications of this self-disclosure?

5. How can a supervisor communicate status in her or his office?

6

Selectivity Process

Selective Exposure • Selective Attention • Selective Perception • Selective Retention • Selective Recall

Causal Attribution

Causal Attribution Defined • Attribution Sources • Attribution Conditions • Basic Attribution Error

Selectivity and Attribution

OBJECTIVES

- Understand the selectivity process that receivers go through when attending to messages.

- Understand the concept of causal attribution and how it affects receivers.

- Define and explain *basic attribution error*.

Getting through to people is not an easy task under the best of circumstances. Even if we have another person who is highly motivated to communicate effectively with us, the odds are still against success unless we can overcome the selectivity and attribution barriers. The *noise in the receiver*, noted in our model of the rhetorical communication process (Figure 1.1), is not there because other people want it to be; it is there because of the basic psychology of human beings.

Human beings are *information processors*. That is, messages do not simply go directly from their source to the mind of the receiver. They go through a reception and processing system. Most messages do not get through that system at all. Those that do may be modified greatly before the meaning they generate is stored in the receiver's mind. That meaning may be only remotely related to the meaning the source was attempting to communicate with the message (McCroskey, Larson, & Knapp, 1971; McCroskey, Richmond, & Stewart, 1986).

We are constantly bombarded by messages and have to select which ones we will attend to in our daily lives.

SELECTIVITY PROCESSES

Actually, trying to get our messages through to produce our intended meaning is like trying to make our way through an obstacle course. The obstacles are the various types of selectivity, as illustrated in Figure 6.1. We must overcome each obstacle in turn, for at any point our message may be blocked from stimulating the meaning we want to communicate. If we fail to recognize an obstacle, or to deal with that obstacle, our communicative goals will be missed.

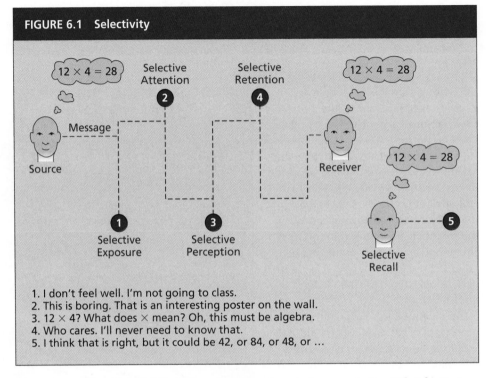

FIGURE 6.1   Selectivity

1. I don't feel well. I'm not going to class.
2. This is boring. That is an interesting poster on the wall.
3. 12 × 4? What does × mean? Oh, this must be algebra.
4. Who cares. I'll never need to know that.
5. I think that is right, but it could be 42, or 84, or 48, or …

Source: McCroskey, J. C. (2006). *An introduction to rhetorical communication* (9th Ed.). Boston: Allyn & Bacon.

As indicated in Figure 6.1, there are four types of selectivity that can directly interfere with initial reception of messages: selective exposure, selective attention, selective perception, and selective retention (McCroskey & Wheeless, 1976). A fifth type of selectivity may occur even after initial reception has occurred: selective recall (McCroskey, Richmond, & McCroskey, 2006). We will look at each of these in turn.

Selective Exposure

Selective exposure refers to a person's conscious or unconscious decision to place her or himself in a position to receive messages from a particular source. We all engage in this type of behavior every day. When we choose a television channel, we have selectively exposed ourselves. Even if we only turn on the TV and watch whatever is on the channel to which it was turned by someone else, we have selectively exposed ourselves, for we choose not to change the channel.

Whether we are interested in influencing someone's behavior or building a better relationship with that person, we cannot do so unless that person is willing to be exposed to our messages. To overcome this first barrier to our effectiveness, then, we need to understand what factors lead to exposure decisions. We will consider four.

Proximity. That which is immediately available is most likely to be chosen. If we want to communicate with someone, obviously we must make ourselves available for communication with that person when he or she is likely to wish to communicate. That is not necessarily the same time *we* want to communicate! Proximity is such an important factor in determining selective exposure that it has even been found the single best predictor of whom a person chooses to marry (Katz & Hill, 1958). Because proximity is such an obvious factor, it often is overlooked, but that does not decrease its importance. How often have you talked with someone who lives in Singapore? Who lives in North Dakota? Who lives on the other side of your town or city? Who lives or works next door to you or in your same building? If the latter are the most frequent, you have a normal relationship between proximity and your communicative exposure. As noted in Figure 6.1, if you don't get past this first obstacle, there will be no successful communication. This obstacle prevents all communication for most of us with most people in the world. This does not speak of obstacles such as the probability of communication with people living or working only a few blocks away from us.

Utility. Things seen as useful are more likely to be selected for exposure than those that have little apparent utility. In addition, those that are *immediately* useful will be more likely to be selected than those that show promise for use later. When we are already interested in buying a new car, we are much more likely to choose to read the advertisements in the magazines and listen to those on television and radio. We are even likely to go to auto dealerships and ask for pamphlets on cars in which we are interested. At a more mundane level, people who think we can help them meet their own needs are more likely to seek communication with us than those who do not perceive us in this way.

Involvement. The more important a topic is to a person, the more the person is likely to expose her or himself to messages on that topic. Avid sports fans seek to communicate about sports. Politically active people want to talk about politics and public policy. The more salient an attitude, belief, or value is, the more involving it is. Communication on topics that relate to salient orientations of people is more likely to get them to expose themselves to it, particularly if it seems likely the communication will be reinforcing (see below).

Reinforcement. People expose themselves to messages they believe will be consistent with their own beliefs. Democrats go to Democratic Party rallies. Republicans go to Republican Party rallies. When we attend athletic events, we sit on "our" side, not "their" side, of the field or floor. Pro-choice people listen to and read messages that support a woman's right to an abortion. Pro-life people listen to and read messages that advocate abolition of abortion. In short, we all want to hear others present messages that agree with our own views. Only infrequently do we choose to expose ourselves to messages that we believe in advance will take positions with which we disagree. We seek advice from people whom we believe see the world the way we do, and we avoid communicating with those who see things differently. It is not surprising, then, that often when people get into conflict with each other, they want little or no communication each other. Some people, of course, are reinforced by getting into arguments with others rather than avoiding them. These people will actively seek to communicate with people who disagree with them, for that is reinforcing.

Whatever the reason people engage in selective exposure, the bottom line remains the same—no exposure, no effective communication. Getting someone else to make themselves available to receive messages from us will not guarantee that we can communicate with them effectively, but failing to get them to expose themselves to us guarantees that we will *not* be effective. Exposure is a necessary, but not sufficient, condition for effective communication.

Selective Attention

There is an old saying that suggests you can bring a horse to water (selective exposure), but can't make it drink (selective attention). We cannot always control the types of messages to which we are exposed. Thus, when we are exposed to messages we would rather avoid, we may simply select to pay attention to something else.

In one sense, *all* attention is selective. Everything in our perceptual world makes some demand on our attention, but we cannot attend to everything at once. Therefore, we may choose to pay attention to something other than a given message, or we may pay more attention to some messages and less to others. In any environment, there are many things competing for our attention—sights, sounds, and odors abound. In a classroom, for example, there are other students, things on the wall, things going on outside of windows, what the teacher is wearing, what the person next to you is wearing, a clock, what the person next to you smells like, what he or she says, what the teacher says, and so on. Many factors contribute to determining which of these things you will pay attention to at any given time. We will consider five of these.

Attention Span.   No matter what we choose to pay attention to, that attention can continue only so long. The amount of time a person can spend attending to one thing before having to shift to something else is called one's *attention span*. How long that span is depends in part on developmental factors. Young children typically have very brief attention spans, whereas adult attention spans are longer. Even for adults, however, attention spans usually are measured in seconds, not minutes. People's attention moves from one thing to another continuously. Even in an important conversation, we are not able to maintain completely undivided attention to what our conversational partner is saying. Thus, if it is vitally important that we communicate a specific idea, we need to be redundant. That is, we need to use more than one message designed to communicate that idea. This will greatly enhance the probability that at least one message will capture the necessary attention to get through.

Novelty.   Things that are unusual attract attention. The routine tends to be ignored. New Yorkers pay little attention to tall buildings, but visitors stare at them. People who live in Hawaii pay little attention to banyan trees and orchids, but tourists pay great attention to both of them. We get used to things in our environment, no matter how unusual those things are to people who are not used to them. Routine memos look like other routine memos, so one on bright green paper catches our attention. If all our memos come on bright green paper, none will be very attention getting. If we want someone to pay attention to our message, we need to make that message stand out from all the other stimuli in the environment.

Concreteness.   Because they are hard to understand, highly abstract messages bore most people. Consequently, people direct their attention away from such messages to others that are more concrete and interesting. Concrete things or ideas, those that relate to the life or experience of the receiver, attract attention. If we want our receiver to pay attention to our message, we should be certain the message relates to what our receiver understands and/or has experienced.

Size.   As a rule, bigger things draw more attention than smaller ones. Big maps, big pictures, big graphs, and even big people will grab attention. Sometimes, of course, things that are unusually small will attract attention because of their novelty. Nevertheless, we tend to notice the bigger things first.

Duration.   Attention is directed toward messages that are moderate in length (written) or duration (time). Very brief messages may be missed—they are over before attention turns to them. Long messages are likely to exceed the receiver's attention span. If we must communicate a large amount of information, it is best that we do so with messages that are devoted to smaller chunks of that information.

Whatever the reason for a receiver's use of selective attention, as we said with selective exposure, the bottom line is the same: no attention, no effective communication. Although attention from our receiver is not sufficient to guarantee effective communication, the absence of attention will guarantee effective communication will *not* occur. Attention is a necessary, but not sufficient, condition for effective communication.

Selective Perception

Perception is the process of attributing meaning to messages. Messages do not "carry" meaning, as we have noted in previous chapters. They *stimulate* meaning in people's minds. The precise meaning that is stimulated depends on both the message and the receiver. Thus, in a sense, all perception is selective. That is, the receiver must select, from all the possible meanings that could be attributed to a message, the particular meaning that we attributed in the given instance. Therefore, it is most likely that different receivers of the same message, because they have different backgrounds and experiences, will attribute different meanings to that message. The problem for the source is to get the receiver to choose the meaning intended by the source rather than another meaning. This outcome is made increasingly likely to occur to the extent that factors that lead to other perceptions are controlled, although it is not usually possible to control, or even recognize, all of the possibilities.

Even if we get our potential receiver to expose her or himself to our messages, and to pay attention to those messages, the desired meaning may not be communicated because the receiver may perceive the messages to mean something different from what we intended. Many factors influence such perceptions or, at least from the source's view, *misperceptions*. We should also recognize that misperception is not only a problem for the source. In fact, it may be much more important to the receiver that he or she perceives the correct meaning in many cases. Students, for example, will be evaluated on how much of the "correct" meaning they learn—correct as defined by the teacher. Whenever we try to obtain information from someone else, it usually is more important to us, as receivers, to perceive messages the way the source intends them than it is to the source. Let us consider several factors that may cause a receiver to select perceptions different from those intended by the source.

Ambiguity of Messages.   Sometimes, messages are very imprecise and open to misunderstanding. Use of words that people use in different ways can lead a receiver, even one who is trying hard to get the source's intended meaning, to select a meaning other than the one intended. Because language is inherently imprecise, careful choice of wording is very important if one hopes to avoid misunderstanding or being misunderstood. Use of abstract rather than concrete words and phrases is particularly problematic. In general, the more abstract a series of messages is, the more ambiguous those messages are. The more concrete and specific a message is, the less likely it will be misperceived. As receivers, we should always remember that if we are not certain we understand a message, we should whenever possible ask the source for additional clarification.

Lack of Message Redundancy.   To the extent a series of messages lacks redundancy, those messages invite misperception. Redundancy permits a second (or third, fourth, and so on) chance for the receiver to capture the intended meaning. Single messages are far more likely to be misunderstood than multiple messages directed toward stimulating the same meaning. Again, receivers should never hesitate to ask for clarification when there is not sufficient redundancy in a source's messages to assure the receiver of the intended meaning.

Lack of Receiver Schemata.   People learn by placing information into categories with information that is similar. Category systems of this kind are known as *schema* (plural, *schemata*). Imagine, please, you are in a post office that has mailboxes. The postal clerk invites you to walk around back so you can see the boxes from the back side. What you see is row after row of boxes, all connected to one another. In a small town, these boxes may have people's names marked on them. In a larger city, the boxes are more likely to have only numbers. The postal clerk sorts through the mail and puts various pieces in the various boxes, and has some mail left over that does not go in any of the boxes. That mail must be returned, or another method must be employed to find the person for whom it is intended.

People's schema systems are somewhat like the mailboxes. As a message is received, we place it in one of our mental boxes if we believe we have one for it. If no box can be found for it, it must be shunted aside to be considered later, or simply ignored (in one ear and out the other!). If people do not have appropriate schemata for the ideas included in our messages, they may not be able to cope with those ideas. Therefore, we must avoid "talking over someone's head."

Missing schemata, of course, are not only problems for sources. Missing schemata have their most direct effect on us as receivers. When we hear a message and find no place for it, the idea the source was trying to communicate most likely will only pass on through our perceptual system and not really be perceived at all. Or, possibly even worse, we may find a place we think is appropriate, though it is not, and perceive that message as if it really did belong there. Children sometimes perceive an "invisible nation" rather than an "indivisible nation" in the Pledge of Allegiance. This occurs because an adult is not smart enough to realize the child is too young to have a schema system that can cope with the concept of "indivisible."

Previous Experiences.   We know the world through our experiences with the world. The experiences of a person who was a child in the 1950s are different from the experiences of a person who was a child in the 1990s. The 1950s child has a breadth of experience with cold war politics and with black-and-white television (and no television at all), and has fond memories of entertainers the 1990s child has never heard of. However, the 1950s child may have to ask the 1990s child how to set her or his VCR or operate a personal computer, things the 1990s child can't believe anyone doesn't already know.

Just as generations have different experiences, so too do people in the same age group who live in different cultures, or even different co-cultures within a broader culture. Whenever people do not have similar backgrounds and experiences, they are highly likely to perceive messages differently.

Expectancies and Biases.   An expectancy is anticipation of a future occurrence. A bias is an unjustified evaluation. All people have both expectancies and biases. Whenever the receiver has either an expectancy or a bias related to a source's message, it is probable that the message will be perceived in a way that is consistent with that expectancy or bias. Unfortunately, this is more the norm than the exception. People tend to perceive what they expect to see or hear and are most likely to interpret messages in a manner such that they conform to their biases.

Selective perception is a difficult problem for us to control, as either a source or a receiver, because it will always occur to some extent. Even after overcoming selective exposure and attention, communication can fail to be effective due to misperception of messages. One positive thing is that even if misperception occurs, if the misperception can be identified, it can be corrected. Thus, we should seek as much feedback and questioning from our potential receivers as possible, and provide such feedback and questions to other sources. It is only in this manner that misperceptions can be prevented from causing ineffective communication.

People under 30 have spent their entire lives surrounded by technology, while people who grew up before the influx of technology are often still learning about new technology.

Selective Retention

Selective retention may be the problem that is the most frustrating. People interact with one another, they pay attention to one another, and they even perceive one another's messages correctly. However, a few days (or sometimes minutes) later, it is as if the conversation never existed. Nothing is retained. *Selective retention* refers to the decision to store or not store information in one's long-term memory. As with the other selectivity factors, this process also occurs primarily at the nonconscious level, but the selection sometimes is made consciously. Several factors are known to influence selective retention.

Lack of Highlighting.   Although not restricted to instructional settings, this factor has a major impact in those settings. When important ideas are not highlighted by teachers, students often do not realize they are important. This is one of the reasons why providing students with learning objectives is such a good idea (like those at the beginning of the chapter). Although this is only one of many means of highlighting, it represents a clear message to the student about what the teacher expects will be retained. Have you ever gone through your notes after a test and found something that was the answer to a test question? Possibly something you did not even remember writing down? If you had been told that was important to learn—in other words, had it been highlighted—it would have been much more likely you would have learned it.

Lack of Redundancy.   In general, the more we hear something, the more important we think it is, and the more likely we are to remember it. Redundancy capitalizes on this premise. Sometimes, people simply do not think something is important until they hear about it several times. For children, this idea is particularly important. In contrast to adults, children are exposed to vastly more "new" things each day. They cannot be expected to retain everything new they initially learn. Thus, if we expect a child to learn something and retain it more than a short time, it is important that the child hear it several times. It is only slightly less important for adults.

Lack of Schema.   Although schemata are very important to initial learning, they are absolutely critical for retention. If there is no system for storage (schema) available, the outcome of communication is simple to predict. There will be no storage. It is like trying to store information on a computer that has no hard disk. You turn it off, and the information is gone. The receiver's schema is the hard disk. If it is missing or defective, retention will not occur.

Lack of Concrete Application.   Retention often depends on applying new ideas or information to real, concrete concerns. Retaining information for use at some indefinite time in the future is particularly difficult. The old saying "Use it or lose it" is particularly appropriate in this instance. That which is used is retained.

Principles of Primacy and Recency.   In the 1940s and 1950s, social scientists were very interested in persuasion. They sought to find out whether things that were covered first in a message (the primacy principle) or things that were covered last (the recency principle) were most remembered (Hovland, Janis, & Kelley, 1953). After many studies, clearly neither primacy nor recency had a universally stronger effect than the other. However, it was seen that things that were presented near either the beginning or the ending of the message would be more effective than things presented in the middle. What is said first and what is said last are what are most likely to be remembered.

The conclusion concerning selective retention is that you are not likely to get someone to retain much from your communication unless you take steps to increase the probability of retention. As we have noted previously, telling is not communicating.

Simply presenting messages will not assure retention. You must design your message to produce retention if you expect it to do so.

Selective Recall

Selective retention and selective recall are often confused and sometimes thought to be the same thing. It is important to distinguish between these two forms of selectivity because they are quite different, although related.

Selective retention has to do with the *storage* of information, whereas selective recall has to do with the *retrieval* of information. Of course, if information is not stored (retained) in the first place, it cannot be retrieved (recalled) later. However, just because something is retained does not necessarily mean it will be recalled at any given point in time. Have you ever had a hard time recalling something at one time, but had it come back to you at another? It was stored away in your brain both times, but it was retrieved only once.

All of us have many things stored away in our long-term memories. Many of these things do not come back to us with ease. We need something to trigger the recall response. Things are learned in a context, and part of what is stored is information related to that context. When we try to recall the information in another context, it may not come back quickly, or even come back at all, unless we can find an appropriate trigger. Sometimes we may not even want to recall something, particularly something that was unpleasant. We all repress some memories.

Effective communication is not easy. There are major barriers in the way, and these selectivity processes number among those most problematic. If one is not aware of these processes and/or does not take appropriate steps to overcome selectivity, effective communication can be expected to occur only by chance. And that is a remote chance!

CAUSAL ATTRIBUTION

Our nature as human beings is such that we perceive events and circumstances to have causes. It is not enough for us simply to know that something happens; it is human nature to want to know why it happens. Even when we are uncertain about the actual causes of events, we tend to assign causes to them. We may pass the scene of an automobile accident during a thunderstorm, for example, and attribute the cause to bad weather. In terms of interpersonal behavior, we may observe a friend ridicule and belittle another person and attribute our friend's behavior to the fact that he or she has the flu and is feeling a bit testy.

Causal Attribution Defined

Attribution of causality is *the perception process by which we make sense out of the behavior of others.* We see people behave in certain ways, verbally or nonverbally, and attempt to make sense out of their behavior by assigning some probable cause to it. If, for instance, your mother has suddenly begun sending you extra money, you might attribute it to the fact that she has received a raise. Or if your dating partner has recently been treating you unusually nicely, you may attribute it to the possibility that he or she is jealous of your "new friend."

Generally, we engage in this process of causal attribution because we want to know why a behavior occurs and what it might mean (Kelley, 1973). In this sense, causal attribution is a process of uncertainty reduction. If we can pin down the probable cause of another person's behavior, we gain a better understanding of that behavior and become more certain of its implications for ourselves, the other person, and our relationship with that person.

Attribution Sources

The causes we may attribute to another person's behavior stem from one of two sources: *internal factors* or *external factors*. When we attribute a person's behavior to internal causes, we are attributing the person's behavior to her or his personality. For example, when someone asks you why you think another person has done something in particular and you reply, "I guess that is just the way she is," you are attributing the person's behavior to internal causes. The words *the way she is* suggest that the person has some predisposition or trait that makes her engage in certain behavior. Similarly, when you suggest to a classmate that your high test scores are due to the instructor being "a really nice person," you are explaining the instructor's personality as the cause for giving students good grades.

Attributing people's behavior to external factors, however, explains their behavior as caused by certain situational influences, which may include other people with whom they are associated. For example, when your roommate arrives home one evening in an angry mood and you think to yourself, "Snowy weather always makes her act this way," you are attributing her behavior to situational causes. It is not her personality or general emotional state that makes her act that way, but rather the weather, an external cause. Also, when a friend explains your good cooking because of well-written recipes and a finely tuned microwave oven, he or she is attributing its cause to certain aspects of the environment rather than to your culinary talent (which would be internal).

Whenever we attribute a person's behavior to other people, we are also making external attributions. For instance, when parents explain that their child's poor conduct is due to "that crowd" he or she associates with, they are attributing the child's behavior to factors external to the child rather than to internal factors such as personality.

Attribution Conditions

Our explanations of a person's behavior at any given time as caused by either internal or external factors are typically based on one of three conditions.

Consensus.   The first attribution condition is *consensus*, or whether the individual acts in a way similar to the way other people act in a given situation. If consensus is high—that is, the person does act in a way similar to others—we tend to attribute the person's actions to external causes because he or she is responding to the particular situation and perhaps is conforming to how others in the situation are acting. However, if consensus is low—the person is not acting like others in the situation—then we are likely to attribute her or his behavior to internal causes because we will perceive that the individual is acting out of her or his own accord and not necessarily out of response to others or the situation. An example of this might be the individual who sits in the corner at parties and ignores what is happening, keeping to her or himself while others mingle and converse.

Consistency.   The second condition on which we base attributions is consistency, or whether the individual behaves the same way in the same situation at different times. When consistency is high—that is, the person always acts the same way in the same situation—we tend to attribute her or his behavior to external causes. This is because it is most likely that some aspect of the situation is causing the person to behave in a particular way. Situational-bound communication apprehension is an example of high consistency; although most of us tend to remain comfortable in face-to-face interactions, we become quite apprehensive in public-speaking situations. Low consistency occurs when the individual behaves differently in the same situation at different times, in which case we are likely to attribute the person's behavior to internal causes. If you are quite nervous about giving a speech on one occasion but are rather calm about it on another, then we probably will attribute your reactions to your mood. You are not necessarily free of anxiety on the second occasion, but perhaps you just feel more enthusiastic and better prepared at the time.

Distinctiveness.   The third condition that determines to what causes we attribute a person's behavior is *distinctiveness*, or whether the individual behaves the same way in different situations. When distinctiveness is high—that is, the person acts differently in response to different situations—we are likely to attribute the individual's behavior to external causes. For example, if your mother cusses when she bumps her toe on a table leg but generally does not cuss on other occasions, we would tend to attribute her exclamation to the pain and frustration that come with hurting one's toe and not to her personality. If distinctiveness is low—the person acts the same way in different situations—then we attribute causality to internal factors. Your mother may cuss when she hurts her toe, is late for work, welcomes you home, and sees a picture of Elvis, and observing her in these varied situations may lead one to attribute her cussing to her personality or her "salty" vocabulary.

Given the three conditions on which we base attributions of causality, we can see that our judgments about a person's behavior are simply our perceptions. That is, we perceive the person either as having control over the situation in which we observe her or him, or as under the influence of situational constraints. The accuracy of these perceptions, and thus the accuracy of our attributions, depends greatly on how well we know the other person. The better we know the other individual, the more accurate our causal attributions of their behavior will be. For example, you likely can explain with much greater precision why your parents would be disappointed with a bad test score you made than you can explain why a new acquaintance would be upset. Simply put, the more information we have about a situation and the people in it with whom we interact, the more precise our judgments will be.

Basic Attribution Error

Closely linked with this information–attribution relationship are interpersonal orientations. The better we know someone, the more likely we are to share the person's attitudes; the greater our knowledge and understanding of the person's attitudes, the more likely we are to accurately judge their behavior and its causes. We can attribute the individual's behavior to the person or to the environment. If we know the person well, we probably can deduce that he or she is acting based on some attitude, belief, or value; if we do not know the person well, the best we can do is to speculate as to the cause of her or his behavior, and likely ascribe it to situational or other external causes. Such attributions usually are inaccurate and derive from the basic attribution error.

The *basic attribution error* occurs when we attribute the causes of our own behavior to external factors and the causes of another person's behavior to internal causes. The "error" is that we more often perceive our behavior as due to situational matters beyond our control and other people's behavior as due to their personality or emotional state. In actuality, neither may be the case. For example, when your boyfriend or girlfriend is late for a date or fails to answer the phone, it is *her* or *his* fault. When you find yourself in these circumstances, however, you are likely to blame a late-running class or being in the shower. The likelihood of this error occurring can partly be determined by the attitudes, beliefs, and values held by us and the other person. Consider the following example.

Assume that you have borrowed a friend's new car for an evening on the town with your date. You and your date enjoy an exceptionally good time at several popular establishments and become rowdy. As your rowdiness heightens, so does your bravery. You decide to challenge some hotshot to a drag race, he in his car and you in your friend's. Without going into the gory details, let's suppose that you crash the car into a cow pasture. Fortunately, no one is injured. Understandably, your friend is a bit displeased about the incident. You try to reason things out anyway. Your friend is irate and has promised not to forgive you. You offer to pay for the damages, but your friend is not satisfied, claiming that your money cannot account for the emotional anguish resulting from the car's loss. Finally, you decide to wait until your friend has had a chance to calm down before you finish discussing how to settle the situation. You understand well the predicament your friend is in and the frustration it is causing. You share your friend's attitude about the incident ("It was stupid") and the value held for the car. With this knowledge, you can attribute your friend's hostile behavior to the situation. Generally, your friend is a good-natured, easygoing person, but most anyone would get upset about her or his new car being totaled. Suppose now that you invite your friend to your parents' home for dinner, a sort of peace offering you think might help soothe the situation.

The invitation is accepted, but your friend's attitude and behavior have not changed much since the accident—there is still much animosity. This animosity is detected by your parents at the dinner table, but they do not know your friend well at all and are yet unaware of the incident. Having had no previous interactions with your friend and having no knowledge of why the person behaves so coldly toward you, they attribute the cause to personality and general disposition. Have your parents made an error in judgment? Essentially, yes; they have made an attribution error, attributing your friend's behavior and attitude to personality factors when they are a function of situational factors. Their perceptions are quite different from yours and result from a difference in knowledge of the person and situation.

Thus, we do make errors in our perceptions of others. Typically, this error occurs from a lack of knowledge of the other person and/or the situation in which we observe her or him. The better we know the individual, however, and the more we share that person's orientations about the situation, the less likely we are to make attribution errors.

The process of causal attribution is very important in the total process of human communication. People behave in a certain fashion, and others observe and interpret that behavior. In turn, the latter's behavior is observed and interpreted by the former. Thus, the attribution process follows directly the transactional process of interpersonal communication. Its functional accuracy is tied not only to more general personal perceptions but also to interpersonal orientations—their direction, intensity, salience, and consistency.

 **KEY TERMS**

causal attribution 134
consensus 135

distinctiveness 136
external attribution 135

internal attribution 135
selective exposure 126

REFERENCES

Hovland, C. I., Janis, I. L., & Kelley, H. H. (1953). *Communication and persuasion*. New Haven, CT: Yale University Press.

Katz, A. M., & Hill, R. (1958). Residential propinquity and marital selection: A review of theory, method, and fact. *Marriage and Family Living, 20,* 27–35.

Kelley, H. H. (1973). The process of causal attribution. *American Psychologist, 28,* 107–128.

McCroskey, J. C., Richmond, V. P., & McCroskey, L. L. (2006). *An introduction to communication in the classroom: The role of communication in teaching and training*. Boston: Allyn & Bacon.

McCroskey, J. C., Larson, C. E., & Knapp, M. L. (1971). *An introduction to interpersonal communication* (pp. 54–76). Englewood Cliffs, NJ: Prentice-Hall.

McCroskey, J. C., Richmond, V. P., & Stewart, R. A. (1986). *One on one: The foundations of interpersonal communication* (pp. 68–84). Englewood Cliffs, NJ: Prentice-Hall.

McCroskey, J. C., & Wheeless, L. R. (1976). *Introduction to human communication* (pp. 264–289). Boston: Allyn & Bacon.

DISCUSSION QUESTIONS

1. How has the multitude of television channels affected selective exposure?

2. Why are people less likely to pay attention to nonconcrete information as compared to concrete information?

3. Why is message redundancy important when attempting to get people to pay attention?

4. What is a schema? Why is it important in the selectivity process?

5. What are the principles of primacy and recency? How are they important during the selectivity process?

7

Understanding and Influencing Attitudes and Behaviors

OBJECTIVES

- Define and explain *attitude*.

- Define and explain *belief*.

- Define and explain *value*.

- Differentiate between statements of attitudes, beliefs, and values.

- Explain the three dimensions of attitudes, beliefs, and values.

- Understand the different theoretical positions on how we develop attitudes, beliefs, and values.

- Explain the principle of consistency and how it relates to balance theory.

Our attitudes, beliefs, and values, and those of the people with whom we communicate, are very important to the success of our communication. These orientations determine how we are likely to respond to one another and the extent to which our communication with each other will be effective and meaningful. Often, such orientations are even the very subject of the communication between us. As a minimum, these orientations serve as a screen through which we receive and decode the messages sent to us by others (Albarra_in, Johnson, & Zanna, 2006).

How we interpret other people's messages, therefore, is largely a function of our own attitudes, beliefs, and values. Of course, the way others interpret our messages is largely a function of similar, or dissimilar, orientations they have. To understand why communication efforts are often unsuccessful when they seem like they should be successful, we need to understand the kinds of orientations we all have.

We begin our discussion of these orientations by exploring their nature and structure. Next, we will consider how attitudes, beliefs, and values are developed; why they are subject to change; and finally how we respond to their change.

◨ THE NATURE OF ATTITUDES, BELIEFS, AND VALUES

If you are like most people, you use the terms *attitude, belief,* and *value* in many of your daily conversations without really knowing how they differ from one another. Many people use the terms interchangeably, and

People have different attitudes toward political hot buttons like abortion, and those attitudes can lead to protesting.

as a result never really understand this important aspect of the psychology of communication. Unfortunately, such an understanding often is critical to being an effective communicator.

Attitudes

Coach to sports commentator: That player's attitude has improved 100 percent this season.

Teacher to student: You would get a lot more out of this class if you had a more positive attitude about what you're learning from it.

Girlfriend to boyfriend: Your attitude stinks!

We hear and say expressions such as these almost every day. What are we talking about when we make a statement about someone else's attitude? What is an attitude? Well, attitude can mean whatever we choose to say it means, because it is only a word. It is very useful, however, for us to know what experts in communication and psychology mean when they use the term. An attitude is defined as *a predisposition to respond to people, ideas, or objects in an evaluative way*. Let's examine this definition a little more closely.

When we define an attitude as a predisposition, we mean that an attitude is a tendency that we have to do something. Here, it is a tendency to *evaluate* people, ideas, or objects. The word *evaluative* in this definition means making judgments of good or bad, desirable or undesirable, or likable or unlikable. Thus, an attitude is our tendency to judge a person, an idea, or an object as either good or bad.

It is important to note that our definition of attitude considers not only people but also ideas and objects. Take the examples above. The coach is probably referring to the player's attitude about the sport he or she plays, the teacher is referring to the student's attitude about the content of the course, and the girlfriend may be referring to her boyfriend's attitude about her. Thus, our evaluative judgments about people are similar to our evaluative judgments about physical objects or entities, such as the game of basketball, and about abstract or concrete ideas, such as the information acquired in a particular course. Just as we evaluated objects and ideas as good or bad, we also evaluate people around us as good or bad.

Attitude, like belief and value, is what is known as a *hypothetical construct*. We can't see, touch, or smell hypothetical constructs. They are presumed (thought) to exist only in people's minds (as thoughts or constructs), therefore the technical term. It is critical, then, that we have a way of measuring these orientations. To do so, we must have the cooperation of the person who has the attitude. That person must be willing to complete some sort of measure.

Scale 18 in the appendix presents an instrument commonly used to measure attitudes. It was developed by McCroskey (1966) based on the research of Bogardus (1925) to measure attitudes in a study McCroskey was doing as a part of his doctoral dissertation. In the scale, the attitude being measured is the respondent's attitude toward capital punishment. The same bipolar scales used to measure attitude toward capital punishment can be used to measure thousands of other attitudes, because the scales used are not topic (attitude) dependent (McCroskey & Richmond, 1989). For example, you can replace "Capital Punishment" with "Gun Control," "Abortion," "Sex Education," or much less controversial topics such as "Broccoli," "Green Beans," or "Peanut Butter."

The attitude measure presented in Scale 17 is a very direct measure. It asks for a series of *evaluations,* the essence of our definition of the term *attitude.* Scale 18 in the appendix, on the other hand, presents a different kind of attitude measure (known technically as a *Likert-type scale*—named after its developer) and is based on the research by Likert (1932). This scale is more indirect in that it asks people to respond to beliefs that are thought to be related to the underlying attitude of interest. This measure also was developed for the dissertation mentioned above (McCroskey, 1966). This measure, unlike the previous one, is very attitude specific. Obviously, it cannot be used to measure your attitude toward "Broccoli"! Although these two types of attitude measure are very different, they are capable of measuring the same attitude. If you are familiar with some basic statistics, the scores from the two measures correlate above $r = .90$ ($r = 1.00$ is perfect, or there would be a perfect relationship between the two variables).

Attitudes are important to human communication for one major reason—it is through communication that we discover how similar our own attitudes are to those of other people. It is the way we establish attitudinal similarity with others. If your attitude about a particular course is similar to that of your teacher, you are more likely to accept the teacher's information than is someone whose attitude is very different from the teacher's. Similarly, if your attitude toward your romantic relationship is similar to that of your romantic partner, there is less likelihood that he or she will tell you, "Your attitude stinks!"

Attitudes, then, are our evaluative responses to things around us, whether they are ideas, objects, or other people. It is assumed that our behavior is controlled, at least in part, by our attitudes. The way we evaluate something, in other words, helps decide how we will behave toward it. Thus, many people prefer to define attitude as *an individual's predisposition to behave in a particular way in response to something in their environment.* Although this is a reasonable view, we believe it is more useful to restrict our use of the term *attitude* to evaluative orientations. We use the term *predisposition to behave* to refer to behavioral dispositions or tendencies.

Beliefs

In the previous paragraph, we used the term *believe.* We meant to imply that for us (not necessarily for everyone else), the differentiation between the terms *attitude* and *predisposition to behave* is a true, correct, appropriate, right way to look at things. We "believe" in the distinction. We also think the distinction is "good," so we have a positive attitude toward it. Belief has to do with our perceptions of reality, whereas attitude has to do with our evaluation of that reality.

With this distinction, we hope that you can see that attitudes and beliefs are qualitatively different. Attitudes concern our *evaluation* of whether someone or something is good or bad. Beliefs concern our *perception of reality* about whether something is true or false. Consider the following belief statements:

1. Guns don't kill people—people kill people.
2. Abortion is killing a living human being.
3. Welfare subsidizes laziness and promiscuity.
4. The barometric pressure is 29.10—very low.
5. State and federal income taxes together are between 50 and 55 percent for many middle-income couples' earnings in some states. Counting social security taxes and local income taxes, the total is over 70 percent in twelve states.

Now consider the following attitude statements and pick the one in each pair that goes with each of the belief statements stated above:

1-A. I favor gun control.

1-B. I oppose gun control.

2-A. Abortion should be outlawed.

2-B. A woman has the right to control her own body.

3-A. The welfare system should be abolished.

3-B. The welfare system is very valuable for society.

4-A. Going on a picnic is a great idea.

4-B. Going on a picnic is a stupid idea.

5-A. Income taxes are good.

5-B. Income taxes are bad.

If you picked 1-B, 2-A, 3-A, 4-B, and 5-B, you clearly understand the relationship between attitudes and beliefs. If you had trouble with number 4, it probably was because you did not know the relationship between barometric pressure and rain. The more the pressure is below 30.00, the more likely it will rain. As it approaches 29.00, it becomes virtually certain there is a major storm nearby—not the day to go on a picnic! If you picked 5-A, this probably indicates you have yet to pay income taxes.

Beliefs, like attitudes, are "hypothetical constructs." To deal with them, we first need to measure them. Scale 19 in the appendix presents an instrument we have used often to measure beliefs. Note that, like the attitude measure in Scale 19 in the appendix, all you have to do is change the belief statement at the top to measure a different belief. This is a fairly sophisticated belief measure. As we noted, each item in the measure presented in Scale 19 in the appendix measures a single belief. Such individual-item measures tend to be less valid and reliable than more sophisticated ones. Nevertheless, the single-item type of measure is the kind used by most polling groups and many marketing researchers, so they have some value.

Attitudes and beliefs tend to go together, as the above exercise hopefully shows, however, this does not mean they always do. It is possible, for example, for two people to agree on the belief that capital punishment does not deter crime. And yet one person could favor capital punishment, and the other person oppose it. The one may oppose it because it is not a deterrent, and the other may still favor it because it severely punishes the offender. The reason their attitudes are different, although their beliefs are the same, is that they are using different criteria for their evaluations. Often, the criteria for evaluation boil down to the person's values.

Values

Values are more complex than are attitudes and beliefs. Values are *our enduring conceptions of the nature of right and wrong, and good and bad.* The key to this definition is the term *enduring.* This is what forms the difference between values, on one hand, and beliefs and attitudes, on the other. Attitudes and beliefs are typically subject to change. We may find our attitudes about some things fluctuating daily, and perhaps some of our beliefs as well. Values are not so easily subject to change. They are highly resistant to change and tend to endure over very long periods of time, some of them a lifetime. Values are the foundation on which we form our attitudes and beliefs about people, objects, and ideas.

People in a given culture tend to share similar values, and to some extent many values are shared by different cultures. Over 2,500 years ago Aristotle, in his work entitled *The Rhetoric,* listed values that he felt the people of his time used to distinguish between that which is good and that which is evil (McCroskey, 2006). The rough translation of the Aristotelian value list is happiness, justice, courage, moderation, splendor, health, beauty, wealth, friendship, honor, reputation, power, wisdom, and life. Are these still major measures of "good" versus "bad" in today's society? Although not an exhaustive list, by any means, we think *most* of these are values held by *most* of us.

Many of us might agree that we hold most of these values. It is highly unlikely, however, that any two people, if asked to rank these values, would rank them in the same order. The ordering of values in comparison with each other is critical. Most of the people who disagree with each other on the issue of abortion probably hold a positive value for the life of an embryo. They also hold a positive value for the right of a woman to make decisions about her own body. They do *not* have these two values in the same order in their hierarchy of values, therefore there is a very strong difference in attitude about the "goodness" or "badness" of abortion.

Consider some other values that many Americans would share: scientific research, attending church, treating children well, being kind to one's spouse, being loyal to one's community, being neat and clean, being efficient, having common sense, being educated, being financially well off, working hard, and being a good sport. Rank these for yourself, and then have someone whom you think is a lot like you rank them. Then compare your responses. You will probably find that you don't think as much alike as you had believed previously. But do not write this person off as a friend! You are likely to have conflict only when discussing an issue for which competing values place one of you on one side and one on the other. The farther the two of you are apart in your ranking of those values, the more serious your disagreement will be.

Thus, attitudes and beliefs may be viewed as short-term expressions of our values. Values are long-term expressions of our judgments about good and bad, and right and wrong, and they form the basis for our attitudes and beliefs. Our attitudes and beliefs about a given person, idea, or object may change quite easily. Our values regarding that person, idea, or thing are much more difficult to change. If you are an avid football fan, you value your favorite school, city, or state team very much. Although the team is having a losing season and your attitude about them is negative and you no longer believe they will make the play-offs, you still place much value on the team. Your attitude and beliefs about the team may change from season to season, but the value you place on the team endures relatively unchanged.

DIMENSIONS OF ATTITUDES, BELIEFS, AND VALUES

At this point, you should have a general understanding of the nature of attitudes, beliefs, and values and of how they differ from one another. In this section, we will elaborate on the multidimensional aspect of attitudes, beliefs, and values. We have used the term *multidimensional* in previous chapters without really explaining, so perhaps we should do so here. When we say that a concept is multidimensional, we mean that it is composed of several different dimensions, or critical characteristics, that we must understand to fully understand the idea itself. A multidimensional concept is analogous to a multidimensional physical object, such as a desk. As you most likely remember from elementary school, physical objects have three dimensions—length, width, and depth. To understand the physical nature of a desk, we have to be able to answer the following questions: how long is it? How wide is it? How deep (or high) is it?

Similarly, many psychological concepts have multiple dimensions. Attitudes, beliefs, and values are each composed of three dimensions—*direction, intensity*, and *salience.* Just as it is important to know the various dimensions of a physical object in order to fully understand it, it is also important to know something about the three dimensions of attitudes, beliefs, and values to more fully understand these orientations. We need to know its direction (positive versus negative), its intensity (how extreme it is), and its salience (how important this orientation is compared to others).

Direction

We have already noted that attitudes range on a continuum from good to bad (or desirable to undesirable, favorable to unfavorable, and so on), and that beliefs range on a continuum from true to false. Values also range on a good-bad continuum. Within each of these ranges, there also exists a neutral or undecided position. Thus, people may have a negative, positive, or neutral attitude about some person or thing; they may have a belief that something is true or false, or they may be undecided about it; and they may have a positive, negative, or neutral value toward something. These ranges represent the possible *directions* that attitudes, beliefs, and values may take.

To illustrate this dimension for each orientation, let's take the example of three people's directional orientations toward sports cars. Darla likes sports cars, Javier doesn't think much about them one way or the other, and Jim dislikes them. The direction of Darla's attitude toward sports cars is positive, the direction of Jim's is negative, and Javier's is neutral. Based solely on these different attitude directions, we would expect Darla to be likely to want to buy a sports car, read about sports cars, talk about sports cars, and so on. Javier would not be likely to buy a sports car but might, from time to time, read an ad for sports cars or take notice of a particularly attractive one in a parking lot. Jim would not be likely to consider buying a sports car, would not read articles or advertisements about them, and might dismiss them curtly if the topic comes up in conversations.

Because we know that people's beliefs tend to be consistent with their attitudes, we would expect that Darla believed things like sports cars represent a good value for the price, are fun to drive, and make a positive impression on other people—all positive beliefs. Jim could be expected to believe that sports cars are overpriced, uncomfortable, and/or dangerous to drive, and that people who are seen driving them are thought of as vain and/or frivolous—all negative beliefs. Javier could be expected to agree with Darla on some things, but with Jim on others. He might think sports cars are fun to drive, for example, but too expensive. He might not have any particular beliefs at all—he just doesn't spend time thinking about sports cars.

As we turn to considering the direction of values that these three people might have, it is important to remember that values are strong and enduring, and, as a result, tend to shape our attitudes and beliefs. Our values lead us to form certain beliefs and attitudes. In the case of Darla, she may have positive values for status and impression making, or for excitement and danger. Jim may have positive values for frugality and safety, or negative values for risk taking or debt. Javier's values may be ambiguous on the issue—positive for excitement but negative for debt, for example.

The direction dimension of attitude, belief, and value orientations references the polar-opposite orientations that people may have, *if they have a directional position at all.* It is important to recognize that we do not have attitudes, beliefs, and values about everything in our environment. We really don't know much about many things, and many we may know a little about, but not care at all. In such cases, if we think about that person, object, or whatever, we are most likely to be like Javier—just plain neutral. No one could predict we would be forthcoming with any relevant behavior, not even ourselves! Direction, then, must develop for us to really have an orientation of any importance.

Intensity

The second dimension of personal orientations concerns the *strength* of attitudes, beliefs, or values about people, ideas, or objects. This strength is called *intensity.* Though the direction of two people's attitudes, beliefs, or values may be similar, the strength with which they feel those orientations may differ. This variation in strength of orientations is accounted for by the intensity dimension.

The predictions we made above concerning Darla, Javier, and Jim's orientations and likelihoods of behavior were very simple ones. Their accuracy might be better than chance guessing, but not much better. Knowing direction of attitude, belief, or value is not enough. We must know how intense that orientation is. Does everyone who likes sports cars buy one? Of course not. Some like them a whole lot more than others, enough so that they might sacrifice going into serious debt or not going to college to get one. Others may like them a lot, but not that intensely. Intensity, then, has to do with extremity. Highly intense attitudes, beliefs, and values are extreme ones. They are the ones most likely to lead to behavior. They are the ones that are least likely to be changed through communication with others, for reasons we will discuss at length in the next chapter.

Let us refer you back to Scales 17, 18, and 19 in the appendix. Each of these measures is designed to get an indication of both direction and intensity. The neutral point on each measure separates those who have positive attitudes or beliefs from those who have negative attitudes or beliefs. The more the person's score moves from the neutral position, either toward the positive extreme (highest possible score) or the negative extreme (lowest possible score), the more intense is the person's orientation.

Although the scores on the instruments in the figures have finite ranges, of necessity, it may be easier for you to grasp the concept of intensity if you think of attitudes, beliefs, and values as being scored on a range from zero intensity to infinity. The more of it you have, the more intense you are, the more likely your behavior will be consistent with your orientations, but the less likely your orientations will be changed because of communication with others. Of course, the same may be said for other people's orientations and behaviors as well.

To visualize intensity concerning beliefs, it is useful to think of probability in terms of percentage, like commonly is done in weather reports—"There is 90 percent probability of rain for this afternoon." When we hear this forecast, if we believe the forecaster, we are likely to cancel our picnic plans. When the forecast is for a 20 percent probability of bad weather, of course, we are likely to behave in an opposite manner.

Salience

The third dimension comprising the multidimensional orientations of attitude, belief, and value is *salience*. Salience can be defined as *perceived importance of an attitude, a belief, or a value to the individual.* Two teenagers, Brian and Kristen, may have similar attitudes, beliefs, and values related to playing football. Often, those orientations probably are much more salient for Brian than for Kristen. Brian is more likely to be expected to play football than Kristen.

The essence of salience is involvement. The more involved we are with something, the more salient it is, and the more impact our relevant attitudes, beliefs, and values will have on our behavior. This may best be illustrated by considering the salience of values. Two people may have very similar positive attitudes and beliefs toward sports cars, as Darla did in our earlier example. Both may have positive values for both honesty and excitement. Which of those two values, honesty or excitement, is most salient to the individual will decide which person will be more likely to steal a sports car and which one will not. As we noted before, our values tend to shape both our attitudes and our behaviors. The salience of those values tends to determine our behaviors.

 ## DEVELOPMENT OF ATTITUDES, BELIEFS, AND VALUES

We are born without attitudes, beliefs, and values. These orientations are developed as we grow and mature; they are products of our life experiences, not our genetics. Thus, attitudes, beliefs, and values are *learned.* There is no one theory that best explains how these orientations are learned. However, *reinforcement theory* is a useful paradigm for describing the process by which attitudes, beliefs, and values are learned.

Reinforcement theory maintains that we respond to various stimuli according to whether these responses lead to rewarding or nonrewarding results for us. Responses that are rewarded become part of our habitual response pattern. Responses that are not rewarded or that result in punishment for us tend to decrease in frequency of occurrence, often to a point at which they cease to be a part of our response pattern.

Take, for example, your own attitude toward communicating with others. If you were raised in a home in which you were reinforced (received reward) for communicating, you probably communicate more and may place much value on communication. In that environment, you may have found that by communicating in certain ways—saying and doing certain things—you received very positive responses from those around you. Those positive responses served to reinforce your communication behavior so that eventually that behavior became habitual for you. On the other hand, if you were raised in a home in which communication was not reinforced or was punished, you likely communicate less and your attitude toward and value for communication may be negative. Perhaps in that environment you were told, "Don't speak unless you're spoken to" or "Children are to be seen and not heard." Such responses from other people were nonrewarding or even punishing to your communication behavior. Thus, you may have decreased your use of that behavior. Consequently, you are likely to have developed quite negative attitudes and values about communication, even a belief that communication is not very important. If our negative attitudes, beliefs, and values concerning communication are extreme, we may well develop deficiencies in our communicative behaviors—deficiencies such as inadequate skills and a "bad attitude."

Many of our attitudes, beliefs, and values are formed through types of reinforcement that are less direct than that exemplified above. A capacity we have as human beings is to generalize our responses to similar stimuli. For example, if in the past you had a very positive relationship with a tall, green-eyed, redheaded person you were romantically attracted to, you may have developed a positive attitude toward that person. You may also have developed a favorable attitude toward redheads in general. That we generalize our orientations in this way explains why we have many preferences in our lives: it explains why we prefer to go out with a certain type of person, why we choose to engage in a particular hobby, why we have our favorite style of music, why we like some foods over others, and why we are more comfortable in certain situations than in others. As long as our responses to these stimuli are reinforced, we are likely to maintain our favorable orientations toward them. When we experience no reinforcement for any given response, we are likely to make a different behavior choice (for example, start to go out with a different type of person, develop tastes for new foods, and so on).

Indirect reinforcement, like when we see someone else receive a reward for some behavior that we may consider engaging in also, is known as *vicarious reinforcement*. Vicarious reinforcement may come from reading or watching movies or videos in which we see others being rewarded for certain behaviors. Of course, our communication with real people can help develop many of our attitudes, beliefs, and values. Orientations we have toward sex, careers, politics, religion, war, and the like develop in our youth, in large part from our interactions with others. Largely, then, the attitudes, beliefs, and values of other people tend to "rub off" on us. To some extent, therefore, we can predict a person's orientations based on the orientations held by the people with whom he or she associates.

Together, the people who serve to shape an individual's orientations are that individual's *reference group*. A reference group, however, may be a group with whom the individual is not directly affiliated but whose opinions the individual values. When the individual's attitudes, beliefs, and values are similar to those of members of the reference group, the individual is likely to be accepted by the group and to be reinforced for her or his behavior. Conversely, if the individual's orientations are different from those of the reference group, the individual is apt to find their orientations unacceptable and may receive punishment from the group in the form of alienation. An example of this process can be drawn from your decision about whether to join a sorority or fraternity. If you have chosen not to be a "Greek," it may be because you do not share many attitudes, beliefs, and values generally held by such organizations. Of course, if you have chosen to join a sorority or fraternity, it is probably because you share the orientations of such groups. Moreover, attitudes, beliefs, and values vary from one fraternity or sorority to another. Therefore, your decision to join a particular organization is determined largely by how similar you perceive your own orientations to be to those of that group.

Attitudes, beliefs, and values are learned responses. These responses are learned from direct and vicarious everyday experiences. Other orientations are learned from generalizing to new or similar experiences. When we have no direct or vicarious experience on which to form our own orientations, we tend to rely on the attitudes, beliefs, and values of people around us. Our life experiences continue for as long as we live. Thus, there is always potential for our attitudes, beliefs, and values to change. In the final section of this chapter, we discuss different theories that attempt to explain changes in our orientations.

Changes in Attitudes

Because attitudes and beliefs are products of our life experiences, they tend to change from time to time as we encounter new experiences and develop new interpersonal relationships. Values, too, may change, although they endure much longer than attitudes and beliefs. Just how and why these orientations undergo change has been a major area of theory and research in social psychology and communication through the decades since World War II. Although most of this work has been labeled *attitude-change* theory and research, it applies equally well to beliefs and values as it does to attitudes. The theory that we believe has particular relevance to communication is consistency theory.

A U.S. Soldier talks with a group of Iraqi youth.

▣ CONSISTENCY THEORY

Contemporary social psychologists explain the role of the message source, and how a receiver responds to a message, in terms of several theories that collectively have generated what has come to be known as the "principle of consistency" (Brown, 1965; Festinger, 1957; Heider, 1946; Osgood & Tannenbaum, 1955). The essence of this principle is that if two attitudes (or perceptions, or beliefs, or values) are inconsistent with each other, change in one or both occurs because of the mind's efforts to establish and maintain consistency. This need for consistency is seen as a need of all people. Although we can tolerate some inconsistency, the greater it becomes, the more pressure there is on us to resolve inconsistencies.

People of all cultures and backgrounds are also seen as having certain common beliefs. You most likely share these beliefs. They include things like the following: "Good people agree with me." "Bad people disagree with me." "Good people tell the truth." "Bad people lie." When we hear someone we like say something we dislike, then we are pressured to change our minds about the person, what they say, or both. The stronger our liking and respect for the person, the more difficult it is for us to disregard what they say or reject it as false or irrelevant. The attitudes we have or those held by the source may change (become inconsistent) anytime, thus affecting perceptions and ultimately our communication behaviors. Let's look now at a particular consistency theory, the one known as *balance theory* (Heider, 1946; Newcomb, 1958).

Based on the principle of consistency, balance theory maintains that (1) a person needs consistency or "balance" among her or his attitudes, beliefs, and values; (2) when a person becomes aware of inconsistency or "imbalance" among attitudes, beliefs, and values, this leads to a state of tension; and (3) a person will seek to reduce this tension by altering one or more attitudes, beliefs, or values. As it applies to communication, the balance or consistency we are concerned with is that among the attitudes, beliefs, and values held by two communicators for each other and whatever it is they are communicating about. These orientations can be illustrated in a model such as that in Figure 7.1, where A represents one person, B represents the other person, and X represents something they are communicating about or may discuss.

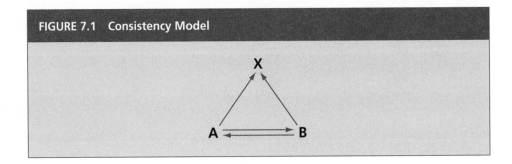

FIGURE 7.1   **Consistency Model**

The theory holds that persons A and B have balanced orientations when their attitudes toward each other and toward X are consistent. That is, balance exists in any condition in which person A's attitudes toward B and X are consistent with person B's attitudes toward A and X. Two communicators—for example, Willie and Hank—can have balanced orientations in two ways, as illustrated in Figure 7.2. Willie and Hank are discussing the 2003 U.S. military campaign Operation Iraqi Freedom. In condition (a), Willie and Hank have positive attitudes toward each other and positive attitudes toward Operation Iraqi Freedom. This situation is balanced because when two people feel positively toward one another, it follows that they should have similar attitudes toward a topic of discussion. Thus, balance would also exist when Willie and Hank like each other but look with disfavor on Operation Iraqi Freedom. In condition (b), Willie and Hank have opposing orientations toward Operation Iraqi Freedom, and they dislike each other. This is also a balanced situation because when two people do not look favorably toward one another, it follows that they should have dissimilar attitudes toward a subject of discussion. In other words, we do not expect two people who feel negatively toward one another to agree with each other.

To put Figure 7.2 into clearer terms, balance theory maintains that we expect people whom we like to favor things we approve of and to disfavor things we disapprove of—condition (a). Moreover, we expect people whom we dislike to disapprove of things we approve of and to approve of things we disapprove of—condition (b). Thus, balance theory holds that a communicative situation is balanced when our expectations about the similarity between our orientations and another person's orientations are consistent. When the other person shows an orientation different from what is consistent with our expectations, we have an unbalanced situation. Figure 7.3 illustrates two possible situations in which orientations are unbalanced.

In condition (a) of Figure 7.3, Willie and Hank both approve of Operation Iraqi Freedom, but they dislike one another. This situation is unbalanced because we would not expect two people who look negatively toward each other to agree on a subject. Thus, imbalance also exists when Willie and Hank dislike each other but both look with disfavor on Operation Iraqi Freedom.

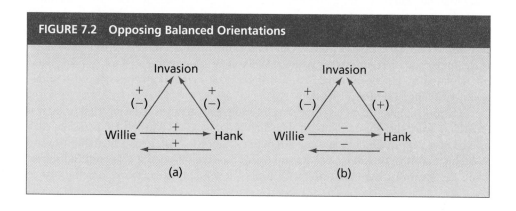

FIGURE 7.2   Opposing Balanced Orientations

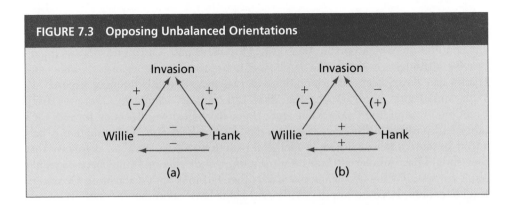

FIGURE 7.3   **Opposing Unbalanced Orientations**

Condition (b) illustrates the situation in which Willie and Hank like each other but disagree in their orientations about Operation Iraqi Freedom. This is an unbalanced situation because we would not expect that two people who like each other would have opposing viewpoints on a topic of discussion.

Consistency theory would predict that no change of orientations will occur in the balanced conditions depicted in Figure 7.2. However, change in attitudes or beliefs would be predicted in the conditions illustrated in Figure 7.3. Because, as the theory states, tension is produced by inconsistency, reduction of tension requires some change in orientations. There are several ways that consistency can be restored in situations in which orientations are unbalanced. Each is considered in the following section.

Restoring Consistency

Inconsistency is present in a communicative situation in which the receiver perceives that the source expresses attitudes different from what he or she expected the source would express. This inconsistency is likely to cause some tension in the receiver, tension that is potentially detrimental to communication outcomes. To alleviate this tension so that outcomes can be better achieved, the receiver must somehow resolve the inconsistency. One way that consistency can be restored is for the receiver to alter her or his attitude toward the subject of communication. This is what the source would want the receiver to do. In the case in which Willie and Hank like each other and disagree on the topic, for example, to restore consistency Willie may attempt to get Hank to take a view of Operation Iraqi Freedom that is similar to his own, so that both either approve or disapprove of Operation Iraqi Freedom.

A second option the receiver has for restoring consistency is to change her or his orientation toward the source. Thus, in the situation in which Willie and Hank dislike each other but agree on Operation Iraqi Freedom, Hank may alter his orientation toward Willie in a positive direction. This would be an especially favorable option if the source wants the receiver to like her or him. Of course, it would be less favorable in the case in which the two individuals disagree on the topic but like each other. That would require that the receiver adopt a negative attitude toward the source to restore consistency.

Given the two options above, one may ask which attitude is most likely to change when the receiver experiences a state of inconsistency—attitude toward the subject or attitude toward the source? Attitude-change research suggests that the attitude most likely to change is the one that is *least intense* for the receiver. Thus, if Hank's attitude for Willie in either condition is more intense for him than is his attitude for the war, he is more likely to change his attitude about the intervention. On the other hand, if Hank were somehow personally involved with the war—perhaps he had a brother serving with the troops—then he is more likely to alter his attitude about Willie. Sometimes, however, the receiver may choose not to change either of her or his attitudes and to turn instead to another option for restoring consistency.

This third way of resolving inconsistency is called *leaving the field.* This is a form of communication withdrawal that may take either a physical or a psychological form. In the physical sense, leaving the field assumes a literal dimension. Knowing that he and Willie disagree about Iraq, for example, Hank may simply remove himself from Willie's company when the topic arises. We all leave the field from time to time, particularly when a topic for which we have an intense attitude is brought up by someone whom we like very much but whose attitude toward the topic is quite different from our own. Recall a time in high school when your parents wanted to "discuss" with you your late school-night hours!

Psychological withdrawal from the communication situation occurs more often than physically leaving the field. Often, it is simply inappropriate or impossible to remove ourselves from the other person's presence. If, for example, Hank knows that his good friend Willie disagrees with him on the topic of the war, Hank can avoid bringing up the subject when talking to him. Or if Hank values highly both his friendship with Willie and Operation Iraqi Freedom, he may unconsciously selectively misinterpret what Willie is saying about the subject, a topic we considered in more detail in the previous chapter. He may perceive what Willie is saying to be the opposite of what he actually feels, he may perceive a reason other than the real reason for why Willie is saying what he is, or he may just tune out and not pay attention to Willie.

Perhaps the most often employed means for restoring consistency through psychologically leaving the field is "forgetting." Hank realizes that his and Willie's attitudes are inconsistent, but he finds it very difficult or undesirable to alter his own, so he may just try to forget the entire transaction concerning the war.

Thus, several options are available for restoring consistency in those communicative situations in which two people's attitudes toward each other and the subject of discussion do not fit one or the other person's expectations. When we partition the communication process into separate source and receiver processes and variables, the whole matter of interpersonal orientations and consistency among them perhaps has greater import for the receiver than for the source. This is because—as we have emphasized throughout this and the previous two chapters—how the receiver perceives and responds to the source has significant impact on communication outcomes. Central to those perceptions are the receiver's attitudes, beliefs, and values, and how similarly the receiver perceives these to be to the attitudes, beliefs, and values of the source. When the receiver perceives inconsistency between her or his own orientations and those of the source, tension results; the need to alleviate that tension leads to the receiver making some choice for restoring consistency. Despite which option the receiver selects to employ, some change in orientations and/or perceptions and behavior occur, and ultimately some change in communication also occurs. Depending on the nature of the transaction, these changes can serve either to enhance the achievement of communication outcomes or to inhibit their achievement.

KEY TERMS

attitude 142
belief 143

intensity 146
principle of consistency 152

salience 146
values 145

REFERENCES

Albarra_in, D., Johnson, B. T., & Zanna, M. P. (Eds.). (2006). *The handbook of attitudes.* Mahwah, NJ: Lawrence Erlbaum.

Bogardus, E. S. (1925). Measuring social distance. *Journal of Applied Sociology, 9,* 299–308.

Brown, R. (1965). *Social psychology.* New York: Free Press.

Festinger, L. (1957). *A theory of cognitive dissonance.* New York: Row, Peterson.

Heider, F. (1946). Attitudes and cognitive organization. *Journal of Psychology, 21,* 107–112.

Likert, R. (1932). A technique for the measurement of attitudes. *Archives of Psychology, 140,* 1–55.

McCroskey, J. C. (1966). Experimental studies of the effects of ethos and evidence in persuasive communication. Unpublished doctoral dissertation. Pennsylvania State University.

McCroskey, J. C. (2006) *An introduction to rhetorical communication* (9th ed.). Boston: Allyn & Bacon.

McCroskey, J. C., & Richmond, V. P. (1989). Bipolar scales. In P. Emmert and L. L. Barker (Eds.), *Measurement of communication behavior* (pp. 154–167). New York: Longman.

Newcomb, T. M. (1958). Attitude development as a function of reference groups: The Bennington study. In E. E. Maccoby, T. M. Newcomb, and E. L. Hartley (Eds.), *Readings in social psychology.* New York: Holt, Rinehart & Winston.

Osgood, C. E., & Tannenbaum, P. H. (1955). The principle of congruity in the prediction of attitude change. *Psychological Review, 62,* 42–55.

DISCUSSION QUESTIONS

1. What is your attitude toward the death penalty? How does this relate to your belief humans should not kill? How do both your attitude and your belief relate to your value of life?

2. How does an individual's culture impact her or his values?

3. If someone's belief is highly salient, do you think you can persuade her or him to another position? Why?

4. How can indirect (vicarious) reinforcement explain how we develop communicative patterns?

5. You and your best friend are debating the ethics of reality television. You see reality TV as ethical and your best friend does not. Explain how consistency theory explains what is occurring in this debate.

8

Levels of Influence

Compliance • Identification • Internalization

Power

Assigned Power • Coercive Power • Reward Power • Referent Power • Expert Power

Communication and Interpersonal Influence

Behavior Alteration Techniques (BAT)

Reward BATs • Punishment BATs • Relational BATs • Referent BATs • Assigned or Legitimate BATs • Moral Responsibility BATs • Expert BATs

Power and Influence

OBJECTIVES

- Define and explain *influence*.

- Understand the three levels of influence.

- Define and explain *power*.

- Explain French and Raven's five bases of power.

- Explain the relationship between the seven bases of power and the three levels of influence.

- Understand the relationship between the five bases of power and behavior alteration techniques (BATs) and behavior alteration messages (BAMs).

A primary reason we communicate is to influence others. People have to learn to cooperate to achieve common goals. People also have to learn that influence through interpersonal communication is a primary means of getting people to work together toward common goals. We have already learned that having high credibility, being attractive, and being similar are all prerequisites for changing another's attitude in a direction deemed desirable. When we attempt to influence others, our ultimate goal is to modify their attitudes and behaviors as we discussed in the previous chapter. To meet this goal, the best means of communication is interpersonal. Because of its personal nature and opportunity to supply feedback, interpersonal communication is the most effective type of communication for influencing people and causing behavior change. This chapter examines different strategies that can be employed when trying to influence others. First, we need to examine the types of behavior change we want and the advantages and disadvantages of each.

LEVELS OF INFLUENCE

Three levels of influence are possible through interpersonal communication. We can get people to *comply* with, to *identify* with, or to *internalize* recommended behaviors. For example, an instructor might say that he or she does not expect any cheating during a class exam. Many students comply only when the teacher is watching them. However, many others can identify with this request and support the request without even being asked to comply. Some students understand the importance of learning on one's own and have internalized this model. The goal, of course, in many influence situations is to get the other person to internalize the recommended behavior. For the students who have internalized the teacher's view, cheating is simply not considered an alternative at all.

Compliance

Compliance is the most transitory level of influence (Wheeless, Barraclough, & Stewart, 1983). People comply with another's request because they can see either some potential reward for complying or some potential punishment for not complying. Individuals temporarily accept the idea, not because they believe in it, but to gain specific rewards or avoid specific punishments. Therefore, compliance is mainly a superficial response to an influence attempt (McCroskey, 1992).

The compliant individual does not necessarily believe the behavior is a good one. This is quite common in the classroom. Often, students yield to a teacher's demands because the students feel they will be rewarded or can avoid punishment. However,

Martha Stewart has power over many people in our society because people want to be like her (referent power), because they want to have her talents in the kitchen and at the craft table.

the students' behavior is totally dependent on whether the teacher is capable of carrying out the rewards or punishments. In addition, the demand must be salient or important to students, or they will not comply. If the teacher threatens a student with a poor grade if the student does not stop talking, but the student does not care about the grade, the student is not likely to stop talking. Therefore, the request and the source of the request must be perceived as relevant to the receiver in order for the receiver to consider complying.

The amount of attitude change in the compliance model is usually very minimal, is often short-lived, and generally does not lead to motivation to continue the behavior. It simply leads to movement by the receiver. To guarantee compliance, the source can illustrate *concern, control,* and *scrutiny* to the receiver. *Concern* refers to the source indicating he or she really cares whether the receiver complies, *control* refers to the source indicating he or she can really do something to or for the receiver, and *scrutiny* refers to the source indicating he or she has ways of knowing whether the receiver complies.

Law enforcement agencies of this country have shown their concern about speeding by reducing the speed limit to 65 or 70 mph on interstates. They have shown that they can control speeding with road monitors and that they can watch for speeders by using radar and other technologies. When the above methods are available, compliance with speed laws will probably occur. However, when one of them is missing, compliance may not occur. For example, if the radar is turned off for a day, speeders know that they are not being scrutinized by the police. Speeders will speed even if concern and control are present. Teachers who say they do not want cheating on a test, but then leave the classroom, have just told the class they are not really concerned about the possibility of cheating.

Compliance is the lowest level or outcome of interpersonal influence. Compliance gets people only to conform, not to identify with or internalize a specific behavior. People who comply "just do it." They don't have to like it.

Identification

When people change a behavior because they think the change is a good idea, they are changing at the identification level. This is a more lasting level of influence. Often, people will identify with behavior changes because they also identify with the person recommending the change: "If Martha Stewart thinks it is a good idea, then it is good enough for me." In other cases, the rationale for the change convinces the person that it is a good idea. In either case, the person influenced now "owns" the behavior.

Change achieved at the identification level is much more persistent than that achieved at the compliance level. Changes tend to be long term, and the person who changes may even attempt to influence others to make the same change.

Whereas compliance depends primarily on the source's ability to mediate rewards and punishments, identification depends more on the relationship between the source and the receiver. Although people still conform to a source's recommendation at the identification level, they do so because they believe they are making a good decision. The image of the source is positive and leads the receiver to "buy into" the recommended change.

Internalization

Internalization is the most lasting level of influence, and involves making the new behavior a habit; its desirability becomes meshed with the person's value system. When an idea or behavior is internalized, it is integrated into the individual's existing value system and is a part of the way the person thinks or behaves. It is indistinguishable from the person's already existing behaviors in the same area. For example, if we do not believe in cheating on exams, when the teacher says not to cheat, we take little notice, for the idea of cheating is simply foreign to us. We engage in the recommended behavior because of who we are, not because someone else promises rewards or threatens punishments. It is already just the way we behave.

When internalization is achieved, the individual is induced to perform the behaviors despite the scrutiny of the source. The behavior will be performed because the person is internally motivated and feels this is the good or right thing to do. In interpersonal relationships, when internalization is present, individuals will do things for the other person without even being asked to do so. They will do something because they believe it is right and good and will help in establishing an effective interpersonal relationship. They will engage in desired behaviors without the need for additional communication.

It is not always important that we exert influence to such an extent that we produce internalized behavior change. In most of our interpersonal relationships, simple compliance may be all we will ever want or need. However, if lasting change is wanted, it is very important that the influence be at either the identification or internalization level. Without a very positive relationship with the other person, we will not have the power to produce change at these levels.

▣ POWER

Power, as we will use the term in this chapter, refers to an *individual's ability to have an effect on the behavior of another person or group.* When we exert interpersonal influence, we are exerting our power. *Power* is a word that is used in many ways, so we need to take care to make clear we are not talking here about raw, physical power. The use of guns, fists, and bombs is not what we mean by interpersonal influence. That type of power can reasonably be described as destructive and evil. Not all power is of that type. The power we are concerned with is the power freely granted to one communicator by another. We believe the most useful model of power is the one advanced by French and Raven (1959), in which they explicated the five bases of power: assigned, coercive, reward, referent, and expert.

Assigned Power

Assigned power, sometimes called *legitimate power,* stems from the assigned role of a person in a relationship (such as your spouse, your lover, or your teacher). Assigned power is based on your perception that the other individual has the *right* to make certain demands and requests as a function of her or his position or assigned role. This type of power can have very explicit rules ("You are not allowed to date others while dating me"). This type of power can have implicit rules ("I expect you to be on time for our dates"). Either way, you will comply because they are seen as "legitimate" demands from the other person because of her or his relationship with you.

Assigned power usually only engenders compliance from the other person. However, in a dating or marriage relationship, an individual is likely to identify with some legitimate demands of the other person. In other environments, this may not be the case. For example, in the work and school environments, most legitimate demands lead only to compliance. Often in these environments, assigned power is associated with the power to reward or punish; therefore, many people dislike the use of assigned power.

Coercive Power

Coercive power relates to an individual's capacity to inflict punishment if another does not conform to that person's requests or demands. For example, a teacher's coercive power is contingent on the student's perceptions of how probable it is that the teacher will exact punishment for nonconformance and the degree of negative consequences such punishment would entail, minus the probability of punishment from other sources (peers, for example) if the student *does* comply with the teacher.

Coercive power provides the best example of how power must be granted by one person to another for the power to exist. For example, teachers are assigned the right to grade students. However, students who really do not care whether they pass or fail do not grant the teacher the power to coerce. If threats to fail fall on deaf ears, the teacher is left powerless. In short, if we are willing to accept the punishment, the other person has no coercive power over us. Of course, the reverse is also true. If the other person is willing "to take our best shot," we have no coercive power over them either. Power must be granted; it cannot just be assumed.

Even when used, coercive power will gain only *compliance* on the part of the other individual; it will not create motivation to continue the new behavior. Therefore, for an effective interpersonal relationship, the coercive power model should be avoided at all costs or employed only if necessary to get someone to do something you absolutely must get them to do. (See Figure 8.1.)

FIGURE 8.1 Levels of Influence and Power

Five Bases of Power	Levels of Influence		
	Compliance	Identification	Internalization
Coercive	X		
Reward	X		
Legitimate	X		
Referent	X	X	X
Expert	X	X	X

Reward Power

When an individual has the potential to provide rewards to another for compliance, this is known as *reward* power. For example, if your boyfriend or girlfriend wants you to do something and promises to take you to dinner as a reward, you might engage in the behavior. However, this does not mean that you identify with or internalize the behavior.

Rewards are effective as far as they are ongoing, positive, and consistent. When a reward has been used once (for children under 10, this may vary), it has been used up. The next time, the person may ask, "What have you done for me lately?" However, though reward may lead only to movement, it does set the basis for identification and internalization. It is a much better way to influence someone than the use of coercion. Remember, if reward is used once in a situation, it has to be used again in that situation or the person will feel as if he or she is being punished. For example, if you do something for your friend and he or she takes you to dinner, the next time you are asked to do a similar favor, you will expect to be taken to dinner again. If you aren't, you will feel you were cheated and are not likely to engage in similar behavior again.

Although it often is not recognized, coercive and reward power essentially are the flip sides of the same coin. Coercive power (a threat) involves introducing something unpleasant or removing something pleasant if the person fails to comply. Reward power (a bribe) involves introducing something pleasant or removing something unpleasant if the person does comply. Neither provides a solid basis for identification or internalization.

Former Surgeon General M. Joycelyn Elders, M.D., had expert power over the American public in the area of medicine because the Surgeon General is seen as the nation's primary physician.

Referent Power

An individual's identification with a specific person or group is called *referent* power. It is sometimes called the *power of association*. Specifically, it is based on the desire of the less powerful person to identify with and please the more powerful person. The less powerful person wants to be liked by and/or to become more like the more powerful person, which means adopting that person's attitudes and behaviors. The stronger the less powerful person's attraction to and identification with the more powerful person, the stronger that person's power is.

Whatever the context of the communication, referent power will lead not only to compliance but also to identification and internalization. This means that in the interpersonal relationship, referent power can cause significant behavior change. Referent power in a strong relationship can be a reciprocal process for the persons involved. For example, if your best friend does not cheat on exams, then you may model this behavior and eventually internalize it. At another point in the relationship, your friend might model the way you dress or talk. Thus, the more referent power between two people, the stronger the relationship is likely to become.

Expert Power

Expert power results from an individual's perceiving the other person to be competent and knowledgeable in specific areas. Expert power stems from source credibility. The more one perceives another to be knowledgeable, the more likely one is to go to that person for information or advice. The person whose advice is asked has the potential to be very influential, particularly in terms of being able to direct another person's way of thinking. Expert power leads to compliance, identification, and finally internalization. If the conveyed knowledge is put to use, then the receiver of the information has identified with the person giving the information, and possibly will internalize the information.

 ## COMMUNICATION AND INTERPERSONAL INFLUENCE

The use of power requires communication (McCroskey & Richmond, 1983). Often, power is used to influence without explicit verbal communication. When a teacher tells students to do their homework, it is usually not necessary to add "or I will punish you by lowering your grade," "because I am the teacher and I have the right to demand that you do this," or "because you like me and want to please me." Such appeals to power are implied and are generally recognized by the student without being directly stated.

In other instances, direct power appeals are stated. Coercive power, for example, may be invoked when a teacher says, "If you don't turn in your work on time, I will give you an 'F' for the assignment." Similarly, reward power may be invoked when a teacher says, "If you do this extra problem, I will give you five bonus points." An appeal to referent power may take the form of the teacher asking, "Will someone help me set up this DVD player?"

Whether power appeals are stated directly or implied, in order for a source to influence behavior, the receiver must associate the requested behavior with the power held by the source (Richmond & McCroskey, 1984). All power is based on the receiver's perceptions. If the receiver does not perceive the source to have a certain type of power, a source's appeal to that power, whether direct or implied, is not likely to result in influence. Similarly, even if the receiver perceives the source to have the power, if the influence attempt is not associated with the power, the attempt is likely to be unsuccessful.

▣ BEHAVIOR ALTERATION TECHNIQUES (BAT)

The original five bases of power have been expanded. A range and diversity of power strategies or *behavior alteration techniques* (BATs) available for personal influence have been identified (Kearney, Plax, Richmond, & McCroskey, 1984, 1985). All of the BATs are concerned with getting others to do what you want them to do. Twenty-two representative BATs, or categories, have been identified. Each category is best represented by a combination of messages, which are known as *behavior alteration messages* (BAMs; see Figure 8.2).

Most of the BATs and representative BAMs represent the previously defined five power strategies (Richmond & McCroskey, 1992). The first five BATs fall in the *reward* category. BATs 6–9 are associated with *punishment* (coercion). BATs 12 and 13 comprise the *referent* category. The *assigned* or *legitimate* category is represented by BATs 13 and 14. The *expert* category is represented by BATs 21 and 22. Two new categories have been added. The new category labeled *relational* is represented in BATs 10 and 11. The new *moral responsibility* category is made up of BATs 16–20.

Figure 8.3 presents the individual BATs and the level of influence that we believe probably can be obtained by using each. The remainder of this section examines each BAT and discusses its implications. They are ordered according to the power basis on which they presumably draw.

Reward BATs

Immediate Reward from Behavior.   Based on the topology of BAMs, this BAT promotes a source's attempts to elicit specific receiver behaviors by suggesting that such behaviors will be inherently rewarding and fulfilling. This BAT points out to the receiver that rewarding consequences can be derived from engaging in the desired behavior. This "Try it—you'll like it" approach is likely in situations in which receivers are reluctant to engage in behaviors that represent deviations from the old way of doing things. This approach is particularly relevant in a new relationship in which the people are feeling out each other's likes and dislikes. This BAT would be a way to develop some similarity between two people and help in the development of a trusting relationship. The key is to make sure the receiver is rewarded for engaging in the new behavior, or else it may be discontinued. For example, an author of this text was told by a close friend that a martini is the best drink around. She tried one, believing the reward would be the adoption of a

FIGURE 8.2 Behavior Alteration Techniques (BATs) and Behavior Alteration Messages (BAMs)	
Category (BATs)	**Sample Statements (BAMs)**
1. Immediate reward from behavior	You will enjoy it. It will make you happy. Because it's fun. You'll find it rewarding/interesting. It's a good experience.
2. Deferred reward from behavior	It will help you later on in life. It will prepare you for college (or high school, job, etc.). It will prepare you for your future. It will help you with upcoming relationships.
3. Reward from source	I will give you a reward if you do. I will make it beneficial to you. You will be rewarded if you do this.
4. Reward from others	Others will respect you if you do. Others will be proud of you. Your friends will like you if you do. Your parents will be pleased.
5. Internal reward: self-esteem	You will feel good about yourself if you do. You are the best person to do it. You are good at it. You always do such a good job. Because you're capable!
6. Punishment from behavior	You will lose if you don't. You will be unhappy if you don't. You will be hurt if you don't. It's your loss. You'll feel bad if you don't.
7. Punishment from source	I will punish you if you don't. I will make it miserable for you. I'll get others to punish you. You will be an outcast.
8. Punishment from others	No one will like you. Your friends will make fun of you. Your parents will punish you if you don't. Your friends will reject you.
9. Internal punishment: guilt	If you don't, others will be hurt. You'll make others unhappy if you don't. Your parents will feel bad if you don't. Others will be punished if you don't.
10. Source–receiver relationship: positive	I will like you better if you do. I will respect you. I will think more highly of you. I will appreciate you more if you do. I will be proud of you.
11. Source–receiver relationship: negative	I will dislike you if you don't. I will lose respect for you. I will think less of you if you don't. I won't be proud of you. I'll be disappointed in you.
12. Peer modeling	Your friends do it. People you respect do it. The friends you admire do it. Other students you like do it. All your friends are doing it.
13. Source modeling	This is the way I always do it. When I was your age, I did it. People who are like me do it. I had to do this when I was in school. People you respect do it.

(Continued)

FIGURE 8.2   Behavior Alteration Techniques (BATs) (*Continued*)

	Category (BATs)	Sample Statements (BAMs)
14.	Legitimate—higher authority	Do it; I'm just telling you what I was told. It is a rule. I have to do it and so do you. Others expect you to do it.
15.	Legitimate—source authority	Because I told you to. You don't have a choice. You're here to work. I'm the person you answer to. I'm in charge, not you. Don't ask; just do it.
16.	Receiver responsibility	It is your obligation. It is your turn. Everyone has to do his or her share. It's your job. Everyone has to pull his or her own weight.
17.	Responsibility to referent group	Your group needs it done. The class depends on you. All your friends are counting on you. Don't let your group down. You'll ruin it for the rest of the group.
18.	Responsibility to system—normative rules	We voted, and the majority rules. All of your friends are doing it. Everyone else has to do it. The rest of the group is doing it. It's part of growing up.
19.	Debt to source	You owe me one. Pay your debt. You promised to do it. I did it the last time. You said you'd try this time.
20.	Altruism toward others	If you do this, it will help others. Others will benefit if you do. It will make others happy if you do. I'm not asking you to do it for yourself; do it for the good of the group or others.
21.	Source identification with receiver or source verification	Because I need to know how well you understand this. Because I need to see how well I've told you. Because I need to see how well you can do it. It will help me know your problem areas. Let me verify if I told you the right things to do.
22.	Expertness	From my experience, it is a good idea. From what I have learned, it is what you should do. This has always worked for me. Trust me—I know what I'm doing. I had to do this before, and I got good at this.

new, good-tasting drink. However, she did not like the martini and to this day has not had another. The author's trust for that person as an opinion leader on alcoholic beverages was lowered. Remember, a reward for one person may not be a reward for another.

This BAT is not likely to be effective much beyond the compliance level of influence. Reward usually leads only to movement, not to motivation to adopt and continue the new idea, unless the reward is highly wanted and virtually always is obtained when the behavior is performed.

FIGURE 8.3 BATs, BAMs, and Influence			
	Levels of Influence		
BATS	Compliance	Identification	Internalization
1. Punishment from behavior	X		
2. Punishment from source	X		
3. Punishment from others	X		
4. Internal punishment—guilt	X		
5. Immediate reward from behavior	X		
6. Deferred reward from behavior	X	X	
7. Reward from source	X		
8. Reward from others	X		
9. Internal reward—self-esteem	X	X	X
10. Source–receiver relationship: positive	X	X	X
11. Source–receiver relationship: negative	X		
12. Peer modeling	X	X	X
13. Source modeling	X	X	X
14. Legitimate—higher authority	X		
15. Legitimate—source authority	X		
16. Receiver responsibility	X		
17. Responsibility to referent group	X	X	
18. Responsibility to system—normative rules	X		
19. Debt to source	X		
20. Altruism toward others	X	X	
21. Source identification with receiver or source verification	X	X	
22. Expertness	X	X	X

Source: Richmond, V. P., & McCroskey, J.C. (1983). *Interpersonal influence in relationships.* Unpublished manuscript. West Virginia University, Morgantown.

Deferred Reward from Behavior. The BAMs that reflect this BAT combine into another type of reward appeal. People who use this BAT are concerned with the reward coming later in life or in the relationship. This BAT is supposed to prepare one to cope with similar circumstances later in life. The main problem with this BAT is that it is not immediately reinforcing; therefore, the receiver may not engage in the behavior because he or she cannot see how it will help in future relationships. For example, the teacher who says to students, "This will help you on tests in college," is trying to get the students to comply now with the understanding that it will help them later. Often, this simply does not work. To make some future reward appealing, one must give exact circumstances in which the behavior will be rewarded in the future. For example, if you want to change the way someone dresses, show that person how this will help in getting the job he or she wants in the future, and then the person might adopt the new behavior. Generally, this BAT will lead to compliance only at a particular point in time, not to identification and internalization, because many people cannot see the future reward.

Reward from Source.   This BAT reflects another reward-type appeal. It should be noted that this BAT most closely resembles French and Raven's reward power. It is primarily concerned with giving receivers a reward if they comply with the source's request. Some consider this the "bribe" category: if you do something I want you to do, I will reward you. Parents use this frequently with small children, but after a while the children learn to ask for bigger and better rewards. This type of power leads only to movement, not to motivation to continue the behavior; therefore, only compliance will be obtained.

Reward from Others.   This BAT is another one of the reward-type appeals. It is concerned with others being proud of the receiver or respecting the receiver for engaging in some desired behavior. In this BAT, the receiver will do something because others will be pleased, which may or may not be reinforcing for the receiver. This BAT generally leads to movement to please others; therefore, there is little chance for identification and internalization.

Internal Reward: Self-Esteem.   This reward appeal centers on receivers' feeling good about themselves for engaging in a new behavior. It says, "You will feel good about yourself if you do this." Generally, if you feel good about something you have done, you are likely to continue it; this will lead to compliance, and sometimes to identification or internalization. However, until receivers have engaged in the desired behavior and felt good about themselves, there will be no identification or internalization.

Punishment BATs

Punishment from Behavior.   This BAT is an appeal either to do something or to lose and be unhappy. It says if the behavior is not engaged in, the receiver will feel a loss and be hurt by her or his lack of compliance with another. This BAT, as with the punishment-coercive power, leads only to compliance, not to identification or internalization. Receivers may engage in the behavior, but only because there is an implied threat; they will not internalize the behavior (McCroskey, Richmond, Plax, & Kearney, 1985).

Punishment from Source.   This BAT is the flip side of the *reward from source* BAT. By using this BAT, the source has said the receiver will be punished if he or she does not engage in the behavior the source wants. For example, the mother says to the small child, "Clean up your room, or I will spank you." In interpersonal relationships, people use this BAT frequently, and then they cannot understand why the other does not identify with the behavior. For example, a male will imply to his girlfriend, "Go to bed with me, or I will stop dating you." He has in effect said, "I will punish you and make your life miserable if you don't sleep with me." This strategy is not likely to get many women into bed. In fact, it is likely to make them reply, "Go to h—! I hear you're not that good." If someone is going to use the above strategy on another, then he or she should make sure that the threatened punishment can be carried out and that it is perceived as punishment by the receiver. If it is not perceived as punishment, it is totally useless in gaining compliance. Obviously, this strategy leads only to compliance, not to internalization.

Punishment from Others. The plea of this BAT is that others will not like the receiver if he or she does not engage in the desired behavior. The underlying premise is that others (friends) will reject the receiver for not engaging in the behavior. This BAT is very powerful for getting people to do something they don't want to do, but it does not lead to identification or internalization. People will do many things they wouldn't normally do to please others; however, it is only *movement* on their part to please the other—it will not be internalized. A person should be wary about overusing this BAT because it loses its appeal quickly. After a while, the receiver will say, "So what—if they don't like me, I don't like them anyway."

Internal Punishment: Guilt. BAMs in this category suggest that the receiver will comply because others will be hurt or unhappy if he or she does not. This BAT is commonly used by college professors: "How will your parents feel when you bring home an 'F' in this course?" The appeal is to the receiver's inner self. It is an appeal to guilt about how one's significant others will feel if one does not comply. This BAT will lead to compliance, but it generally does not lead to identification or internalization. If the receiver complies with a source's request because others will be hurt, that is little more than compliance. The receiver is doing it for someone else and may not even buy into the request except to keep others happy. When those others (such as parents and friends) are not involved, the receiver will not comply with the request.

The use of punishment-oriented BATs will gain only compliance, not identification or internalization. Punishment BATs are negatively associated with identification and internalization. Coercive BATs should be avoided at all costs in any interpersonal relationship and, if used, should be used only as a last resort. Generally, the use of punishment BATs leads only to negative outcomes—dislike for the source, mistrust, and maybe even a breakup in the friendship.

Relational BATs

Source–Receiver Relationship: Positive. BAMs in this BAT category suggest that the source will like the receiver more if the receiver will comply. Essentially, this BAT is concerned with the source's increased respect for the receiver. This BAT tends to be very powerful, particularly if the source is a referent model or a significant other for the receiver. This means that the receiver not only will comply but also may identify with and internalize the behavior.

Source–Receiver Relationship: Negative.   This BAT is the flip side of the previous one. It suggests that the source will dislike and lose respect for the receiver if the receiver does not comply with the source's request. This is negative referent power, which is akin to some punishment strategies, and this type of power may lead only to compliance, not to identification and internalization. After a while, receivers will start thinking that the relationship is negative if they have to comply with the source's requests in order not to disappoint the source. Receivers will feel they are being unfairly manipulated. The relationship could be destroyed by this negative use of referent power.

Referent BATs

Peer Modeling.   The BAMs within this category suggest that the receiver should comply with the source's demands because the receiver's friends and admired peers are already engaging in the behavior. It suggests that people who are liked and respected by their peer group engage in this behavior. This is a very potent power strategy because it leads to modeling of the peer group. From this modeling, much reinforcement will be given by the peer group, and often internalization takes place.

Source Modeling.   This BAT suggests that the receiver should model the source because the source will like and respect the receiver for doing so. If the receiver respects the source as an opinion leader, the receiver is likely to model the source and identify with and internalize the source's ways of thinking and acting. This power strategy obviously may lead to identification and internalization by the receiver, but only if the receiver respects the source.

Assigned or Legitimate BATs

Legitimate Higher Authority.   The BAMs in this category suggest that the receiver should do what the source asks because both the source and others in the system are expected to do it by some higher authority. Often, people will comply with higher authority (students comply with principals) if the request seems reasonable. However, if the request is unreasonable, the receiver will try to find a way not to comply. Then the source has to resort to punishment-oriented types of power, which are very detrimental to an effective interpersonal relationship. This BAT will lead only to compliance, not to identification or internalization.

Legitimate Source Authority.   The BAMs that reflect this BAT are source oriented. This BAT says that the receiver should comply with the source's demands because the source has the legitimate right to ask the receiver to comply. For example, the teacher has the legitimate right to ask students to be on time for class. This BAT will guarantee only compliance, not identification and internalization.

In conclusion, the authority BATs just discussed are concerned with the use of assigned power. Assigned power, although not perceived as negatively as the punishment types, is still perceived by receivers in a somewhat negative light. The positiveness or negativeness of assigned power is primarily decided by the respect the receiver has for the source of higher authority and for the source. If the source is respected by the receiver, compliance will be obtained without resorting to threats. However, if the receiver does not respect and like the source, the legitimate power often must be accompanied by threats or the punishment-oriented strategies.

Moral Responsibility BATs

Receiver Responsibility.   The BAMs within this category suggest that compliance is derived from the receiver's sense of responsibility. The source tries to get the receiver to conform by pointing out that everyone has to do her or his share and "It's your turn to do your share." This obligatory type of power generally leads only to compliance by the receiver. However, it does not often lead to negative feelings toward the source as do the punishment-oriented or legitimate strategies.

Responsibility to Referent Group.   This appeal is made when the source suggests that the receiver's referent group is depending on the receiver's compliance. It suggests that the receiver will let down friends or a group if he or she does not comply with the source's demands. This BAT may get receivers to comply and even identify with the source's demands, but they may not internalize the demands. The appeal is dependent on how receivers feel about their referent group. Because they are a referent group, the receiver probably feels very close to them and will comply and perhaps identify with the value of the source's demands for the referent group. But the receiver may never internalize. For example, athletes know they should not smoke; therefore, they will comply for many reasons. They may identify with the no-smoking rule because it is their obligation to the group. However, they may never internalize the no-smoking rule. When they no longer are on the team, they may smoke.

Responsibility to System—Normative Rules.   This BAT is concerned with majority rule, or the idea that the receiver should conform because friends are doing it. Many people will conform to demands because these are the norm during that period in their lives; however, they may never really identify with or internalize the demands. For example, a group of first-year college students takes their first drink based on this premise. It is the norm to drink to be accepted by the group, so they drink. They never identify with or internalize drinking, however. When they leave college, most drop the habit and pick up habits of their primary work group.

Debt to Source.   Similar to the previous responsibility BATs, this BAT is concerned with the receiver's feelings that he or she owes it to the source to carry out the source's requests. The source might even go as far as to say to the receiver, "You owe it to me to do this." Paying back a debt leads only to compliance, not to identification and internalization.

Altruism toward Others.   This BAT suggests that if the receiver complies with the source, others will benefit and be happier. The motto here is "Try it; others will benefit from it." This BAT asks the receiver to comply for the good of others; there is no particular benefit to the receiver other than seeing others pleased. This is similar to referent group responsibility in that it could lead to compliance, and perhaps identification, because it will benefit someone.

These five responsibility BATs have all dealt with the receiver's feeling some responsibility to comply for the benefit of the source or some other people. As we can see from the above, the only responsibility BATs that are likely to lead beyond compliance are *responsibility to referent group* and *altruism toward others*. These two may lead to identification because we tend to identify with particular groups and see them as extensions of ourselves. As has been suggested before, altruism may be little more than enlightened self-interest.

Expert BATs

Source Responsiveness.   The concentration of the BAMs under this BAT shows that the source needs to see the receiver comply with her or his request to determine whether the receiver understood what the source wanted. The receiver must comply by either performing the request or at least explaining the request to the source. Then the source knows whether the receiver understood what he or she was expected to do. If the source can get verification about whether the receiver understood the request, then the source can help the receiver with any problem areas in carrying out the request. This technique is really more for clarification of the request than it is to encourage the receiver to carry out the request. However, this technique lets the receiver realize how important it is to carry out the request. Therefore, compliance and identification could result.

Expert Source.   Like French and Raven's notion of expert power, the BAMs in this category suggest that the receiver should comply with the source's request because the source is an expert and has had previous experience in this area. As in French and Raven's expert power strategy, this BAT may lead to compliance, identification, or internalization.

Finally, it is important to stress that an individual should avoid the use of the punishment (coercive) BATs. An individual should also refrain as much as possible from using the assigned (legitimate) BATs in establishing and maintaining effective interpersonal relationships. Although the reward BATs may not lead to internalization, they can be used initially as a way to move to or establish the referent and expert BATs.

The BATs presented here are valuable tools for the establishment and maintenance of effective interpersonal relationships (Richmond, McCroskey, & Roach, 1997; Richmond, Wagner, & McCroskey, 1983; Richmond, McCroskey, & Davis, 1986; Richmond, McCroskey, Kearney, & Plax, 1987). Furthermore, the BATs have been shown to have an impact on education (Plax, Kearney, McCroskey, & Richmond, 1986; Richmond, 1990). Also, BATs have also been shown to have an impact on the day-to-day running of organizations (Richmond, Davis, Saylor, & McCroskey, 1984; Richmond, McCroskey, & Davis, 1982). However, one must remember to try to communicate with only the more desirable BATs and use combinations of desirable BATs. Personal influence is fairly easy to achieve without sacrificing friendship if only these prosocial BATs are used. If, however, you choose to employ the more antisocial BATs, you can expect to have your relationship deteriorate sharply or disintegrate completely. Few behavioral alterations are worth such extremely negative relational side effects.

 KEY TERMS

coercive power 163	influence 159	power 162
compliance 159	internalization 161	referent power 165
expert power 165	legitimate power 162	relational power 166
identification 161	moral responsibility power 166	reward power 164

 REFERENCES

French, J. R. P., & Raven, B. (1959). The bases for social power. In D. Cartwright (Ed.), *Studies in social power*. Ann Arbor, MI: Institute for Social Research.

Kearney, P., Plax, T. G., Richmond, V. P., & McCroskey, J. C. (1984). Power in the classroom IV: Teacher communication techniques as alternatives to discipline. In R. N. Bostrom (Ed.), *Communication Yearbook 8* (pp. 724–746). Beverly Hills, CA: Sage.

Kearney, P., Plax, T. G., Richmond, V. P., & McCroskey, J. C. (1985). Power in the classroom III: Teacher communication techniques and messages. *Communication Education, 34*, 19–28.

McCroskey, J. C. (1992). *An introduction to communication in the classroom* (Ch. 8). Edina, MN: Burgess International Group.

McCroskey, J. C., & Richmond, V. P. (1983). Power in the classroom I: Teacher and student perceptions. *Communication Education, 32*, 175–184.

McCroskey, J. C., Richmond, V. P., Plax, T. G., & Kearney, P. (1985). Power in the classroom V: Behavior alteration techniques, communication training, and learning. *Communication Education, 34*, 214–226.

Plax, T. G., Kearney, P., McCroskey, J. C., & Richmond, V. P. (1986). Power in the classroom VI: Verbal control strategies, nonverbal immediacy, and affective learning. *Communication Education, 35*, 43–55.

Richmond, V. P. (1990). Communication in the classroom: Power and motivation. *Communication Education, 39*, 181–184.

Richmond, V. P., Davis, L. M., Saylor, K., & McCroskey, J. C. (1984). Power in organizations: Communication techniques and messages. *Human Communication Research, 11*, 85–108.

Richmond, V. P., & McCroskey, J. C. (1984). Power in the classroom II: Power and learning. *Communication Education, 33*, 125–136.

Richmond, V. P., & McCroskey, J. C. (Eds.). (1992). *Power in the classroom: Communication, control, and concern*. Hillsdale, NJ: Lawrence Erlbaum.

Richmond, V. P., McCroskey, J. C., & Davis, L. M. (1982). Individual differences among employees, management communication style, and employee satisfaction: Replication and satisfaction. *Human Communication Research, 8*, 170–188.

Richmond, V. P., McCroskey, J. C., & Davis, L. M. (1986). The relationship of supervisor use of power and affinity-seeking strategies with subordinate satisfaction. *Communication Quarterly, 34,* 178–193.

Richmond, V. P., McCroskey, J. C., Kearney, P, & Plax, T. G. (1987). Power in the classroom VII: Linking behavior alteration techniques to cognitive learning. *Communication Education, 36,* 1–12.

Richmond, V. P., McCroskey, J. C., & Roach, D. K. (1997). Communication and decision making styles, power base usage, and satisfaction in marital dyads. *Communication Quarterly, 45,* 410–426.

Richmond, V. P., Wagner, J. P., & McCroskey, J. C. (1983). The impact of perceptions of leadership style, use of power, and conflict management style on organizational outcomes. *Communication Quarterly, 31,* 27–36.

Wheeless, L. R., Barraclough, R., & Stewart, R. (1983). Compliance-gaining and power in persuasion. In R. N. Bostrom (Ed.), *Communication Yearbook 7* (pp. 105–145). Beverly Hills, CA: Sage.

DISCUSSION QUESTIONS

1. What is the relationship between power and influence?

2. As a student in a classroom, what type(s) of power do you think you possess?

3. If you are attempting to create an advertising campaign to get teens to stop smoking, what type of power do you think is important?

4. In the health care setting, which type of influence do you think is possible to achieve? Why?

5. You are having an argument with your roommate about taking out the trash. Which behavioral alteration technique do you think would be the most effective to get her or him to take out the trash? Why?

9

Public Speaking

OBJECTIVES

- Explain why public speaking is considered monological.

- Explain the two disadvantages of the public speaking format.

- Understand how communication apprehension is exhibited in the public context.

- Differentiate between the three general purposes of speeches.

- Understand the different ways to organize a speech.

- Explain the steps in Monroe's motivated sequence.

- Understand why memorizing a speech can be detrimental to a speaker's performance.

- Explain why both verbal and nonverbal immediacy are important in public speaking.

- Explain what is meant by *extemporaneous speaking*.

- Understand how to effectively handle question-and-answer periods.

- Differentiate between hearing and listening.

- Understand why receivers may not be able to listen to a message.

- Explain the seven things receivers need to do to be critical listeners.

Public speaking is one of the most written about topics in Western history. The first known document written about public speaking was the *Precepts* written by Ptah-Hotep for the Pharaoh Djedkare Izezi's son as guidance in effective communication around 2200 B.C. Since Ptah-Hotep wrote the *Precepts*, many thinkers have written about how to effectively speak in public. Although many people have written about public speaking, today few people deliver more than a small handful of formal public speeches in their entire lives. Yet, in a national survey of citizens of the United States, it was found that fear of public speaking is the number one fear of Americans.

Most students have given only a few speeches by the time they enter college, and many think they have given far fewer than they actually have. Speech making is a common activity in elementary and secondary schools, although it often goes under other names: show and tell, oral reading, oral book reports, current events, science projects, and so on.

Some schools offer formal classes in public speaking, and many have debate and forensics (competitive speech and oral interpretation of literature) programs for students who want to enhance their speaking skills. However, the vast majority of students graduating from high school have no formal training in public speaking. Most students are expected to speak in public with no training while being publicly evaluated on their performance! Would we send a football team on the field without having ever practiced or learned the game? Of course not! It certainly is not surprising that people feel

Senator Barack Obama addresses the 2004 Democratic National Convention.

apprehensive about public speaking because they do not know how to deliver speeches in public effectively.

This chapter is not designed to ensure that you will be a polished public speaker. The chapter is designed to give you a more realistic perspective on your chances of being a successful speaker. This chapter will point to the basic skills that you can master to speak in public with a modicum of confidence and success.

NATURE OF PUBLIC SPEAKING

Public speaking is *oral communication in a one-to-many, monological format*. Let's break down this definition by looking at the various parts of the definition. *One-to-many* suggests only one person is functioning as the primary source of verbal and nonverbal messages at a given time, but the source of the message has many receivers. Although a speaker can deliver a speech to only one person, more likely a speaker and the audience member would switch into dyadic interaction under such circumstances. The planned public speech would most likely not be given as planned because the rhetorical situation (the situation in which an individual's understanding or behavior can be changed through a given message) has been altered.

The number of people in the audience for a public speech may vary from a few to a few hundred, if the speaker can speak loudly. An audience may grow to a few thousand with an effective microphone (public address) system, or the audience may grow to several million with the assistance of radio, television, and/or film. In this chapter, we will restrict ourselves to the live, nonmediated level of public speaking, which is the one most people will encounter. We will, however, take note of the impact of media on all forms of communication in Chapter 14.

When we use the term *monological*, we are referring to the public speaker being the only person talking for a given period—the length of the speech. This is the normal pattern for public speaking, although many experienced speakers, particularly when talking to relatively small audiences, will invite audience members to stop the speaker in order to ask questions or add comments. However, audiences usually do not expect such an invitation to interrupt, and without that invitation, most people will avoid breaking in because it is considered very rude. It is much more common for people to hold any questions or comments until the speaker has finished and formally requests such interaction with the audience.

Often, there is more than one speaker present. Such formats as a symposium or debate provide for *serial* monologues—one person speaking after another without real interaction between the speakers. These are generally quite formal occasions at which no one is expected to interrupt except a designated moderator who introduces speakers and lets the speakers know when their time is expired. The audience may be invited to ask questions when all the speakers have completed their presentations, but in the case of debates, audiences rarely have the opportunity to actively engage the speakers.

Although not explicitly included in our definition of public speaking, audience feedback is an important factor in nonmediated public speaking events. Audience feedback permits the speaker to judge how her or his ideas are being received, and allows the speaker to adapt during the speech to make it more effective. How the audience responds not only has a major impact on the speaker (Gardiner, 1972), but also can have a major impact on the members of the audience itself (Hylton, 1971).

These three characteristics of public speaking (monological, large number of receivers, and availability of feedback) provide important advantages to the communicator. Because public speaking is monological, the speaker can carefully prepare a speech in advance so the verbal message will be exactly the way he or she wants. Having many receivers permits greater impact with less effort than would be necessary to contact each audience member individually. Having available feedback permits the speaker to adjust the verbal and nonverbal messages to better fit the audience and increase the likelihood of achieving the purpose of the speech.

There are two disadvantages of the public speaking format. The first disadvantage is that public speaking usually is noninteractive; therefore, audience feedback for the most part is completely nonverbal. Misunderstandings and disagreements by audience members may not become known to the source, so the speech may fail without the speaker knowing that the speech has failed or why it failed. This disadvantage can be overcome, however, if the speaker is willing to enable audience participation during a speech by asking her or his audience questions and allowing the audience to make comments. In this way, the interactive nature of interpersonal communication can supplement the traditionally monological nature of public speaking.

The second disadvantage to public speaking is that this communication context is likely to be accompanied by much higher apprehension by the speaker than any other context. Research in the area of communication apprehension (CA) discussed in Chapter 3 has shown that public CA is by far the most common form of CA. This problem can be dealt with if the speaker can gain an accurate perspective on the public speaking process. Richmond and McCroskey (1995) noted, "While only 20 percent of the population experiences high traitlike communication apprehension, estimates run as high as 80 percent of the population for generalized context communication apprehension—over 70 percent for the public speaking context alone" (p. 46). In essence, the vast majority of people are "scared speechless."

GAINING PERSPECTIVE

Fear of the unknown is normal. Remember when you were a child and became frightened when the lights were turned off? What happened when the lights were turned back on? If you were like most children (or adults, for that matter), the fear went away immediately when you saw there was nothing to be afraid of in your room.

Fear or anxiety about public speaking for many is much like fear of the dark. If you don't know "what is out there waiting for you," it is reasonable to be fearful and anxious. For most, however, when the "light is turned on," the boogeyman goes away. Just reading this chapter and Chapter 3 on communication apprehension can help you gain perspective, and therefore gain more control of the public speaking experience. The more you know about the public-speaking process, the more light is shed on what was previously the unknown. There are many books that explain the public communication process in considerable detail (e.g., McCroskey, 2006; Richmond & Hickson, 2002), and reading such a book can add a great deal of light to the situation, as can taking a formal course in public speaking.

There are two things you should remember. First, most people are not asked to give many speeches in their lives, and even when they are, it is often possible to refuse with no major penalty. Second, if you are one of those who must give speeches, you can learn more about the process, and as you get more experience you are likely to get better at it—and become less fearful.

Let's go ahead and reexamine your scores on the public-context portion of the Personal Report of Communication Apprehension–24 (PRCA-24) you filled out in Scale 11 in the appendix. Check to see what your score was on the public speaking dimension. If it is above 18, that indicates you feel a good bit of apprehension about speaking in this context. Be aware that if you score between 18 and 30, **YOU ARE NORMAL**. That is what most people, of all ages, score.

Yes, most people are apprehensive about giving speeches. When you see and listen to people speak, you may or may not be aware they are anxious. Some people while speaking will turn red, shake, shift their weight constantly, pace, sweat, and so on. If you recognize their fear, how do you feel about them? If you answer, "Sympathetic," you are like most people. That is the way most people will also feel about *you* if you appear frightened while speaking before them. Just like you would be if you were in the audience, they are cheering for you and hoping you will succeed. Of course, there may be some jerks who would like to see you really mess up your speech. Who cares what those jerks think?

Finally, you should recognize there is no such thing as fear, anxiety, stage fright, or whatever you want to call it. These are only labels people use to represent their physiological activation. Others use labels like *excitement*, *thrill*, and *exhilaration* to represent the same activation. The difference is in one's mind. If you can change the label, you probably can change the experience. Fear of public speaking, or the thrill of public speaking, is analogous to the fear of roller coasters or the thrill of roller coasters. People who fear roller coasters and people who are thrilled by such rides actually are experiencing much the same physiological reaction. They simply give it different labels, and experience it differently. Recognize that as you approach a public speaking opportunity, your body is becoming physiologically aroused to allow you to be "on top of your game" as you talk to your audience. Recognizing that activation as your friend, rather than your enemy, will go a long way toward making stage fright a memory rather than a presence.

▣ THE BASIC SKILLS

To become an outstanding and highly effective public speaker is not easy, and it requires concentrated study and much experience. You probably have little or no need to set such excellence as your goal. However, if you plan to be a member of the clergy, be a trial attorney, run for political office, be a college professor, or enter another occupation that requires you to be a professional public speaker, you should constantly hone your public speaking skills. You should try to get as much experience in as many different public speaking settings as you can while you are in school because such training and experience are very costly outside the college environment.

If your desired profession does not involve a great amount of public speaking, then you probably can become a satisfactory speaker for most occasions by learning a few basics. Mastery of these basic skills can prepare you to deal with most public speaking demands in your everyday life. These basic skills include topic selection, organizing the speech, introductions, conclusions, and delivery. We will consider each in turn.

Topic Selection

The choice of a topic on which to give a speech often is an intimidating decision to people taking classes in public speaking. Students often just don't know what to talk about in their speeches. The plight is real; however, many students really are not motivated to talk at all about anything. They have no purpose to accomplish. Students often feel that the class does not really want to hear them talk about anything, either; or, worse yet, students may feel they really do not know anything the other class members do not already know. However, in classrooms students cannot choose the option that any sensible person would choose in the "real" world—refuse the invitation to speak! In fact, you may be required to give a speech in the class for which you're reading this textbook. Don't worry—we are going to present you with some clear ideas on how to select a killer speech topic.

Choosing a speech topic in the "real world" is generally very easy because you have very specific guidelines given to you or goals you personally want to accomplish through your speech. You may even choose to seek the opportunity to speak because you have a purpose to accomplish that is important to you. Others request that you speak to them because they believe (rightly or wrongly) that you have expertise or views that they will benefit from by hearing you. In both cases, you will know what you are talking about, or the public speaking opportunity is highly unlikely to arise. If you don't have an objective to accomplish or if some other people do not believe you have something important to share with them, then why are you giving a speech?

In public speaking, we often refer to three basic reasons, or purposes, why people give speeches. A speaker's *general purpose* designates the intent behind the speech, and is usually phrased in the form of a basic prepositional phrase starting with the word *to* followed by one of three different actions: inform, persuade, or entertain (evoke). A speaker should be aware of her or his general purpose because the different purposes lend themselves to different types of speech material and practices. Speeches that are designed to inform, for example, are information generation speeches, and are developed with the sole purpose of giving information to one's audience, not trying to convince an audience to agree with the information or make a behavioral or psychological change. On the other hand, speeches that are designed to persuade are purely designed with the purpose of giving a speech to an audience that will cause the audience to agree with the information or make a behavioral or psychological change in favor of the speaker's point of view. Lastly, speeches that are designed to entertain are designed to evoke some level of emotion from the audience. Speeches that fall into this category include speeches in which a person presents another speaker or a group of speakers, someone roasts another person, or someone simply tries to entertain her or his audience. In fact, there are professional speakers called *humorists* whose career is to entertain large audiences with their speaking abilities.

Once you know what your general purpose for speaking is, it is very important that you keep this purpose in mind while speaking. If you want to persuade a group of people to give you something, giving an informative speech would not be very useful because people are rarely moved by simple information. Conversely, if you have been asked to give a speech on an informative topic, people will get very offended if you spend the entire time trying to persuade them to a specific position.

In the real world, the choice of topic may or may not be given to you. Meeting planners (people in charge of all planning for a meeting, which includes logistics, meals, hotel arrangements, room sets, travel, and hiring speakers) often have a specific topic in mind for an audience and then will seek out speakers who are perceived as experts on that topic. If you want to learn more about the professional world of public speaking, Dottie and Lilly Walters's *Speak and Grow Rich* (2002) is seen as the industry bible for professional speaking. In this book, you will learn how to create speeches that meeting planners will be interested in and how to catapult yourself to expert status. When it comes to creating a speech topic that you want to be seen as an expert in, the speech topic should be something you know about and something you have reason to be motivated to talk about. If you are not motivated and excited about your topic, your audience will not be excited about your topic either. Furthermore, if a meeting planner asks you to deliver a speech on a specific topic, and some benefit to you is promised or implicit, giving the speech you've been asked to give is a necessity. If you do not feel that you are an expert in the area the meeting planner is asking you to speak on, either suggest an alternative speaker you know who is an expert or refuse the invitation. Nothing is worse than getting up and giving a speech knowing that you are not the expert on the topic and shouldn't be the one delivering the speech at all.

Organizing the Speech

Speeches have three parts: the introduction, body, and conclusion. The body of the speech should be prepared first; then it will be relatively easy to introduce it and conclude it. The body of the speech contains the main content. Generally, speeches can be organized in a variety of ways. In this section, we are going to examine the following speech organization types that can be used for either informative or persuasive speeches: chronological, topical, cause and effect, biographical, comparison and contrast, problem–cause–solution, spatial, and psychological. We will also discuss one speech organization type specifically designed for persuasive speeches: Monroe's motivated sequence.

Chronological.   The first speech pattern for arranging main ideas is what is referred to as the *chronological pattern*. The chronological pattern places the main ideas in the order in which items appear—whether backwards or forwards. For example, if you wanted to give a speech on the first three American presidents, you would first talk about George Washington, then discuss John Adams, and lastly discuss Thomas Jefferson. You could also reverse the list and start your speech with Thomas Jefferson, then work your way backwards in history to George Washington.

Topical/Categorical.   The topical, or categorical, speech format involves dividing the content into its logical subpoints. Each subpoint is a major idea for your speech. There should never be more than a few such subpoints—three to five in most speeches. They may be arbitrary categories (oranges, watermelons, and grapes) or employ some system that arises out of the topic. Examples include past, present, and future; African issues, Asian issues, Australian issues, European issues, South American issues, and North American issues; straight female behaviors, straight male behaviors, gay male behaviors, and lesbian behaviors; before 1800, the nineteenth century, and the twentieth century; hereditary diseases, viral diseases, and bacterial diseases; and so on. Topical sequences emerge from an examination of the topic itself. Usually, the ordering that should be used is clear. If the ordering of the subtopics isn't clear, you will probably have no problems keeping your audience with you, but make sure the audience can easily move from subtopic to subtopic along with you.

Cause and Effect.   The cause-and-effect speech format is used to explain what causes a specific situation and what the effects of that situation are. For example, consider the statement that there is currently a problem in the United States with teenage smoking, which is caused by a lack of parental involvement. The effect of teen smoking on the health care system could be an increased likelihood of lung cancer later in life. In this example, whether the above statements are right or wrong is not the question, but rather how the format is employed. If you are organizing a cause-and-effect speech, you will first start with a simple discussion of what the problem is. Then you will discuss what you believe has caused the problem, and then lastly end with a discussion about the effects of the problem you are addressing.

Biographical.   Another common format is the biographical speech format. The biographical format is generally used when a speaker wants to describe a person's life. If you are going to give a speech about a biography of a famous athlete, you might use her or his childhood, her or his teenage years, and the athlete's professional career as your three main points. In essence, the biographical format is simply a telling of someone's life in narrative form, but you create a series of specific life periods that you clearly discuss.

Comparison and Contrast.   Another method for creating main points is the comparison-and-contrast method. Although this format clearly lends itself to two main points, you can easily create a third point by giving basic information about what is being compared and what is being contrasted. For example, if you are giving a speech about two different modes of transportation, you could start by discussing what the two modes of transportation are separately. Then you could talk about the similarities and differences between the two modes of transportation.

Problem–Cause–Solution.   Another format for creating distinct main points is the problem–cause–solution format. In this specific format, you discuss what a problem is, what is causing the problem to occur, and then what the solution should be to correct the problem. This format clearly lends itself to a persuasive topic because you will be offering a solution to your audience. For example, if you wanted to give a speech on the problems with outsourcing jobs to foreign countries, you could start by explaining how many U.S. citizens are losing their jobs (the problem). You could then explain how many corporations find it cheaper to hire skilled labor in Third World countries and pay them considerably less (the cause). And lastly, you could discuss how Congress needs to step in and penalize corporations that send U.S. jobs overseas (the solution).

Spatial.   The spatial order format for main point development is best used when you have different locations that can exist independently as your main points. For example, if you want to give a speech about the countries that border Israel, you could start by talking about Jordan, then talk about Syria, Lebanon, and lastly Egypt. Another example would be talking about different structures within the body: the brain, the heart, and the gastrointestinal tract. The basic reason for choosing this format for organizing your main points is to make it clear that the main points have specific locations.

Psychological.   The last way to organize your main ideas within a speech is through a psychological order, or *a* leads to *b* and *b* leads to *c*. One speaker we know uses a psychological order to speak about how she became a world-renowned advertising agent. She first talks about how hard it was for her as a mother of a baby girl to find work (a). She started pushing her baby's carriage from business to business, looking for businesses that needed a freelance writer for advertising copy (b). She ultimately turned her little advertising copy business into a multimillion dollar business and became the first prominent female advertising executive in the world (c). This speech is contingent on all four areas. If the speaker had not been a single mother looking for work, who knows where her professional life may have taken her?

Monroe's Motivated Sequence.   The motivated sequence was introduced into the study of communication about sixty years ago by Monroe and remains one of the most useful pervasive organizational patterns yet devised (Gronbeck, McKerrow, Ehninger, & Monroe, 1994). It is particularly well suited to the speech designed to elicit change in behavior. It includes five steps: attention, need, satisfaction, visualization, and action.

1. *Attention step.* This essentially is what we have called the introduction to the speech. It is designed to get the audience in the mood to hear what we have to say.
2. *Need step.* This is the first step in the body of the speech. It addresses what is wrong with what is currently going on, that is, what the problem is. It identifies causes and effects, and explains them to the audience.
3. *Satisfaction step.* This is the solution to the problem that is outlined in the need step. The solution itself is explained, and then it is related to the problem so that the audience can see how it would satisfy the need for a change. Enough detail

should be provided to be certain the audience understands how the solution will work, but not so much as to overpower them with those details.

4. *Visualization step.* This step functions as a transition from the body of the speech to the conclusion. It helps the audience see what things should be like once this solution has been put into place. *Positive* visualization outlines how good things will be if the proposed solution is adopted. *Negative* visualization, in contrast, outlines how bad things will be if the proposed solution is *not* adopted.

5. *Action step.* This step lets the audience know exactly what is expected of them, when, and how. It includes an appeal to them to behave in certain ways. This step is what we normally call the conclusion to the speech.

These organizational sequences should be adequate for most speeches you will need to give. They are simple and straightforward. They should help make your speech clear and avoid audience confusion.

When developing the body of the speech, always remember the KISS injunction—"Keep it simple, stupid!" As one cynic once put it, "No one ever failed at public speaking by *underestimating* the ability of their audience to understand." Listening to a speech is not like reading a technical manual. If you don't get the speech right the first time, your audience can't just reread or rewind the speech to determine what you meant. Therefore, clarity and simplicity are very positive virtues in public speaking. *Clarity* refers to making sure that the words coming out of your mouth can be clearly interpreted by your audience members, so avoid jargon and complex words that are not necessary. As for simplicity, always choose the path that is easiest for your audience.

One thing to remember is the principles of primacy and recency when developing a speech. *Primacy* is the idea that people will remember the information delivered at the beginning of a speech, whereas *recency* is the idea that people remember the information delivered right at the end of a speech. For this reason, you want to make sure that your speech's introduction and conclusion are very strong.

Introducing the Speech

The purpose of the introduction within a speech is to capture the audience's attention and direct that attention toward the following content. Generally, you should tell your audience what you are going to talk about and why you are going to talk about that topic. Emphasis should be placed on why the audience should care about what you are going to say. If the audience can't see why they should care, they most likely will not listen to you.

The two reasons speech introductions fall flat before a live audience are when a speaker (1) apologizes for not being a good speaker ("Unaccustomed as I am to public speaking . . .") or (2) tells a "funny" joke that no one else thinks is funny ("On the way over here today, I encountered two pygmy ponies. . . ."). Be assured, if you are a lousy speaker, you will not need to inform the audience of that; they will figure it out soon enough! Your apology will not overcome the fact that you have wasted their time or bored them to tears. On the other hand, without the warning, they may not notice your shortcomings at all, particularly if you really are an adequate speaker.

Concluding the Speech

When approaching the conclusion of a speech, it is good to keep in mind the three S's of public speaking: stand up, speak up, and shut up. These three injunctions roughly relate to the introduction (stand up), body (speak up), and conclusion (shut up) of the speech, respectively. Many speakers find the final injunction to be the most difficult to follow because they just can't sit down and shut up. You hear the speaker say, "In conclusion," but ten minutes later he or she is still rambling on and the audience begins to look like corpses in chairs. Usually when a speaker has a hard time concluding her or his speech, it is because he or she has not planned the speech's conclusion in advance. Speakers may have worked on the body of the speech, and even the introduction, but thought the conclusion would just take care of itself. It won't.

The primary function of a speech's conclusion is to let the audience know what you most want your audience to remember or do, so the conclusion should be focused on this objective. Sometimes it is good to summarize the main points you have discussed. In other cases the conclusion should focus on exactly what you want the audience to do or think. Just as you should not apologize in your introduction, you should not thank your audience in your conclusion—unless you really have imposed on them. If you sought them out and encouraged them to come to hear you, such as happens for a political candidate, a gracious "Thank you" certainly is in order. However, often people say thanks because they can't think of anything else to say at the end, so make sure you plan your conclusion because it may be harder to shut up and sit down than you think!

▣ DELIVERING THE SPEECH

Preparing the speech is one thing; delivering it is quite another. For the most part, anyone with a small amount of intelligence can prepare a very good speech. As you have seen by reading the sections above, preparing a speech really isn't that hard, but actually standing up before a live audience and giving the speech is when many people fail.

However, giving a speech really isn't too difficult either. Let us begin with the advice that is easiest to follow. (1) Never write out and read (or try to memorize) your speech unless your speech will occur in a very formal situation when any inadvertent misstatement could have very serious repercussions. And (2) if you do not write or memorize your speech, do have easy-to-read notes showing your main ideas so that if you have a mental block, you can quickly get yourself back on track. Even professional speakers with years of experience can go blank while giving a speech, so always make sure you have notes on hand just in case you forget what you're supposed to be saying.

Some novice speakers are so intent on being fully prepared they write out their entire speech so nothing will be forgotten. This practice virtually ensures a poor presentation. Few of us are trained to be good oral readers. Therefore, the reading will sound awkward and cause the audience to question your competence. People often make this mistake at professional conventions. As a result, many sessions are poorly attended, many people leave during presentations, and often the few people in the audience are totally bored. In fact, Toastmasters, the largest international organization devoted to teaching people public speaking skills, does not allow speakers to use manuscripts until their final speech in the program because manuscript speeches are so hard to pull off successfully.

This student is delivering a speech in front of her peers.

Even if one is a good reader, by reading a speech manuscript you lose your ability to change your speech based on audience feedback while speaking. Furthermore, when you read a speech it is hard for you as a speaker to pay attention to audience feedback. And even if feedback is noticed, there is little the reading speaker can do about it because speech adaptation is not really possible when the speech is already written out word for word.

The only thing worse than reading a speech is memorizing the speech. If you have the slightest tendency to be nervous, forget ever memorizing your speech. Nothing makes memory go away faster than a little nervousness. Standing in front of an audience, not remembering what to say next, has to be one of the most unpleasant experiences a person could have. One of the authors of this textbook competed in forensics through high school and college and had a serious memorization mishap. Once while giving a ten-minute memorized speech, he completely blanked during the introduction. While he was trying to remember where he was in his speech, his mind started racing and a variety of inappropriate and colorful words started racing around in his head. Unfortunately, he later found out that not only was he thinking about the inappropriate and colorful words, but those words were actually coming out of his mouth as well. In essence, although memorization may seem like a good idea while practicing a speech, memorization can be very problematic if a speaker is not very skilled and able to handle "brain farts," which are inevitable.

Instead of memorizing or reading, we recommend you present your speech "extemporaneously." Do not confuse this with "impromptu" speaking. When you deliver an impromptu speech, you have no advance preparation. You are called on, you speak, so you must prepare as you go. Extemporaneous speaking, in contrast, includes careful preparation, following the advice in the previous sections of this chapter. The speaker will have the main points of her or his speech outlined on note cards or the first page of a legal pad. These notes can be held by the speaker or placed conveniently nearby on a table, desk, or lectern; however, many people end up hiding behind their notes, which really hurts their nonverbal delivery while speaking. Although you shouldn't hide behind your notes, you should not attempt to hide the notes either. The audience is going to know you have notes—and they couldn't care less, unless you appear to be sneaking peaks at them.

Having notes and speaking extemporaneously permit you to do the most important thing to ensure effective delivery: *be verbally and nonverbally immediate with your audience*. As we noted in Chapter 5, immediacy is at the core of effective communication. Get close to your audience. Avoid standing behind a podium or lectern because it places a barrier between you and your audience. Also, don't use a microphone unless absolutely necessary because technology can be more problematic than it is worth. If you do have to use a microphone, try to get one that is not attached and doesn't require you to hold it (e.g., a wireless lavaliere or headset microphone). Furthermore, avoid electrical audio-visual aids (videos, slide shows, PowerPoint, etc.) whenever you can. If you must show something to the audience, remember that a visual aid is just that—an *aid*. Too often, speakers get *so* completely wrapped up in creating their visual aids that they completely forget about the content of their speech. No one wants to see a flashy speech that is devoid of good content. One alternative to an electronic visual aid is a handout. Handouts are useful either as an alternative or in addition to a visual aid because they enable the audience to continue to pay attention to a speaker while the speaker explains what is on the handout (as opposed to frantically trying to write down notes from the visual aid), and the audience can take the handout home with them when the speaker is finished speaking. When it comes to electronic visual aids, Murphy's Law is virtually absolute for novice speakers: if the electronic device on which you depend can break down, it will break down. All electronic devices *can* break down, so you must be prepared for breakage if you use electronic visual aids, and always have a backup plan ready to go.

Immediate delivery includes always maintaining eye contact with your audience when you are not glancing at your notes. Never let an audience member feel they can look away from you without your noticing their inattention. By demanding their eye contact, you ensure their attention. If you don't look at your audience, they will stop looking at you, and eventually stop paying attention to you. Don't give them that chance.

Extemporaneous, immediate delivery permits you to *interact* with your audience rather than *present* your speech. You can, if the audience is not too large, invite them to ask questions while you are talking with (not *at*) them. This gives the public speaking event the atmosphere and electricity of the interpersonal interaction and permits you to adapt to the responses of the audience. Remember, if you forget where you are in your speech, you have your notes nearby.

Other aspects of immediacy should also be remembered: move around the room rather than stand still in one place—but avoid just pacing back and forth; face the audience directly as much as possible (never talk to the screen when a visual aid is projected); use meaningful gestures such as illustrators and emblems, but avoid adaptors that will distract the audience; wear apparel that is appropriate but not too formal; avoid wearing artifacts that may distract the audience; watch your use of time, because going substantially overtime is very discourteous and is virtually certain to cause a loss of attention; and use lots of vocal variety, because nothing kills attention like a monotonous voice.

If the above seems to sound a lot like advice one would give to a person who asks how to be a good conversationalist, that is no accident. These are the same communication skills discussed earlier for interpersonal interactions, just applied to slightly different communication contexts.

Handling Questions

The final part of many public speaking events consists of responding to questions from audience members. Of course, audience questions need not be held until the end unless you have some good reason to do so. In any event, the way to handle questions is the same in either case, so we recommend the following:

1. *Repeat the question before answering it*. This accomplishes two things. First, people sitting behind the questioner are not likely to hear the question otherwise. Second, in case you have misunderstood the question, the questioner has the opportunity to clear up the confusion before you waste time answering the wrong question.

2. *Be direct with your answer, if possible*. Do not attempt to evade answering a question. If you don't want to answer it, say so, and explain why. Otherwise, just answer the question simply and clearly.

3. *Don't be afraid to say you don't know*. Never try to bluff your way out of a question. If you don't know the answer to an audience member's question, just say so. Audiences usually are very understanding when a speaker acknowledges that he or she does not have all the answers. Sometimes it is effective to tell the questioner you don't know but will try to find out and get back to her or him with an answer later. Of course, it is acceptable to speculate about what the answer might be—if you clearly indicate that is what you are doing.

4. *Try to take questions from various parts of the audience*. People of like mind often sit together in an audience. To get as much variety in perspectives as possible, pick questioners from different places in your audience.

5. *If possible, stay after the scheduled concluding time so that other audience members may ask questions*. Sometimes speakers run out of time before some important questions get asked. In other cases, some people who really want to ask a question just can't bring themselves to do so in front of all of the other people, but they can ask one-on-one. Give them that opportunity if you can.

Recognize that the more immediate you are, the more effective you are likely to be. Also, the more effective you are, the more likely people will have questions. If no one has a question for you, it may be because you have been so clear there just is nothing more to ask. Or it may be because the audience members are so bored they just want to get it over and get out of there. Usually, it is easy to tell which is the case in the given situation.

EFFECTIVE LISTENING

The last part of this chapter is going to look at public speaking from the receiver's viewpoint and talk about how to effectively listen to speeches. One of the first things an individual must understand to learn about effective listening is the difference between hearing and active listening (Wolff & Marsnik, 1992). Hearing is the physiological process in which an individual interprets sounds. For example, when you walk into a crowded room, you will probably hear many different conversations going on at once, but this does not mean you are listening to all of them. Active listening, on the other hand, is an acquired and refined skill, and refers to the ability to listen to a speech in a nonjudgmental fashion while weighing the validity of the speaker's arguments. Although most people can hear a speech with no problems (assuming an individual is not hearing impaired), not everyone has the ability to listen actively while a person is speaking. There are a number of reasons why a person may not be able to actively listen to a speaker.

The first reason a person may not listen actively to a speaker relates to receiver distractions. Often, receivers are not in a frame of mind to actively listen to a speaker because the receivers are distracted by noise, both external and internal (Nabelek, Tampas, & Burchfield, 2004). For example, maybe you're trying to listen to a speech during class while one of the groundskeepers is mowing right outside the window of the classroom. The sound caused by the mowing (physical distraction) could literally prevent a receiver from being able to hear what is being said, which would also prevent active listening from occurring. Another receiver may be feeling sick (internal-physiological distraction) or have just broken up with her or his significant other (internal-psychological distraction), and cannot focus on what a speaker is saying. Anytime a receiver is not able to focus 100 percent of her or his energy on a speaker's message, the receiver cannot actively listen to the speaker's message.

A second reason why people may not be able to actively listen relates to an individual's attention span. Although there is no perfect time limit for a speech, speakers should avoid lengthy speeches because people will quickly start to tune them out, even if they want to be there. One of the authors of this textbook remembers sitting through a six-hour lecture and slide presentation one evening by a well-sought-after professional speaker. Even though he had been waiting for months to view this lecture, it was physically impossible for the speaker to keep his attention that long.

A third reason why people may not be able to actively listen during a speech relates to receiver biases about either the speaker or the topic. For example, if a receiver is absolutely opposed to the death penalty, no matter how persuasive or effective a pro–death penalty speaker is, the receiver will not be able to attend to the message without creating a negative bias against the speaker. Any flaw that the receiver sees in the speaker's message will be exaggerated because the receiver is actively looking for reasons to disagree with the message, not trying to listen to the message itself.

A final reason why a receiver may not be able to critically listen to a speaker's message relates to receiver apprehension. Wheeless (1975) identified receiver apprehension as one of the potential reasons why many individuals have difficulty decoding messages. Wheeless (1975) defined receiver apprehension as "the fear of misinterpreting, inadequately processing, and/or not being able to adjust psychologically to messages sent by others" (p. 263). Basically, receiver apprehension occurs when individuals are cognitively unable to process information correctly because of internal factors (biological) or external factors (sender or noise). When information that is being presented is highly technical, the receiver may feel that the information is above the receiver and may start to question her or his own ability to understand the information, which can cause people to experience anxiety (Beatty & Payne, 1981). Once anxiety gets a hold of a receiver, the receiver then becomes focused more on the anxiety and less on the message being communicated. Wheeless, Preiss, and Gayle (1997) found that receiver apprehension was positively related to communication apprehension, so people who are apprehensive about being the source of a message are also apprehensive about being the receiver as well.

Up to this point, we've looked at reasons why receivers may not listen, but there is another communication trait that also is important when discussing listening: a person's willingness to listen. *Willingness to listen* is defined as a person's general level of desire to listen to others. A person's willingness to listen is the flip side to a person's willingness to communicate. Whereas willingness to communicate has a person acting as a source of information, willingness to listen has someone acting as a receiver of information (Richmond & Hickson, 2002). Scale 20 in the appendix contains the Willingness to Listen Scale created by Richmond and Hickson (2002). Scores on this scale should be between 24 and 120, with scores over 80 indicating a high willingness to listen and scores under 50 indicating a low willingness to listen. People who are highly willing to listen to other people view listening as an opportunity to gain information from other people, so they actively listen to other people regularly. People with a low willingness to listen are generally uncomfortable listening to information and probably will miss important information when it is presented to them.

Research has also shown that we can increase another person's willingness to listen. One way to increase another person's willingness to listen to a speech is to have a strong introduction. Andeweg and de Jong (1998) examined different types of introductions and found that anecdotes actually increased the audience's willingness to listen when compared to introductions that highlighted the speaker's credibility, introductions that showed how the speech topic related to the audience, and speeches with no introduction at all. Although Andeweg and de Jong suggest that demonstrating credibility and showing an audience how the speech relates to them personally are important, an anecdote can be used to gain attention better than the other two. Another way to increase your receivers' willingness to listen is to be a good listener yourself (Batty-Herbert, 2003). When people see you actively listening, they are more likely to listen to you when it is your turn to talk. However, if you are clearly not paying attention to the other person, they will not listen to you either, which is true whether you are listening to speeches or listening to people interpersonally.

Willingness to listen has also been shown to be related to a number of the personality and communication variables previously discussed in this textbook (Chapter 2). In a study conducted by Roberts and Vinson (1998), the researchers examined the relationships among willingness to listen, receiver apprehension, communication apprehension, and dogmatism. Overall, a person's willingness to listen was negatively related to all three variables. In essence, people who are afraid of information coming in are not going to be very willing to listen to that information. Also, people who experience anxiety as a source of information are not willing to listen to information as a receiver as well. Lastly, people who are highly dogmatic, or are very rigid in their thinking, are not very willing to listen to other people.

So far, we have looked at the differences between hearing and critical listening, and why people may not be able to critically listen during a speech. Now we're going to switch gears and talk about a number of strategies for increasing a receiver's ability to critically listen. There are two primary ways to help focus yourself as a receiver of a speech to ensure that you set yourself up to critically listen to a speaker. The first method listeners can employ is mapping. Mapping is the process in which a receiver of a message mentally analyzes a message as it occurs. In many ways, mapping is like grading a speech. First, you ask yourself about the purpose of the speech. Although picking out a speaker's purpose sounds easy, figuring out what a speaker is actually speaking about can often be fairly hard. Next, you want to determine what the main points of the speech are and whether the main points adequately support the speaker's purpose. The basic goal of mapping is to determine the argument(s) that a speaker is making. Once you know what a speaker's argument is, you can then determine whether the argument was supported by the speaker during her or his speech.

A second way a receiver can help focus her or himself to listen critically is by taking notes. Note taking is a written form of mapping. The key to note taking is realizing that it is impossible to write down every word a speaker says, so using key words in an outline format will help you as a receiver follow the speech more closely. While keeping a running outline of the speech, you will also want to jot down your own thoughts about what the speaker is saying. When you combine the speaker's thoughts with your thoughts, you will be able to evaluate the speech as a whole more clearly.

The last part of critical listening is often the most time-consuming part because it requires critical thinking. Most people in our world today do not delve into the content and arguments of the messages they hear. As a result, people are often persuaded to think and do things because they are not critically attending to the messages people send them. One type of message that people often do not critically analyze is advertising messages. Experts even suggest that people in the United States may witness six to nine thousand advertising messages a day, but many people do not even think that they are affected by advertising messages. Ask any parent whose child has seen any number of cereal commercials, and they'll tell you how effective advertising is. If advertising messages were not effective, companies would not spend billions of dollars annually trying to get consumers to buy products. Unfortunately, most people just listen to the messages and never really pay attention to what they are listening to, but when they enter a store, all of those messages follow them around and influence their buying habits. In order to become a more critical listener of messages, receivers need to think about seven different things.

1. Avoid accepting assertions based on faith. In other words, do not listen to a speaker and agree with her or him just because he or she told you so.

2. Recognize the difference between facts and opinions. Everyone has an opinion on something, but having an opinion doesn't make it true. Opinions innately have error

built into them because there is uncertainty. Facts are concrete and verifiable, so determine if a speaker's arguments are based on facts or based on her or his opinions.

3. See if the speaker's arguments are based on assumptions, or gaps in a logical sequence that people attempt to fill with information that may or may not be accurate. When listening to a speaker, try to see what kinds of assumptions he or she is making. Are the assumptions credible or faulty? And are there facts that would negate those assumptions?

4. Strive to be as nonjudgmental and open to a speech and speaker as possible. This does not mean that we have to agree with the speech when the speaker is done, but during the speech we need to listen as openly as possible.

5. Apply your own sense of reason and common sense to new ideas when you encounter them. If you are listening to a speaker and her or his speech just does not make sense to you logically, then you are probably listening to an illogical argument.

6. Take a speaker's ideas and apply them to ideas that you already have yourself. When you are trying to understand information, often it is easiest to understand the information in light of something you do know.

7. You need to know what kind of listener you are. Watson, Barker, and Weaver (1995) argued that there are four different listening styles: people, action, content, and time. The people-oriented listener is someone who attends to and is concerned with a source's emotional state. Listeners who are people oriented tend to empathize with their sources and are probably responsive communicators (Johnston, Weaver, Watson, & Barker, 2000). The second listening style, content-oriented listening, consists of listening behaviors that analyze the content of a source's message. Content-oriented listeners listen for logical argumentation within a message, prefer to listen to credible speakers, and will ask questions if they need more information to form an adequate opinion of the message itself. The third listening style, action-oriented listening, consists of listening behaviors that are focused on the desired action a source is asking for in her or his message. Action-oriented listeners tend to be task focused and really do not want to spend a lot of time listening. Action-oriented listeners want a source to tell them what action needs to be taken, and then either complete the task or not complete the task. For this reason, action-oriented listening is sometimes referred to as *task-oriented listening* and is contrasted with people-oriented listening. The last listening style, time-oriented listening, consists of listening behaviors that are focused with time limitations. Time-oriented listeners determine how much time they have to listen to a source's message and will interrupt a source if her or his message is boring or the source's time is up. Time-oriented listeners quite often use both verbal interruptions and nonverbal cues (e.g., no eye contact, playing with artifacts, or clearly looking at a watch or clock) to indicate that the interaction should wrap up quickly. Although Watson et al. (1995) believe there are four listening styles, this does not mean that each person falls into one of the four styles alone. In fact, Weaver, Richendoller, and Kirtley (1995) found that 40 percent of people listen with two or more distinct styles. In other words, it is very common for people to use different listening styles depending on their audience or the communicative context (Weaver et al., 1995).

In a study by Bodie and Villaume (2003), the researchers examined the relationships among the four listening styles, communication apprehension, and receiver apprehension. Overall, the results indicated that people-oriented listeners were not likely to be anxious when receiving information or when they are the sources of information interpersonally or in small groups. Furthermore, action-oriented and time-oriented listeners were slightly more likely to be apprehensive while receiving information and less likely to experience interpersonal communication apprehension. Ultimately, these results clearly indicate that knowing one's listening style is extremely important for active listening. To be an active listener, one must balance the relational-oriented and task-oriented listening styles.

CONCLUSION

Although public speaking may be the number one fear in the United States, our society is still built greatly on an individual's ability to speak. Political campaigns, religious meetings, classroom teaching, and business endeavors are all highly based on the ability of at least one person to engage in public speaking well. Although this chapter has not discussed every facet of public speaking, we do hope that this chapter has shown you how to start creating speeches, how to properly deliver them both verbally and nonverbally, and how to be a critical listener when listening to another person's speeches.

 ## KEY TERMS

action-oriented listening style 195
content-oriented listening style 195
people-oriented listening style 195

primacy 187
receiver apprehension 192
recency 187

time-oriented listening style 195
willingness to listen 193

 ## REFERENCES

Andeweg, B. A., & de Jong, J. C. (1998). "May I have your attention?" Exordial techniques in information oral presentations. *Technical Communication Quarterly*, 7, 271–284.

Batty-Herbert, K. (2003). Attention trainers: Are you a model listener? *Listening Professional*, 2, 14–19.

Beatty, M. J., & Payne, S. K. (1981). Receiver apprehension and cognitive complexity. *Western Journal of Speech Communication*, 45, 363–369.

Bodie, G. D., & Villaume, W. A. (2003). Aspects of receiving information: The relationship between listening preferences, communication apprehension, receiver apprehension, and communicator style. *International Journal of Listening*, 17, 47–67.

Gardiner, J. C. (1972). The effects of expected and perceived receiver response on source attitudes. *Journal of Communication*, 22, 289–299.

Gronbeck, B. E., McKerrow, R. E., Ehninger, D., & Monroe, A. H. (1994). *Principles and types of speech communication* (12th ed.). Glenview, IL: Scott, Foresman.

Hylton, C. (1971). Intra-audience effects: Observable audience response. *Journal of Communication*, 21, 253–265.

Johnston, M. K., Weaver, J. B., III, Watson, K. W., & Barker, L. B. (2000). Listening styles: Biological or psychological differences? *International Journal of Listening, 14*, 32–46.

McCroskey, J. C. (2006). *An introduction to rhetorical communication: A Western rhetorical perspective* (9th ed.). Boston: Allyn & Bacon.

Nabelek, A. K., Tampas, J. W., & Burchfield, S. B. (2004). Comparison of speech perception in background noise with acceptance of background noise in aided and unaided conditions. *Journal of Speech, Language & Hearing Research, 47*, 1001–1011.

Richmond, V. P., & Hickson, M., III. (2002). *Going public: A practical guide to public talk*. Boston: Allyn & Bacon.

Richmond, V. P., & McCroskey, J. C. (1995). *Communication: Apprehension, avodiance, and effectiveness* (4th ed.). Scottsdale, AZ: Gorsuch Scarisbrick

Roberts, C. V., & Vinson, L. (1998). Relationship among willingness to listen, receiver apprehension, communication apprehension, communication competence, and dogmatism. *International Journal of Listening, 12*, 40–56.

Walters, D., & Walters, L. (2002). *Speak and grow rich* (3rd ed.). Upper Saddle River, NJ: Prentice Hall.

Watson, K. W., Barker, L. L., & Weaver, J. B., III. (1995). The Listening Styles Profile (lsp-16): Development and validation of an instrument to assess four listening styles. *International Journal of Listening, 9*, 1–13.

Weaver, J. B., III, Richendoller, N. R., & Kirtley, M. D. (1995, November). Individual differences in communication style. Paper presented at the annual meeting of the Speech Communication Association, San Antonio, TX.

Wheeless, L. R. (1975). An investigation of receiver apprehension and social context dimensions of communication apprehension. *Speech Teacher, 24*, 261–268.

Wheeless, L. R., Preiss, R. W., & Gayle, B. M. (1997). Receiver apprehension, informational receptivity, and cognitive processing. In J. A. Daly, J. C. McCroskey, J. Ayers, T. Hopf, & D. Ayres (Eds.), *Avoiding communication: Shyness, reticence, and communication apprehension* (2nd ed.) (pp. 151–187). Cresskill, NJ: Hampton Press.

Wolff, F. I., & Marsnik, N. C. (1992). *Perceptive listening* (2nd ed.). Fort Worth, TX: Harcourt Brace Jovanovich.

FURTHER READING

Borchers, G. L. (1936). An approach to the problem of oral style. *Quarterly Journal of Speech, 22*, 14–117.

DeVito, J. A. (2000). *The elements of public speaking* (7th ed.). New York: Longman.

Grice, G. L., & Skinner, J. F. (2004). *Mastering public speaking* (5th ed.). Boston: Allyn & Bacon.

Lucas, S. F. (2001). *The art of public speaking* (7th ed.). Boston: McGraw-Hill.

McCroskey, J. C., Wrench, J. S., & Richmond, V. P. (2003). *Principles of public speaking*. Indianapolis, IN: College Network.

O'Hair, D., Rubenstein, H., & Stewart, R. (2004). *Pocket guide to public speaking*. Boston: Bedford St. Martin's.

Verderber, R. F. (2000). *The challenge of effective speaking* (11th ed.). Belmont, CA: Wadsworth.

Walters, L. (1993). *Secrets of successful speakers: How you can motivate, captivate, & persuade*. New York: McGraw-Hill.

Walters, L. (1995). *What to say when . . . you're dying on the platform: A complete resource for speakers, trainers, and executives*. New York: McGraw-Hill.

Walters, L. (2000). *Secrets of superstar speakers: Wisdom from the greatest motivators of our time*. New York: McGraw-Hill.

Winans, J. A. (1938). *Speech-making*. New York: Appleton-Century-Crofts.

DISCUSSION QUESTIONS

1. Give an example of when each general purpose of speaking is appropriate.

2. If you want to give a speech on Victorian dress, which speech organizational type would you want to use? Why?

3. Use the five parts of Monroe's motivated sequence to generate a speech on why dogs and cats should be neutered or spayed.

4. Why does speech memorization tend to backfire during an actual speech? How, then, should you prepare for a speech?

5. Why is it important to be a critical listener as compared to a passive hearer?

10

The Nature of Interpersonal Relationships

Characteristics of Relationships • Stages of Relationship Development • Coming Together • Coming Apart

Relational Expectancies

Short-Term Expectancies • Long-Term Expectancies

Gaining Affinity: Getting Others to Like *You*

Managing Interpersonal Conflict

The Nature of Conflict • Tolerance for Disagreement • Conflict Management Techniques • Preventing Conflict

Developing and Maintaining Interpersonal Relationships

OBJECTIVES

- Explain Schutz's three social needs that people attain through interpersonal communication.

- Explain the eight factors of interpersonal relationships.

- Explain Knapp's five stages of relationship development (coming together).

- Explain Knapp's five stages of relationship dissolution (coming apart).

- Understand why expectancies are important for both short-term and long-term relationships.

- Understand the short-term expectancies individuals have for interpersonal relationships.

- Understand the long-term expectancies individuals have for interpersonal relationships.

- Define and explain *affinity seeking*.

- Understand the various affinity-seeking strategies.

- Explain the basic nature of conflict.

- Define and explain *tolerance for disagreement*.

- Understand the relationship among disagreements, tolerance for disagreement, and incidence of actual conflicts.

- Explain the four conflict management techniques.

- Understand the relationship between behavior alteration techniques (BATs) and affinity building.

A fundamental component of the interpersonal communication process is the achievement of goals. Although a myriad of possible goals can be achieved through interpersonal communication, perhaps none is as central to our social survival as that of developing interpersonal relationships. We may not think of interpersonal relationship development as one of our focal concerns with communication, but it is. Just as our survival depends on the fulfillment of certain physiological and psychological needs, so too does it depend on our satisfying certain social needs.

Schutz (1960) maintains that we strive to satisfy three social needs through interpersonal communication: inclusion, control, and affection. *Inclusion* needs are those we attempt to fulfill to satisfy our need for belonging and association. Through interpersonal communication, we develop relationships with others to fit our need for social affiliation. To some extent, our attempt to satisfy these needs is what leads us to join fraternities, sororities, civic groups, professional associations, religious denominations, and the like. *Control* needs are those we strive to satisfy to fulfill our need to have influence over others. Control is the need to take charge of various social situations, and to use our leadership abilities. In trying to fulfill these needs, we are likely to take the upper hand in given situations. We may assume responsibility for the actions of ourselves and others, and engage in certain duties and actions to which other people would prefer to submit. Finally, *affection* needs are those we try to fulfill to satisfy our need to be liked and to like others. When we feel this type of need, we tend to do favors for others and to show them that we

This couple is engaging in interpersonal communication.

care for them. We often become quite responsive to their expressions of liking and concern for us.

According to Schutz (1960), the only way to satisfy needs for inclusion, control, and affection is by interacting with others. Largely, however, interpersonal interaction by itself is insufficient for fulfilling our social needs. What essentially allows us to satisfy these needs is the development of interpersonal relationships with others. Thus, the goal of relationship development through interpersonal communication is a major way of meeting some of our basic social needs.

In this chapter, we explore interpersonal relationship development and mainte-nance. We define and consider different characteristics of relationships. In addition, we define the stages through which relationships develop, how we go about getting people to "like" us, and various expectancies we have about our relationships. We also examine the problem of conflict and how it can undermine relationships.

 ## THE NATURE OF INTERPERSONAL RELATIONSHIPS

Characteristics of Relationships

The term *relationship*, as we will use it here and throughout the remainder of the book, refers to a variety of social affiliations (Phillips & Wood, 1983; Rubin, 1966). When we mention interpersonal relationships, we are not concerned only with intimate romantic relationships. We are also concerned with relationships such as those between siblings, parent and child, employer and employee, teacher and student, physician and patient, minister and churchgoer, and people of the same and opposite sexes. Perhaps the biggest difference between any two of these types of relationships rests with the role played by the respective member of each relationship (for example, teacher versus stu-dent, and sister versus brother). Beyond this difference, however, most interpersonal relationships are characterized by several factors. This section focuses on eight of these factors: variability, duration, frequency, revelation, meshing, support, anxiety reduction, and proximity.

Variability.   Variability is the characteristic of interpersonal relationships that indi-cates that the partners in the relationship engage in many different types of interactions. For example, two friends who work together at the same job interact in task-related sit-uations at work and in social situations after work. Similarly, a Catholic who has estab-lished a close friendship with her or his priest is likely to interact with the priest in a very formal way at church but in an informal way outside church.

Duration.   That interpersonal relationships last over some period is shown by the characteristic of *duration*. Any interpersonal relationship requires a considerable amount of time to fully develop. Because the parties to the relationship continue to receive rewards from their relationship, all else being equal, their relationship should endure. Generally, the longer a relationship's duration, the stronger that relationship is. Weak relationships tend not to endure.

Frequency.   Closely linked with duration is *frequency.* This characteristic indicates that people involved in an interpersonal relationship engage in interactions with each other regularly and often. Both duration and frequency are important to interpersonal relationships because the more we interact with an individual, the better we come to know that person. Contrast, for example, a teacher whom you have had as an instructor for more than one class with a teacher with whom you have had only one class. Chances are you know the former much better than the latter, simply because you have interacted with that person more often and for longer periods of time.

Revelation.   As an interpersonal relationship develops and matures, the individuals involved in the relationship share with each other their basic as well as their more personal attitudes and beliefs. This characteristic of relationships is known as *revelation,* and it satisfies one of our more essential interpersonal needs—revealing our thoughts and feelings to others. The amount of revelation we engage in is—up to a point—determined by the duration and frequency factors mentioned above. Generally, the longer we have known someone, and the more often we have interacted with that person, the more we are willing to reveal about ourselves to that person. High self-disclosure, as we noted in Chapter 5 usually does not occur early in relationships. Thus, more revelation can be expected to occur in a long-term relationship than in a relationship in which the individuals are new acquaintances.

Examining revelation in relationships stems from a theory called *social penetration theory* developed by Altman and Taylor (1973). Altman and Taylor theorized that initial relationships are characterized by a breadth of topics. *Breadth* refers to the number of topics discussed in a relationship (e.g., biographical data; preferences in clothing, food, and entertainment; and goals and aspirations). Early in relationships, people cover many topics but typically do not spend a lot of time deeply discussing any of those topics. After someone knows another person for a while, the breadth of topics starts to diminish, and people then start self-disclosing more intimate information about themselves, which is referred to as *depth* (e.g., topics relating to religious convictions, deeply held fears and fantasies, concept of self, and understanding of how we fit into the greater universe). Ultimately, social penetration theory states that in initial interactions, people opt for a breadth of topics, and as relationships become more intimate, the depth of topics discussed becomes more intimate, or deep, as well (West & Turner, 2004). Think of this theory like a giant onion. In the breadth part of self-disclosure, you're dealing with the external layer of the onion. Each layer of the onion represents a more intimate level of self-disclosure (Davis, 1973; Derlaga & Chaikin, 1973). External-layer self-disclosures may be things like "I like green beans" or "I'm a communication studies major." By the time you get to the very inner core of the onion, depth, you would disclose things like "I'm afraid of dying alone" or "I think I may be obsessive-compulsive." Clearly, there is a difference between the two types of self-disclosure. A second aspect of this theory posits that as relationships progress, we expect people to self-disclose at the same level we are disclosing for the relationship to continue being intimate. If we are revealing that we "truly are afraid of dying alone" and our interaction partner responds with "I love green beans," we're going to rethink how much depth we should be disclosing in the relationship. Ultimately, self-disclosure in a relationship is about building trust and determining how much information we can give another person (Pearce, 1974). The greater the depth of a self-disclosure, the more opportunities there are for an individual to feel vulnerable in the relationship. The caution in disclosive communication is that if too much private information is revealed early in the relationship (you go too deep, too fast), your partner may feel uncomfortable, and this may motivate her or him to end your relationship. Self-disclosure should always be thoughtful and appropriate.

Meshing.   A fifth characteristic of interpersonal relationships is *meshing*. This refers to how the behavior of two people in a relationship is organized and interpreted with respect to each other. In some relationships, each partner's behavior is *complementary* to the other person's. For example, in a relationship in which one person is a communication apprehensive and the other is not, one person's quietness complements the other person's great amount of talk and vice versa. In other relationships, however, each partner's behavior is *symmetrical* to that of the other person. This occurs when both individuals perceive their behavior as quite similar. For example, two communicative-apprehensive individuals involved in a relationship with each other are likely to be symmetrical in their verbal behavior. Likewise, a young boy who imitates some of his father's unique behaviors exemplifies a symmetrical interpersonal relationship, one for which we have a popular cliché: "Like father, like son." Thus, *meshing* refers to that aspect of interpersonal relationships that conveys the complementary or symmetrical nature of the behavior of the individuals in the relationship.

Support.   A sixth characteristic of interpersonal relationships is *support*. Support occurs in a relationship when the actions of each partner are conducive to the well-being of the other person. Consider two siblings who seem to bicker with each other constantly. When an outsider presents some sort of threat to one of them, however, one sibling is quick to come to the other's aid. Support can be of several types: physical, emotional, and intellectual. One type of emotional support, *anxiety reduction*, is also another characteristic of interpersonal relationships.

Anxiety Reduction.   Anxiety reduction can be thought of as a basic social need, the satisfaction of which comes through having interpersonal relationships. We all have fears, anxieties, and stresses, and sometimes these can be alleviated through the support given to us by the individual with whom we have a particular relationship. For example, the anxieties we might feel about a given course can be lessened by establishing a closer relationship with the teacher or with a fellow student in the same class. Similarly, our job-related stresses are more easily coped with when we seek and receive support from those who work with us.

Proximity.   The final characteristic of interpersonal relationships we want to discuss is *proximity*. This refers to the physical distance between the individuals in a relationship. An interpersonal relationship is characterized by the spatial closeness of its partners. Proximity may be the most important of the eight characteristics we have discussed. Research has found that proximity is the greatest predictor of initial interaction between two people. That is, we are more likely to initiate communication, and thus to establish a relationship, with an individual who is spatially close to us than with one who is more distant from us. This may sound like common sense. However, we do tend to take proximity for granted until we are separated by a great distance from someone about whom we care very much. Have you ever had a "long-distance relationship," one in which two people carry on their relationship although separated by many miles? Such relationships are common among college students who are away from their "high school sweethearts." Lack of close proximity is perhaps the primary cause of failure in long-distance relationships. It reduces frequency and variability of interaction with the other person and leads to a lack of adequate support and revelation from the other person.

One new exception to this rule of proximity in relationships has been the increase of both friendship and romantic relationships online. Many people are now meeting and even dating over thousands of miles because of Internet technology. Although these relationships can be very close psychologically, they are not close physically. There are even cases in which couples have gotten married and never actually touched each other or seen each other face-to-face (FtF) before they finished their vows online. With this said, there does come the point in *every* relationship at which proximity does become necessary if it is to progress. Even in these unusual cases in which people have married through the Internet, they did eventually meet, have sex, and create a family unit together. Although proximity isn't a necessity for initiating relationships, it does become important later on in the relationship. One study actually showed that 80 percent of college students had met their online best friend for an FtF interaction at least once (Wrench, 2004). Of those students who initiated friendships online, most students eventually started real-time friendships with that individual after meeting FtF.

Ongoing, well-established interpersonal relationships typically are characterized by close proximity between the partners. This is not to suggest that relationships characterized by longer distances always fail. However, greater distance does make such relationships more difficult to maintain because of its potentially negative influence on other factors.

The eight characteristics discussed above are interdependent. In other words, for any given relationship, a change in one characteristic is likely to lead to changes in several other characteristics. This is best exemplified by what happens between two partners in a relationship when there is an increase in spatial distance. The eight relational characteristics are also important to the satisfaction of our social needs and the achievement of our interpersonal goals. To the extent that these characteristics comprise our relationships, we can expect to have certain of our needs satisfied and our goals achieved. Notice, though, that most of these characteristics are based on and will encourage interpersonal communication. For this reason, people with high levels of communication apprehension experience many problems in interpersonal social relationships.

Social relationships require communication for their establishment and maintenance. Typically, when someone doesn't want to talk with us, we disregard that person and move on to someone else. As we noted in Chapter 3, low talkers are perceived as less friendly and less attractive than talkative people. Low talkers have fewer dating relationships than talkative people, and, to some extent, they have fewer people whom they can call friends. In one study that asked high communication apprehensives and low communication apprehensives to indicate how many people they knew who they could classify as "good friends," the high apprehensives indicated a range from 0 to 2, with more than one-third indicating none. More interesting was the finding that, when asked to list the names of their good friends, the high apprehensives most often named relatives, whereas the low apprehensives seldom listed relatives. Based on these results, it seems that low talkers tend to fare less well in the general social environment than do talkative people.

Moreover, the relational characteristics, along with social needs, interpersonal goals, and personality traits, determine the course any particular relationship will take in its development. In the following section, we outline a general developmental path followed by most interpersonal relationships.

Stages of Relationship Development

Several communication researchers and social psychologists have offered different models of the process of relationship development. Most of these models can be broken down into three separate but related processes: relationship *building*, relationship *maintenance*, and relationship *deterioration*. One model we consider to be especially useful is that proposed by Knapp (1978, 1983). This model accounts for ten stages of relationship development. Five of these stages—*initiating, experimenting, intensifying, integrating,* and *bonding*—comprise the developmental process of "coming together." The remaining five stages—*differentiating, circumscribing, stagnating, avoiding,* and *terminating*—comprise "coming apart." We will examine these stages with emphasis on communication behavior representative of each stage.

First, however, it is important to understand that although we present the stages in a sequential, ordered fashion, many interpersonal relationships do not follow this specified sequence in their progress through the stages. Also, the amount of time necessary to complete a given stage and to move through the various stages will differ from relationship to relationship.

Coming Together

Initiating.   The first stage of "coming together" is *initiating*. This is a conventional stage and usually lasts only a few seconds, a few minutes at most. The primary decision we try to make at this stage is whether to initiate verbal communication with the other person. Thus, it involves a good deal of scanning the other person. We look at the person, consider the person's familiarity and attractiveness to us, and decide if the person is open to an interaction with us. We typically move through this stage with much caution, wanting to put our best foot forward and to make a good impression on the other. Verbally, this stage is characterized by exchanges such as the following: "Hi, I'm Tom." "I'm Mary." "Pleased to meet you." "Nice to meet you too."

Experimenting.   Once we have successfully initiated an encounter, we move to the *experimenting* stage. At this stage, we try to discover how similar the other person is to us. A colleague of ours has drawn an analogy between this stage and the "sniffing-out" behavior engaged in by dogs when they greet each other. Indeed, we do engage in somewhat of a "sniffing-out" of the other person at this stage. We attempt to isolate interests we have in common, discover similarities in our backgrounds and experiences, and find a basis for deciding whether to allow the relationship to progress farther. Our verbal exchange at this stage is exemplified by such statements as "I see you like country music" and "Yeah; I used to be into rock, but I like country better now." It also involves a great amount of small talk. Knapp contends that commitment is limited at the experimenting stage and that most of our relationships do not move very far beyond this stage. One reason may be that we have only a certain amount of time to devote to each of our relationships. Therefore, we allow only a few to progress to more developed stages and let most of the others remain at the experimenting level. Here they remain noncommittal, casual, and comparatively unimportant to us.

Intensifying.   Progress through the experimenting stage can take a relatively short time or may extend over months or years. When a relationship moves out of experimenting, it typically moves into the *intensifying* stage. Relationships with people we call *close friends* or *intimates* are maintained at this stage. Interaction here involves much deeper and broader self-disclosure or revelation. We tell the other person some of our most confidential secrets, our deepest feelings, and our worst frustrations and failures.

At the intensifying stage, verbal interaction often employs the first-person plural (*we*). There are also more direct expressions of commitment, such as "You really are a good friend," or "I'm really in love with you." The use of nicknames and terms of endearment becomes very important for a relationship at this stage (Harre, Morgan, & O'Neill, 1979); the partners attempt to decrease formality and establish private symbols unique to their relationship. Aside from verbal cues, however, nonverbal cues (like those discussed in Chapter 4) become especially important at this stage as ways of communicating messages about the relationship; touch, for example, may become a substitute for many words. The partners' clothing becomes more coordinated, and they begin to share and exchange many physical possessions.

Integrating.   After completing the intensifying stage, a maturing relationship moves into the *integrating* stage. Occurring at this stage is a fusion of the two partners at both a psychological and a social level. Not only do they think of themselves as "one," but they also want others to recognize them as one. You probably experienced this stage with someone you dated for quite a long time. You went "everywhere" and did "everything" together as a couple. You considered the relationship special, unique, and unlike any you or anyone else had before. You exchanged pictures, rings, or bracelets to emphasize your oneness with each other. Perhaps others began emphasizing your oneness by asking you to travel and do things "together," by sending you a single letter, or by giving you one gift. You began claiming common property, such as "our song," "our restaurant," or "our car," and spoke to each other thus: "You're such a big part of me. I'd feel incomplete without you."

We should probably note, however, that the integrating stage does not involve complete togetherness. Although both partners commit much of themselves to the other, they still maintain a large portion of their individuality. Thus, although they want to feel like a single "unit" much of the time, there are other times when they need their "selves" apart from the other.

Bonding.   The final stage of coming together involves a formal and contractual integration known as *bonding*. The United States recognizes bonding most often in opposite-sex relationships, such as going steady, engagement, and marriage. However, in Canada, Spain, Denmark, and Massachusetts, same-sex marriages are legally recognized. Furthermore, many states in the United States legally recognize domestic partnerships and grant rights to both same-sex and opposite-sex domestic partnerships as legitimate expressions of bonding. Bonding is different from integrating in several ways. First, it is formal and public. Moreover, bonding is institutionalized and therefore more difficult to break off. It is a lasting commitment to a future together. Finally, bonding involves specified rules and regulations for guiding the relationship and expressing and maintaining its commitment. Much of the communication at this stage is based on the "contract," or commitment, and often entails talk about the future.

Coming Apart

Some relationships have a very positive future; they may last until one person in the relationship dies, and at least psychologically continue even after that for the surviving partner (Baxter, 1984). Other relationships do not fare so well. They eventually come apart.

Differentiating.   The first stage of "coming apart" is *differentiating*. This stage essentially is the opposite of the integrating stage of coming together. Thus, in the differentiating stage of coming apart, the individuals focus on their differences and disagreements. Verbally, the partners move away from using the *we* and *our* statements characteristic of integrating and use more *I, me,* and *mine* statements. This often is the first sign that a relationship is moving from a highly immediate or intimate status to a more nonimmediate one. Much of the communication serves to emphasize how different the people are in attitudes, values, beliefs, and behaviors (see Chapter 7); they talk about *not* having certain commonalities. The stage is marked by verbal exchanges such as "I thought you liked watching *Lost!*" "I always hated that show—I watched it just because you did!" Fighting and conflicts are obvious communicative signs of differentiating, although the stage can progress without explicit oral conflict.

Circumscribing.   A relationship that comes apart beyond differentiating may move into the *circumscribing* stage. At this stage, both the quantity and the quality of communication decrease. Topics of discussion between the individuals are restrained to safe areas; touchy subjects are avoided. Interaction frequency and duration begin to decrease. This stage is marked by less revelation and fewer expressions of commitment. Statements exemplifying this stage may include "Let's leave religion out of this." "I don't want to hear about your day at work." "Can't we just be friends?"

Stagnating.   After circumscribing comes the *stagnating* stage of coming apart. If a dog's sniffing-out behavior is analogous to the experimenting stage, then a stagnated pond is analogous to this stage. A stagnating relationship is one that has ceased to be active and functional. Much of the communication at this stage is nonverbal and negative. The participants feel that saying anything is unnecessary because they "know" what will be said anyway. Their attitude, spoken or unspoken, says, "What is there to talk about? You know what I'll say, and I know what you'll say." Many of the couple's interactions are similar to those engaged in with strangers. Their communication becomes rigid, difficult, narrow, and awkward. Just as a stagnating pond loses its means to support organic life, a stagnating relationship loses its means to support communicative life.

Avoiding.   The process of stagnating in a relationship usually occurs while the individuals are in close proximity. The next stage, *avoiding*, involves an attempt to increase physical distance. Communication at this stage is done for the sole purpose of avoiding direct interaction with the other person. The message being conveyed is "I don't want to see you or speak with you." Sometimes, it is sent implicitly through nonverbal channels—one party simply avoids being in the same place with the other party. When physical separation is not possible, one party may simply ignore the other. Sometimes, the message is sent more explicitly through verbal channels, exemplified by statements such as the following: "I'm too busy to talk to you." "If the phone rings, I won't answer." "Go away!"

Terminating.   The final stage of coming apart is *terminating*. This stage can occur anytime and for any number of reasons. Two people may simply "grow apart." One person may die. Long distances between the individuals may perpetuate deterioration of their relationship. Or one party may suddenly say, "Goodbye." Messages exchanged at this stage can vary as widely as their reasons. Knapp contends, however, that communication during termination is generally characterized by messages of distance and disassociation. Messages of *distance* put psychological and physical barriers between the two individuals. Such messages may take the form of actual physical separation, or they may be conveyed through certain other nonverbal behaviors and verbal expressions. A statement like "I just can't stand your face anymore" would serve to express distance. Messages of *disassociation* convey concern for one's own interests while emphasizing differences from the other person. A message such as "You never did appreciate what I'm doing. I've got my own life to live, so pack up and get out" would convey disassociation.

As already mentioned, termination can occur anywhere within the general process of relationship development. It can happen just as easily after a single "Hello" as it can after a twenty-year marriage. Like the termination stage, any stage beyond initiation can begin after any other stage. Indeed, in their developmental process, most long-term interpersonal relationships fluctuate back and forth between the stages of coming together and coming apart. Thus, any given relationship may progress, for example, from experimenting straight to stagnating, back to experimenting, then to intensifying and integrating, from there to circumscribing, back to intensifying, and finally to bonding. Some relationships cease progressing and remain at the second or third stage of their development. Others never get beyond initiating, ending with "A great-looking guy, but his breath would kill a mule!"

We hope that the discussion to this point has given you a deeper understanding of the nature of interpersonal relationships. Specifically, by now you probably can realize that all interpersonal relationships have basically the same characteristics. You should also know that interpersonal relationships develop in and out of a series of stages. Keep in mind, however, that the importance and function of these characteristics and stages will differ along with differences in people, particularly their needs and goals. We want now to look a bit closer at the individual in relationships by considering what expectancies people have for their relationships.

RELATIONAL EXPECTANCIES

Think for a moment about this question: what do you expect out of your relationships with others? That may be a difficult question to answer. Most of us do not think about "expecting" anything from our relationships. We may think about it, however, when it comes up in a conversation or something happens in a given relationship that causes us to think about what we expect out of the relationship. In short, we tend to take relational expectancies for granted. At best, most of us have only a stereotyped perception of what a relationship should be. We expect it to begin easily, for there to be mutual attraction, to have fun, and to "live happily ever after." In reality, however, people have some specific expectancies for their interpersonal relationships. Some of these are expectancies about a relationship in the short term, and others are expectancies for a relationship in the long term.

Short-Term Expectancies

When we first enter a relationship with another, we have certain expectations about how we and the other individual will behave and interact early in the relationship. Thus, short-term relational expectancies are most readily developed in the early stages of coming together (initiating, experimenting, and intensifying). Moreover, our focus on these expectancies and the importance we place on them will affect our communication in the stages of development. Mostly, they will determine how we communicate with the other person and what we communicate about. The seven short-term relational expectancies we want to consider are interest, peace, rule obedience, amusement, appearance, presence, and affection.

Interest. Early in a relationship, we expect to be interested in what the other person says and does. We expect them to be similarly interested in what we say and do. This is the primary purpose of the experimenting stage: to communicate so that we can isolate commonalities between us and the other person. Realization of such commonalities reinforces our desire to interact with the other person. Should our expectancy for mutual interests not be met, we may find continued interaction with the individual unrewarding and dissatisfying.

Peace. When we begin a new interpersonal relationship, we expect it to be free of discord, strife, and fighting. This expectancy is likely formed in the experimenting stage, in which interaction has shown to us that we can get along with the other person. Thus, it may serve as a catalyst for moving into the intensifying stage. Violation of the peace expectancy in the earliest stages of coming together may quickly lead to coming apart. We neither want nor expect conflict in the short term, so when it occurs we may decide to stop interacting with the person.

Rule Obedience. In the earliest stages of a new relationship, we expect the other party and ourselves to follow certain relational rules. Some of these rules are learned through experience and observation; others are unspecified until agreed on by the partners to a given relationship. An example of this expectancy can be drawn from an organizational context. When you begin a new job, you and the person you go to work for expect you to follow certain rules related to the job. These rules relate to when you are to arrive at work, whom you are to work with, whom you are to report to, how to carry out given procedures, and how often you can have access to the copying machine, among other things. The purpose of many, if not all, work rules is to allow your employer to develop a basis for trust in you. Once trust has been established, you may be allowed to "bend the rules a little." Expectancies of rule obedience operate in much the same way for more personal relationships. You and a new dating partner, for example, may follow certain rules for dating. After you have dated each other for a time and have developed trust for one another, you probably can overlook some disobedience of the rules. However, when this expectancy is violated in the short term—for example, when you say hello to a new acquaintance and he or she ignores you—the outcome is apt to be dissatisfaction with and disinterest in the other person. Thus, rule obedience is an important expectancy for communication in the early stages of relationship development. We are turned off by people who cannot follow the rules for interacting, whatever they may be.

Amusement. How often have you initiated an interaction with a joke or a one-liner? We expect to have fun early in our relationships. We expect the other person to be entertaining and to find us entertaining. This expectancy is closely linked to the expectancy of interest. People find amusing people interesting. Thus, much of our communication in the initiating and experimenting stages may consist of lighthearted, comical messages. Conversely, people find nonhumorous people boring. If early in a relationship we perceive the other person to have no sense of humor, it may cause us to lose interest in that individual. Have you ever heard the line "You're just no fun anymore"? As we begin relationships, we expect to have fun. As the relationship progresses and some fun disappears, we miss the fun the relationship had.

Appearance.   Most of us realize the importance of personal appearance in making a first impression on someone. Because of this, we tend to have fairly strong expectancies about physical appearance early in our relationships. This is perhaps more true when initiating a relationship with a possible romantic or sex partner. Even with nonromantic relationships, we generally expect people with whom we are establishing a relationship to dress in a way we consider appropriate. Often we expect the other to dress quite similarly to the way we dress ourselves.

How are expectancies about appearance related to interpersonal communication? As pointed out in Chapter 4, one's attire sends many interpersonal messages. Through our choices of clothing we can either turn each other on or turn each other off. Even the brand of clothing you are wearing can turn people on or off. First impressions are critical for successfully establishing relationships, and the way we dress is often critical to making first impressions on others.

Presence.   We mentioned earlier that proximity is a major predictor of initial interaction with others. Once we have established a relationship with someone, we develop an expectancy related to the proximity principle—we expect that person to want to be near us. Because we often establish relationships with others who must remain far away from us—due to their occupation, school, and the like—this expectancy may be less consistent and more situational than other short-term expectancies. That is, even in relationships with people who are a great distance from us, we expect them to *want* to be with us from time to time and that they will *try* to be with us whenever possible.

This expectancy is reinforced and upheld whenever the other person communicates messages to us that show her or his desire to be in our presence—whether those messages are transmitted via phone calls, e-mail, letters, face-to-face conversations, or third parties. When the other person fails to send such messages, we are likely to interpret this as a lack of interest and are likely to lose interest too. Realize, however, that the other person will most likely have the same expectancy for us. There is much to be said for the slogan "Reach out and touch someone!"

Affection.   In the experimenting and intensifying stages of coming together, affection may be the most important short-term expectancy. When establishing a relationship, we expect the other person to be at least moderately attentive to us and to show liking for us. During interactions with the other person, verbal expressions such as "You have an interesting background" and "I like how you do that" help fulfill this expectancy. It can be reinforced nonverbally through certain gestures, eye behavior, touch, and postures that convey openness and responsiveness. Our expectancy for affection stems from our social need for affection. We seek out and establish relationships with persons who are likable and who express liking for us.

Long-Term Expectancies

As a relationship enters and progresses through the latter stages of coming together—intensifying, integrating, and bonding—we develop a set of expectations about how the relationship should operate in the long term. Some of these expectancies concern the long-term value placed on the relationship by us and our partner. For example, a major expectancy might be how we expect each other to express and maintain value for the relationship. Two of these are extensions of the amusement and affection expectancies developed for the short term. Others we will discuss are commitment equity, fidelity equity, contracting, twosome, recognition, frankness, and averaging.

Amusement. Our short-term expectancy for amusement extends to a long-term expectancy as we progress through the intensifying stage and move on to integrating. Much of what leads us to be drawn emotionally closer to another person rests with the enjoyment and fun we experience when with the person. As we look ahead to the future of our relationship, we expect the fun and enjoyment to continue. Naturally, this expectancy stems from our continued interactions with the other person. We feel that because the person has expressed a positive sense of humor in the past, he or she will continue to do so for as long as the relationship lasts.

Affection. As important as the affection expectancy is in the short term, it probably is even more so in the long term (Fitzpatrick & Best, 1979). The very nature of the latter stages of coming together requires affection. As we interact with the other person during these stages, we expect affection to be continually provided. During integrating and bonding, we expect affection to be expressed in ways that are more intimate and private than how it is expressed in earlier stages. Moreover, the messages upholding this expectancy become more powerful in the latter stages. These messages can be conveyed through such statements as "I love you" and "We have a great 'thing' going, so let's not lose it."

Commitment Equity. As we become psychologically tied to another person, we expect each other to have an equal commitment to the relationship. This commitment can be expressed in many ways, and perhaps differently by each partner. You and your roommate, for example, expect each other to be similarly committed to your friendship. You don't expect to violate each other's trust or in any way threaten your liking for one another. As long as each of you perceives the commitment to be equal, it matters little how you express it. When this expectancy is violated, trust is easily lost and interactions may convey distance and disassociation.

Fidelity Equity.   One way to express our commitment to a relationship is to remain faithful to our partner. Our expectancy for equal fidelity is most prominent in intimate relationships in which we expect our partner to share our sexual faithfulness. We often have a similar expectancy in other relationships. On the job, for example, we might feel that our supervisor's expressed favoritism toward a coworker is something akin to infidelity. When we assume that a relational partner is being unfaithful to us, it is often the result of misunderstanding and misinterpretation of the other's behavior. Feelings of jealousy, for example, usually occur when we perceive our partner to be showing more interest in someone else. Our partner's interest in another is in itself little cause to suspect infidelity. However, the fulfillment of our expectancy for affection is easily threatened by other relationships involving our partner. Thus, we tend to expect our partner to adhere to the idea that "I won't if you won't." In other words, we expect a mutual level and expression of fidelity.

Contracting.   In the latter stages of coming together, as two people develop a sense of oneness, they expect each other to adhere to certain implicit "contracts." For example, an unspoken contract between your parents may hold that your mother cooks and your father repairs, or he buys the groceries and she fixes the car. Less intimate relationships have similar contracts. A contract exists between you and your teacher, for example. Such a contract might say that as long as you satisfactorily complete your assignments in the allotted time, he or she will assign you an appropriate grade. The formulation of such contracts is usually not discussed and agreed on outright by two relational partners. Rather, the expectancy develops in a predominantly nonverbal way as the two parties progress through their relationship. Experience has taught you, for example, that when you do your homework you will get a grade for it. The specifics about how to do the assignments and how they will be graded may be specified verbally. Seldom do you need to be told how to keep up your end of the teacher–student contract.

Twosome.   Recall that in the integrating stage, two people begin to feel as one and perceive themselves as a "couple." This fusion leads to an expectancy that, as the relationship continues to grow over time, each partner will think in terms of *us* rather than *you and me*. It is expected that each partner will depend on the other. This expectancy is fulfilled through interactions characteristic of integration, in which expressions such as "What happens to you happens to me" predominate in the communication. Our expectancy for being a twosome strengthens our expectancies for commitment and fidelity equity. As long as we remain a couple, we will remain committed and faithful to our relationship.

Recognition.   Just as we expect each other to think in terms of *us* in an integrated relationship, we expect others to see us as a couple. We perpetuate this expectancy through various verbal and nonverbal expressions, all of which convey the message "We're a pair." We may attend social gatherings together, share the same class and study schedule, wear identical clothing, hold hands while walking down the street, and hang out her-and-his towels. The ultimate fulfillment of this expectancy is a formal bonding.

Frankness.   In the early stages of coming together, we tend to hide some facts about ourselves and feelings that we have. Often we will distort information to stimulate the other person to have a certain impression of us. As our relationship intensifies and moves into a stage of integration, however, we expect to be more honest with each other. Basically, we expect each other to be more open about feelings and opinions and to be more responsive to the feelings and opinions of the other. Moreover, we expect not only increased frankness from each other but also more honesty with each other than with other people. In an intimate dating relationship, for example, we are likely to express certain hopes, fears, and anxieties to our partner that we would not express to others. Frankness is a very critical expectancy in intensifying and integrating relationships because its fulfillment serves as the foundation for trust and solidarity between the partners. Lack of frankness and violation of its expectation may lead quickly to disintegration.

Averaging.   This expectancy concerns a balance in our relationships between the good times and the bad times. Essentially, in integrated relationships we expect that the pluses will outweigh the minuses eventually. Anyone with a sense of reality is well aware that any relationship will have its negative aspects, that there will be strife, conflict, and other threats to the relationship. Yet the very fact that we can intensify a relationship and move into a stage of integration substantiates that we expect such a relationship to offer more good than bad. If we expected otherwise, chances are we would progress no further than the experimenting stage. When we have this expectancy, we accept that our relationships will have their problems. As long as the expectancy is fulfilled—the pluses do outweigh the minuses—we are better able to cope with the problems. Many people do not have this expectancy and thus are unrealistic in their view of what should happen in a relationship. They think everything should be positive. These people are likely to find it very difficult to have other long-term expectancies met as well.

In summary, our expectancies for a given relationship help us clarify for ourselves what the nature of that relationship is now and what it is likely to be in the future. Expectancies give us a sense of how well developed a relationship is and how we can go about developing it further. Whether our relational expectancies are met depends on the nature of communication within the relationship. If our concern is with the contracting expectancy, for example, consistent messages that appear to violate the contract will violate our expectancy. Important to note here is that *violation*, or lack of a single expectancy, is unlikely to cause much dissatisfaction with the relationship. Dissatisfaction most often occurs when several expectancies continually fail to be met. We should emphasize also that the expectancies we have discussed are not meant to be a completion of the list—many others are bound to exist. Our list was developed through research conducted by John Daly, a colleague of ours at the University of Texas. His hope (also ours) is that future research will continue to enlighten us on the types of relational expectancies that do exist and how they affect and are affected by interpersonal communication.

To this point, we have covered the characteristics of interpersonal relationships, the stages through which relationships develop, and some expectancies we have about our relationships. It is now time to address the most important question when one wants to establish a relationship—romantic, social, business, academic, or any other kind: how can I get people to like me?

▣ GAINING AFFINITY: GETTING OTHERS TO LIKE *YOU*

The degree to which we feel social needs for affection and inclusion often manifests itself in our attempts to get other people to like and/or appreciate us. This is known as *affinity seeking* (Daly & Kreiser, 1992; Richmond & McCroskey, 2005). We are probably more concerned about gaining another person's affinity in the experimenting and intensifying stages of coming together. It is in these stages that our needs for affection and inclusion are likely to be high. Affinity seeking should be of less concern in the latter stages of coming together, because these stages assume that liking and belonging already exist.

The process of affinity seeking is important to most of our interpersonal relationships. We engage in the process when coming together in new relationships and when trying to salvage relationships that are coming apart. Often, we use affinity seeking to gain the positive regard of our teachers (McCroskey & McCroskey, 1986), coworkers (McCroskey & Richmond, 1992), and superiors (Richmond, McCroskey, & Davis, 1992). We may try anew to seek the affinity of a dating partner whose respect for us has diminished for some reason. Affinity seeking is quite useful in our attempts to make positive first impressions on new acquaintances. Thus, affinity seeking is a process that has a major role in our everyday interpersonal transactions and relationships. As pervasive as this process is in our social lives, however, researchers have only recently begun to investigate what it is that people do to gain others' affinity.

Affinity seeking was first addressed by McCroskey and Wheeless (1976). They suggested seven techniques for increasing another person's affinity for us: control physical appearance, increase positive self-disclosure, stress areas of positive similarity, provide positive reinforcement, express cooperation, comply with the other person's wishes, and fulfill the other person's needs. Each of these suggestions has been supported by subsequent research.

The research that has had the most impact on our understanding of affinity seeking was the series of studies conducted by Bell and Daly (1984). In the first of these studies, they asked several groups of undergraduate and graduate students to produce a list of things that people can do to get others to like them. The lists generated by these groups were pooled together and then divided into categories of affinity-seeking behaviors. The results are presented in Figure 10.1. Each category, such as *altruism, dynamism, listening,* and so forth, represents a series or combination of behaviors used to gain another's affinity. Used together, the behaviors in any given category represent an

FIGURE 10.1 Typology of Affinity-Seeking Strategies	
Altruism	People attempting to get another individual to like them try to be of help to this individual. For example, the person holds the door for this individual, offers to get him or her something to drink, takes his or her coat, and is generally available to run errands for this individual. He or she also gives advice when it is requested.
Assume Control	People attempting to get another individual to like them present themselves as a leader, a person who has control over what goes on. For example, these people direct the conversations held with the other person, take charge of the activities the two engage in, and mention examples in which they have taken charge or served as a leader in the past.
Assume Equality	The person using this strategy presents him or herself as an equal of the other person. For example, the person avoids showing off, does not act superior or snobbish, and does not play "one-upmanship" games. If the person attempting to be liked is of lower status, he or she treats the other individual as an equal rather than a superior.
Comfortable Self	The person attempting to get another individual to like him or her acts comfortable in the setting in which the two find themselves, comfortable with him or herself, and comfortable with the other person. He or she is relaxed, at ease, casual, and context. Distractions and disturbances in the environment are ignored (e.g., loud noises and obnoxious people). The person tries to look as if he or she is having fun, even if this is not the case. The impression this person tries to convey is that "nothing bothers me."
Concede Control	People using this strategy allow the other person to control the relationship and situations the two individuals find themselves in. For example, they let the other take charge of their conversations and decide what they do and where they go. The person attempting to be liked also lets the other individual influence his or her actions by not acting dominant.
Conversational Rule Keeping	People attempting to get another individual to like them follow closely the culture's rules for how people are to socialize with one another by demonstrating cooperation, friendliness, and politeness. These people work hard at giving relevant answers to questions, saying "the right thing," acting interested and involved in the conversation, and adapting messages to the particular characteristics of the other party. They avoid changing the topic of conversation too soon, interrupting the other person, being pushy, dominating the conversation, and using excessive self-references. When talking to strangers and acquaintances, they engage in small talk rather than serious discussions. They also avoid topics that are not of common interest to both parties.

(Continued)

FIGURE 10.1 Typology of Affinity-Seeking Strategies *(Continued)*

Dynamism	Here the person attempting to get another individual to like him or her presents him or herself as a dynamic, active, and enthusiastic person. For example, the person acts physically animated and very lively when with the other person, varies his or her intonation and other vocal characteristics, and is outgoing and extraverted in the presence of the other person.
Elicit Others' Disclosures	People who use this strategy encourage others to talk by asking questions and reinforcing the other person for talking. They inquire about the other person's interests, feelings, opinions, views, and so on; respond as if these are important and interesting; and continue to ask more questions of the other person.
Facilitate Enjoyment	In this strategy, people attempting to get another individual to like them seek to make the situations in which the two are together very enjoyable experiences. The person does the things the other will enjoy, is entertaining, tells jokes and interesting stories, talks about interesting topics, says funny things, and tries to make the environment conducive to enjoyment.
Inclusive of Other	The person attempting to get another individual to like him or her includes this person in his or her social activities and groups of friends. He or she makes the person feel like "one of the guys" or "one of the girls."
Influence Perceptions of Closeness	People who want another individual to like them engage in behaviors that lead this person to perceive the relationship as closer and more established than it has actually been. For example, they use nicknames when addressing the other and talk about "we" rather than "you" and "I." They also mention any prior activities that include both of them.
Listening	In this strategy, individuals pay close attention to what the other person says, listening very actively. They focus attention solely on this person, paying strict attention to what is said. Moreover, the person attempting to be liked demonstrates that he or she listens by being responsive to the other's ideas, asking for clarification of ambiguities, being open-minded, and remembering things the other says.
Nonverbal Immediacy	Here the person signals interest and liking through various nonverbal cues. For example, the person frequently tries to make eye contact with the other person, stands or sits close to him or her, and smiles at the person. He or she also uses nonverbal signs of interest, such as leaning forward, nodding the head frequently, and directing much of his or her gaze toward the other person. All of these indicate that this person is very much interested in the other individual and in what he or she has to say.

FIGURE 10.1 Typology of Affinity-Seeking Strategies *(Continued)*	
Openness	In this strategy, people are open about themselves. They disclose information about their background, interests, and views. They may even disclose very personal information about their insecurities, weaknesses, and fears to make the other individual feel very special and trusted (e.g., "Just between you and me").
Optimism	People attempting to get another individual to like them present themselves as positive individuals—optimists—so that they will appear to be cheerful, and look on the positive side of things. They avoid complaining about things, talking about depressing topics, and being critical of self and others. In short, the person makes a concerted effort to avoid being a "drag."
Personal Autonomy	The person attempting to get another individual to like him or her presents him or herself as an independent, free-thinking person—the kind of person who stands on one's own, speaks one's mind regardless of the consequences, refuses to change behavior to meet the expectations of others, and knows where he or she is going in life. For instance, if the person attempting to be liked finds that he or she disagrees with the other individual on some issue, that person states an opinion anyway, is confident that his or her view is right, and may even try to change the mind of the other person.
Physical Attractiveness	People employing this strategy try to look as attractive as possible in appearance and attire. They wear fashionable clothes, practice good grooming, show concern for proper hygiene, stand up straight, and monitor their appearance.
Present Interesting Self	In this strategy, the person presents him or herself as a person who would be interesting to know. For example, he or she highlights past accomplishments and positive qualities, emphasizes things that make him or her especially interesting, expresses unique ideas, and demonstrates intelligence and knowledge. The person may also try to discreetly drop the names of impressive people he or she knows. Such individuals may even do outlandish things to appear unpredictable, wild, or offbeat.
Reward Association	People who use this strategy in getting another individual to like them present themselves as important figures who can reward this individual for associating with them. For instance, they offer to do favors for the other, and they give this person gifts and valuable information. The message to this individual is "If you like me, you will gain something."
Self-Concept Confirmation	People attempting to get another individual to like them demonstrate respect for this individual and help the person feel good about him or herself. For example, they treat the individual as a very important person, give compliments, say only positive things about him or her, and view the things this individual says as very important information. They may also tell others what a great person this individual is in hopes that the comment will get back to the person through third parties.

(Continued)

FIGURE 10.1	Typology of Affinity-Seeking Strategies *(Continued)*
Self-Inclusion	In this strategy, the person attempting to get another individual to like him or her sets up frequent encounters with this person. For example, he or she initiates casual encounters with this individual, attempts to schedule future encounters, places him or herself physically close to the other person, and puts him or herself in a position to be invited to participate in the other person's social activities.
Sensitivity	People attempting to get another individual to like them act in a warm, empathic manner toward this individual in order to communicate concern and caring. They also show sympathy for this person's problems and anxieties, work at understanding how this individual sees life, and accept what the individual says as an honest response. The message these people attempt to send is "I care about you as a person."
Similarity	In this strategy, the person tries to make the other individual think that the two of them are similar in attitudes, values, interests, preferences, personality, and so forth. He or she expresses views that are similar to the views the other person holds, agrees with what the other person says, and points out things that the two have in common. Moreover, the person deliberately avoids engaging in behaviors that would suggest differences between the two parties.
Supportiveness	The person attempting to get another individual to like him or her is supportive of this individual and his or her positions by being encouraging, agreeable, and reinforcing. The person also avoids criticizing the other or saying anything that might hurt this person's feelings, and sides with this person in any disagreements he or she has with others.
Trustworthiness	People using this strategy present themselves as trustworthy and reliable. They emphasize their responsibility, reliability, fairness, dedication, honesty, and sincerity. They also maintain consistency in their stated beliefs and behaviors, fulfill any commitments made to the individual, and avoid "false fronts" by acting natural at all times.

affinity-seeking strategy. Thus, such behaviors as holding a door open for someone, getting her or him a drink, and running errands for the person comprise the affinity-seeking strategy called *altruism* (which means helping others).

Following their initial study, Bell and Daly conducted subsequent investigations to find out if any of the affinity-seeking strategies are used more often than other strategies. They were also concerned with which strategies have the greatest likelihood of being used, and whether people's selection and use of strategies depend on personality and sex differences. Strategies found to occur most frequently in basic interpersonal relationships are *conversational rule keeping, self-concept confirmation, elicit other's disclosure, nonverbal immediacy, self-inclusion, listening, facilitate enjoyment,* and *altruism.* Those strategies that respondents said they are most likely to use for gaining affinity are *optimism, trustworthiness, physical attractiveness, listening, conversational rule keeping,* and *sensitivity.* Thus, it appears that people will employ affinity-seeking strategies that help them form a positive impression on another person. This tendency seems to agree with what we have already discussed as communication patterns and relational expectancies characteristic of relationships in the early stages of coming together. That is, we have short-term expectancies for interest, rule obedience, and appearance; such affinity-seeking strategies as *elicit other's disclosure, conversational rule keeping,* and *physical attractiveness* parallel those expectancies.

Personality and biological sex have an impact on people's likelihood of using particular affinity-seeking strategies. Let's now examine how affinity-seeking behaviors can be applied to a number of the personality traits discussed in previous chapters. Highly communication-apprehensive individuals, it was found, prefer using more passive strategies for gaining affinity than do low apprehensives. High apprehensives in the Bell and Daly study were more likely to use the strategies of *concede control* and *supportiveness* than they were other strategies. People who were identified in the study as highly Machiavellian preferred to use the strategies of *openness, present interesting self,* and *reward association.* These results suggest that highly manipulative individuals attempt to gain affinity by emphasizing how rewarding interaction with them can be. Finally, in terms of sex differences, Bell and Daly found that females are more likely than males to use relatively passive and other-directed strategies for gaining affinity. Females showed much greater preference than did males for the strategies of *conversational rule keeping, elicit other's disclosures, listening, sensitivity,* and *similarity.*

The research findings collected by Bell and Daly suggest that, although people generally prefer some affinity-seeking strategies over others, a person's personality and sex play a part in the choice of which strategies to use. Thus, it can be expected that if you exhibit certain personality characteristics, you will use affinity-seeking strategies that are different from those of someone whose personality is unlike yours. If you are a relatively quiet and reserved person, you are likely to use more passive strategies than someone who is more outgoing and talkative. Similarly, if you are a male we can expect that your strategies for getting others to like you are somewhat more aggressive than those used by a female.

The research cited above also found that people's choices of affinity-seeking strategies differ from situation to situation. In a social situation, for example, people seem more likely to use strategies such as *inclusion of other, assume equality,* and *concede control;* whereas in a task situation, they are more likely to use the strategies of *openness* and *dynamism.* These results suggest that strategies used to gain affinity with others may differ not only according to our specific personal characteristics but also according to the situation in which we and the other person are interacting. Thus, you are likely to vary in your use of strategies for gaining affinity with a new acquaintance—the student sitting next to you, your teacher, and someone you would like to date. Other research has confirmed many observations reported by Bell and Daly. This research has pointed to similarities and differences in effectiveness of different strategies between general peer relationships and those involving teacher–student and supervisor–subordinate relationships.

Yelling is a non-productive form of conflict management.

To summarize, the process of getting others to like us has its greatest impact in the early stages of relationship development. The process is related both to how we communicate in those stages and to the expectancies we have about a given relationship. The studies by Bell and Daly have identified twenty-five strategies that people choose from for gaining affinity with others. People tend generally to prefer several strategies over others. However, people's ultimate likelihood of using various strategies depends on their personalities, their gender, and the context. Because people strive to satisfy their needs for inclusion and affection, they will engage in the process of affinity seeking. This tendency is a fundamental reason for establishing and maintaining interpersonal relationships.

▣ MANAGING INTERPERSONAL CONFLICT

It is often said that only two unpleasant things are inevitable in the human experience—death and taxes. Although these two unpleasant realities confront all of us, another unpleasant fact of human experience is equally inevitable—conflict. The number one threat to relationships is interpersonal conflict.

Conflict is something that almost everyone wishes to avoid. However, because we are in contact with other human beings, there is little chance of being completely successful in doing so. Conflict is an inherent part of interpersonal relationships, whether those relationships are between parent and child, teacher and student, supervisor and subordinate, or lovers. Although the occurrence of conflict in interpersonal relationships is inevitable, the frequency with which it occurs, and the severity of the conflict, can be reduced by effective communicators. Thus, although we cannot reasonably expect to eliminate conflict from our interpersonal communication, we can learn to manage it and keep it under control.

The Nature of Conflict

To build an understanding of how to manage conflict, we must first understand what conflict is. Here is how McCroskey and Wheeless (1976) have defined it:

> Conflict between people can be viewed as the opposite or antithesis of affinity. In this sense, interpersonal conflict is the breaking down of attraction and the development of repulsion, the dissolution of perceived homophily (similarity) and the increased perception of incompatible, irreconcilable differences, the loss of perceptions of credibility and the development of disrespect. (p. 247)

To understand the nature of conflict, one needs to distinguish between conflict and disagreement. Disagreement is simply a difference of opinion. We may disagree on facts, on what the facts imply, or on what we might wish to do about those facts (Richmond & McCroskey, 1979). Disagreement does not necessarily lead to conflict. People may disagree, and even disagree extremely strongly, without entering into conflict.

Conflict is characterized by hostility, distrust, suspicion, and antagonism. Disagreement can lead to conflict, but this will occur mainly when the level of affinity between the communicators is not high. If we really like another person and that feeling is reciprocal, the incidence of conflict is greatly reduced, and when it does occur, it is usually short-lived. Consequently, conflict is sometimes defined as "disagreement plus negative affect."

Disagreement is a critical component in conflict. However, the way a person habitually deals with disagreement has more to do with whether disagreement will lead to conflict than does the simple presence or absence of disagreement. People differ in the extent to which they can tolerate disagreement and, thus, avoid entering conflict.

Tolerance for Disagreement

Perhaps you have noticed that some people with whom you interact tend to become hostile whenever you disagree with anything they say. Yet others tend to remain relatively unemotional even when you take a view directly counter to theirs. If these people respond to others in ways similar to the ways they respond to you, they are evidencing differing levels of tolerance for disagreement. Scale 21 in the appendix contains a

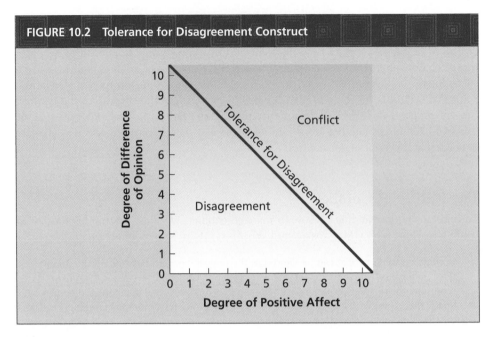

FIGURE 10.2   Tolerance for Disagreement Construct

Source: McCroskey, J. C. (2006). *An introduction to rhetorical communication* (9th Ed.). Boston: Allyn & Bacon.

research scale designed to measure an individual's degree of tolerance for disagreement (Teven, Richmond, & McCroskey, 1998). Take a minute to go ahead and fill out this scale now.

Figure 10.2 provides a basic illustration of the tolerance for disagreement construct, and it notes the distinction between disagreement and conflict. This figure shows that, other things being equal, the lower the degree of difference of opinion and/or the higher the degree of positive affect, the less likely it is that communication between people will enter into conflict. Thus, if little difference of opinion is expressed, or high affinity is present, the likelihood of conflict occurring is greatly reduced.

The pattern illustrated in Figure 10.2 represents the general relationship between conflict and disagreement and notes that tolerance for disagreement separates those two conditions. It does not consider that people differ in the way they respond to communication in which differences of opinion are expressed.

People differ in terms of how much disagreement they can tolerate. They differ even when degree of difference of opinion and degree of positive affect are held constant. Figures 10.3 and 10.4 illustrate these differences among people. Figure 10.3 presents the type of situation in which a person, or both people in an interaction, has a low tolerance for disagreement. Even a modest level of difference of opinion will lead to conflict, as will even a modest reduction in positive affect. People with this type of personality orientation are likely to be in conflict much of the time. Other people have

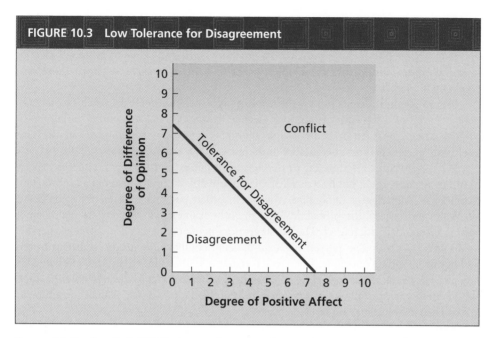

Source: McCroskey, J. C. (2006). *An introduction to rhetorical communication* (9th Ed.). Boston: Allyn & Bacon.

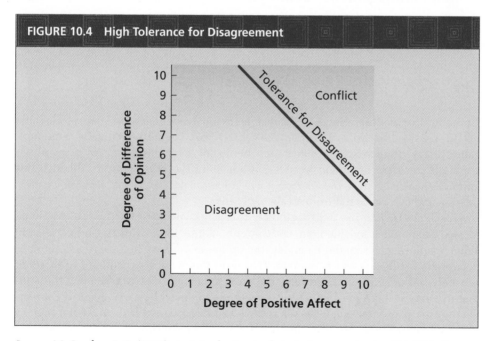

Source: McCroskey, J. C. (2006). *An introduction to rhetorical communication* (9th Ed.). Boston: Allyn & Bacon.

to be extremely careful in their communication with such people to avoid conflict with them. This becomes doubly difficult because such people tend not to be liked by others; one must try hard to make friends with a person who does not like to avoid conflict. In many communication contexts, people do not feel this is worth the effort; therefore, conflict will most likely occur.

Figure 10.4 represents exactly the opposite type of situation. For conflict to occur, a major degree of difference of opinion must be expressed or a substantial reduction in positive affect must be present. People with this type of personality orientation are likely to experience very little conflict in their everyday communication.

What is not illustrated in any of the figures discussed here is that conflict is experienced by an *individual,* not by a dyad. It is quite possible for one person in an interaction to perceive a high degree of conflict, whereas the other person experiences no conflict at all. When this occurs, the probability that the other person will also experience conflict later is substantially increased. The person experiencing conflict is likely to react harshly to the other person. The person not experiencing conflict may not be sensitive to the feelings of the other person and may voice statements that exacerbate the conflict. This scenario illustrates a basic principle concerning conflict: *conflict feeds on communication.* When conflict is present, communication is more likely to *increase* it than to reduce it. We will expand on this point later.

Conflict Management Techniques

We will discuss methods for preventing conflict from arising. However, you should recognize that although much conflict can be prevented, in the real world we are not going to be able to create a conflict-free existence. We are going to find ourselves in conflict from time to time in spite of our best efforts. It is important, then, to understand the options we have when such situations arise. We will consider four of these.

Leaving the Field.   Because conflict feeds on communication, one of the first options we should consider is *leaving the field.* By this, we mean halting the communication that is stimulating the conflict. One method of doing this is to leave physically, to break off communication and leave the presence of the other person. Although this approach may not reduce the conflict, it will at least make the conflict less immediately relevant and may prevent it from escalating farther.

A second leaving-the-field method is to leave psychologically. By this, we mean to stop communication (at least verbally) about the topic with the other person. When employing this method, one lets the other person have her or his say, but does not respond with a contrary opinion. If you do this, you may continue to disagree privately but not say so. Therefore, the communication that would allow the conflict to escalate is not present. This is a method employed by many married couples. One person knows the other person's views and disagrees with them. If the topic is not absolutely critical, one may simply not express the contrary views. Then, because disagreement is not present in the communication, the potential for conflict is greatly reduced.

The final leaving-the-field method is to change the topic of discussion. Sometimes we can simply note that the present disagreement cannot be resolved. Thus, there is no useful purpose served by discussing the topic further. A person skillfully employing this technique will shift the topic of discussion to one that the parties agree on. Because disagreement is no longer being expressed, the level of conflict can drop sharply in a relatively brief period.

It must be stressed that the leaving-the-field option is *not* a method of resolving disagreement. Rather, it is an effective method for putting the disagreement out of sight for a time and reducing the potential for conflict. Disagreements cannot be resolved in the presence of serious conflict. Thus, this method should be seen as a first step toward such resolution, not as a resolution. An example of this distinction may be drawn from marital conflict. In years past, when a married couple was in conflict, a common method of attempting to help them was to bring them together to "talk it out." The result was often a screaming session that only made things worse. Today it is generally recognized that when a marriage is in serious distress, the couple should be separated. This reduces the potential for destructive communication, as a first step. This does not solve the couple's problems, but it does make it possible to prevent the problems from becoming more severe. It is a first step toward solving the problems themselves.

Restoring Trust.   When serious interpersonal conflict has developed, one way of breaking out of a self-perpetuating cycle is to deal with suspicion and distrust. The goal is to restore a sufficient amount of trust so that real communication can occur. Trust exists when someone feels free to make a risky decision, to self-disclose, to stick one's neck out. When trust is present, we are willing to give a little, to take a chance that could potentially result in harm to us.

Trust is more likely to be present when people have had previous experiences of positive orientations toward each other's welfare. If husband and wife, father and son, student and teacher, supervisor and subordinate, or two coworkers have previously acted positively toward each other, then the restoration of trust is more likely. Trust can be developed even when the people in conflict have not previously had a positive relationship; it is just more difficult to achieve.

By setting up certain conditions, we can help the restoration or establishment of trust. Trust may develop when each person has some guarantee, or knows with some certainty, what the other person will do before each makes an irreversible decision to trust the other. For example, in marital problems, the promise or "solemn oath" not to repeat some behavior is often sought. Labor unions seek legal contracts before they return to work after a labor dispute. Trust may also develop when there is both the opportunity to communicate about mutual responsibilities and the means to deal with violations of trust. Marriage counselors often focus on these elements. Two people having conflict over a class project they are working on together may discuss such issues. The "father and son talk" (when the father does most of the talking about the son's behavior) frequently deals with mutual responsibilities and actions that will be taken if trust is violated.

In addition, we can facilitate trust if we have the power to influence other people's choice to trust by rewarding their trustworthy decisions and punishing their untrustworthy ones. This technique is often used in child rearing. At times, mothers inform daughters of their responsibility to return home from a date by a particular hour, especially if their trust has been violated in the past. Actions that will be taken when this trust is violated are also frequently noted. We have a similar ability, if we hold the right position or rank, in complex business organizations or in the military.

Finally, we can facilitate trust with the use of a third party. A third person or agency can point out how losses to either party because of violations of trust are detrimental to both people in the conflict. Interpersonal disputes and personal marital problems are often solved by the instigation of trust through a third party.

Reinstating Communication.   A major problem in conflict management is reinstating communication between the two parties involved. This problem represents a paradox, or at least a "two-edged sword." Communication probably initiated the conflict in the first place—some verbal statement or nonverbal behavior was interpreted in a way that increased hostility, competition, or distrust. On the other hand, lack of communication may perpetuate the conflict. The restoration of communication, therefore, is no guarantee that the conflict will be reduced. It may even be increased. There is some evidence to suggest that too much communication may often be detrimental to interpersonal relationships. For example, disclosure patterns in marriage may focus on undesirable elements, and high disclosure is often associated with disturbed (i.e., in conflict) marriages. Further, in negotiation, completely free communication may be used to convey information such as threats and insults, which intensify hostilities rather than reduce them. Consequently, reinstatement of communication must be carefully planned and, to some extent, controlled.

To be useful in managing conflict, communication must be limited and directed toward actions that are vital to reduction of the conflict.

1. Communication should be directed toward restoring trust. Note the ways we have proposed in which this might be accomplished. Some evidence suggests that reinstated communication without trust is not very useful.

2. Communication should focus on common goals. From our previous discussion of factors related to affinity and attraction, we would expect common goals to have an effect.

3. Communication should focus on other areas of similarity, such as common attitudes, beliefs, and values.

4. Communication should be positive and as reinforcing as possible. This is particularly true of self-disclosure in conflict situations. Care should be given to positive and reinforcing disclosures.

5. Expressions of cooperation and compliance in areas indirectly related to the dispute should be sought.

6. Past behaviors showing positive orientations should be discussed.

Free ventilation and disclosure of feelings should not be the essential nature of the communication exchange. These can lead to greater conflict. Recitation of platitudes and principles is seldom helpful. In conflict situations, we are seldom influenced by injunctions to "turn the other cheek," or that "it is better to give than receive." The conflict itself shows that we have abandoned these as working axioms in this situation. Similarly, communication that focuses on the common enemy has only a temporary effect in resolving the conflict and merely transfers the conflict to others.

A now classic study conducted under the direction of social psychologist Muzafer Sherif experimented with some of these conflict variables in a secluded boys' camp (Sherif & Sherif, 1954). The experimenters created two groups in the camp that were in conflict with each other. They tested most of the above methods of resolving conflict and found the common goal approach to work most successfully. When the boys were brought together in the accomplishment of a superordinate goal (survival), the process of conflict resolution was begun. Their cooperation was necessary for achieving the goal, which in turn built strong bonds. Through many of these experiences, the experimenters could resolve the conflict between the two groups.

Compromise and Negotiation. Even when some measure of trust has been restored and communication has been reinstated and directed, it is likely that conflict will still not be completely eliminated, except in very minor problem situations. The ground has been prepared for compromise and negotiation. Compromise and negotiation assume that sufficiently strong mutual interests are at stake. Some common goals must be established at the outset. Marriage partners in conflict frequently compromise by both "giving in a little" and changing their behaviors because of underlying strong bonds and common goals, such as child rearing.

In the negotiation phase, communication should be directed toward discovering the ranges or latitudes of acceptable and unacceptable solutions to both parties involved. If there is an overlap of acceptable solutions (although not the most desired by either), then compromise in this area of overlap can produce resolution. This frequently occurs in labor–management disputes that are settled fairly quickly. When there is no overlap between each party's range of acceptable solutions, further communication must follow. The two parties must be influenced to expand their range of acceptable solutions so that there is an area of overlap in which compromise can be reached.

Communication in this setting functions in three ways: (1) communication is used to discover what settlements both parties are likely to accept, (2) communication is used to influence or persuade both parties to modify their range of acceptable solutions, and (3) communication is used to provide both parties with rationalizations for acceptance of previously unacceptable positions or solutions.

In the compromise and negotiation setting, there is usually mutual pressure for reaching agreement early in the exchange. Communication is usually less threatening and more cooperative at that point. As time goes on, however, people in a conflict are less likely to agree. Communication may become more competitive and lose sight of common goals. Again, too much communication, especially free ventilation between conflicting parties, may be detrimental to compromise and the restoration of affinity. In the last analysis, some level of tolerance may always be needed.

Preventing Conflict

Clearly, the superior method of managing conflict is to prevent it from occurring in the first place. To prevent conflict from occurring, three options are possible: (1) raise a person's level of tolerance for disagreement, (2) reduce the importance of the issues in your communication, and (3) increase the level of affinity between communicators. The first option has very limited potential. We can have little effect on the basic personalities of others around us, and short of intervention by a skilled psychologist, our own personality is likely to change little. As for the second option, sometimes it is possible to deemphasize or reduce the importance of issues in our communication. It is not uncommon for people to get into heated arguments over issues that are not worth their time to discuss. However, issues are the very reason for the existence of much of our communication, and the issues are important. Therefore, this option, like the first, frequently offers little potential.

Our third option, increasing the level of affinity between communicators, holds the most promise for preventing conflict in our everyday lives. If we find we do not like another person, it is largely the other person's task to change our view. However, we still have substantial control over the way in which others view us. We can, in other words, determine to a major extent the affinity others have for us. Therefore, we have at our disposal a method for greatly reducing the amount of conflict we will need to experience in our lives—and, additionally, increasing the amount of influence we have over the attitudes and behaviors of others. The basis for this control is our use of communication to seek affinity directly and to effect behavior alteration in others.

Behavior Alteration Techniques.   In Chapter 8, we outlined twenty-two behavior alteration techniques (BATs) that we generated from a series of research projects. These are essentially the options we have available for getting others to change their behaviors or their attitudes. When employing such techniques, our primary concern is behavior change on the part of the other person. However, a secondary concern should not be overlooked—maintaining affinity for us in the person we are attempting to influence.

Our research suggests that attempting to alter another's behavior generally is not an effective method of increasing affect. That is really not surprising. People generally do not want to change their behavior. Thus, to try to change them causes some stress, at best.

Only two of the twenty-two BATs have been found consistently related to increased affinity. These are *deferred reward from behavior* and *internal reward: self-esteem.* In other words, if you try to get people to change their behavior by indicating they will be rewarded sometime in the future and/or they will feel better about themselves, they are likely to increase their regard for you.

In contrast, eight of the twenty-two BATs have been found consistently related to *decreased* affinity. These are *punishment from source* ("I will punish you if you don't"), *punishment from others* ("Others will dislike you if you don't"), *guilt* ("If you don't, others will be hurt"), *source–receiver relationship: negative* ("I will dislike you if you don't"), *legitimate higher authority* ("Do it; I'm just telling you what I was told"), *legitimate source authority* ("Because I told you to"), *receiver responsibility* ("It is your obligation"), and *debt to source* ("You owe me one"). Clearly, use of these techniques leads to a reduction in affinity and an increased probability that conflict will occur. Other techniques should be chosen whenever possible, and usually it *is* possible to use others.

The remaining twelve BATs have not been found consistently related to affinity, either positively or negatively. Thus, it is not necessary to use only *deferred reward from behavior* or *internal reward: self-esteem* to influence others. The remaining twelve BATs are based primarily on one's ability to reward others, or on a positive affinity relationship between the communicators. Thus, if a good relationship is built initially, efforts to modify another person's behavior need not lead to either increased conflict or decreased affinity. The eight BATs that we cited in the preceding paragraph, those that are most associated with decreased affinity, are most likely to be used when there is already a bad relationship between people. Their use only leads to a worse one. The key, then, is to build affinity directly at the outset and continue to cultivate it as the relationship continues.

Building Affinity.   Earlier in this chapter, we outlined twenty-five affinity-seeking strategies. Our research suggests that most of these are associated with increased affinity between communicators, although they do not all appear to be equally effective.

Two of the strategies, *dynamism* and *personal autonomy*, seem helpful in building affinity only if used in moderation. Extensive use leads to negative results. Six of the strategies seem only modestly helpful. These are *altruism, concede control, influence perceptions of closeness, reward association, self-inclusion,* and *similarity.* The remaining seventeen strategies are all strongly associated with increased affinity. Thus, one has a substantial array of choices when seeking to increase affinity with others. We will go as far as to suggest that the primary reason a person will not build affinity with another must be that the person doesn't *want* to!

 **KEY TERMS**

affinity seeking 214
disagreement 206

interpersonal conflict 220
tolerance for disagreement 221

REFERENCES

Altman, I., & Taylor, D. A. (1973). *Social penetration.* New York: Holt, Rinehart & Winston.

Baxter, L. A. (1984). Trajectories of relationship disengagement. *Journal of Social and Personal Relationships, 1,* 29–48.

Bell, R. A., & Daly, J. A. (1984). The affinity-seeking function of communication. *Communication Monographs, 51,* 91–115.

Daly, J. A., & Kreiser, P. O. (1992). Affinity in the classroom. In V. P. Richmond and J. C. McCroskey (Eds.), *Power in the classroom: Communication, concern, and control.* Hillsdale, NJ: Lawrence Erlbaum.

Davis, M. S. (1973). *Intimate relations.* New York: Free Press.

Derlaga, V. J., & Chaikin, A. L. (1975). *Sharing intimacy: What we reveal to others and why.* Englewood Cliffs, NJ: Prentice-Hall.

Fitzpatrick, M. A., & Best, P. (1979). Dyadic adjustment in relational types: Consensus, cohesion, affectional expression, and satisfaction in enduring relationships. *Communication Monographs, 47,* 167–178.

Knapp, M. L. (1978). *Social intercourse: From greeting to good-bye.* Boston: Allyn & Bacon.

Knapp, M. L. (1983). *Interpersonal communication and human relationships.* Boston: Allyn & Bacon.

McCroskey, J. C., & McCroskey, L. L. (1986). The affinity-seeking of classroom teachers. *Communication Research Reports, 3,* 158–167.

McCroskey, J. C., & Richmond, V. P. (1992). *Communication in educational organizations.* Edina, MN: Burgess International Group.

McCroskey, J. C., & Wheeless, L. R. (1976). *An introduction to human communication.* Boston: Allyn & Bacon.

Newcomb, T. M. (1953). An approach to the study of communicative acts. *Psychological Review, 60,* 393–404.

Pearce, W. B. (1974). Trust in interpersonal communication. *Speech Monographs, 41,* 236–244.

Phillips, G. M., & Wood, J. T. (1983). *Communication and human relationships: The study of interpersonal communication.* New York: Macmillan.

Richmond, V. P., & McCroskey, J. C. (1979). Management communication style, tolerance for disagreement, and innovativeness as predictors of employee satisfaction: A comparison of single-factor, two-factor, and multiple-factor approaches. In D. Nimmo (Ed.), *Communication Yearbook 3* (pp. 359–373). New Brunswick, NJ: Transaction Books.

Richmond, V. P., & McCroskey, J. C. (2005). *Organizational communication for survival: Making work, work.* Boston: Allyn & Bacon.

Richmond, V. P., McCroskey, J. C., & Davis, L. M. (1992). The relationship of supervisor use of power and affinity seeking strategies with subordinate satisfaction. *Communication Quarterly, 34,* 178–193.

Rubin, W. C. (1966). *The interpersonal underworld.* Palo Alto, CA: Science & Behavior Books.

Schutz, W. C. (1960). *FIRO: A three dimensional theory of interpersonal behavior.* New York: Holt, Rinehart & Winston.

Sherif, M., & Sherif, C. (1954). *Groups in harmony and tension.* New York: Harper & Row.

Teven, J. J., Richmond, V. P., & McCroskey, J. C. (1998). Measuring tolerance for disagreement. *Communication Research Reports, 15,* 209–217.

West, R., & Turner, L. H. (2004). *Introducing communication theory: Analysis and application* (2nd ed.). Boston: McGraw-Hill.

Wrench, J. S. (2004, November). Face-to-face v. online friendships: An examination of friendship intimacy, interpersonal communication satisfaction, and interpersonal communication motives. Paper presented at the National Communication Association's Convention, Chicago.

DISCUSSION QUESTIONS

1. Think of five relationships in which you are currently involved. Which of Schutz's three social needs is being met in each relationship?

2. Use one of your own relationships in life to illustrate Knapp's five stages of relationship development. Did you follow the pattern exactly, or did

you slip into relationship dissolution at some point?

3. Looking at the list of short-term relationship expectancies, which do think are the most important for your own relationships?

4. If you are trying to get your boss to like you, which affinity-seeking strategies do you think would work best? Why?

5. If you have a high tolerance for disagreement about religion and you interact with someone who has a low tolerance for disagreement about religion, what do you think will happen?

11

Intercultural Communication

OBJECTIVES

- Define and explain *culture*.

- Explain the concept of *co-culture*.

- Explain each of the following constructs: intracultural, intercultural, cross-cultural, international, interethnic, interracial, and pancultural.

- Define and explain *intercultural communication apprehension*.

- Explain the concept of ethnocentrism.

- Understand the positive and negative aspects of ethnocentrism.

- Understand the relationship between stereotypes and prejudices.

- Understand the relationships among ethnocentrism, homonegativity, and human temperament.

- Understand the relationships among religious fundamentalism, religious communication apprehension, intercultural communication apprehension, and ethnocentrism.

- List and explain the five levels of ethnocentrism.

- Understand the twelve suggestions for improving intercultural communication.

All communication occurs within a context. Therefore, context is considered one of the critical components of the communication process. As we noted in Chapter 1, context focuses on *roles* and *rules*. Because culture is the largest, and often most important, aspect of context, it is primarily responsible for defining communication roles and setting forth the rules we must follow in our communication with others.

When we are communicating with people from our own culture in everyday interactions, we seldom recognize the extent we are dependent on our understanding of our culture to know how and when to communicate. Even though we have spent much of our lives figuring out how to communicate appropriately and effectively with others, it is usually only when we must communicate with someone from another culture that we realize how helpless to communicate we become when we don't understand where the other person is "coming from."

In this picture, Condoleezza Rice, U.S. Secretary of State during George W. Bush's administration, talks to people from other countries at the United Nations. Dr. Rice's communication in this picture is an example of international communication.

Sensitivity to cultural differences is increasing in the United States. Although there are many areas in the United States that remain very homogeneous, and all of the people are from a single cultural grouping, this has never been true in large cities and is becoming less true in most other communities across the country. The United States was built on the "melting pot" model, in which people from all the world's cultures were welcome to come here so long as they were willing to blend in to form a new "American" culture. The degree to which this has effectively occurred is now subject to considerable debate, a debate into which we shall not enter here. It suffices to say that the melting pot metaphor is no longer the preferred choice for many new immigrants to this country (Gudykunst & Kim, 2002). More commonly today, we hear calls for the acceptance of "diversity" of cultural perspectives. As a consequence, there are many different sets of roles and rules that are considered correct by different people with whom we are likely to come in contact.

Of course, there have always been many cultures with many different views of appropriate roles and rules for communication. Some people have been concerned with communication between people from different cultures for a long time. Today, however, *all* of us are highly likely to find ourselves in intercultural communication contexts on any given day. In fact, many of us are finding such contacts increasingly routine. When contact with other cultures was primarily the province of the wealthy, who could afford the expense of a trip by ship to a foreign land, few needed to study the problems of intercultural communication. Now such contacts can be had by driving a few blocks, or flying a few hundred miles for a few hundred dollars, or connecting to the Internet and communicating with a person from thousands of miles away virtually for free. Today, intercultural communication is everybody's concern.

■ THE NATURE OF CULTURE

The term *culture* has a somewhat negative image for many people. When some hear this word, they think of opera and classical music, and have a very negative response. If you think opera is "Italian theater" and symphonic orchestras play "German elevator music," you can relax. This was a view of the elite in the United States when it was just beginning and did not truly have a culture of its own, but rather was dependant on a conglomerate of European cultures. Although many Americans truly appreciate both opera and classical music, neither is a central aspect of American culture. And, even if they were, they would have little bearing on that which we are concerned with here.

When we use the term *culture*, we are referring to "a group of people who through a process of learning are able to share perceptions of the world which influence their beliefs, values, norms, and rules, which eventually affect behavior" (Wrench, 2001, p. 12). Culture, as defined here,

> refers to the relatively specialized life-style of a group of people—consisting of their values, beliefs, artifacts, ways of behaving, and ways of communicating—that is passed on

from one generation to the next. Included in culture would be all that members of a social group have produced and developed—their language, modes of thinking, art, laws, and religion. (DeVito, 1994, p. 420)

A culture may be thought of as "a set of rules for constructing, interpreting, and adapting to the world" (Klopf, 2005). As Samovar and Porter (1991) suggest, a culture encompasses all of the knowledge, experience, beliefs, values, attitudes, meanings, hierarchies, religion, notion of time, roles, spatial relations, concepts of the universe, and material objects and possessions a group of people acquires over the course of generations. A simple definition of culture, which has broad applicability, is "a group of people with similar backgrounds who think, act, and communicate a lot alike" (Richmond, McCroskey, & McCroskey, 2005).

It is useful to think of a culture like a living thing. Cultures grow and change very slowly, and have many means of protecting themselves. They have very high "self-esteem," and their devotees are fiercely loyal. A culture is cumulative: it grows, expands, and adapts to changes. A group's culture is passed on to its children through a process called *enculturation*. Although schools are the most obvious instrument of enculturation for children, religious groups, parents, peers, senior members of communities, writers and artists, the mass media, and even government agents function to enculturate the young. When new people move into a culture, the host people attempt to "acculturate" the newcomers by directly and indirectly influencing them to adopt new ways of thinking and doing things— the ways of the host culture (McCroskey, 2006). Acculturation is almost always in this direction—host culture influencing newcomer. Efforts by newcomers to change the host culture are usually rejected, and often newcomers who persist in making such attempts will be ejected from the host culture or at least made to feel extremely unwelcome. In the United States, most immigrants are heavily acculturated through our media.

Although you may have grown up in one of the many "less sophisticated" areas in North America, even if you hate opera and classical music, fear not—you are cultured! You are a part of the general North American culture. You probably take certain things pretty much for granted, such as "American" music in one or more of its various forms (jazz, rock, country, Broadway, rap, gospel, etc.), supermarkets, movie theaters, fast food, interstate highways, talk radio, commercial TV, cable TV, free public education, Dr. Pepper, diet soft drinks, apple pie, grits, black-eyed peas, tacos, barbecue, public colleges and universities, football (not soccer!), basketball, baseball, pickup trucks, rodeo, cowboy boots, jeans, aloha shirts, button-down collars, and deodorant. You might be surprised to learn that some cultures have *none* of these things! That is the way culture is—it is so omnipresent that we seldom notice our own culture except when we are somewhere where it *isn't!*

But culture is not only about things like fast food and jeans. It is also about much more serious things, like how people think. People in the general North American culture tend to have certain beliefs ingrained in them, although some people in the culture may not identify with all of the beliefs and attitudes of the general culture. Some common beliefs in this culture are that everyone should have an opportunity to achieve a better life, that working hard will eventually pay off, that people should strive to do well and succeed, that one should help people who are poor or less fortunate than themselves, that democracy is the best form of government, that people should be free to worship as they please, that everyone should learn to communicate in American English, and that "the American way is the best way, and if everyone were like us, the world would be a much better place."

Co-culture is a term we need to consider before we go much farther, for you may have looked at the list of "things American" above and found some that "just don't fit into" what you see as your culture, whereas many others do (Wrench, 2001). Within all very large cultural groups exist subgroups that share not only many of the characteristics of the larger culture but also characteristics within their group that are not shared by the larger culture. For example, every organization has a culture of its own; generally, the older the organization, the stronger and more unique is its culture

A group of children play Irish tin whistles in a band marching in the St. Patrick's Day parade in St. Louis. St. Patrick Day parades celebrate the Irish American co-culture.

(Richmond et al., 2005). New organizations typically have weak cultures that are much more subject to change than those of older organizations. Organizational subcultures live within larger general cultures, and those general cultures often have a strong impact on them.

Members of some subcultures, particularly ethnically based subcultures, prefer their group to be thought of as a *co-culture* because the prefix *sub* is interpreted by them as indicating something below or suppressed. In reality, smaller cultural groups can live alongside a larger culture without suppression. The term *co-cultures* refers to cultures not below or suppressed by the larger culture, but instead to a unique cultural group that exists inside of a larger culture. The most commonly recognized co-cultures within the general North American culture stem from ancestry (membership in racial or ethnic minority groups) and/or geographical residency. There are, however, many subcultures that are not co-cultures.

There is an enormous number of "hyphenated" Americans in the United States. In fact, most U.S. citizens have some identification with an ancestry group, whether it be Native American, German American, Asian American, African American, Japanese American, Chinese American, Mexican American, Irish American, English American, Italian American, Cuban American, Swedish American, or one of dozens of others. Members of each of these co-cultures share important similarities with each other that are not shared with the larger culture. However, although each person's identification with that co-culture may be strong, odds are very good that *culturally* the person is more like people in one of the other hyphenated American groups than he or she is like the people who currently live in the ancestral home. The exception to this general rule, of course, is people who are very recent immigrants to this country.

Current residency also represents potential for important co-culture groupings. Certainly, Canadians don't like being mistaken for U.S. residents, and within Canada the distinction between the French-speaking and English-speaking groups is very important. Within the United States, there are important regional co-culture groupings—such as New England, West Coast, Midwestern, Great Plains, Southern, Eastern, Alaska, Hawaii, and Texas (as their tourist bureau says, "Texas, It's Like a Whole Other Country!"). Although people in any two of these regions are far more alike than they are like Rumanians, they each have unique cultural characteristics in which they take pride and that they think make their co-culture better than others.

THE CULTURAL CONTEXT OF COMMUNICATION

A central tenet of modern communication theory, which we advanced and discussed early in this book, is that "meanings are in people, not words (or nonverbal behaviors)" (Richmond & McCroskey, 2004). Consequently, if we are to communicate effectively with you about the area of intercultural communication, it is important that we explain how some terms related to intercultural communication are commonly used in this field. Although culture provides the general context for all communicative encounters, the nature of that context may take many forms.

Intracultural Communication

Intracultural communication refers to communication between members of the same cultural or co-cultural group. In this form of communication (the most common for most people), the proportion of shared meanings for words and nonverbal behaviors (i.e., communicative messages) is quite high, because these meanings develop differently within cultures, but people within a given culture learn what these messages are intended to mean as a function of both schooling and experience in everyday interaction.

When most of us think about communicating with others around us, this is the communication context we have in mind. However, we must keep in mind that even within this context, major differences may be present as a function of membership in different groupings within the same general culture. Consider the differences in orientations within a single culture between females and males, heterosexuals and homosexuals, teenagers and senior citizens, blind and sighted, hearing and deaf, physically handicapped and non-handicapped, Christians and Jews, doctors and patients, teachers and students, and even people employed in two different organizations (which are often referred to as having different *organizational cultures*). Some people prefer to consider all of these to be instances of "intercultural" communication. Although we understand this view, we prefer to reserve the term *intercultural* for contexts in which the basic culture is not the same. This is not meant to trivialize the differences between people in these categories, for they can be large and very important and are deserving of study in their own right. Here, however, our attention is directed toward the larger cultural context.

Intercultural Communication

Intercultural communication refers to communication between members of different cultural groups. This term is also used to refer to communication between members of two co-cultures within a larger culture, particularly when the co-cultural differences are seen as quite substantial.

Cross-Cultural Communication

Cross-cultural often is used interchangeably with *intercultural* to reference communication between members of different cultural groups. However, it is more commonly used to reference comparisons of communication behaviors across different cultures and the study of specific communication issues on a comparative basis in two or more cultures. We make "cross-cultural" comparisons of nonverbal communication behaviors, for example, in Chapter 4.

International Communication

International communication generally refers to communication between governmental representatives of different countries. Such contacts can represent very great cultural differences (England and Japan) or comparatively small differences (Canada and the United States). Most international communication, however, is plagued with all of the problems that individuals face in intercultural communication, plus the added ones produced by governmental concerns. This is thought by some to be the most difficult context for communication that humans regularly encounter. When nongovernmental conferences are attended by many people from divergent countries, the participants also perceive themselves and other conferees as interacting with people from other countries and functioning in many cases as informal representatives of their own country.

Interethnic Communication

Interethnic communication is communication between members of different ethnic groups that represent co-cultures within a larger, overall culture. For example, an Irish American communicating with an Italian American would be engaging in interethnic communication. Similarly, an African American communicating with a Korean American would be considered interethnic communication.

Interracial Communication

Interracial communication is communication between members of different racial groups. Most interracial communication is also interethnic communication, as exemplified by our African American–Korean American example used above. However, the reverse is not true. That is, much interethnic communication involves members of the same racial group, as in our Irish American–Italian American example above.

Whatever the cultural context for communication, the level of a person's ethnocentrism plays a critical role in determining the effectiveness of that communication. Although ethnocentrism tends to make *intracultural* communication *more* effective, it raises severe problems for communication in all other cultural contexts. Ethnocentrism is discussed in further detail below.

CULTURAL COMMUNICATION APPREHENSION

Many people feel various forms of apprehension when communicating with individuals from different cultures. Some people are apprehensive because they are afraid of saying something offensive or because of the novelty of the situation itself. In fact, every reason we discussed for communication apprehension in Chapter 3 applies to cultural communication apprehension as well. Realizing that this was an area that needed further exploration, Neuliep and McCroskey (1997a) developed a measure called the Personal Report of Intercultural Communication Apprehension (PRICA) to examine this phenomenon. The PRICA can be seen in Scale 22 in the appendix.

Scores on the PRICA can range from 16 to 80. Higher scores indicate elevated levels of communication apprehension when interacting with individuals from other cultures. Most people who fill out the PRICA score between 28 and 32.

Neuliep and McCroskey (1997b) took the PRICA one step further and retooled the instrument to examine individual levels of communication apprehension when interacting with individuals from various ethnic groups in a scale that is now called the Personal Report of Interethnic Communication Apprehension (PRECA). The PRECA can be seen in Scale 23 in the appendix. Your scores on the PRICA and PRECA will most likely be fairly similar because the concepts are highly related. Research by Neuliep and Ryan (1998) found that people with high levels of intercultural communication apprehension were less competent at reducing uncertainty during initial interactions with someone from another country, which was also reconfirmed by Lin and Rancer (2003).

Let's now switch gears and look at some of the problems that individuals can have when interacting with people in other cultures. The first of these is ethnocentrism.

▣ ETHNOCENTRISM

Although people in other cultures do not necessarily agree with any of the other general North American beliefs, they all tend to agree with the last one noted earlier—"The American way is the best way, and if everyone were like us, the world would be a much better place." That is, they agree with it except that they substitute their own group's name in place of *American*. The Russians, Chinese, Australians, South Africans, Finns, Brazilians, Egyptians, Iranians, Egyptians, Singaporeans, Puerto Ricans, and Japanese all feel their way "is the best way," and that if everyone would just behave like "us," the world would be much better off. There are few things that have been found to be truly "pancultural," that is, the same across all cultures. But this view of one's own culture being superior to all the rest does seem to be pancultural. The view that the customs and practices of one's own culture are superior to those of other cultures is known as *ethnocentrism*. People in all cultures are ethnocentric in varying degrees. Even if they move to a new culture, they tend to retain their ethnocentric attitude about their former culture—which often makes them far less than welcome in the new culture! In Scale 24 in the appendix is the Generalized Ethnocentrism (GENE) Scale developed by McCroskey and Neuliep (1997b) and Neuliep (2002).

Ethnocentrism comes from the combination of two Greek words. *Ethnos* is Greek for "nation" and *kentron* is Greek for "center" (Klopf, 2005). In combination, they suggest that our own nation is the center of the universe. When one holds ethnocentric views, as virtually everyone does, one's own culture is used as the standard by which all other cultures will be evaluated. Most importantly, any deviation from that standard is most likely (but not always) to be seen as negative and an indication of the inferiority of the other culture and the people from that culture. Thus, because in North America we play "American" (or Canadian) football, another form of football (which we call *soccer*) is inferior and the males who play such a game are not like "real men" who play "real" football.

Favorable Aspects of Ethnocentrism

Although we have implied above that ethnocentrism may have very unfavorable implications, we will return to that consideration later. For now, we need to consider the favorable impact of ethnocentrism, for if its impact were only unfavorable there would be no reason for it to continue to exist and it might die out, as many have before it. Ethnocentrism performs a very valuable function for cultures and co-cultures. It helps maintain the integrity of the culture in the face of external threats and in the presence of interface with other cultures or co-cultures (whose members also think their culture is superior).

Ethnocentrism gives the people of a culture an identity and helps make them more homogeneous and cohesive, and as a result it promotes positive and effective communication among members of the culture. This also makes people more willing to go along with the formal and informal rules of the culture. After all, those rules are *right* and the *best* rules around! When things go wrong in communication with people from other cultures, blame can be placed externally and there is less need for internal conflict. Ethnocentrism serves as the foundation for such noble values as patriotism—for if our system is the best, it certainly is worth defending, and possibly even worth dying for! Wars have been fought to "preserve democracy." And more people have been killed in wars to protect or advance a religion than for all other reasons combined throughout human history. Additionally, the basic concept of patriotism is ethnocentric in its orientation. The foundation of patriotism is the belief that your country is right, honest, just, and good, so when you have strong patriotic beliefs, you are being ethnocentric.

Ethnocentrism, then, is the first line of defense for a culture. Without ethnocentric views in its people, a culture is open to rapid and extreme changes, and is subject to losing its existence as a culture. For this reason, people who lead co-culture groups that are living within a larger general culture, but deviate in some ways from that culture (ways that usually are important to them), often resort to very militant communication in the ethnocentric defense of their co-culture and their attacks on the larger culture. They recognize that in the absence of high ethnocentrism among the members of the co-culture, it will lose its distinctiveness and blend into the larger culture (and the leaders will lose their leadership status). If no one thinks a co-culture is worth preserving, it will not be preserved.

Unfavorable Aspects of Ethnocentrism

Like most things, ethnocentrism in moderation can be favorable. But like most other things in life, if taken too far, ethnocentrism can become a very unfavorable orientation. Equally as dangerous is for people to have strongly ethnocentric beliefs and not recognize that they do. It is always easy to see ethnocentrism in others, but it usually is difficult to see in oneself. Let us examine four potential problems for communication that can emanate from ethnocentrism: culture shock, stereotyping, prejudice, and violence.

Culture shock.   First described by Oberg (1960), culture shock is something almost everyone experiences when they move to a new cultural environment. Whether the move is from one continent to another, one state to another, or just from home to a nearby college, some degree of trauma is likely to be experienced. That trauma has been dubbed *culture shock*. If you ever have experienced it, "shock" will not seem strong enough to describe what you feel.

Most people go through stages when they move to a new culture. Usually, the move is preceded by considerable anticipation, and often with great enthusiasm. This excitement and pleasure usually are enhanced in the early days after arrival in the new environment. All of the newness is exciting, and one enjoys being introduced to new ideas, people, places, and ways of doing things. Not too much later, however, the person has to deal with the new world he or she is in—has to deal with problems relating to housing, what to eat, where to shop, how to get to work or school, where to get money, and what is expected by neighbors. In short, one has to deal with an everyday world that just is not the everyday world he or she is used to. Frequently, people feel like *everything* is different, even if only a small portion really is. This is the point at which culture shock begins to be experienced. Often, it is experienced through depression and fear of everything—other people, the water, the food, the bedding, the buildings, the weather, the traffic. This may be accompanied by severe loneliness, a longing to be "back home," and a desperate need for some things that one is used to—their favorite soft drink, a pizza, some peanut butter or other familiar food, and someone to talk to "who makes sense."

This period of shock is a critical period for the individual. Many cannot survive it and flee as rapidly as they can and return to their home culture. Others, who want to leave but cannot, often become resentful and irritable. They are apt to withdraw from contact and become very lethargic. When they come in contact with members of the new culture, they are likely to view friendly suggestions as criticisms and lash out or communicate in very negative ways at the least provocation. This is an extremely unpleasant experience for the individual, or the family if it has moved as a group. It increases self-doubt and feelings of inadequacy. Some people even go so far as to commit suicide during this stage. Others communicate in such negative ways that they alienate those around them in the new culture with whom they otherwise might have been able to become friends.

Although individuals often don't think so at the time, most people pass through this stage in a few weeks, or a few months for the more extreme sufferers. Gradually, most people begin to adapt to the new cultural environment. Some even come to view the new culture as their home, and the new culture as their own; but the latter typically happens only over many years.

A person's level of ethnocentrism is a very good predictor of the severity of the culture shock he or she is likely to experience. The more ethnocentric the person, the more severe the shock. This makes sense, for if the old ways are perfect and all the good people live in those ways, that must mean that the new ways are defective and the people who live like that are not good people, right? That really is what ethnocentrism is all about. If you want to experience other cultures, reduce your ethnocentrism first, or your intercultural experience may be one of the worst experiences of your life.

Stereotyping.   When we view a group of people from a culture or co-culture as sharing one or several common characteristics, we have formed a generalization commonly known as a *stereotype* (Lee, Jussim, & McCauley, 1995). Such generalizations are a means of organizing our experiences and interactions with others. They help us make sense out of the differences we observe among individuals and groups. We need these kinds of generalizations so that we may better predict how people around us are likely to behave in response to our communicative efforts or everyday behavior.

It is simply impossible to respond to everyone in the world as an individual and adjust our perceptions and communication to her or him personally. First, there are simply too many people to make this response feasible. Second, we know so little about most people that any responses we attempt to individualize are likely to be wrong because we don't know enough about the person to adapt appropriately.

Stereotypes are a way of making sense out of the variations in people and behavior in our environment. Such generalizations are necessary for thinking and communicating. As we come into contact with people, we need to avoid those who fit within our stereotype of "potentially dangerous." We initiate interaction with those fitting our stereotypes of either "probably interesting" or "likely pleasant to be with." We gauge our communication and other behavior to our stereotypes of various types of people as we come in contact with them: professor, student, male, female, server, police officer, parking attendant, store clerk, and child. Although each one we meet will certainly be at least somewhat different from others we have met before, we must depend on our stereotype to get us started in our initial encounter.

There is no question, then, whether a person will make the kinds of generalizations we call stereotypes. All people do, and they must in order to function. The problem comes when we stereotype within the context of high ethnocentrism. If we are highly ethnocentric, it is likely that we positively evaluate those who are very much like ourselves (that is, are good representatives of our culture) and negatively evaluate others (all, or nearly all, others). This is why we hear so many negative expressions about stereotypes. People who do not fit into the stereotype of "a lot like me" tend to be placed in a variety of very negative stereotypical categories.

When we stereotype, we tend to make three kinds of errors: overestimate differences, underestimate differences, and see what we expect to see. We will consider each in turn. The first common error we make when stereotyping is overestimating the differences between groups. Stereotypes typically exaggerate differences between cultural groups. They emphasize a few obvious differences while ignoring many similarities; therefore, the other group is seen as odd, unfamiliar, and even dangerous because it is so much "not like us." Such stereotypes lead to avoiding communication with people from another group because of fear or distrust. It is only a short step from there to disliking or even hating the stereotyped group.

The second type of error is to underestimate differences among people from another culture. Although we usually recognize that there are great differences among people in our own culture (some of whom are wonderful people, and others who are really rotten eggs!), we tend to stereotype people from other cultures as all being the same. We fail to acknowledge within our stereotype that such variability is probably present in the other culture's people as well. One rude taxi driver or hotel clerk, and our stereotype of New Yorkers becomes that of "rude people." One bad meal in a French restaurant, and "French food is terrible"—we don't acknowledge that restaurants probably range from great to awful in France just like they do "back home." We meet one group of tourists from Japan all carrying cameras and wearing aloha shirts, and our image of Japanese people takes on those characteristics.

The final type of error is the one that lets us keep our stereotype even though we have evidence of its weakness right before us. We tend to selectively perceive what our stereotype causes us to expect to perceive. If we see evidence that the stereotype is wrong, we just consider this observation as an exceptional one and discount it. If our stereotype is that purple people who live on farms are dumb, we will center our attention on the purple people who live on farms and are indeed dumb, and look at any smart purple people living on farms as exceptions—even if the "dumb" purple people account for only a small percentage of the purple people we meet who live on farms.

Given these common errors to which we are all prone, it is no wonder that once stereotypes are formed, they are highly resistant to change. In fact, if we enter a culture with such stereotypes firmly in place, we are likely to reinforce those stereotypes through our selective perceptions of those around us and our choices of people with whom to communicate in that culture—for those who fit our stereotype will be easier for us to deal with in many cases.

Prejudice.   Essentially, *prejudice* refers to *a priori judgments based on stereotypes* (Allport, 1954). The term *a priori judgments* references judgments that are made in advance of the time when they are employed. That is, we may form the judgment today but not have cause to use it for days or months into the future. When we say the judgment is based on stereotypes, we indicate that the judgments are not based on the best of information. Although the judgment may be applied to a person we have never even met or a behavior we have never observed, it is determined on the basis of limited information about a group of people about whom we may know very little and whose behavioral tendencies may be the subject of only conjecture. In short, prejudice means to prejudge a person or a person's behavior on the basis of limited information about the culture or co-culture of which that person is a member.

Although it is quite possible for such prejudgments to be positive, in actual practice most prejudice is very negative. Although most people can come up with an example or two of positive prejudices, the availability of negative examples runs far beyond those that are positive many times over. Hence, it is appropriate to think of prejudice in negative terms. It seldom helps anyone, and it usually is harmful to all it touches.

Like stereotyping, the root cause of prejudice is ethnocentrism. Because it is normal to be at least somewhat ethnocentric, and it is normal to need to place people around us into groups and then generalize about those groups in order to make sense of our environment, most (if not all) people have prejudices about some groups of people and their culturally based behaviors, including communication behaviors. We often refer to high levels of prejudice as the *isms,* which include racism, sexism, ageism, heterosexism, ableism, and lookism. In racism, we hold negative views against people from different ethnic and racial groups. Sexism is the negative view of an individual because of her or his biological sex. Ageism is prejudice against an individual because of her or his age. Heterosexism is the belief that everyone should be heterosexual and behave in a traditionally prescribed heterosexual manner. Ableism is the belief that anyone who is fully abled is superior to those who are disabled. And lookism is the negative view that some people may hold about specific individuals based on their physical appearance (hair color, eye color, weight, height, etc.). Most of these prejudices are very negative and put people in those groups in a very negative light.

We also need to emphasize that prejudice does not mean that you are discriminating against someone. Discrimination is the withholding of rights from individuals because of a group to which they belong. In the 1960s, there were many white Southerners who were racist but did not discriminate against African Americans. Ethnocentrism is a thought process; discrimination is a behavioral process. One modern group that still faces legal discrimination are gays, lesbians, and bisexuals within the United States. Although vocal forms of racism are not appropriately uttered about ethnic and racial groups, it is still very common to hear people use derogatory words for gays, lesbians, and bisexuals in normal language. On the playground, you'll often hear little boys taunting another little boy by calling him a *fag.* Teenagers today actually refer to anything they don't agree with or like as *gay* (as in "That's so gay"). The use of these terms in this manner is just as offensive to gay and lesbian individuals as various racial slurs are for racial groups, but the gay and lesbian slurs are still considered socially "OK." Scale 25 in the appendix contains the Homonegativity Short Form, created by Wrench (2001) and then shortened by Wrench (2005). This scale was designed to examine heterosexual perceptions of gay and lesbian individuals. Although this scale was specifically designed to examine perceptions of gay and lesbians, it could be rewritten to look at a number of different cultural groups.

Wrench and McCroskey (2003) examined the relationship between homonegativity, ethnocentrism, and human temperament. They found that, yes, a human's level of ethnocentrism was largely responsible for her or his level of homonegativity. However, neither ethnocentrism nor homonegativity was related to Eysenck's supertraits extraversion, neuroticism, and psychoticism. In essence, this suggests we are not biologically hardwired to not like other groups of people; we are culturally conditioned to do so. In another study conducted by Wrench (2005), the researcher examined the relationships among sociocommunicative orientation, ethnocentrism, and homonegativity. Although ethnocentrism and homonegativity were strongly, positively related constructs, only homonegativity showed a small positive relationship with assertiveness. Both ethnocentrism and homonegativity were moderately, negatively related to responsiveness. In other words, the more someone considers other's feelings, listens to what others have to say, and recognizes the needs of others, the less likely he or she will be ethnocentric or homonegative.

Another variable that has often been shown to be strongly related to ethnocentrism is religious fundamentalism. Gordon Allport (1954), a famous psychologist who spent years studying how prejudice functions, first questioned the role of religion in the creation of prejudice when he wrote,

> The role of religion is paradoxical. It makes prejudice and it unmakes prejudice. While the creeds of the great religions are universalistic, all stressing brotherhood, the practice of these creeds is frequently divisive and brutal. The solemnity of religious ideals is offset by the horrors of persecution in the name of these same ideals. (p. 444)

Two Canadian researchers in the 1990s, Altemeyer and Hunsberger, started examining the relationship between religious fundamentalism and right-wing authoritarianism. Altemeyer and Hunsberger (1992) defined *religious fundamentalism* as

> the belief that there is one set of religious teachings that clearly contains the fundamental, basic, intrinsic, essential, inerrant truth about humanity and deity; that this essential truth is fundamentally opposed by forces of evil which must be vigorously fought; that this truth must be followed today according to the fundamental, unchangeable practices of the past; and that those who believe and follow these teachings have a special relationship with the deity. (p. 118)

In this perspective, religious fundamentalism can be applied to a number of religious traditions ranging from Hinduism to Islam to Judaism to Christianity. Altemeyer and Hunsberger (1992) believed there was a second variable, right-wing authoritarianism, that needed to be referenced when examining the influence of religion on prejudice as well. Right-wing authoritarianism is the tendency of one person to believe that others should be submissive and go along with the status quo, and if someone is not submissive and going along with the status quo, then it is perfectly all right to punish that person through physical violence. In fact, Altemeyer and Hunsberger found that religious fundamentalism and right-wing authoritarianism were positively related to an individual's belief that if the government someday outlawed "radical" and "extremist" political movements, they would publicly endorse such a view, tell police about any radicals they knew, help hunt down and attack members of the outlawed organizations, and support torturing and executing them. Overall, religious fundamentalism is positively related with a number of variables: belief in creation science, belief in the traditional god, Christian orthodoxy, dogmatism, ethnocentrism, frequency of church attendance, hostility toward homosexuals, racial and ethnic prejudice, religious ethnocentrism, and right-wing authoritarianism. Religious fundamentalism has also been negatively correlated with a number of variables: doubt about religion, quest for spirituality, and intrinsic religious beliefs.

More recently, the research team comprising Wrench, Corrigan, McCroskey, and Punyanunt-Carter (2006) have started investigating religion and how it relates to communication. The first in a series of studies, Wrench et al. (2006), examined the relationships among religious fundamentalism, intercultural communication, ethnocentrism, intercultural communication apprehension, homonegativity, and tolerance for religious disagreements. Ethnocentrism was positively related to intercultural communication apprehension, religious fundamentalism, and homonegativity, and was negatively related to tolerance for religious disagreements. Intercultural communication apprehension was not related to religious fundamentalism, but was positively related to homonegativity and negatively related to tolerance for religious disagreements. In essence, this study illustrates that religious fundamentalism clearly impacts how people are able to engage in intercultural communication.

In a second study conducted by Punyanunt-Carter, Wrench, Corrigan, and McCroskey (2006), the researchers examined the relationship among religious communication apprehension (apprehension one has when talking about religion with someone of a differing religion), religious receiver apprehension, tolerance for religious disagreement, and willingness to communicate about religion. Specifically, Punyanunt-Carter et al. (2006) found a positive relationship between religious communication apprehension and religious receiver apprehension. Furthermore, the researchers reported a negative relationship between religious communication apprehension and both tolerance for religious disagreements and willingness to communicate about religion. Overall, religious communication apprehension impacts how people interact with others with regard to religious convictions.

COPING WITH ETHNOCENTRISM—YOURS AND MINE

The problems that stem from ethnocentrism, as we have seen, can be very severe. Communication can be problematic, at best, in the presence of even moderate levels of ethnocentrism—even if only one person in an interaction is behaving ethnocentrically. Communication can become absolutely destructive under circumstances in which more ethnocentrism is present, with either one person being highly ethnocentric or both people being moderately ethnocentric with regard to each other's culture. Intercultural communication, then, is fraught with potential problems, for at least some ethnocentrism is likely to exist in any intercultural communication encounter (Lustig & Koester, 1993). *Your* ethnocentrism added to *my* ethnocentrism equals *our* communicative disaster!

DeVito (1994) has outlined an ethnocentrism continuum and identified five steps along that continuum. Each step has considerable implications for the nature of intercultural communication. We will examine each of these steps.

Equality

This is the lowest level of ethnocentrism. The person at this level communicates with others on the basis of equality. Although differences in cultural practices and ways of behaving are acknowledged, they are not considered inferior to one's own, just different. If both interactants approach the communication situation with this orientation, the probability of effective communication is quite high. Unfortunately, this is the least common circumstance under which intercultural communication is likely to be undertaken.

Sensitivity

This is a moderately low level of ethnocentrism. The person at this level is sensitive to the fact that he or she is somewhat ethnocentric, and wants to communicate without offending the person from another culture. If both people in an intercultural communication encounter are at this level of ethnocentrism or lower, the likelihood of successful communication is good. This is the type of intercultural communication encounter that is likely to occur at international conferences in which everyone is "on their best behavior" and is highly sensitive to the potential problems that intercultural communication encounters may confront.

Indifference

This is a moderate level of ethnocentrism, the amount a typical person would have in a typical culture. Such people are happy with their own culture, or at least they don't think negatively about it. Such people really don't know or care much about how people from other cultures or co-cultures differ from people in their own culture. They prefer to communicate with people who are very much like themselves, and prefer not to think about people with different attitudes and values at all. If they are forced to interact with people from other cultures or co-cultures, they are likely to become much *more* ethnocentric as a result. The likelihood of a successful intercultural encounter when even one of the participants has this level of ethnocentrism is low.

Avoidance

This is a moderately high level of ethnocentrism. This person knows they are ethnocentric (although they may not have ever heard the term!), and they want little to do with people from other cultures or co-cultures. Although this person may be able to be around such people in everyday life, they will have a very difficult time communicating effectively enough with them to have a good working relationship with them, much less a personal relationship. Such people want to avoid communication with people from other cultures and co-cultures, and that is a wise choice, for the chances of effective intercultural communication with this person are very low.

Disparagement

This is a very high level of ethnocentrism. A person with this high a level is likely to be thought of by others as a racist, a sexist, and/or a jerk. The communication of this person with one from another culture or co-culture is most likely to involve hostility. He or she is likely to belittle the other person and their culture, and make a major point of talking about the positive qualities of her or his own culture, particularly in contrast to that of the other person. The probability of effective intercultural communication with this person is nil.

Many people suggest that we should learn to assume a position of *cultural relativism* when entering intercultural communication encounters in order to keep our own ethnocentrism under control. Although we can still maintain our preference for our own culture (remain ethnocentric, in other words), we need to learn to understand how other cultures see things from their vantage point rather than through the evaluative filter of our own belief system. Understanding another culture does not mandate that we personally approve of it or even that we think it to be reasonable. Understanding the other culture simply means that we are aware of what attitudes, beliefs, and values are held by members of that culture, and what implications that has for the behavior of people in that culture.

The ability to take on a culturally relativistic position is vital to our capacity to engage in effective intercultural communication. It is what makes it possible for us to function at the "sensitivity" level of ethnocentrism, the highest level at which successful interpersonal communication is likely to occur (and the lowest level most of us will ever be able to achieve!).

If cultural and co-cultural groups are to maintain positive civil relationships with each other, it is critical that children in all such groups be taught how to assume the culturally relativistic position. This position means that we accept other people *as they are,* and not expect them to change to what we would prefer them to be. We must leave our "missionary zeal" at home when we enter into intercultural communication encounters. People are not likely to change their cultural orientation as a function of others pushing them to do so, and certainly are even less likely to do so when those others are stating or implying that the people's culture is somehow inferior to that of the persuader.

For children (or adults) to learn the skill of assuming a culturally relativistic position, the skill most central to being an effective intercultural communicator, it is vital that they be taught the nature of culture and its influence on people's behavior. At present, most societies do a very good job of enculturating their children, but a very poor job of preparing those children to communicate in a world of people with alien cultures.

IMPROVING INTERCULTURAL COMMUNICATION

In a sense, everything we have talked about in the previous chapters of this book can be employed to improve your intercultural communication. At the bottom line, competent intracultural communicators have the best opportunity to become competent intercultural communicators. However, that achievement will not come without special effort and attention to the unique problems relating to communication in intercultural contexts.

Our purpose in this section is to provide several suggestions you should consider if you wish to become a more effective intercultural communicator. Attention directed to even a few of these suggestions should result in meaningful improvement.

1. *Recognize your own ethnocentrism.* As we have noted above, ethnocentrism is the number one enemy of effective intercultural communication. Although you are entitled to think that your culture is the best culture in the world, it is vital that you also recognize that such judgments are a matter of opinion, not a matter of fact, and that a person from *any* other culture is most likely not to agree with you.

2. *Avoid derogating anyone else's culture.* Be sensitive to the ethnocentric feelings of people of other cultures. They, like you, are proud of their culture. You can gain nothing by making negative references to the other person's cultural views or practices. Such references will only serve to "make an enemy" and ruin your chances for establishing effective intercultural communication. Remember: the more someone attacks a person's culture, the more ethnocentric that person will become.

3. *Demonstrate respect for the other person and her or his culture.* The principle of reciprocity that we discussed with respect to intracultural communication also applies to intercultural communication. If you show respect and sensitivity to the other person and her or his culture, it is more likely you will be shown similar respect in return. Remember: intercultural communicators do not have to like one another's cultural orientations, but they do need to be sensitive to them and show respect for them if there is to be effective intercultural communication.

4. *Be empathic.* Try to see things from the vantage point of the other person's culture. You may see them differently, but if you can empathize with the other person and understand why he or she has a view different from your own, it is more likely that the two of you can reach some common ground through your communication.

5. *Develop a higher tolerance for ambiguity.* Intercultural communication encounters often present one with situations for which one has no previous experience. Imagine being invited to a person's home and shown throughout the rooms of what we would call a mansion in this country. Then, after seeing a beautifully appointed bathroom, you request to use it but are shuttled out back to an "outhouse." If you were not aware that it was common in that culture to have fancy bathrooms that are for show only, for there is no sewer system in most areas, you could be very offended and reciprocate in very negative ways. If, however, you develop a high tolerance for ambiguity, you are more likely to presume that there is some good reason for this strange behavior, go along with it, and find out later what was going on.

6. *Reduce the level of evaluation in your messages.* People in the general North American culture tend to be highly evaluative in observations of the world around them. When people from this culture communicate with people from other cultures, most of whom are far less openly evaluative, it is important that this level of evaluation be reduced. Try to be more descriptive—"That seems somewhat strange to me; can you explain why it is done?"—in contrast to "I hate that."

7. *Be exceptionally careful in interaction management.* The cues that people follow for turn taking, initiating communication, and terminating communication are all culturally determined. You can be reasonably certain that the way you have learned to manage interaction is not the same as the way a person from another culture has learned to do so. In order not to offend, the best rule is that when in doubt, defer to the other person.

8. *Be sensitive to relational and social needs.* North Americans tend to be very straightforward and business-like. After the business is over, it is time to socialize and relate to others. That approach is not shared by many other cultures. In many cases, the cultural norm is to avoid business until people have established a very

good social relationship. If that cannot be done, no business will be allowed! In many cases, moving toward business too quickly will guarantee failure of the communication. In general, it is wise to assume that the needs for a social relationship are at least as important as the task relationship, and to attend to those needs before moving on to business.

9. *Do not assume that nonverbal messages are pancultural.* We learn our nonverbal behavior from our culture, and we learn it so well we assume it is "natural human behavior" that every human uses. It isn't. In fact, some of the most innocuous nonverbal behaviors in one culture are obscene in other cultures. Also, nodding the head in some cultures means "yes," whereas in others it means "no." Standing or sitting very close to someone while communicating is normal in some cultures, but offensive in others. When anticipating an intercultural encounter, such as traveling to another country, it is wise to read about the nonverbal behaviors characteristic of people in that culture. Otherwise, the probability of misunderstanding and/or offense is very high.

10. *Be sensitive to both differences and similarities.* In intercultural encounters, it is easy to become overly focused on the differences between people. It is, indeed, important to recognize those differences, as we have noted above, but it is equally important to look for real similarities between you and the other person. Just as is the case in intracultural communication, in intercultural communication homophily is a powerful influence toward effective communication. In some cases, a small number of important similarities will go a long way toward overcoming problems caused by less important differences. International mediation and conflict resolution often boil down to the search for important similarities on which to build common understandings.

11. *Work to build better stereotypes.* In the ideal world, there would be no stereotyping for there would be no need for stereotypes. Unfortunately, intercultural communication does not occur in such an ideal world. You are going to find it necessary to build generalizations about how to expect people to behave in various cultures. The more you read about and study a culture, the better generalizations you will be able to make. Similarly, the more contact with people from a given culture you have, the more your stereotypes can be refined.

12. *Never forget that meanings are in people, not in cultures.* Remember that people in any culture do not all behave alike. Therefore, although it is fine to start with cultural stereotypes, try to monitor the behavior of the individual with whom you are communicating in order to identify the important ways that person is different from the cultural stereotype.

The twelve suggestions above are not the "Twelve Commandments," but if followed they will increase the likelihood that your intercultural communication experiences will be more positive and effective. Unfortunately, the other person's ethnocentrism could be so high that nothing you do could overcome it and permit the two of you to communicate effectively. All we can expect of one person is to meet the other person halfway. If you follow these suggestions, you will at least have some assurance that you have done what you could.

KEY TERMS

REFERENCES

Allport, G. W. (1954). *The nature of prejudice* (25th anniversary ed.). Cambridge, MA: Perseus.

Altemeyer, B., & Hunsberger, B. (1992). Authoritarianism, religious fundamentalism, quest, and prejudice. *The International Journal for the Psychology of Religion, 2*, 113–133.

DeVito, J. A. (1994). *Human communication: The basic course* (6th ed.). New York: HarperCollins.

Gudykunst, W. B., & Kim, Y. Y. (2002). *Communicating with strangers: An approach to intercultural communication* (4th ed.). New York: McGraw-Hill.

Klopf, D. W. (2005). *Intercultural encounters: The fundamentals of intercultural communication.* Englewood, CO: Morton.

Lee, Y. T., Jussim, L. J., & McCauley, C. R. (Eds.). (1995). *Stereotype accuracy: Toward appreciating group differences.* Washington, DC: American Psychological Association.

Lin, Y., & Rancer, A. S. (2003). Ethnocentrism, intercultural communication apprehension, intercultural willingness-to-communicate, and intentions to participate in an intercultural dialogue program: Testing a proposed model. *Communication Research Reports, 20*, 62–72.

Lustig, M. W., & Koester, J. (1993). *Intercultural competence: Interpersonal communication across cultures.* New York: HarperCollins.

McCroskey, J. C. (2006). *An introduction to rhetorical communication* (9th ed.). Boston: Allyn & Bacon.

McCroskey, J. C., & Neuliep, J. W. (1997a). The development of intercultural and interethnic communication apprehension scales. *Communication Research Reports, 14*, 385–398.

Neuliep, J. W. (2002). Assessing the reliability and validity of the Generalized Ethnocentrism Scale. *Journal of Intercultural Communication Research, 31*, 201–215.

Neuliep, J. W., & McCroskey, J. C. (1997b). Development of a U.S. and generalized ethnocentrism scale. *Communication Research Reports, 14*, 145–156.

Neuliep, J. W., & Ryan, D. J. (1998). The influence of intercultural communication apprehension and sociocommunicative orientation on uncertainty reduction during initial cross-cultural interaction. *Communication Quarterly, 46*, 88–99.

Oberg, K. (1960). Cultural shock: Adjustment to new cultural environments. *Practical Anthropology, 7*, 176–182.

Punyanunt-Carter, N. M., Wrench, J. S., Corrigan, M. W., & McCroskey, J. C. (2006, November). The development and validation of a Religious Communication Apprehension Scale. Paper presented at the National Communication Association's Convention, San Antonio, TX.

Richmond, V. P., & McCroskey, J. C. (2004). *Nonverbal behavior in interpersonal relationships* (5th ed.). Boston: Allyn & Bacon.

Richmond, V. P., McCroskey, J. C., & McCroskey, L. L. (2005). *Organizational communication for survival: Making work, work.* Boston: Allyn & Bacon.

Samovar, L. A., & Porter, R. E. (1991). *Communication between cultures.* Belmont, CA: Wadsworth.

Wrench, J. S. (2001). *Intercultural communication: Power in context.* Acton, MA: Tapestry Press.

Wrench, J. S. (2005). Development and validity testing of the homonegativity short form. *Journal of Intercultural Communication Research, 34*, 152–165.

Wrench, J. S., Corrigan, M. W., McCroskey, J. C., & Punyanunt-Carter N. M. (2006). Religious fundamentalism and intercultural communication: The relationships among ethnocentrism, intercultural communication apprehension, religious fundamentalism, homonegativity, and tolerance for religious disagreements. *Journal of Intercultural Communication Research, 35,* 23–44.

Wrench, J. S., & McCroskey, J. C. (2003). A communibiological explanation of ethnocentrism and homophobia. *Communication Research Reports, 20,* 24–33.

 ## DISCUSSION QUESTIONS

1. Based on the definition of culture provided in the chapter, is a fraternity a culture? Why?

2. What are three co-cultures you belong to in life? How have these co-cultures influenced your communicative behaviors?

3. How is patriotism a form of ethnocentrism?

4. Explain a time when you've experienced culture shock.

5. How does stereotyping lead to prejudice?

12

Biological Sex and Gender in Communication

OBJECTIVES

- Explain the concept of *sex roles*.

- Differentiate between differences of kind and differences of degree.

- Understand the biological differences that exist between females and males.

- Understand how expectations at the cultural and interpersonal levels lead to the creation of sex roles.

- Differentiate between biological sex and psychological gender orientation.

- Define and explain *androgyny*.

- Define and explain *metrosexual*.

- Explain the types of communication in which females and males differ.

- Explain the sex differences in nonverbal communication.

- Differentiate between female–female, male–male, and female–male friendships.

- Define and explain *sexual communication satisfaction*.

- Define and explain *verbal sexual communication* and *nonverbal sexual communication*.

- Explain the four types of sexual communicators and why sexual communication is important in intimate relationships.

Culture is the foundation on which systems of communication are built. As we noted in the previous chapter, each culture builds its own system of communication. Culture determines the roles each of us must play in our everyday lives and the rules that we must follow. Culture is a major portion of the contextual variation from one communication situation to another. Its impact, though often not recognized immediately, is overpowering. Possibly the most important impact of culture, which frequently is not recognized, is its impact on the way we see males and females in our society (Gamble & Gamble, 2003). The earliest discussions of gender and communication date back to the early 1970s and talked about the need to form a political group within the field to identify and challenge sexist practices within the Speech Communication

Biological sex and psychological gender affect even a simple dinner party.

Association, now the National Communication Association (Dow & Wood, 2006). After this discussion, there was an increase in feminist scholarship within the field of communication, but the first textbook on the subject of gender and communication didn't appear until the mid-1980s (Pearson, 1985). Since the publication of Pearson's (1985) text, gender and communication has become a consistent area of study within the field of human communication.

From early childhood we know how boys differ from girls, and how each is expected to behave (or *mis*behave). If we don't behave in the expected ways, parents, teachers, peers, and sometimes even strangers are quick to put us back in our "place." Although we grow up thinking that biology determines how boys and girls (and, later, men and women) behave, the reality is that biology is only part of behavior. The culture in which children are raised greatly determines how they will be shaped to behave as men and women. Most important in that shaping process is how children are taught to communicate according to their biological sex.

As we noted in Chapter 1, communication changes from one context to another, and how we must communicate in various contexts depends on our *roles* in different interactions and the *rules* associated with those interactions. Roles pertain to the "part" we play in a given situation (friend, lover, teacher, student, parent, child, and so forth). Rules are the generally unspoken cultural norms that dictate how we are to play our part as a communicator in that situation. To the extent that our roles change from situation to situation, which in turn calls for a different set of rules by which to carry out interaction, communication also changes.

The way that roles are defined and rules are established in any given culture depends heavily on how that culture determines appropriate behavior differentially for females and males. These *sex roles* and how they impact our communication behaviors is the central focus of this chapter. We believe it is important to consider sex roles because they have significant impact on how each of us communicates with others in our environment. Specifically, we will look at how sex roles develop, our psychological orientations toward femininity and masculinity, how females and males differ in their use of verbal and nonverbal communication behaviors, and how they differ respective to their attitudes about, and behavior in, both intimate and nonintimate communicative relationships.

Because culture dominates how we see female and male communicative behaviors, as well as communication between females and males, it is important that we make clear at the outset the framework in which this chapter is presented. We are looking at gender and communication from the vantage point of the dominant North American culture. That culture has its distant heritage in Europe and is centered on heterosexual orientations. It should not be expected, therefore, that feminine and masculine distinctions noted here will be equally applicable to people with other cultural backgrounds and/or orientations, including many North Americans representing diverse co-cultures. Each reader, however, is invited to compare her or his own cultural orientations with those outlined here.

In the realm of biological sex, researchers generally talk about two types of differences: differences of kind and differences of degree (Allen, 1998). Differences of kind are differences that occur when two groups do different things associated with their groups.

One example of a difference of kind is menstruation. Women menstruate, and men cannot menstruate. There is a difference in how women and men are physiologically built that causes this difference to occur. However, most differences between the sexes are not differences of kind, but rather differences of degree. A difference of degree occurs when two groups have differing degrees on a trait that they both display. For example, research has shown that women smile more than men. Does this mean that men do not smile at all? Of course not. What this indicates is that women to a greater degree smile more than men. Does this mean that no men smile more than women? The answer is still no. There are many men who smile more than many women, and there are many women who simply do not smile at all. However, researchers do not look at the people at the extremes of groups (men who smile a lot and women who never smile) because the extremes are not indicative of the whole group's behavior. Instead, researchers focus on the average of a group's behavior, and then compare this average to other group(s) average(s). For example, maybe researchers find that women, on average, smile twenty times in a two-minute conversation, and men only smile an average of five times in a two-minute conversation. Researchers will then use statistical tests to determine if this is an actual difference, or a difference that can be accounted for by some kind of error. All in all, it is extremely important to realize that most of the differences discussed in this chapter are differences of degree, and not differences of kind.

 # BIOLOGICAL DIFFERENCES BETWEEN MALES AND FEMALES

The most obvious, although certainly not the most important, difference between females and males is the biological (or anatomical) one (Anderson, 2006). Beyond this basic physical difference, few other "natural" differences exist between males and females. Although there are many communicative differences between females and males that clearly occur because of our culture, we cannot completely negate the impact that biology has on communication. For example, hormonal differences between females and males create communication patterns that are different. One clear example of this biologically impacted difference between females and males is in the area of aggression (Wrench, 2002). In the wild, male mammals are always more aggressive than female mammals. This is not to say that female mammals are not aggressive. Female mammals can be quite aggressive when they feel the need to protect themselves or their young. Male mammals, on the other hand, are aggressive because of goal-oriented needs: food, position in a hierarchy, space, and mating partners. In addition to these goal-oriented reasons for aggression, male mammals are often just aggressive for the pure joy of being aggressive.

Neuroscientist Simon LeVay (1993) has found that aggressive behavior in humans has primarily been linked to a portion of the brain called the *amygdala* (the Greek word for almond). The amygdala in humans is the central point for many behaviors that have strong emotional loadings such as aggression, fear-driven behavior, and sexual behavior. Females and males actually have differing amygdala structures, which has led researchers to believe that this is one reason why males are more aggressive than females. In fact, when humans injure their amygdala, we usually see decreases in physical aggression. It is not uncommon in India for highly aggressive and uncontrolled individuals to undergo an operation (bilateral ablation of the amygdala, or removal of the amygdala) to decrease their aggressive behavior (LeVay, 1993).

Another area of communication that has been shown to be impacted greatly by biology is in the area of verbal fluency (Anderson, 2006). Women are generally much more adept at stringing together series of words related to a specific topic. Brain researchers suspect that this difference between females and males on verbal fluency has to do with the way that female and male brains actually process information. In most individuals, of both sexes, verbal information is primarily processed in the left hemisphere of the brain. However, women tend to have at least some level of activity in the right hemisphere when processing verbal information. This extra boost of brain power is also related to why women tend to recover verbal abilities much faster when they have suffered from a stroke in the left hemisphere.

However, we cannot say that simple anatomical structures in the brain are the only needed explanation for sex differences on both aggression and verbal fluency. Other research has shown that hormone production actually is extremely important to understanding biological sex differences. The amygdala sends messages to the hypothalamus to turn on the sympathetic nervous system (our fight-or-flight tendencies). The hypothalamus also links the nervous system to the endocrine system, which controls the secretion of hormones from the pituitary gland. In other words, the amygdala is directly linked to the process of hormone production within the human body. Obviously, the two primary hormones that are important to sex are testosterone (in men) and estrogen (in women). If hormones are important in human communication, then the addition of testosterone to females and estrogen to males should result in changes in behavior.

Scientists, however, cannot run around injecting men and women with hormones just to see what happens, but scientists have studied individuals undergoing gender reassignment surgery (both male-to-female and female-to-male). Male-to-female (MtF) transsexuals are people who are born biologically male, suffer from gender identity disorder (when a person is born as one biological sex but identifies as belonging to the opposite biological sex), and decide to have gender reassignment surgery to become females. Female-to-male (FtM) transsexuals are people who are born biologically female and undergo medical treatments to become males. Individuals who are undergoing gender reassignment surgery usually start hormonal treatments prior to undergoing surgery to help the transition from one biological sex to the other. In a study conducted by researchers at the John Hopkins School of Medicine by Moore, Wisniewski, and Dobs (2003), the researchers found that when MtF transsexuals are given estrogen, their levels of aggression decrease; on the other hand, FtM transsexuals, when given testosterone, tend to have increased aggressive behavior. Clearly, these findings illustrate how hormones actually impact behavior. Further research has also examined the impact that hormones have on verbal abilities. In a study conducted by Miles, Green, Sanders, and Hines (1998) in the United Kingdom, the researchers found that estrogen therapy in MtF transsexuals increased verbal ability; whereas research conducted by Pennebaker, Groom, Loew, and Dabbs (2004) found that FtM transsexuals undergoing testosterone therapy saw a decrease in verbal ability. Yet again, clearly hormones do affect our ability to communicate. Aggression and verbal ability are two examples of behavioral biological research that has demonstrated how biology impacts how females and males differ in communication behavior. However, research conducted by Canary and Hause (1993) indicated that only around 1 percent of communicative behavior is truly attributable to biological sex. Although the authors of this book realize that biology clearly impacts the differences often seen between female and male communication, a lot of differences seen between men and women are not biological, but rather are a result of our cultural practices. For this reason, let's now focus on the development of sex roles in our culture.

THE DEVELOPMENT OF SEX ROLES

At the *cultural* level, we expect each sex to behave in certain ways based on our cultural background (Eagly & Koening, 2006). Most of us know, for example, that females and males in many Asian and Middle Eastern countries interact and are perceived differently from those in North America. At the *societal* level, our expectations for the behavior of each sex are based on the norms currently prevalent within our given society. They involve such things as what clothing a person is expected to wear, what kind of job one is expected to have (if any), what kind of leisure activities one is expected to find enjoyable, and how much education one is expected to have. Because such norms are subject to change over time, societal expectancies also may change. In this society, for example, only recently has it been generally accepted in some areas that females and males are "equal" in their intellectual and emotional capacities. Earlier, males were seen as more intellectual and less emotional than females. Expectations such as these are generated through the general social (educational, occupational, religious, and political) norms characterizing our society.

Expectations at the *interpersonal* level are based on our individual interactions with "significant others"—our family, close friends, and opinion leaders. These people help to shape not only our morals, beliefs, and values about life in general, but also our views about appropriate sex roles in particular (Carlson, 1976; Galvin & Brommel, 1982). Thus, you may have been raised believing that males and females are equal in every aspect and should be treated in that way, or you may have been raised with the view that "a woman's place is in the home" and that "the man is expected to bring home the bacon."

All of these expectations are generated through our interpersonal and mass communication experiences with others and are reflective of the culture as it exists around us. Most of us never have really *chosen* how we view the roles of men and women. We have just *acquired* a view, and unless we have run into someone who has a view that is strongly divergent from our own, we probably have never really thought much about the differences between men and women at all. After all, such differences are just *natural*, right? Of course! Ours is the right culture, it is normal, and what it says is right, is right. See the discussion of "ethnocentrism" in Chapter 11!

The types of expectations just described are important to understanding perceptions of female–male differences because they lead to stereotypical perceptions of what roles males and females should fill (Carlson, 1976). When these perceptions become strong enough and prevalent enough, they become, in effect, norms for sex roles. Since its beginnings, the general North American culture has adhered to the norm that the role of males is primarily *instrumental* and that of females is primarily *expressive*. The norm of the instrumental male role suggests that males are mostly task oriented, their major concern being to get things done—complete an education, compete with others, be an occupational success, and so forth. The norms of the female expressive role suggest that females are mostly other oriented, their major concern being to develop socially, show care for others, share self with others, be a mother and a wife, and so forth. In terms of communication differences, then, sex-role norms imply that male communication behavior will be mostly task oriented (much talk about work, future goals, making money, and sports) and that female communication will be mostly other oriented (much talk about social affairs, the family, interpersonal relations, and so forth).

Although much has been made of greater equality between the sexes over the past four decades, the primary socialization of children today is not greatly different from how it was several decades ago. In particular, socialization of males still focuses on the instrumental and generally ignores, for the most part, the expressive. In many communities in North America, however, females are receiving more socialization toward the instrumental than they have in the past. Thus, males continue to be socialized toward the single, instrumental role, but females are frequently are being socialized toward dual (instrumental and expressive) roles.

It is important at this point to make a distinction between two general kinds of roles. *Ascribed roles* are those we are born into and cannot avoid, such as our ethnic group, nationality, family position (e.g. firstborn or later born), and biological sex. *Achieved roles* are those we fill by earning a particular position, such as college student, supervisor, professor, foreperson, lieutenant, and husband or wife. Although we have no control over our ascribed roles, we can influence the achieved roles we fill. If you want to earn your doctorate in communication, you will work and study to do so. If you want to marry and become a husband or wife, you will structure your social life so as to find a suitable mate. Essentially, and this is the major point here, females can achieve a normative instrumental male role, and males can achieve a normative expressive female role, if they individually choose to do so. But society will not push either the female or the male in these directions. Nevertheless, females and males are achieving these non-sex-typed roles today. Contemporary examples include females who are filling traditionally male-dominated positions in business and industry, government, the military, and politics. Also, males are achieving expressive roles as elementary teachers, nurses, secretaries, and "househusbands."

Sex-role norms can be and often are violated. This is much more acceptable today than it was two or three generations ago. At that time, it was practically unheard of that a mother of two children could also be a successful public relations executive, just as it was unheard of that a father could stay home with the kids and do the housekeeping while his wife earned the family income. Inasmuch as these violations lead to changes in sex-role norms, they also lead to changes in perceptions of appropriate communication behavior. Hence, we are becoming accustomed to visiting with female physicians, voting for (or against) female politicians, talking with our child's male first grade teacher, and asking a male telephone operator for assistance. Our perceptions are changing such that it is becoming "acceptable" for males to be more expressive and other oriented in their communication behavior and for females to be more assertive and task oriented. Changes in norms in sex-role expectations are leading to changes in our orientations toward females and males and the differences between them. Essentially, these orientations are psychological in nature and relate to our self-identification with femininity and masculinity.

PSYCHOLOGICAL GENDER ORIENTATION

When researchers and scholars in the social sciences use the terms *male* and *female*, they usually are referring to anatomical (or biological) sex (Dindia & Canary, 2006). When the terms *feminine* and *masculine* are used, however, reference is being made to *gender*, a type of personality orientation. Thus, describing someone as *feminine* does not necessarily mean a person is female, nor does describing a person as *masculine* mean the person is male. Rather, masculinity and femininity concern one's identification with and use of behaviors that are generally characterized in the culture as either masculine or feminine behaviors. This identification is called one's *psychological gender orientation.*

A person's psychological gender orientation is her or his level of self-identification with both dominance (instrumentality) and submissiveness (expressiveness) in interactions with others. That is, it is the person's overall orientation represented by communication behaviors that reflect dominance or submissiveness toward those with whom he or she interacts. A person with a highly feminine gender orientation is one who employs mostly submissive communication behaviors. The person's communication behaviors will express helpfulness, cheerfulness, affection, sympathy, sensitivity to others' needs, understanding, compassion, sincerity, an eagerness to soothe hurt feelings, warmth, tenderness, and gentleness. On the other hand, a person with a highly masculine gender orientation is one who employs mostly dominant communication behaviors. The person's communication behaviors will express competitiveness, aggressiveness, a willingness to lead, self-sufficiency, forcefulness, assertiveness, and independence. In short, a very masculine individual expresses strong control needs, and a very feminine individual expresses strong affection needs.

The development of gender orientation is related to the development of self-concept (the way one views oneself as a person) and stems from our social experiences and background. Essentially, how others respond to us as either a female or a male affects how we view ourselves. As little boys or girls, for example, we are dressed in either blue or pink, play with either balls or dolls, and pretend that we are either "daddies" or "mommies." A little girl may further observe and be taught that girls are supposed to be nice, are not to get dirty, are supposed to learn piano, are not to hit or play rough with others, and are to portray appropriate manners. A little boy is likely to be taught that he shouldn't play with dolls, should play to win, shouldn't fear getting into a fight or taking risks, and should never cry. Thus, females and males at an early age develop masculine and feminine role expectations and learn behaviors associated with each of these roles.

Generally, boys develop masculine behaviors and receive reinforcement for them. Likewise, girls generally develop and receive reinforcement for feminine behaviors. To the extent that these expectations are fulfilled through interactions with others, individuals will develop a view of themselves that indicates, "This is the way I am supposed to be." This self-view eventually develops into a particular gender orientation that is manifested in the types of dominant or submissive communicative behaviors we have mentioned. That is, females tend to be taught to communicate in submissive, nurturing, and expressive ways, whereas males typically are taught to communicate in dominant, instrumental, and competitive ways.

Females who have a high feminine orientation and males who have a high masculine orientation are said to be *sex typed*. Sex-typed females, then, are those who exhibit mostly submissive communication behaviors when interacting with others, and sex-typed males are those who display mostly dominant communication behaviors. However, you may know people of both sexes who most often exhibit behaviors typically thought to be those of the opposite sex. A "tomboy," for example, is a female who generally exhibits dominant, competitive, "masculine" behaviors, and a "sissy" is a male who most often displays submissive, expressive, "feminine" behaviors. These individuals are said to be *sex reversed* because their behaviors indicate a gender orientation opposite of their biological sex. It is likely that they have developed such an orientation because, like the sex-typed individual, they have some need to engage in their respective behaviors and have received reinforcement for doing so.

You may be thinking by now that there are times when you feel that you exhibit mostly submissive behaviors, other times when you show more dominant behaviors, and still other times when you feel that you express a combination of both. In other words, you may be the type of person who engages in specific behaviors according to the demands of the given situation. If so, you may have an *androgynous* gender orientation.

The term *androgyny* is a combination of the Greek words *andros,* meaning "man," and *gyne,* meaning "woman" (Bem, 1974). Thus, an androgynous person is one who can exhibit both masculine and feminine characteristics. In terms of psychological gender orientation, this type of individual is able to adapt to a variety of roles by engaging in either instrumental or expressive behaviors, depending on the situation. Essentially, then, the androgynous individual can be warm, compassionate, sincere, helpful, sympathetic, and submissive in one situation, and turn right around and be competitive, risk taking, aggressive, independent, and dominant in another situation. An example of an androgynous female might be the college student majoring in petroleum engineering (a traditionally male major) who not only spends her Saturdays and Sundays watching college and professional football (a typically masculine recreation) but also enjoys going shopping (a typically feminine recreation) and studying dance (a traditionally feminine interest). An androgynous male might be exemplified by the firefighter (a traditionally male occupation) who spends one of his days off each month doing volunteer work at a day care center (a typically feminine, nurturing activity).

Generally, then, the person with an androgynous gender orientation is highly flexible in her or his behavior. These individuals do not feel limited in their communication with others and are fully aware of and adaptable to their affection and control needs. Thus, androgynous individuals are able to sense another person's needs to be dominant in a given situation and, if they deem it appropriate, will engage in submissive behaviors. Similarly, this type of individual recognizes when the partner in an interaction requires compassion and warmth and is quite able to meet those needs. On the other hand, persons who are either highly sex typed or highly sex reversed are quite limited in their behavior. Specifically, they are not as adaptable to varying situational demands as are androgynous people. The highly masculine person, for example, may have difficulty expressing sympathy for another, whereas the highly feminine individual might have trouble coping with a very competitive and aggressive interaction. In sum, our psychological gender orientation develops from our social interactions—the way others respond to us affects how we see ourselves and our roles as females or males, and these effects appear in our interpersonal communication behavior.

Now that you have a basic understanding of sex roles and psychological gender orientation, we can turn to a more general discussion of female–male difference in communication behavior. We wish to reiterate at this point that females and males communicate differently not just because they are anatomically different but because they are taught to accept certain sex roles and gender orientations that are proscribed by their culture. Each gender orientation represents certain communication patterns that the culture determines are appropriate means of expressing femininity or masculinity. In short, we do what we are taught to do, not just what we are biologically predetermined to do.

In our discussion of communicative differences between females and males below, we will be making comparisons that have been found to exist in the general North American culture. Such differences should not be expected to exist to the same extent, or even in the same direction, in other cultures—or even in all co-cultures within the general North American culture. Remember: gender differences are primarily a function of cultural conditioning—different cultures produce different differences. Today, however, we are seeing a growing movement against traditional gender norms. One such group of individuals not adhering to gender norms is called the metrosexual.

Recently, a lot of people have been talking about a new wave of psychologically related gender issues specifically related to heterosexual men. The new term for gender scholars and advertising executives is *metrosexual*. A metrosexual is defined as a "dandyish narcissist in love with not only himself, but also his urban lifestyle; a straight man who is in touch with his feminine side" (Simpson, 2002). Simpson argues that the line between heterosexual male behaviors and their gay counterparts is quickly disappearing. Simpson went on to say in his 2002 article "Meet the Metrosexual" that the

> [t]ypical metrosexual is a young man with money to spend, living in or within easy reach of a metropolis—because that's where all the best shops, clubs, gyms, and hairdressers are. He might be officially gay, straight, or bisexual, but this is utterly immaterial because he has clearly taken himself as his own love object and pleasure as his sexual preference. Particular professions, such as modeling, waiting tables, media, pop music, and nowadays, sport, seem to attract them but, truth be told, like male vanity products and herpes, they're pretty much everywhere.

Although Simpson's comments were originally intended to be viewed as sarcasm, advertising executives quickly realized that metrosexuals were an untapped market that could be easily targeted through advertising messages. Even television shows like the

David Beckham, a former British footballer who currently plays for the Los Angeles Galaxy, is the epitome of metrosexual.

acclaimed 2003 summer hit *Queer Eye for the Straight Guy* tapped into this genre that is quickly becoming a norm.

For gender scholars, the metrosexual is less a narcissist than a male who has openly accepted the role of gender androgyny within our society. Males in the United States are beginning to realize that a lot of the gender propaganda they were raised with simply isn't true: being aggressive and domineering won't always help you in the business world, women do expect males to take care of themselves physically, and there is nothing unmasculine about treating yourself with respect and wanting to present yourself in a positive light.

By this point, you most likely have recognized that gender differences are highly associated with the three components of basic communication competence which we discussed in Chapter 3—assertiveness, responsiveness, and versatility. Take a second and look up your score. In the general North American culture, males are taught to be more assertive, and this is taken in this culture to be a positive sign of masculinity. In contrast, females are taught to be more responsive, and this is taken to be a positive sign of femininity. They are also taught to avoid engaging in the behaviors of the other gender—to be consistently masculine or feminine, not versatile. Thus, children of both genders are taught to be "half-competent." They are encouraged to exhibit the communication behaviors culturally appropriate for their gender and avoid those behaviors that are culturally inappropriate for their gender. These differences in behavior are reflected in both verbal and nonverbal communication behaviors. Before we start talking about gender differences and communication, we previously noted that Canary and Hause (1993) analyzed 1,200 research articles and found that only about 1 percent of social behavior can be attributed to a person's biological sex. This notion clearly differs greatly from that of pop psychology, which has tried to say that males and females are so drastically different in how they communicate that they come from different planets. The next few sections will examine what we really do know about men and women and how they communicate.

SEX DIFFERENCES IN VERBAL COMMUNICATION

Differences between males and females in verbal communication are most evident in the type and amount of information they disclose, the language they use, and the subject matter they discuss. We consider each of these areas below.

Self-Disclosure

According to most of the research in the general North American culture, females disclose more information about themselves than do males. Although several studies in this area of communication have found women *not* to be significantly more disclosive than men, none have found men to be more disclosive (Aries, 2006; Cline, 1982, 1983). Women sometimes self-disclose a greater amount of information, with longer duration, and with more intimate topics than do men. Moreover, females are less guarded and more honest about disclosing negative information about themselves than are males. Females also disclose more intimate information to other females than they do to males. On the other hand, males tend to reserve their most intimate disclosures for females with whom they are close, being quite non-intimate in self-disclosure to other males. Males typically do not self-disclose much negative information to either sex. Some research suggests that sex differences in disclosure may be related to socioeconomic level and geographic region. For example, studies utilizing students from some "prestigious" universities show no difference in the amount of disclosure between females and males.

North American females generally have been found to be more disclosive than British females. In both cultures, when sex differences have been found, women are consistently more self-disclosive than men. The most plausible explanation for this pattern would seem to be the greater expressiveness of females over males in these societies, a function of the feminine gender orientation. As we have already noted, the norm in the general North American culture is for females to be more outgoing, expressive, friendly, and other-oriented than males. The female who adheres to this sex-role expectancy is quite likely to be more self-disclosive in her communication with others.

Language Use

Have you ever felt that your male friends use different types of words and phrases than do your female friends? Such differences do indeed exist. As we have already noted in earlier chapters, the language we use both constructs and reflects our perceptions of reality. Thus, much research in recent years has sought to determine the effects of certain word usages on perceptions of the sexes (Bate, 1988; Mulac, 2006). This body of research has examined the use of particular nouns, verbs, and pronouns and found that some do indeed affect how we perceive males and females (Mulac, 2006). For example, studies have found females to be (1) labeled more frequently than males by informal terms (first names or nicknames), (2) labeled more often in terms of the men with whom they are associated rather than by their own identity (*Bill's wife*, *Mrs. Jones*, *Mr. Smith's girl*), and (3) identified more than males as sex objects (*fox, doll, babe*). Studies have found that females, on the other hand, use more euphemisms (substituting more acceptable or polite terms for embarrassing terms; for example, "He is intellectually challenged" instead of "He really is stupid"), more emotional terms ("I just *love* that!" instead of "That is very nice"), and more intensifiers ("enormous" as opposed to "large" or "big") than do males.

A great deal of research in this area has looked at the use of *generic* pronouns, those used to refer to people in general rather than gender-specific references. The most notable of these terms in the English language is the generic *he*. This pronoun has served for centuries in both written and oral communication as a referent for both males and females, particularly when the actual referent is unknown. When a female referent is known, however, the pronoun *she* is used instead, although *he* remains when a male referent is known. It is perhaps because of this dual usage of *he* that it has been found to be an unsatisfactory generic for many readers and listeners. Not surprisingly, studies have shown that the use of masculine terms as generics causes readers and listeners to think of the referent as male. Such language use shapes our perceptions in unintended ways—we read or hear a generic such as *he* and envision something specifically sex typed, which is what use of generic terms is specifically designed to avoid in the first place. Many feminist religious scholars have taken issue with the use of the pronoun *He* in reference to religious deities that are not known to have a biological sex.

Finally, we tend to use different types of verbs in reference to females and males. For males we generally use verbs expressed in the active voice; for females, however, we more often use verbs expressed in the passive voice. Talking about Moesha and Phillip going to the market, for example, we are more likely to say, "Phillip took Moesha to the market" (active verb "took") or "Moesha was taken to the market" (passive verb was "taken") as opposed to "Moesha rode to the market with Phillip."

Thus, females and males both use and are referenced by different types of words and word patterns. Again, the source of this differential usage most likely stems from the differences in sex-role expectations we have for feminine and masculine behavior. Different language usage allows us to fulfill and maintain those culturally based expectations. For a complete analysis of the differences in female and male speech patterns, read Mulac (2006).

Subject Matter

We have already noted that females and males differ in the types of information that they disclose to others. On a more basic and less intimate level, males and females also differ relative to the types of topics with which they most frequently begin conversations. These differences occur in both same-sex and opposite-sex interactions. Some of the patterns may surprise you. When females initiate conversation with other females, the most likely subjects they will discuss are men, clothing, and other women. When men initiate conversation with other men, the most likely topics of discussion will be business, money, and sports or other amusements. In opposite-sex dyads, when females initiate conversation with males, they are most likely to discuss men and other women. When males initiate conversation with females, however, they are most likely to begin with a discussion of sports or other amusements. When such differences occur, they can probably be attributed to the instrumental, external orientation of males in contrast to the expressive, internal orientation of females. These orientations, of course, are remnants of cultural norms and expectations. Thus, normative expressive behavior of females explains their likelihood of beginning and carrying on conversations about other people, both men and women. Clothing, by the way, is a highly expressive subject for females. Similarly, the normative instrumental behavior of males explains their likelihood of initiating interactions on the subjects of work, money, or amusements.

Females and males do indeed differ in their verbal communication with others. Most of these differences stem from cultural norms and expectations we have developed about female and male behavior. Perhaps more noticeable than the verbal differences on an interpersonal level, however, are the nonverbal differences between the sexes.

SEX DIFFERENCES IN NONVERBAL COMMUNICATION

Differences between females and males in nonverbal communication have been consistently reported by research on eye behavior and facial expressions, posture, use of personal space, and touching behavior (Richmond & McCroskey, 2004). Because these areas were considered more fully in Chapter 3, this section focuses solely on how the sexes differ in their use and interpretation of them.

Eye Behavior and Facial Expressions

Eye behavior differs for females and males in terms of the frequency, duration, and distance of eye contact between interactants (Exline, Gray, & Schwette, 1965; Exline & Winters, 1965). Generally, females have a greater frequency and longer duration of eye contact with others than do males. Females also look more when talking and when others are talking to them. Males tend to share gaze with a partner at greater distances, whereas females maintain mutual gaze at closer distances. Although these findings seem rather straightforward, several factors impinge on male and female gaze behavior. When interacting with an opposite-sex acquaintance, for example, both sexes tend to try to increase physical distance between themselves and their partner in an apparent effort to reduce eye contact (Kendon & Look, 1969). Other factors that affect differences in eye behavior are verbal intimacy, anxiety, body orientation (posture), age, and degree of friendship.

Relative to facial expressions, differences appear in the amount of emotion a person reveals. Because they are inhibited in our society from showing their emotions, males tend not to display as much facial emotion as females do. Both females and males smile more when they are seeking social approval from others. Generally, however, females smile more often than do males, particularly females from the Southern U.S. subculture. Males, of course, are highly unlikely to exhibit crying and are more likely than females to display displeasure through their facial expressions.

Posture and Gestures

The next time you are sitting in a classroom, look around and see if you notice any differences in the way females and males sit. Make a similar observation the next time you are in or near a mixed-sex group of people; take note if there are any differences between the sexes in their use of gestures. Typically, you will find that males sit or stand with their legs apart, hold their hands against their hips, keep their heads erect, maintain an upright stance, and take up space to a greater extent than females (Richmond & McCroskey, 2004). Although males are more likely to use pointing gestures in interactions, females are more likely to clasp their hands together, fold their arms across their midsections, or pat their hair. Finally, when seated during a dyadic interaction, males are likely to engage in many more seat-shifting movements than are females.

Personal Space

In general, females maintain closer physical distances in their interactions than do males (Leibman, 1970; Sommer, 1959; Willis, 1966). As with eye behavior, however, several variables seem to affect this trend. The sex of the interaction partner is perhaps the most influential of these. Several studies have shown that females tend to sit closer to other females than do males. It seems that males simply require more space than females. They are, however, likely to sit closer to females than to other males. The direction of the other person's approach also affects use of space. For example, females let others approach them more closely from the sides, whereas males let people approach them more closely from the front. In terms of their own approach, females are likely to approach closer to a "best friend" and to remain further away than males from "mere friends."

Touching Behavior

Several interesting relationships have been found between touching behavior and one's sex. First, the norm for adults of both sexes in our society is one of very limited and infrequent physical contact. Touching behavior appears to be much more frequent for both sexes early in life, with frequency of touch steadily decreasing as the individual gets older. Studies show that the greatest frequency of touch occurs during infancy, when much consistent contact is maintained between mother and infant. Generally, however, male infants receive more touch during the first six months of life, and thereafter females increasingly receive more touch from both parents.

An interesting facet of this research, that has received attention is touch avoidance, a person's unwillingness or lack of desire to have much physical contact with others. Research has discovered gender differences in touch avoidance. Specifically, heterosexual males tend to show much higher levels of touch avoidance toward other males than do heterosexual females toward other females (Leibowitz & Andersen, 1978). Conversely, females show a tendency toward higher touch avoidance toward males than do males toward females. Moreover, both of these trends are consistent over various age groupings.

Finally, it is interesting to consider how females and males interpret different types of touch. Studies show that both females and males view a "pat" as the most friendly and playful form of touch, and a "stroke" as the most loving, sexual, and pleasant form. Although both sexes indicate that touch to the genital areas communicates a sexual meaning, differences between the sexes appear in that males are more likely to view genital/sexual touch by females as positive, whereas females view such touch from males more negatively. One important note: These findings were for unmarried females; married females perceive sexual touch quite positively. It is likely that the research environment had a major impact on the results of this research.

As for understanding and interpreting nonverbal communication, research has shown that females tend to be more nonverbally sensitive than males (Hall, 2006). In essence, females appear to be more adept at understanding both their own sex's nonverbal communication and the nonverbal communication from males as well. Although some scholars argue that women may be biologically more adept at interpreting nonverbal information (Anderson, 2006), other scholars argue that women may be socialized through their social roles to be more nonverbally sensitive (Eagly & Koening, 2006; Hall, 2006).

Many differences exist in the nonverbal behavior of females and males. In most cases, the origin of the differences can be traced back to cultural norms and general sex stereotypes. To the extent that nonverbal behaviors are expressive and self-disclosive we can expect, based on cultural norms, that females will display more emotional nonverbal behaviors than will males. Conversely, to the extent that nonverbal behaviors indicate dominance and interaction control, we can expect that males will exhibit more of them. It is equally likely, however, that an individual with an androgynous gender orientation will be able to adapt to and utilize a variety of nonverbal communication behaviors across numerous interaction situations. Inasmuch as people's communication behavior is a function of their gender, their perspectives toward interpersonal relationships are also a function of gender.

GENDER AND INTERPERSONAL RELATIONSHIPS

Men and women tend to perceive interpersonal relationships differently. Their differing perspectives on relationships coincide with the varied expectancies and norms that society has for men and women. In general, then, relationships for females revolve around an expressive function; whereas, relationships for males revolve around an instrumental function. This section discusses female and male perspectives on friendships and intimate communicative relationships.

Friendships between Females

Females tend to develop friendships with other females in terms of a communal function. Wright (2006) listed a number of characteristics associated with communal friendships: intimacy, personal/emotional expressiveness, amount of self-disclosure, quality of self-disclosure, confiding, and emotional supportiveness. In essence, women seek out friendships that enable them to satisfy their needs for affection and belonging. Phillips and Wood (1983) have identified three primary reasons why females develop friendships. One is *recreation.* Many female friendships are based on shared activities and events. Examples would be friendships developed at a pilates class, at PTA meetings, or at the hairstylist. These types of friendships serve especially to provide conversation and noncommittal association with another. Thus, the friends who greet and interact with one another in aerobics class will not likely have an association outside that class.

Another reason females develop friendships is for *personal support.* This type of friendship stems from a need to have a confidante with whom to share one's deepest thoughts, feelings, and concerns. Females are more likely to share this kind of information with another female than they are with a male. Moreover, females maintain this type of relationship much longer than do males—females are much more likely than males to have associations with "lifelong" friends. In short, a female's greater expressed need for personal support leads her to expend more energy maintaining close associations with certain other females.

The third reason females develop friendships is for *problem solving.* This type of friendship serves to provide a female with information and experience she might not be able to acquire from anyone else. Housewives, for example, develop friendships with other housewives; most interactions might deal with homemaking ideas, child-rearing problems, and so forth. Similarly, women employed outside the home tend to develop friendships with other employed women, and many of their interactions concern, for example, career goals, sexism, equal pay and opportunity, and corporate responsibility.

One feature of female–female friendships that is less apparent in male–male friendships is *reciprocation.* Females, more so than males, view friendships as dependent on mutual exchange, a give and take. Thus, females tend to put into their friendships with others what they expect to get out of them, and vice versa. Interestingly, however, females are likely to give up a female friendship for a relationship with a male. Essentially, females sustain more female–female relationships than they do female–male relationships, so they may be willing to sacrifice one or more of their female friends to have a relationship with a male.

Friendships between Males

Most male–male friendships are characterized by the notion of agency or are activity centered. This coincides with a male's predominantly task-oriented perspective toward relationships. Males typically develop and maintain relationships with other males that satisfy primarily, the social need for control, but also the need for belonging, so we classify male friendships as agentic, whereas female friendships are communal. However, this does not mean that female and male friendships cannot show atypical sex characteristics (female agentic friendships and male communal friendships), or that females are more likely to be communal and males are more likely to be agentic within their friendships (Gamble & Gamble, 2003; Hays, 1984; Rawlins, 1982, 1992; Wright, 2006). Contrary to female–female friendships, male–male friendships tend to be quite superficial. Males do not share their deepest feelings and problems with each other; they are more likely to turn to females for such disclosure—or not disclose such things at all.

Male friendships develop mostly around activities. A male's closest male friendships are likely to be with men with whom he works, who have the same hobbies he has, or who belong to the same social organization or club. College males, for example, find their closest friendships to be with fraternity brothers or roommates. Moreover, Phillips and Wood (1983) have found that males define friendship in terms of allies and team members. Friends for a male are those who share mutual favors and take sides with each other. Males, perhaps more so than females, socialize with those who are most like themselves. That is why in college you may notice that many male friendships are among people who have the same major, are from the same home town, are members of the same athletic team, or frequent the same night spots.

Like female friendships, male friendships develop because of recreational, personal support, and problem-solving concerns. Unlike females, however, males are unlikely to disclose much about their values, fears, or troubles associated with these concerns. Also, male friendships are less reciprocal than female friendships. In fact, many males refrain from using the term *friend* to describe or refer to their male associations. It would seem, then, that males develop friendships with other males in order to get from the relationships what they can, and they think less about what they can put into the relationship. This isn't to suggest that males are selfish, egocentric ogres. Rather, it is a reflection of their instrumental orientation. Males have a culturally engendered need to be dominant and competitive, and to develop their leadership qualities. It is through their friendships with other males that males are best able to develop and satisfy these needs.

 ## INTIMATE FEMALE–MALE RELATIONSHIPS

No type of interpersonal relationship is as central to a heterosexual's social concerns and desires as is an intimate interpersonal relationship with a member of the opposite sex. However, females and males differ in their perspectives on what intimacy is and how it should be expressed.

Men equate intimacy with sexual activity much more so than do women. In their survey of female and male attitudes toward intimate interpersonal relationships, Phillips and Wood (1983) found that males desire intimate relationships with females who provides not only nurturing and support but also *good sex*. For the males studied, intimacy with females could not be discussed without reference to sex, and many males reported that their first thoughts when meeting a female in a work environment were about her possibilities as a sexual partner. Unlike males, females do not openly admit to seeing sex as highly important in male–female relationships. They tend to feel that opposite-sex relationships can develop and be sustained without implications for sex. As a result, heterosexual females often find nonsexual relationships with gay men to be particularly pleasant. Although females were unlikely to state it openly, the Phillips and Wood (1983) survey revealed that most females do perceive sex as an important issue in their relationships with heterosexual males. Given these discrepant views of female–male relationships, it is no wonder that considerable tension exists in many organizations employing both females and males as a function of contemporary concerns with the definition and prevention of sexual harassment in the workplace.

Given the expressive and instrumental orientations of females and males, respectively, it would appear that most intimate opposite-sex relationships evolve in a complementary fashion. Males seek to develop intimate relationships with a female who will enable them to maintain their self-definition of dominance, self-sufficiency, and independence, but who will also provide them with needed compassion, empathy, affection, understanding, and help. Females desire intimate relationships with a male who will enable them to express their nurturance, compassion, and affection, and who in turn will provide responsibility and leadership when it is needed. These orientations may appear boringly traditional and may seem to leave out the independent woman and the compassionate man. They do, however, represent the norm for complementary opposite-sex relationships in our society, and they stem from the expectancies formed by the cultural norms for males and females.

Many intimate female–male relationships are symmetrical. These are relationships in which the partners are "balanced" in most ways. Thus, some female–male relationships may involve partners who share equal orientations toward issues, share interests and activities, perceive themselves equal in status and ability, and perhaps even have the same career objectives and goals. The advantage of this type of relationship is that it allows both partners a wide margin of independence and power in the relationship.

When does communication come into play with intimate opposite-sex relationships? As Chapter 10 emphasized on relationship development, communication *is* the relationship. Thus, the level of intimacy experienced between two partners in a relationship is a function of their communication. To the extent that communication is intimate, the relationship will be intimate. Intimacy is, of course, communicated in different ways among people and relationships. Much intimacy is communicated verbally ("I love you"; "We are meant for each other"), but a great deal of it is communicated nonverbally through such general modes as touch, eye contact, and facial expression. For intimacy to be fully and adequately expressed between two partners, however, it should be conveyed through both verbal *and* nonverbal messages. That is, for most partners it will not be sufficient to be told "I love you" without actions to back it up, nor will the actions stand alone without appropriate verbal support.

In many opposite-sex relationships, sexual activity serves as an important indicator of intimacy. Moreover, a person's satisfaction with sexual relations within the relationship may be important to general satisfaction with her or his partner and their association. Communication researchers have attended to this aspect of intimacy and have developed the concept of *sexual communication satisfaction.* This is defined as "satisfaction with communication about sexual behavior and the satisfaction that sexual behavior itself communicates" (Wheeless, Wheeless, & Baus, 1981, p. 2).

Sexual communication satisfaction is reflected by (1) satisfaction with communication about sexual behavior, (2) communication about what kind of sexual behavior is satisfying, (3) satisfaction from what is communicated by certain sexual behaviors, and (4) willingness and/or ability to communicate about sex with one's partner. In the appendix, you will find a copy of a scale designed to examine the extent to which couples communicate both verbally and nonverbally during sex in Scale 26.

Research has shown that individuals are more satisfied during sex when their sexual partner communicates both verbally and nonverbally. From this conceptualization, it can be deduced that sexual behavior is both a verbal and a nonverbal form of communication. It involves not only engaging in sexual activity but also talking about those activities with one's partner. Also, sexual communication satisfaction pertains to a wide variety of sexual activities ranging from winking at one's partner to having sexual intercourse. That it is indicative of the level of intimacy is substantiated by research that has shown sexual satisfaction to be highest for partners whose relationships are highly developed, and lowest in relationships that are just beginning and those that are completing termination (Wheeless et. al., 1981).

According to the research conducted by Wrench, Brogan, and Fiore (2005), people who communicated using verbal sexual communication (degree to which an individual tells her or his sexual partner what he or she enjoys sexually) were perceived as being highly extraverted and not neurotic. Furthermore, people who communicated using verbal sexual communication were also perceived as being highly responsive, but not assertive. Lastly, people who had sexual partners who communicated using verbal sexual communication reported that they were more likely to be sexually satisfied, and were more likely to discuss their sexual relationship outside of sexual situations. As for people who communicated using nonverbal sexual communication (degree to which an individual shows or demonstrates to her or his sexual partner what he or she enjoys sexually), an individual's temperament or sociocommunicative orientation did not impact their use of nonverbal sexual communication. However, people who had partners who communicated using nonverbal sexual communication were more sexually satisfied and more likely to discuss their sexual relationship outside of sexual situations.

Figure 12.1 illustrates the four different types of sexual communicators found in the Wrench et al. (2005) research. The first type of sexual communicator is seen in Quadrant 1 and is labeled the competent sexual communicator and exhibits both high nonverbal and high verbal sexual communication. As a whole, people were more sexually satisfied with partners who were both verbally and nonverbally communicative. Quadrant 2 represents sexual communicators who tell their partners what they enjoy sexually, but do not communicate their desires in a nonverbal fashion. Quadrant 3 represents those sexual communicators who show or demonstrate to their partners what they enjoy sexually, but do not verbally communicate their desires. Lastly, Quadrant 4 represents people who neither verbally nor nonverbally communicate sexual desires to their partners. As a whole, people who are noncompetent sexual communicators have the least satisfying sexual relationships and are less likely to communicate about sex outside of sexual situations. Overall, noncompetent sexual communicators will likely have many problems in their intimate relationships relating to their lack of sexual communication.

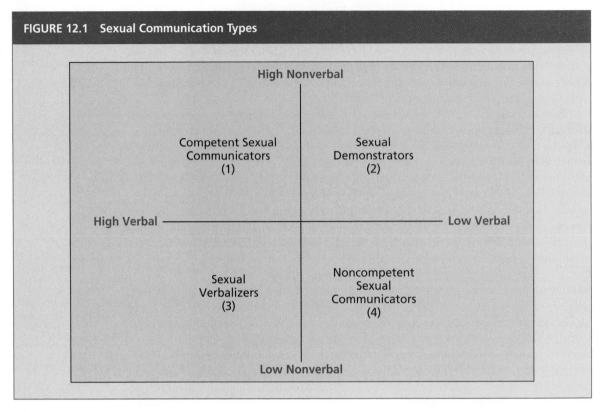

FIGURE 12.1   Sexual Communication Types

High Nonverbal

Competent Sexual
Communicators
(1)

Sexual
Demonstrators
(2)

High Verbal ———————————————————— Low Verbal

Sexual
Verbalizers
(3)

Noncompetent
Sexual
Communicators
(4)

Low Nonverbal

Source: Wrench, J. S., Fiore, A. M., & Brogan, S. M. (2005, November). The development and validity testing of the Sexual Communication Style Scale. Paper presented at the National Communication Association's convention, Boston.

CONCLUSION

In summary, different expectancies and norms for males and females manifest themselves in the sexes' different perspectives on relationships. Males view friendships as mostly instrumental; females view them mainly in an expressive way. Females and males conceive of intimate opposite-sex relationships in somewhat opposing ways, but both feel that sex should be an integral concern within such relationships. Indeed, sexual activity and one's satisfaction with it may be one of the major factors determining the level of intimacy in an opposite-sex relationship.

Gender and culture are intertwined in framing the context for communication among humans. Although biological differences exist between the sexes, every culture tells its members how to interpret and react to those differences. The culture determines the nature of relationships between members of both the same sex and the opposite sex. Although differences between what is considered appropriate masculine and feminine communication behaviors exist in all cultures, it is important to remember that males and females in a given culture are likely to communicate *more like one another* than they are to communicate like members of their own sex from another culture.

KEY TERMS

agentic friendships 271   nonverbal sexual communication 273   sex-typed orientations 260
communal friendships 270   psychological gender orientation 261   verbal sexual communication 273

REFERENCES

Allen, M. (1998). Methodological considerations when examining a gendered world. In D. J. Canary and K. Dindia (Eds.), *Sex differences and similarities in communication: Critical essays and empirical investigations of sex and gender in interaction* (pp. 427–444). Mahwah, NJ: Lawrence Erlbaum.

Anderson, P. A. (2006). The evolution of biological sex differences in communication. In K. Dindia and D. J. Canary (Eds.), *Sex differences and similarities in communication* (2nd ed.; pp. 117–136). Mahwah, NJ: Lawrence Erlbaum.

Aries, E. (2006). Sex differences in interaction: A reexamination. In K. Dindia and D. J. Canary (Eds.), *Sex differences and similarities in communication* (2nd ed.; pp. 21–36). Mahwah, NJ: Lawrence Erlbaum.

Bate, B. (1988). *Communication and the sexes.* New York: Harper & Row.

Bem, S. L. (1974). The measurement of psychological androgyny. *Journal of Consulting and Clinical Psychology, 47,* 155–162.

Canary, D. J., & Hause, I. S. (1993). Is there any reason to research sex differences in communication? *Communication Quarterly, 41,* 129–141.

Carlson, J. (1976). The sexual role. In F. I. Nye (Ed.), *Role structure and analysis of the family.* Beverly Hills, CA: Sage.

Cline, R. J. (1982). Revealing and relating: A review of self-disclosure theory and research. Paper presented at the International Communication Association convention, Boston.

Cline, R. J. (1983). The politics of intimacy: Costs and benefits determining disclosure intimacy in male-female dyads. Paper presented at the Speech Communication Association convention, Washington, DC.

Dindia, K., & Canary, D. J. (Eds.). (2006). *Sex differences and similarities in communication: Critical essays and empirical investigations of sex and gender in interaction* (2nd ed.). Mahwah, NJ: Lawrence Erlbaum.

Dow, B. J., & Wood, J. T. (2006). The evolution of gender and communication research: Intersections of theory, politics, and scholarship. In B. J. Dow and J. T. Wood (Eds.), *The SAGE handbook of gender and communication* (pp. ix–xxiv). Thousand Oaks, CA: Sage.

Eagly, A. H., & Koening, A. M. (2006). Social role theory of sex differences and similarities: Implication for prosocial behavior. In K. Dindia and D. J. Canary (Eds.), *Sex differences and similarities in communication* (2nd ed.; pp. 161–178). Mahwah, NJ: Lawrence Erlbaum.

Exline, R. V., Gray, D., & Schwette, D. (1965). Visual behavior in a dyad as affected by interview context and sex of respondent. *Journal of Personality and Social Psychology, 1,* 201–209.

Exline, R. V., & Winters, L. C. (1965). Affective relations and mutual glances in dyads. In S. S. Tomkins and C. E. Izard (Eds.), *Affect, cognition, and personality.* New York: Springer.

Galvin, K. M., & Brommel, B. J. (1982). *Family communication: Cohesion and change.* Glenview, IL: Scott, Foresman.

Gamble, T. K., & Gamble, M. W. (2003). *The gender communication connection.* Boston: Houghton Mifflin.

Hall, J. A. (2006). How big are nonverbal sex differences? The case of smiling and nonverbal sensitivity. In K. Dindia and D. J. Canary (Eds.), *Sex differences and similarities in communication* (2nd ed.; pp. 59–82). Mahwah, NJ: Lawrence Erlbaum.

Hays, R. B. (1984). The development and maintenance of friendship. *Journal of Social and Personal Relationships, 1,* 75–98.

Kendon, A., & Look, M. (1969). The consistency of gaze patterns in social interaction. *British Journal of Psychology, 60,* 481–494.

Leibman, M. (1970). The effects of sex and race norms on personal space. *Environment and Behavior, 2,* 208–246.

Leibowitz, K., & Andersen, P. (1978). The development and nature of the construct touch avoidance. *Environmental Psychology and Nonverbal Behavior, 3,* 89–106.

LeVay, S. (1993). *The sexual brain.* Cambridge, MA: MIT Press.

Miles, C., Green, R., Sanders, G., & Hines, M. (1998). Estrogen and memory in a transsexual population. *Hormones and Behavior, 34,* 199–208.

Moore, E., Wisniewski, A., & Dobs, A. (2003). Endocrine treatment of transsexual people: A review of treatment regimens, outcomes, and adverse effects. *Journal of Clinical Endocrinology & Metabolism, 88,* 3467–3473.

Mulac, A. (2006). The gender-linked language effect: Do language differences really make a difference? In K. Dindia and D. J. Canary (Eds.), *Sex differences and similarities in communication* (2nd ed.; pp. 219–240). Mahwah, NJ: Lawrence Erlbaum.

Pearson, J. C. (1985). *Gender and communication.* Dubuque, IA: Wm. C. Brown.

Pennebaker, J. W., Groom, C. J., Loew, D., & Dabbs, J. M. (2004). Testosterone as a social inhibitor: Two case studies of the effect of testosterone treatment on language. *Journal of Abnormal Psychology, 113,* 172–175.

Phillips, G. M., & Wood, J. T. (1983). *Communication and human relationships: The study of interpersonal communication.* New York: Macmillan.

Rawlins, W. K. (1982). Cross-sex friendship and the communicative management of sex-role expectations. *Communication Research Reports, 30,* 343–352.

Rawlins, W. (1992). *Friendship matters: Communication, dialectics, and the life course.* New York: Aldine de Gruyter.

Richmond, V. P., & McCroskey, J. C. (2004). *Nonverbal behavior in interpersonal relationships* (5th ed.). Boston: Allyn & Bacon.

Simpson, M. (2002, July 22). *Meet the metrosexual.* Salon.com. Retrieved December 5, 2006, from http://www.marksimpson.com/pages/journalism/metrosexual_beckham.html.

Sommer, R. (1959). Studies in personal space. *Sociometry, 22,* 247–260.

Wheeless, L. R., Wheeless, V. E., & Baus, R. (1981). Communication satisfaction and interpersonal solidarity in relationship development. Paper presented at the annual convention of the Speech Communication Association of Puerto Rico, San Juan.

Willis, F. N. (1966). Initial speaking distance as a function of the speakers' relationship. *Psychonomic Science, 5,* 221–222.

Wrench, J. S. (2002). The impact of sexual orientation and temperament on physical and verbal aggression. *Journal of Intercultural Communication Research, 31,* 85–106.

Wrench, J. S., Brogan, S. M., Fiore, & A. M. (2005, November). *The development and validity testing of the Sexual Communication Style Scale.* Paper presented at the National Communication Association's Convention, Boston.

Wright, P. H. (2006). Toward an expanded orientation to the comparative study of women's and men's same-sex friendships. In K. Dindia and D. J. Canary (Eds.), *Sex differences and similarities in communication* (2nd ed.; pp. 37-57). Mahwah, NJ: Lawrence Erlbaum.

DISCUSSION QUESTIONS

1. How does sex-type play (e.g., girls play with dolls and boys play with guns) impact our sex-role development?

2. What is your psychological gender orientation? How does it influence your communicative interactions with other people?

3. Does the "metrosexual" actually exist, or is it a marketing ploy run wild? Why?

4. Can heterosexual females and males be in friendships with each other without sexuality playing a part, or will sexuality always exist in cross-sex friendships even if it is not openly discussed?

5. Why is communication during sexual intimacy important for relationship stability?

13

Health Communication

OBJECTIVES

- Define and explain *health communication*.

- Explain a patient's actual reason for coming (ARC) and why it is important.

- Understand how physicians use verbal, nonverbal, and mediated channels in health communication.

- Understand how patient perceptions of physician credibility, patient satisfaction, and perceived quality of medical care influence health communication.

- Understand how patients' personalities can negatively affect health communication.

- Explain how gender affects health communication.

- Understand the basic communication skills for patients.

- Explain the purpose of the medical interview.

- Understand what a SOAP note and a SOAP-ER note are.

- Define and explain *risk* and *risk communication*.

- Explain technical and democratic risk communication.

- Differentiate among the four types of risk communicators.

- Understand how source credibility, sociocommunicative style, humor, and nonverbal immediacy affect patients' perceptions of their physicians.

Everyday, millions of people around the United States engage in some form of communication with a health practitioner. People talk to physicians, nurses, pharmacists, radiology technicians, emergency medical technicians, psychologists, dentists, optometrists, and many other individuals whose sole occupational purpose is to manage an individual's health and wellness while making decisions that can either improve or detract from that individual's quality of life. Because health communication affects all of us, knowledge of effective health communication can have large ramifications on our lives. Our ability, or inability, to communicate about our problems, both physical and psychological, impacts our life. For example, it is much harder for an individual who is both mute and a quadriplegic (cannot talk or move) to inform her or his physician about any necessary symptoms causing pain. This chapter includes three unique parts. The first part will examine the definition of health communication and the health communication model. The second section will examine patient communication. And the third section will cover physician communication.

WHAT IS HEALTH COMMUNICATION?

The term *health communication* has just as many meanings to health providers and researchers as does the

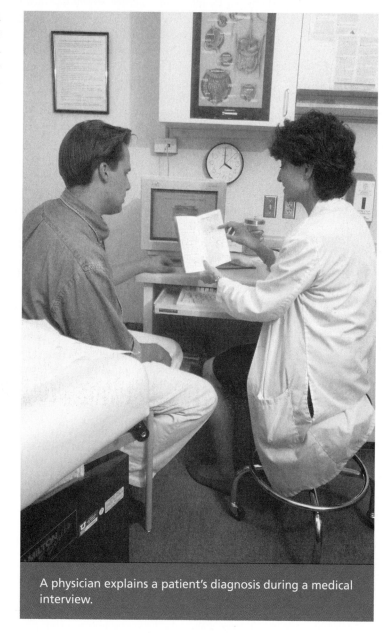

A physician explains a patient's diagnosis during a medical interview.

term *communication* within the communication community. Many people only think of physician–patient interaction when they conjure up the term *health communication*. Although the physician–patient interaction is extremely important, it is not the only form of health communication that exists. Health communication can be defined as *the process by which one person stimulates meaning in the mind(s) of another person (or persons) through verbal and nonverbal messages specifically related to the physical and psychological well-being of another person (or persons)*. In essence, health communication is any form of communication about the physical (body) and/or psychological (mind) wellness of an individual.

Our bodies are truly amazing machines. When our bodies are running effectively, we can do all kinds of phenomenal acts. When something goes wrong with our body, it will go to great lengths to naturally heal itself, but often the body is simply unable to do so. When we can't heal ourselves, we look for outside practitioners who specialize in healing our bodies. If there is something wrong with your teeth, you go see a dentist. If your eyes don't function as they use to and you need glasses, you go to an optometrist. If your eyes have developed cataracts, on the other hand, and you need surgery, you go to a specialized physician called an ophthalmologist. When it comes to physicians, there are hundreds of specializations that exist to help you maintain your body.

Our minds, on the other hand, are often harder to diagnose when they are not functioning effectively. When your arm gets chopped off, you can easily look in the mirror and see that something has gone wrong. You can also tell people what has happened and how it feels. If someone gets depressed, on the other hand, it's much harder to explain what is going on. Often people who suffer from long-term depression don't even realize that they are depressed. Instead, they just know that life isn't as much fun as it once was. This lack of understanding is often why psychiatrists and psychologists are so important in the diagnosing and treatment of many problems.

Now that we've defined what health communication is and examined the two primary avenues of health communication (physical and mental), let's now discuss health communication in light of the interpersonal communication model originally discussed in Chapter 1.

Model of Health Communication

In the interpersonal communication model, the patient/client functions as the source of most of the communication that occurs within the health communication context. As a patient/client, when you knowingly enter into the health practitioner's office it is your responsibility to present a message (encode) to the health practitioner explaining why you are there and what you expect to happen. In other words, if you go see your family physician, you have to explain to her or him why you are there.

Although this may sound extremely easy, many patients/clients have extreme difficulty encoding why they have gone to see a health practitioner. One reason patients/clients have problems encoding why they have gone to a health practitioner is because patients/clients often have problems verbalizing their Actual Reason for Coming—ARC (Sloane, 2002). As discussed above, often people do not know what is wrong with them when they go see their family physician; they just know something isn't right. For example, a 65-year-old man can go to his family physician complaining of insomnia (inability to sleep), and think he is physically defective. In reality, it could be that this same gentleman has recently gotten divorced or there has been a death in the family, so he is not suffering from a physical ailment but rather a psychological one. People often suffer from unexplained illnesses after a traumatic event or crisis. People often have what are called psychosomatic illnesses, or illnesses that cause physiological problems but are caused by psychologically related problems.

Another problem that can occur when trying to determine someone's ARC has to do with embarrassing problems. Western cultures tend to be very shy and embarrassed about anything related to the human body. Often, when people who have a problem in one of their "nether" or unspeakable regions, it can cause extreme embarrassment. After Pfizer Pharmaceuticals released the drug Viagra (a drug that helps some men with male impotence), many men suddenly found themselves talking with their physicians about issues and problems that had never been discussed outside the bedroom. Many of these men would go to their physicians and talk about every possible insignificant thing that was wrong with them, and then at the very end of the visit they would say something like "Oh yeah, can I get a prescription for Viagra?" Although the other "insignificant" issues may have been important, often these men's ARC was to get a prescription for Viagra. Other touchy issues that can be embarrassing or hard to openly discuss are eating disorders, physical/mental abuse, suicidal ideations (thoughts of suicide), depression, sexual orientation, contraception, safe sex, pregnancy termination, sexually transmitted infections, death and dying, and many other very sensitive topics.

Once the patient/client has encoded her or his message, he or she then needs to transmit this message using verbal, nonverbal, and/or mediated channels. Often, the verbal channel is used to explain to a health practitioner when there are no physical symptoms that can easily be detected. Psychologists often refer to therapy as the "talking cure" because they rely heavily on information presented to them verbally from their clients. Nonverbal channels are also extremely important in health communication. Nonverbal communication can occur in one of two primary ways: directly through contact with the individual, or through testing. In the first case, patients/clients will often show health practitioners parts of their body that are hurting or not functioning correctly. Health practitioners can also determine the intensity of the problem by examining the body. If an individual notices a strange lump on her or his breast, her or his physician will want to see the lump and feel it (and yes, men *can* get breast cancer).

The second form of nonverbal communication that is often used in the health communication context occurs in the form of lab tests and results. Although these tests are the decision of the health practitioner, they help her or him better determine the actual problem. Trained medical practitioners can learn a lot about a patient/client's problems simply by examining lab results, X-rays, PET scans, MRIs, CAT scans, and so on. Psychologists and psychiatrists also use questionnaires as a way of testing an individual to get a more holistic view of the individual and her or his problems. In emergency situations, emergency physicians, nurses, and medical technicians are often left only to their perceptions of an individual's nonverbal communication to determine what happened and what steps to take to save the patient's life.

Lastly, patients could transmit a specific message through mediated means. Increasingly, health practitioners are having a presence on the Internet. One of the most utilized Web pages in cyberspace is called WebMD, which is a clearinghouse of medical-related information for nonmedical people. Many of these health-related websites have a way for individuals to directly ask questions to a professional, who then posts an answer. This is one way in which patients can use a mediated channel to transmit an encoded health message.

Once a health practitioner receives the message from a patient/client, then the health practitioner must decode the message and make an accurate assessment of the patient/client. As previously mentioned, one common problem that patients/clients have when engaging in health communication deals with the ARC. The ARC problem is often

A patient clearly explains her Actual Reason for Coming (ARC) to her physician.

the greatest challenge for a health practitioner during an interaction with a patient/client. If a health practitioner cannot determine the ARC, then the interaction has been a waste of time for both the patient/client and the health practitioner. Often it can take multiple visits before a patient/client actually explains her or his ARC to the health practitioner. In many ways, the health practitioner has to be a detective when trying to get to the bottom of a patient/client's ARC. To aid in this process, health practitioners often obtain a lot of feedback by asking questions to help draw out a patient's ARC. Of course, the process a health practitioner goes through to determine appropriate questions is encoding.

Another function of encoding that health practitioners go through is when they have to present findings, diagnoses, and treatment options. Each of these requires different forms of messages. It's one thing for a physician to tell someone that he or she is going to take an antibiotic for three days, and something completely different when a physician tells someone that he or she is likely to die in three days.

After a health practitioner encodes a message, he or she can transmit that message through verbal means (telling the patient/client directly), through nonverbal means (showing the patient), or through mediated means (through a brochure, website, or video).

This first section has examined the definition of health communication and how the interpersonal communication model relates to health communication. The next two sections of this chapter are going to look specifically at the patient–physician interpersonal relationship. Although this chapter is focusing on the patient–physician relationship, much of this information can be cross-applied to other health communication contexts as well.

PATIENT COMMUNICATION

The first step in effective health communication is to equip patients with the necessary communication skills. Too often, people just blindly follow their physician's directives without ever asking the question "Why?" In today's arena of modern medicine, we all must be more shrewd and question the treatment we are receiving. This is not to say that physicians are not capable and intelligent, but rather that the state of your life often lies within your own choices and judgments. Ultimately, we have to take responsibility for our own health and wellness. One impacting way to ensure health and wellness is through complete communication with one's primary care physician. If your physician does not know, he or she cannot help you. Let's discuss some communicative tools that can help prepare you as a patient to communicate effectively with your primary care physician. Before we can discuss specific communication skills necessary for patients, let's examine how our own perceptions affect the way we interact with our physicians, some basic problems people can have with patient–physician communication, and how gender affects patient–physician communication.

The Effects of Patient Perception

How people feel and relate to a communicative situation can have severe consequences on how that person communicates. This is very true in the realm of patient–physician interactions. We have all heard the horror stories of callous physicians who scream, yell, and throw things at their patients and staff. If you've ever encountered this physician, I'm sure you are in no hurry to go back. In fact, if you've ever seen a physician fly off the handle in her or his office, we bet it affected your level of willingness to communicate in the medical context. Virtually no one wants to interact with someone who screams and yells. This section is going to look at how a patient's perceptions about the patient–physician interaction can impact her or his quality and quantity of medical care. Specifically, this section is going to examine the impact that a patient's perceptions of physician credibility and personal satisfaction have on a patient's perception of the quality of care he or she received.

Physician Credibility.   As discussed in Chapter 2, credibility is a combination of three basic factors, competence, trustworthiness, and caring/goodwill. In specific relation to the patient–physician context, patients judge their physician's credibility based on a number of factors. Patients will view physicians who are famous as more credible. Many patients just assume that the physician they know and like is credible without even questioning the physician's credibility. The first factor of credibility, competence, refers to a patient's perception of her or his physician's skill and knowledge about medicine. Although we all want to believe our physicians are all-knowing about medicine, it's impossible for your physician to know everything there is to know about medicine. Since the 1960s, there have been more than 12 million medical articles written. The last five years accounts for approximately 18 percent of all medical research that has been conducted and catalogued, and this number is growing rapidly. It is estimated that your family physician would need to read approximately 6,000 research articles per day just to stay up-to-date with current trends in medical research (Wrench, 2003). In fact, according to the Center for Evidence Based Medicine in the United Kingdom, physicians read considerably more in medical school and their residency than when they actually start practicing medicine. Not only do physicians read less, but they also tend to know less about medicine the longer they are out of school. This isn't to say that we should run in fear of the ignorance of our physicians, but we should understand their limitations and realize that they do not know everything.

Trustworthiness is another important factor when considering patient–physician credibility. Simply put, if we trust our physicians, we are more likely to go along with their prescriptions and treatments. If we do not trust our physicians, we are probably going to seek out a second opinion before undertaking serious medical treatments or procedures, or we may just ignore our physician's advice. Trust is also one of the hardest factors to build between people because trust must be built over time. For this reason, it is important to find a physician with whom you are comfortable, and to be willing to develop a long-term relationship with that physician. The more a physician knows about you as a person, the easier it will be for her or him to make accurate diagnoses.

The third factor of credibility, caring/goodwill, is probably the most important factor for patients when making decisions. If I believe that my physician is looking out for my best interests, I'm going to be a lot more likely to go along with anything he or she wants me to do. However, if I believe that my physician could not care less about me as a person, then it does not matter how competent I think he or she is—I'm not going to comply with her or his treatment. Just remember, many mad scientists were competent people who did not care about human life. On the other hand, one of the coauthors of this text has a primary care physician who is not the brightest crayon in the box, but who immensely cares for her patients and her patients know she cares. Every patient who walks into the physician's office is hugged, called various pet names (sweetie, honey, cutie pie, darling, etc.), and treated like a long-lost best friend. As a result of her immense caring, patients flock to her and often recommend her to others, so she has a very busy medical practice. Even though our coauthor often has to second-guess the physician, he has no desire to quit seeing her because she clearly cares. No matter how much pain you are in when you go see this physician, you feel slightly uplifted and feel better just by being greeted by her.

Patient Satisfaction. Consistently, patient satisfaction has been shown to be one of the most important patient perceptions. Fitzpatrick (1993) defined patient satisfaction as the cognitive evaluation of an emotional reaction to health care. When patients are satisfied with their primary care physician, they are more likely to return to that physician in the future (Baker, 1998). Even more important, research has shown that if a patient is satisfied with her or his physician, then the patient is actually going to recover from an illness faster (Becker & Rosenstock, 1984). Patients are also more likely to comply with their physician's prescribed medication and treatments (Lochman, 1983). Ultimately, an individual's satisfaction with her or his physician is extremely important. Richmond, Smith, Heisel, and McCroskey (1998) created a scale for measuring an individual's satisfaction with her or his physician. Take a minute to fill out the Satisfaction with Physician Scale (Scale 27 in the appendix). Scores on this instrument can range from 7 to 21. The higher your score, the more satisfied you are with your current primary care physician. In a study by Richmond, Smith, Heisel, and McCroskey (2002), it was found that patients who were satisfied with their physicians also saw their physicians as competent, caring, and trustworthy. In other words, patients who are satisfied with their physicians also see their physicians as more credible than patients who are not satisfied with their physicians.

Perceived Quality of Medical Care. A patient's perception of the quality of medical care is a construct closely related to patient satisfaction. Theoretically, it is possible to receive excellent care from a scummy physician. Surgeons are notorious for having poor communication skills when interacting with their patients, but can still provide a medical service that is top notch. For this reason, it is also important to understand how patients perceive the quality of their medical care. Richmond et al. (1998) created a scale for measuring a patient's perception of the quality of care he or she received. Take a minute to fill out the Perceived Quality of Medical Care measure (Scale 28 in the appendix). Think of the last time you went to see your primary care physician. If you do not have a primary care physician, just think of the last time you saw any physician.

Scores on the Perceived Quality of Medical Care measure can range from 7 to 42. The higher your score, the more you perceived the quality of the medical care you received. It should also be noted that Richmond et al. (2002) found that individuals who reported high levels of quality of care from their primary physician also perceived their physician as more competent, trustworthy, and caring and were more satisfied. Overall, the concepts of satisfaction, credibility, and perceptions of care are highly intertwined.

Problems with Patient–Physician Communication

There are a number of problems that patients face when trying to communicate with their primary care physician. This section is going to examine four basic problems that must be overcome for effective patient communication to occur: specifying your ARC, giving complete information, overcoming your fears, and locus of control. The first problem that must be overcome by patients is being specific about their ARC. If a physician cannot determine why you are in her or his office, he or she cannot help you. Although feelings of insecurity and embarrassment are often the reasons people cite for withholding their ARC, as patients we have to see our physicians as professionals who are there to help us through our difficult times.

Along the same lines as spelling out your ARC to your primary care physician, we also have to be completely honest with our physicians if they are going to be able to provide us with the best quality of medical care. Too often, people withhold information for fear that they will be seen as socially undesirable by their physicians. The physician will ask a patient if he or she smokes, and the patient will lie, knowing that the physician does not want her or him to smoke. When you lie about something like this to your physician, he or she is unable to provide you with the best care.

Patients often do not adequately communicate about medication and supplements when talking with their primary care physician. As patients, it is extremely important that we always know what kind of medication we are currently taking (name of medication, frequency we take it, and dosage level). Many people will see multiple physicians and go to multiple pharmacies to get their prescriptions filled. It is not uncommon for a person to have a bad drug reaction because two medications interacted with each other, causing harmful results. If your physician and pharmacist do not know what medications you are taking, the possibility of a negative drug reaction is more likely. On that same line, many people in the United States take countless numbers of over-the-counter medications and supplements that can interfere with the effectiveness of a prescription medication or cause negative drug reactions. In essence, if you are putting a foreign chemical of any kind into your body, whether it is prescription medication, over-the-counter medication, herbs, vitamins, muscle-enhancing formula, weight loss pills, or anything else, your physician needs to know in order to more accurately and safely help you.

The next major hurdle that causes problems in the patient–physician interaction is patient fear about communication with a physician. To examine an individual's level of fear or anxiety about either real or perceived communication with her or his physician, Richmond et al. (1998) created a scale to measure an individual's fear of physician (FOP). At this point, find out your score on the Fear of Physician Scale (Scale 29 in the appendix).

Scores on the FOP Scale should be between 5 and 25. If you scored above a 20 on the FOP, you probably have more apprehension and anxiety than the average person when communicating with your physician. If you scored between 10 and 20, you probably have normal levels of apprehension when communicating with your physician. Lastly, if you scored below 10, then you probably have no anxiety at all when communicating with your physician. Richmond et al. (1998) found that people with higher levels of trait communication apprehension tended to have higher levels of apprehension when communicating with physicians. And as we know from previous research done with communication apprehension, people who are more anxious are not going to be as effective at communicating when compared with those who have low levels of apprehension. This pattern is also seen in the patient–physician relationship. Patients who have high levels of communication apprehension will not be as effective in communicating their pain and body dysfunctions as those individuals with lower levels of communication apprehension. All in all, if you scored high on both the PRCA-24 in Chapter 3 and the FOP, you probably are already experiencing problems as a result of ineffective communication with your physician.

Richmond et al. (1998) also found that people who had high levels of anxiety while communicating with their physicians tended to have lower levels of satisfaction and reported lower levels of quality of medical care. Clearly, an individual's apprehension or anxiety about either real or anticipated communication with her or his primary care physician can be very negative for health communication.

The last major problem that often impacts a patient's health relates to her or his health locus of control. An individual's health locus of control is similar to the discussion we had earlier in this book in Chapter 2 about locus of control. Before we continue this discussion, take a second and fill out the Health Locus of Control Scale (Scale 30 in the appendix).

As mentioned in Chapter 2, people can have both internal and external perceptions about the influence of behavior. People who have an internal locus of control believe their behavior and future are a result of what they do themselves. People who have an external locus of control believe that forces outside of their own will control their behavior and future. The health locus of control is based on these two principles, but specifically focuses on the extent to which people believe that their personal health is something they control or is controlled by outside forces. People who have an internal health locus of control believe that the state of their health is largely impacted by their own behaviors. In other words, if I eat healthy foods and exercise appropriately, I should have fairly good health as a result of my choices. Conversely, people who have external health loci of controls believe that fate, not personal choices, causes them to be sick. For these people, it does not matter if they eat healthy or unhealthy foods or whether they exercise. If they get sick, they get sick. There is nothing they can do to prevent sickness, and there is nothing they can do to foster wellness either.

People who have internal health loci of controls are going to be much more apt to comply with a physician's prescription of medication and treatments. If it is my behavior that is making me sick or well, then I will chose behaviors that will enable me to be well and avoid behaviors that place me in harm's way. People who have external health loci of controls basically take little to no responsibility for their health. These people will often make very rash decisions and will not comply with their physician on treatment options or medication. People with external health loci of controls will be more likely to make decisions that will actually increase their chance of morbidity (harm).

Gender and Health Communication

A number of scientific research articles have demonstrated that an individual's biological sex actually has a number of very interesting effects on the patient–physician interaction. In a study by Hall and Roter (2002), it was found that both male and female patients tend to talk more with female physicians than with male physicians. However, in a number of studies, female patients engage in more verbal communication with their physicians when compared to male patients (Wallen, Waitzkin, and Stoeckle, 1979; Waitzkin, 1984, 1985). Hall, Roter, and Katz (1988) found that physicians also communicate more nonverbally with female patients than they do with male patients. One suggested reason for this disparity is that females in the U.S. culture are more likely to take on the role of a sick patient because it is socially acceptable for a woman to show sickness in our culture, but not for men (Hohmann, 1989). Women have also been shown to actually know more about their own health and treatment options than men. Overall, the picture that is painted above clearly indicates that when it comes to health communication, women seem to be ahead of the game. The next section is designed to enhance everyone's skills when communicating with their physicians.

Communication Skills for Patients

Now that we have looked at some of the problems that can affect the overall quality of care an individual receives from her or his physician, let's examine some basic communication skills that can enhance your future patient–physician interactions. Health communication, like most communication situations, can be enhanced by simply preparing yourself for the interaction. In Figure 13.1, you will see an information sheet that you can fill out before you see your physician to help enhance the overall experience. Let's examine each section of this "Patient Information Sheet" in an effort to help you understand your role as a patient in the patient–physician interaction.

Actual Reason for Coming (ARC).   The first, and most important, part of the patient–physician interaction is your reason for going to see your physician. Although the actual reason for coming is often embarrassing, patients must be up-front with their physicians if they want to get the help that is needed. By writing down your ARC before you go to your physician, it may make it easier for you to broach the topic with your physician.

Physical Symptoms.   Physical symptoms refer to any symptoms that can be either felt by the patient or easily seen by both the patient and physician. An example of a physical symptom felt by the patient would be an intense headache. Often a headache will yield no observable symptoms on the outside of your body, but you can still definitely feel it. Physical symptoms that can be seen by both a physician and patient would include things like rashes, bug bites, and a foreign object in your eye. When it comes to explaining your physical symptoms, it is best to make sure that you are complete in your descriptions and do not leave out any important or seemingly unimportant details.

FIGURE 13.1   Patient Information Sheet

Patient Information Sheet

Appointment Date: _____ / _____ / _____   Time: _____   Physician: _____

Actual Reason(s) for Coming

_____
_____
_____
_____

Physical Symptoms

_____
_____
_____
_____

Psychological Symptoms

_____
_____
_____
_____

List of Current Medication

_____
_____
_____

List of Alternative Forms of Medication

_____
_____
_____
_____

Tests or Procedures Conducted

_____
_____
_____
_____

Physician's Diagnosis and Prognosis

_____
_____
_____
_____

Medication and/or Treatments Prescribed

_____
_____
_____
_____

Side Effects of Medication/Treatment?

_____
_____
_____

How Long Should I Expect to Wait before My Symptoms Lessen?

_____

Date/Time of Next Appointment

Date: _____ / _____ / _____   Time: _____

Remember…
- If you don't understand your physician, ask.
- Don't hide any details from your physician.
- Own your appointment; you've paid for it.
- Always get a copy of test results and procedure notes for your own health record.
- Take control of your health.

Psychological Symptoms.   Psychological symptoms are symptoms related to your emotional health. Sadly, people often write off their psychological symptoms, try to find physiological reasons for problems, and end up missing what is actually wrong. Many psychological symptoms we exhibit are manifestations of real biological problems. The only way our physicians can help us overcome these biological problems is by being completely aware of how patients are feeling and behaving.

List of Current Medication.   As we discussed earlier in this chapter, your physician cannot do her or his job if you do not let her or him know the medication you are currently taking. Any time you put foreign chemicals into your body, there is a chance that your body will not like the foreign chemical, leading to mild and serious side effects. One way physicians can prevent side effects from occurring is to make sure that the drugs being prescribed do not have a known negative interaction with each other. It is important for your physician to know the name of the medication, the dosage level, and how often you are currently taking the medication.

List of Alternative Forms of Medication and Therapies.   Complementary medicine, or nontraditional forms of medicine intended to enhance and complement traditional medicine, can be very destructive if you are not a careful consumer. Complementary medicine includes, but is not limited to, the following forms of medicine, including osteopathy, chiropractic, Chinese medicine, acupuncture, magnet therapy, cranial therapy, vitamins, muscle enhancers, and yoga. Each of these can play an important role in the health care of an individual, but your physician should know that you are engaging in any form of complementary medicine to ensure you with the highest standard of quality care.

Recently, at a large mid-Atlantic university, there was a case where a college student went to see a physician in the University Health Center. He complained that his chest felt really tight and he was having problems breathing. The physician assumed that the patient had a condition known as costochondritis (or tightening of the chest muscle). When the physician was done with the examination, the patient stood to leave and collapsed. The patient was rushed to the emergency room, and it was determined that the patient had been taking an over-the-counter performance-enhancing drug originally designed for asthmatics called ephedra. Ephedra is a legal version of speed, and if it is used in large enough quantities it can be very lethal, like this male college student almost found out. If the physician had known the male patient had been taking ephedra, it would have made diagnosing the patient much easier.

Tests of Procedures Conducted.   The first column of information on the Patient Information Sheet is to be completed before you go to the physician; the second column is to be filled out while you are with your physician. This first section asks you to write down any tests or procedures that were conducted during your appointment. This information is helpful in two ways: (1) it lets you keep track of what was done to or for you, and when it happened; and (2) it gives you a way to cross-reference your bill from either your physician or the insurance company. Billing mistakes happen. If you don't keep track of what happens at your physician's office, no one else will.

Physician's Diagnosis and Prognosis.   The next section has you fill in your physician's diagnosis (what is wrong with you) and prognosis (what your physician thinks will happen next). It's always important to know what your physician actually thinks is going on and why. Too often, people are just given medication and told goodbye by their physicians. As patients, we have a right (a legal one, at that) to know what is going on. In the "good old days," what a physician wrote in the medical chart was for her or his eyes only. This is not the case anymore. Medical charts (with the exception of psychiatrist and psychologist notes) can be accessed and read by the patient. It may cost you to get copies of your medical chart, but you do have the right to get a copy. If you are ever moving, always make sure that you get current copies of your medical chart to take with you for future physicians.

Medication and/or Treatments Prescribed.   In this section, you will write a detailed list of the specific medications your physician prescribes for you, along with their dose level and how often you should take the medication. You will also write down any specific treatments that your physician puts you on. Even if the treatment is as simple as getting thirty minutes of exercise per day, write it down on the sheet. By documenting what your physician wants you to do while in the office, you will be more likely to remember her or his exact treatment ideas later.

Side Effects of Medication/Treatment?   In this section, you will list any side effects that the medication or treatment could cause. With any medication or medical treatment, there is always some degree of risk of a negative side effect. Most medications have a long list of possible side effects. Your physician should be able to explain these side effects for you, and what you should do if you experience any of the side effects. If your physician does not know the specifics about possible side effects, it can also be useful to ask your pharmacist. Although your pharmacist will know a lot about the medication, your decision to stay on a medication is one that is strictly between you and your physician.

How Long Should I Expect to Wait before My Symptoms Lessen?   It is always extremely important to ask your physician, "How long should I expect to wait before my symptoms lessen?" Some medications and treatments work instantly, and others can take months or even years before you can see the full effectiveness. Your physician will generally tell you that if your symptoms do not improve in a certain period of time, you should come back for a follow-up. Many people get disappointed when their symptoms do not lessen immediately, and find another physician to go to instead of following up with her or his first physician. As hard as it might be, it is often better to wait and let a medication or treatment play its course than to switch to something midstream. Remember, physicians need to know when treatments and medication work or fail.

Date/Time of Next Appointment.   The next major part of the Patient Information Sheet simply asks you to write in the date and time of your next appointment. Most physician offices have little cards that they will give you that have the date and time of your next appointment, but some people always seem to misplace these little cards. By writing the date and time of your next appointment on the Patient Information Sheet, you will be able to keep all relevant health information on one sheet, and be a bit less likely to forget.

Remember.   The last section on the Patient Information Sheet is made up of five key points that will help you during and after a patient–physician encounter. First, if you don't understand what your physician is saying, ask her or him to repeat it. You should never leave your physician's office confused. If you are confused about something, chances are you will not follow through appropriately, which could ultimately lead to worse problems in the long run.

Second, don't hide any details from your physician. If you are complaining of itching or soreness in the genitalia, don't lie to your physician and tell her or him that you're a virgin when you are not. If you aren't a virgin, your physician could bypass the possibility of a sexually transmitted disease, which could only make the condition more painful in the long run.

Third, own your appointment: you've paid for it. As a patient, you are a customer. You have a right to expect that your physician pay attention to you. If your physician does not appear to want to pay attention, you probably need to find a new physician. This does not mean, however, that you have the right to monopolize your physician's time beyond what is reasonable.

Fourth, always get a copy of your test results and the procedure notes for your own health records. Eventually, we will all probably have a computerized medical file that we can carry with us in our wallets or a wristband, but for now we have to create paper files. The reason why we encourage you to get a copy of your test results and procedure notes is so that you know what is going on with your own body. If you don't know what a lab value on a result sheet means, ask or look it up in a medical book or on the Internet. Lastly, take control of your health. There is nothing more precious to you than your own health.

This section has examined the role of the patient in the patient–physician communication interaction. The next section focuses on the role of the physician in the patient–physician communication interaction.

▣ PHYSICIAN COMMUNICATION

All of us have heard horror stories related to how poorly some physicians actually communicate. All three authors of this book have friends who are physicians, and we all know physicians who are great communicators and some who clearly need a lot of help. This section examines why physician communication is extremely important. Understanding what physicians are thinking about during the medical interview (the question-and-answer session that a physician has with a patient) will help all of us as patients be more effective communicators with our physicians. First, we will explain the medical interview in detail, and then we will look at specific communication variables that impact physician communication.

Medical Interview

As mentioned just above, the medical interview is the process a physician uses in which he or she asks a patient questions and the patient responds with relevant answers. To the physician, the medical interview enables her or him to elicit responses from the patient to come to a quick and accurate diagnosis. As we discussed earlier in this chapter, there are many reasons why the medical interview may not be effective. In a way, physicians work like immensely powerful computers. Physicians take all of the known symptoms (data) and logically come to some kind of a conclusion about those symptoms in the form of a diagnosis. For this process to work correctly, patients have to give their physicians all the necessary information no matter how benign a patient may think the information is. Ultimately, physicians will then come up with a plan of attack in the form of a medical treatment or medication.

Physicians look at the medical interview as an investigation of the problem a patient is presenting in her or his office. When the patient leaves, a physician will write down her or his findings in the patient's medical chart, which is a legal document that can be used in a court of law. During the medical interview, physicians attempt to get enough information from their patients to write a SOAP note. A SOAP note is the acronym device that physicians use for the format of information in a patient's chart. The SOAP note stands for *Subjective, Objective, Assessment,* and *Plan.* Let's look at each of these individually.

Subjective. The subjective part of a SOAP note relates to the information that a patient directly gives a physician primarily through verbal communication. There are many things that a patient can clearly, and not so clearly, tell a physician about her or his current symptoms. Physicians often need all kinds of information from a patient to correctly diagnose a patient's medical problems. Physicians need to know about a patient's past medical history (significant illnesses, major traumas, surgeries, recent medical problems, etc.), family history (diseases that could be genetically passed on, like many forms of cancer), social history (use of drugs, tobacco, alcohol, etc.), psychological history (episodes of depression, suicidal tendencies, hyperactivity, etc.), relational history (single, dating, married, divorced, separated, etc.), and occupational history (on-the-job hazards, occupational accidents, etc.). Also included in the subjective portion of a SOAP note is the patient's present illness or injury. Physicians need to know many different aspects of a patient's current medical problem: duration (when did the injury happen or illness start), character (how does the patient describe the pain or discomfort), location (where is the pain/discomfort the most intense), exacerbation (what causes the pain/discomfort to get worse), positional pain/discomfort (does the pain get worse or better depending on the position of the patient), medications (what prescription and over-the-counter medications is the patient on), allergies (does the patient have any known allergies), and other facts about the illness or injury that can help a physician make a more exact diagnosis.

Objective.   The objective part of a SOAP note relates to information about a patient's illness or injury that a physician finds through a physical examination of the patient. In the case of many emergency room situations, physicians have to rely almost entirely on information they find from physical findings. To complete this process, a physician will often conduct a review of systems. In a review of systems, a physician will systematically examine the major systems of the body (breasts, ears, eyes, cardiac, endocrine, gastrointestinal, genito-reproductive, head, hematologic, immune, mouth, musculoskeletal, neck, nose and sinuses, neurological, psychiatric, respiratory, and urinary). Admittedly, certain physiological symptoms will lead a physician to examine specific body systems and not others. If a child is accidentally dropped and lands on her or his head, the physician will probably pay close attention to the child's face, neck, and neurological systems to make sure nothing was damaged.

Assessment.   Once a physician has completed the subjective and objective portions of a SOAP note, the physician will start to piece the puzzle together to come up with a diagnosis. In other words, the assessment part of a SOAP note is a physician's interpretation of her or his patient's condition. An assessment can be either very simple or very difficult to determine. Many times, a primary care physician will simply not be able to make a correct diagnosis, and he or she will require a patient to receive a consultation from a specialist. Each of the systems we described above in the objective section has its own group of physicians who specialize in the diagnosis and treatment of that system. Many conditions will require the consultation of multiple physicians who will work in a collaborative effort to diagnose and then treat a patient.

Plan.   The last section of a SOAP note is the plan section, or the point in a SOAP note in which a physician determines what is in the best interest of a patient to overcome an illness or injury. There are three basic dimensions to a plan: treatment, procedures, and consultations. The first dimension of a plan consists of the therapeutic treatment a physician decides is necessary for her or his patient. Therapeutic treatments can range from medication, to bandages, to crutches, and so on. The second dimension of a plan consists of the procedures that a physician feels needs to be conducted. Procedures can come in one of two forms, diagnostic and performed. Diagnostic procedures are procedures conducted in order to get a better understanding of what is happening with a specific patient. If you are tired all the time, a doctor may draw blood to see if you are suffering from anemia. Anytime your doctor draws blood, conducts a biopsy, asks for a urinary or fecal sample, or asks for X-rays, PET scans, or MRIs, your physician is conducting a diagnostic procedure. Many physicians will also perform office-based procedures or performed procedures. A performed procedure is a medical procedure that can be completed in the office. If your toenail is highly infected, your primary care physician may perform a simple medical procedure to remove the toenail. If your physician is an osteopathic physician, he or she may perform a form of medicine called osteopathic manipulative medicine. For example, if you slip a rib out of alignment, an osteopathic physician can perform a manipulative technique to help realign your rib cage. Although many people confuse osteopathic physicians (doctors of osteopathy, or

DOs) with chiropractors, DOs are fully licensed and practicing physicians who can be in any specialty of medicine like their counterparts, the allopathic physicians or MDs. The last part of the plan section of a SOAP note is when physicians write about any necessary consultations that a patient should have with a specific specialist. As mentioned in the assessment section, physicians often have to rely on people who specialize in a specific branch of medicine.

At the beginning of this chapter, we mentioned that there are 4,600 medical journals currently published and that your physician would have to read 6,000 medical journal articles a day to stay current with modern medicine. Because there is a huge amount of medical research being conducted, specialists have helped primary care physicians manage this burden because they focus on just one area of medicine. For example, if a patient is depressed, a primary care physician will often attempt to help that patient, but if the patient doesn't respond to conventional therapies the physician will consult with a psychiatrist. Ultimately, it becomes extremely important for a physician to understand what her or his limitations actually are.

In this section, we have explored the traditional SOAP note that is commonly used in medical records. Although the traditional SOAP note only examines the subjective, objective, assessment, and plan, many people now believe that an addition to the SOAP note is necessary. In other words, it is not uncommon now to see *SOAP-ER*. The *E* in *-ER* represents *Patient Education*, and the *R* represents *Return to Clinic*.

Patient Education.   Patient education is one of the most important functions that a physician actually has. Physicians have more schooling than the average person in areas of wellness and health. For this reason, physicians often have to educate patients about specific parts of the body, specific diseases, use of medication, medication side effects, healthy and unhealthy behaviors, and so on.

One common form of patient education is what is known as risk education. Risk education is when an individual (in this case a physician) explains the possible risks of a behavior or hazard (anything that can cause morbidity and/or mortality) to another individual (in this case, the patient). Every behavior from flying in a plane to writing with a pencil has some degree of risk, or the possibility of injury (morbidity) or loss of life (mortality). Clearly, some behaviors we engage in increase the risk of morbidity and mortality (M&M), and some behaviors decrease our risks of M&M. The process by which an individual (in this case a physician) transmits a message about the risk associated with a behavior(s) through verbal and nonverbal messages is called risk communication. Before we continue our discussion of risk communication, take a second to fill out the Risk Communicator Style Scale (Scale 31 in the appendix).

In risk communication, there are two different ways that people can communicate the nature of a risk. The first way many people, including physicians, communicate risks is through the use of scientific explanations and statistics on *technical risk communication*. Risk as general concept is based on science and statistics, so many people will use scientific explanations and statistics when communicating about risks. The second way people can communicate risks involves the tendency to rely on open interaction with the people directly affected by the risks. Because this way of communicating about risks

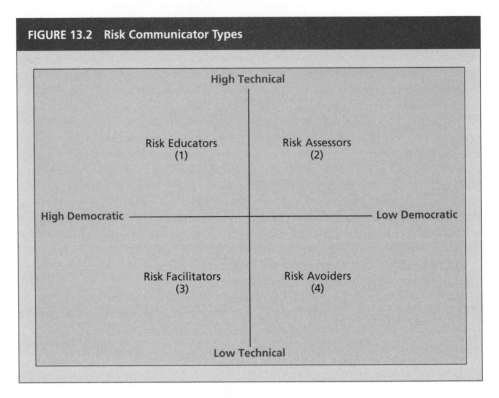

FIGURE 13.2   Risk Communicator Types

High Technical

Risk Educators (1)   Risk Assessors (2)

High Democratic ——————————————— Low Democratic

Risk Facilitators (3)   Risk Avoiders (4)

Low Technical

is about involving stakeholders (people who could be impacted by a risk), we call this form of risk communication *democratic risk communication*. When people communicate about risks, they generally are not technical or democratic but a combination of both forms of communication. In other words, we tend to see variations of risk communicators being both technical and democratic. In Figure 13.2, we see the four basic types of risk communicators broken down by their use of technical and democratic communication strategies while communicating risks.

The term *risk educator* was used for those risk communicators who scored both high on the technical and democratic factors of the Risk Communicator Style Scale (RCSS). The basis of risk communication is the transmission of technical information about a behavior or hazard while taking the patient's emotional perception of the risk into account at the same time. The term *risk assessor* is used for those risk communicators who communicate in very technical manners with little concern for the receiver's perception of the risk. Physicians who are risk assessors are generally seen as detached and scientific in their explanations about risk. Physicians who communicate risks in a highly democratic way without the use of technical language and scientific information are referred to as *risk facilitators*. Physicians who are risk facilitators focus solely on making sure everyone's perception of the risk is clearly discussed and understood. In essence, physicians who are risk facilitators are very concerned with understanding how someone feels about a diagnosis rather than contradicting those feelings with scientific evidence. Those physicians who scored low on both the scientific and affective factors of the RCSS are referred to as *risk avoiders*. Physicians who are risk avoiders do not inter-act with their patients on either an intellectual or emotional level, and are basically seen as avoiding the need for risk messages. Many physicians are just too overwhelmed with the number patients that they need to see in a day that they simply don't talk about risk behaviors with their patients at all.

In the realm of patient satisfaction, Wrench (2001) found that individuals who per-ceived risk communicators as using democratic risk communication were seen as more credible and were more satisfied with their interaction with the risk communicator. How-ever, the use of technical risk communication was not shown to be related with a risk communicator's perceived credibility or an individual's level of satisfaction with the risk communicator. In essence, it is important for physicians to remember that the science part can be used when communicating risks to patients, but you also have to make sure that you are using democratic risk communication at the same time.

Return to Clinic.   The last part of the SOAP-ER process of medical record documen-tation is the section on returning to the clinic. The returning to the clinic section is when a physician writes when and under what circumstances a patient should return to see their physician. Often the initial treatment in an illness or injury is not the most effective treat-ment. For this reason, a physician will almost always say something like "If your headache does not go away in three days, come back and see me." It's also possible that a physician will let you know that if you experience any side effects on her or his prescribed treatment or medication, you should return to her or his office for further evaluation. Like what was mentioned in the patient communication section of this chapter, patients often want relief to be immediate. If that relief is not immediate, a patient will come back the next day or quite possibly go and see a different physician for a second treatment. It is important for a physician to explain the reasoning behind the wait period. Many medications need a few days to get into the body before they actually start relieving or healing anything.

Hopefully, now that you, as a consumer of medical care, understand what a physi-cian is looking for, you will be able to help your primary care physician more accurately diagnose any future problems. Let's now switch gears and examine some basic physician communication variables that research has shown impacts the medical interview.

Communication Variables and Physician Communication

Although for many patients the necessity for a physician to be a competent communica-tor is obvious, many physicians don't understand why good communication skills are important during the medical interview. If you're a physician, if you know one, or if you plan to be one, here is one reason why it is important to be a competent communicator: physicians who have good communication skills receive fewer lawsuits. That's right: in two different articles found in the *Journal of the American Medical Association* (*JAMA*), it was found that physicians with good communication skills had fewer patient complaints and lawsuits (Hickson et al., 2002; Levinson, Roter, Mullooly, Dull, & Frankel, 1997).

If that's not reason enough, good communication skills have also been shown to affect a patient's level of compliance with medication or treatment. Fifty percent of all patients do not comply with the treatments or medication a physician prescribes (Bullman, 1996; Stone, 1979). Although noncompliance may not seem like a huge problem to some people, Giuffrida and Torgerson (1997) found that noncompliance is actually causing everyone's insurance premiums to increase as a result. Bullman (1996) concluded that the most common reason for noncompliance with a physician's prescribed medication and treatments is a direct result of a lack of effective patient–physician communication. So if a physician truly wants to heal people, he or she needs to realize that the way he or she is communicating effects patient compliance.

In the rest of this section we are going to examine four communication behaviors that have been shown to impact patient–physician interactions: perceived credibility, sociocommunicative orientation, humor, and nonverbal immediacy.

Perceived Credibility.   Physician credibility is an extremely important concept to explore in the patient–physician relationship. Credibility as a construct is entirely based on perceptions. In the patient–physician relationship, we examine a patient's perceptions of credibility. Patients will make judgments about a physician's competence, trustworthiness, and caring/goodwill. Wrench and Booth-Butterfield (2003) noted that a patient's perception of a physician's credibility impacts a patient's likelihood of complying with her or his physician's prescribed treatment/medication. As mentioned in the patient communication section of this chapter, patients who see their physicians as credible are more satisfied with their physicians and believe that the quality of their care was better than those patients who do not perceive their physicians as credible.

So what can physicians do to make themselves appear more credible to their patients? Physicians need to exhibit more caring oriented behaviors. In many ways, credibility is akin to what the former president of the National Speaker's Association Cavett Roberts said: "They don't care how much you know, until they know how much you care." In the realm of credibility, research has shown that caring/goodwill is probably the most important initial form of credibility a person can have. If a physician can show a patient that he or she truly cares about that patient, it will increase the patient's perceptions of the physician's credibility. Beyond just demonstrating caring/goodwill, it is important for physicians to demonstrate their competence as well. One way to demonstrate competence is to be aware of major medical studies that get discussed in the media. The media frequently latch on to research causing the research to become national news. Physicians need to know what these studies are saying in order to talk with their patients when they ask questions about the media touted research. Along with this, physicians must learn how to understand and interpret medical research. Lastly, trustworthiness will be strengthened only over time. Although high perceptions of competence and caring/goodwill can boost perceptions of someone's trustworthiness, true trustworthiness only comes after a long period of time. Physicians should encourage the development of long standing patient–physician relationships.

Sociocommunicative Orientation.   A physician's tendency to communicate in assertive and responsive ways does have a clear impact on the way that her or his patients respond during the medical interview. If you need a refresher on sociocommunicative orientation, reread Chapter 2 in this book. In a study conducted by Richmond et al. (2002), it was found that physicians who are both highly assertive and highly responsive are seen as credible physicians. Specifically, patients saw both highly responsive and highly assertive physicians as being competent. However, patients did indicate that highly responsive physicians were more trustworthy and caring than were physicians who were perceived as being highly assertive. In other words, although both assertive and responsive communication patterns can make a physician appear competent, a physician needs to exhibit responsive communication patterns to be seen as trustworthy and caring by her or his patients.

The Richmond et al. (2002) also looked at patient perceptions of satisfaction and the quality of medical care. The researchers found that a physician's level of responsiveness did impact a patient's level of satisfaction and perception of the quality of medical care. However, assertiveness was not shown to help or detract from a patient's level of satisfaction and perception of the quality of medical care.

Humor. A physician's use of humor during the patient–physician interaction is extremely important. Levinson et al. (1997) found that physicians who use humor during the medical interview were less likely to face malpractice lawsuits and had more satisfied patients. Wrench and Booth-Butterfield (2003) found that patients who perceived their physicians as humorous also perceived their physicians as being more credible on all three levels of credibility (competence, trustworthiness, and caring/goodwill). The impact that humor has on the patient–physician relationship and on patient health has been researched for a long time.

Research in the area of medical humor has shown that humor is related to many medical findings such as lower levels of stress-related hormones (Berk, 1989), increased immunoglobulin rates (Lambert & Lambert, 1995; McClelland & Cheriff, 1997), increased helper T-cells (Berk, 1993), lower levels of pain (Adams & McGuire, 1986; Cohen, 1990; Pasquali, 1991), lower blood pressure levels (Fry & Savin, 1982), and faster recovery rates from illnesses (McClelland & Cheriff, 1997). Although these medical terms may not be familiar concepts to you, the fact that exposure to humor can actually change the way your body functions should be pretty impressing. Gaberson (1991) found that patients who were exposed to humorous messages before an operation had lower levels of anxiety before the operation and faster post operation recovery rates. In other words, people actually recover faster if they are exposed to humor. Overall, the inclusion of humor into the medical environment appears to have an overwhelmingly positive effect.

Nonverbal Immediacy. The last specific physician trait that is examined in this section of the chapter is nonverbal immediacy. If you need a refresher on nonverbal immediacy, reread Chapter 5. Like we see in interpersonal relationships, the degree to which a patient perceives that a physician is physically and psychologically close to her or him is extremely important. Richmond, Smith, Heisel, and McCroskey (2001) found that a physician's level of nonverbal immediacy positively impacted patient satisfaction and perceptions of the quality of medical care while decreasing an individual's fear of communication with a physician. The Richmond et al. (2001) study found that patients who perceived their physicians as more nonverbally immediate also were more satisfied and reported higher perceptions of the quality of medical care they received. Patients who perceived their physicians as more nonverbally immediate also reported having lower levels of fear when communicating with their physicians.

 CONCLUSION

This chapter has been an exploration of how we can apply the concepts from the first section of this book to the context of health communication. As an area of research for communication scholars, health communication is still fairly new. Although we are just beginning to understand the importance of competent communication in the health care environment, the benefits are very clear.

 KEY TERMS

actual reason for coming (ARC) 280

health communication 279
medical interview 292

SOAP note 293

 REFERENCES

Adams, E. R., & McGuire, F. A. (1986). Is laughter the best medicine? A study of the effects of humor on perceived pain and affect. *Activities, Adaptation, and Aging, 8,* 156–175.

Baker, S. K. (1998). Improving service and increasing patient satisfaction. *Family Practice Management, 5,* 29–32.

Becker, M. H., & Rosenstock, I. M. (1984). Compliance with medical advice. In A. Steptoe & A. Matthews (Eds.), *Health care and human behavior* (pp. 175–208). London: Academic Press.

Berk, L. S. (1989). Neuroendocrine and stress hormone changes during mirthful laughter. *American Journal of the Medical Sciences, 298,* 390–396.

Berk, L. S. (1993). Eustress of humor associated with laughter modulates specific immune system components. *Annals of Behavioral Medicine, 15,* S111.

Bullman, W. (1996). The National Council on Patient Information and Education: Focusing on communication, compliance, FDA Medguide proposal in 1996. *Formulary, 31,* 389–396.

Cohen, M. (1990). Caring for ourselves can be funny business. *Holistic Nursing Practice, 4,* 1–11.

Fitzpatrick, R. (1993). Scope and measurement of satisfaction. In R. Fitzpatrick & A. Hopkins (Eds.), *A measurement of patients satisfaction with their care.* London: Royal College of Physicians.

Fry, W. F. Jr., & Savin, M. (1982). *Mirthful laughter and blood pressure.* Paper presented at the Third International Conference on Humor. Washington, DC.

Gaberson, K. B. (1991). The effect of humorous distraction on preoperative anxiety. *AORN Journal, 54,* 1259–1263.

Giuffrida, A., & Torgerson, D. J. (1997). Should we pay the patient? Review of financial incentives to enhance patient compliance. *British Medical Journal, 315,* 703–708.

Hall, J. A., & Roter, D. L. (2002). Do patients talk differently to male and female physicians? A meta-analytic review. *Patient education and counseling, 48,* 217–294.

Hall, J. A., Roter, D. L., & Katz, N. R. (1988). Meta-analysis of correlates of provider behavior in medical encounters. *Medical Care, 26,* 657–675.

Hickson, G. B., Federspiel, C. F., Pichert, J. W., Miller, C. S., Gauld-Jaeger, J, & Bost, P. (2002). Patient complaints and malpractice risk. *JAMA, 287,* 2951–2957.

Hohmann, A. A. (1989). Gender bias in psychotropic drug prescribing in primary care. *Medical Care, 27,* 478–490.

Lambert, R. B., & Lambert, N. K. (1995). The effects of humor on secretory immunoglobulin A levels in school-aged children. *Pediatric Nursing, 21,* 16–19.

Levinson, W., Roter, D. L., Mullooly, J. P., Dull, V. T., & Frankel, R. M. (1997). Physician-patient communication: The relationship with malpractice claims among primary care physicians and surgeons. *JAMA, 277,* 553–559.

Lochman, J. E. (1983). Factors related to patients' satisfaction with their medical care. *Journal of Community Health, 9,* 91.

McClelland, D., & Cheriff, A. D. (1997). The immunoenhancing effects of humor on secretory IgA and resistance to respiratory infections. *Psychology and Health, 12,* 329–344.

Pasquali, E. A. (1991). Humor: Preventive therapy for family caregivers. *Home Healthcare Nurse, 9,* 13–17.

Richmond, V. P., Smith, R. S., Heisel, A. M., & McCroskey, J. C. (1998). The impact of communication apprehension and fear of talking with a physician and perceived medical outcomes. *Communication Research Reports, 15,* 344–353.

Richmond, V. P., Smith, R. S., Heisel, A. M., & McCroskey, J. C. (2001). Nonverbal immediacy in the physician/patient relationship. *Communication Research Reports, 18,* 211–216.

Richmond, V. P., Smith, R. S., Heisel, A. M., & McCroskey, J. C. (2002). The association of physician socio-communicative style with physician credibility and patient satisfaction. *Communication Research Reports, 19,* 207–215.

Sloane, P. D. (2002). Approach to common problems in family medicine. In P. D. Sloan, L. M. Slatt, M. H. Ebell, & L. B. Jacques (Eds.), *Essentials of family medicine* (4th ed., pp. 231–240). Baltimore: Lippincott, Williams, & Wilkins.

Stone, G. C. (1979). Patient compliance and the role of the expert. *Journal of Social Issues, 35,* 34–39.

Waitzkin, J. H. (1984). Doctor-patient communication: Clinical implications of social scientific research. *Journal of the American Medical Association, 252,* 2441–2446.

Waitzkin, J. H. (1985). Information giving in medical care. *Journal of Health and Social Behavior, 26,* 81–101.

Wallen, J., Waitzkin, J. H., & Stoeckle, J. (1979). Physician stereotypes about female health and illness. *Women and Health, 4,* 1135–1145.

Wrench, J. S. (2001). *The Development and validity testing of the risk communicator style scale and the risk knowledge index.* Unpublished doctoral dissertation. Morgantown, WV: West Virginia University.

Wrench, J. S. (2003, March). *The STATS Method.* Presentation to the West Virginia School of Osteopathic Medicine. Lewisburg, WV.

Wrench, J. S., & Booth-Butterfield, M. (2003). Increasing patient satisfaction and compliance: An examination of physician humor orientation, compliance-gaining strategies, and perceived credibility. *Communication Quarterly, 51,* 482–503.

DISCUSSION QUESTIONS

1. Have you ever not been completely honest about your actual reason for coming to a physician? If yes, why do you think you had a problem with being completely up-front and honest? If no, why do you think others often are not completely up-front and honest?

2. What problems can you see with the increasing number of websites that offer medical advice?

3. Why do you think fear of physicians negatively influences an individual's medical care?

4. Think of your last trip to the physician. Did your physician complete a SOAP note? If not, what parts of a SOAP note were not clearly covered?

5. Which type of risk communicator do you think would be most effective when dealing with young children? Why?

14

Mediated Communication

OBJECTIVES

- Explain the difference between communication and communications.

- Understand the basic evolution of human communication.

- Differentiate between pictographic and orthographic alphabet systems.

- Know the significance of Johannes Gutenberg's work.

- Understand the types of media that are monological.

- Understand the types of media that are dialogical.

- Explain why mediated group communication is difficult.

- Understand the history of the Internet.

- Define and explain *asynchronous computer-mediated communication* and *synchronous computer-mediated communication*.

- Explain Walther's social information processing (SIP) theory.

- Understand the relationship among communication apprehension, willingness to communicate, communication competence, and computer-mediated communication.

- Understand the future directions in which mediated communications are heading.

The previous chapters of this book have looked at human communication in its most common form—face-to-face, oral interaction. For much of the history of the human race, that was the only form of communication available. It remains the most used, and therefore the most important, form today; but it certainly no longer stands as the only form.

In the first chapter in this book, we defined communications as "transferring messages from place to place" (e.g., mass communications: television, radio, and print media). Ultimately, the difference between communication and communications is that communications requires the use of some sort of mediation. Mediated communications is similar to the more common form except that the source(s) and receiver(s) are not physically in the presence of each other at the same time. They may be separated by distance, time, or both, which makes live interaction either difficult or impossible. Some "medium," therefore, is necessary to link them together.

EVOLUTION OF HUMAN COMMUNICATION

We do not really know when humans started communicating with each other, but we are certain it was a very long time ago. That early communication most likely was little different from the communication we can see today among lower forms of life— monkeys, dogs, bears, birds, whales,

I-pods are being used everywhere, even on a subway.

and so on. Early human communication probably involved nothing more than grunting, squealing, smiling, pushing, and grabbing. Although such communicative efforts certainly were not sophisticated, they did permit these early humans to relate to one another to some extent. This primitive behavior did allow the communication of some very basic emotions, such as anger and affection.

Nonverbal behavior, then, is the foundation on which human communication has evolved. Even today, nonverbal behaviors function as the primary means to communicate emotional, or affective, meanings between humans (McCroskey, 1992; Richmond, 1992; Richmond & McCroskey, 1995). Nonverbal behaviors remain essential to oral languages. Without them, oral languages cannot exist.

After many thousands of years, humans evolved the power of speech. Again, this was probably a very slow process, with very few words being learned during the comparatively short life span of humans at the time. In due course, the few words grew into language with syntax and grammar, and the offspring of the adults with language competence were taught the language of their parents.

As these humans ventured forth to populate various parts of the world, more oral languages evolved. Today, approximately 5,000 oral languages exist on Earth. No single one of these is spoken or understood by a majority of humans, although Mandarin is spoken by more people than any other language. Thus, even today, when people travel to various parts of the world, unless they can find someone who speaks their own language or another language they have learned, they must resort to nonverbal behaviors to communicate. Even if you were to become fluent in a dozen languages, a feat achieved only by rare individuals, you would be unable to communicate in the languages of the overwhelming majority of cultures in the world.

EARLY DEVELOPMENT OF MEDIATED COMMUNICATION

Although it is difficult today for us to imagine a world without writing, writing is a very recent development in the history of human communication. In fact, writing was not the first "medium" developed for communicating with people who were not present. The earliest attempts at recording information for later humans were left as drawings by ancient cave dwellers. Obviously, cave drawings were neither an efficient nor particularly effective method of communicating anything but the most primitive of thoughts. In fact, there are some people who try to make a case for prehistoric extraterrestrial contact based on the drawings found in caves. In essence, people can see pretty much anything they want in a cave drawing, so as a historical tool cave drawings are not very reliable. Such drawings slowly evolved into more complex picture systems.

History of Writing

If the history of human communication were represented by a typical twelve-inch ruler, the history of writing would be included in *less than the last quarter of an inch.* Even today, the overwhelming majority of the 5,000 languages in the world *have no written form.* In fact, only about 100 of them even have an alphabet. Although writing is central to the educational system in the United States today, there are many who believe its time is running out. In the not-too-distant future, humans may have no further use for this very inefficient and imprecise tool! Not too long ago, we wrote books, literally. Now we keyboard them. What's next?

Writing is believed to have evolved from humans' desire to record information for the use of people who came along after them. Early humans recognized that history by hearsay is very imprecise and subject to each teller's biases and fantasies. Early humans realized that as information passes through such a serial communication process (McCroskey, 1992), information is distorted severely and might not even remotely represent what actually happened. The remnants of such oral histories can be seen in the mythologies and religions of the various cultures of the world.

Today we have cultures that continue to use a *pictographic* system (albeit a more sophisticated one) for their written language; Chinese is one of the best examples. In these cultures, there is no pretense that the written language is the same as the oral language. It is recognized that both the oral and the written languages are symbolic representations of ideas the user is trying to communicate, but that they are very different systems.

In other cultures, an alphabet has been developed. In these *orthographic* systems, the alphabetical symbols are put together to approximate the sounds of the oral language. Early on, that relationship may have been fairly close. However, as those of us who have grown up as English speakers are apt to recognize quickly, that approximation is extremely strained in contemporary societies.

The relationship between oral and written English is remote indeed. Although each uses symbols to represent ideas, those symbols have little relationship to each other. People in the U.S. culture continue to consider these radically different language forms to be the same language. The problems this mythology creates for the users of the language, particularly children, are severe indeed (Richmond, McCroskey, & Thompson, 1992).

Even writings from Judaism, Christianity, and Islam, which are at their oldest only 3,000 years old, can be very ambiguous to scholars today. Although there are countless numbers of people who will tell you that they "know" what a religious text says, the actual meanings of the writings are hotly contested by scholars who examine them. For example, cultural idioms of the day, which have found their way into religious writings, may be interpreted in one way today but would have been understood in a different way by the readers of the text at the time when it was written. Imagine in 3,000 years someone reads a paper from today, and he or she reads that Joe Smith was a left fielder for the Pittsburgh Pirates. Well, if they know that pirates were people who were thieves on the sea, and fields are only found on land, was a left fielder a gardener on a boat? Or maybe a left fielder was someone who only stole crops? The fact is you cannot discount the cultural impact on writings, which causes writings to be at best ambiguous to people in other cultures and at worst completely uninterpretable.

Another problem with writings comes in the form of translations of writings from one language to another language. Translation problems are yet another area in which religious texts often have difficulty. In the Greek version of the Christian New Testament, there are 5,437 different words used 138,162 times. From the original Greek to the original version of the King James Version of the Christian Bible, approximately 2,000 changes were made to the text. The New International Version (NIV) has 64,000 fewer words than the King James Version of the Christian Bible. Although biblical scholars still debate the exact number of changes that have been made to various translations, the written text of 1,700 years ago is not the exact written text that you can buy at a bookstore today or pick up in your local motel room. Just go peruse your local bookstore, and you'll find many different modern English translations of the Christian Bible. In fact, there are over fifty different translations currently being sold in the United States alone. Although we are not suggesting that the Christian Bible is a flawed document, we are noting that written texts innately have limitations.

One last major early limitation with written languages was that only highly educated and trained people were able to read, write, and understand written language. Until the invention of the Western printing press by Johannes Gutenberg in 1436 (and completed by 1440), people had to rely on members of the clergy and other trained people to read written texts because written texts were rare. Obviously, this put a lot of power in the hands of clergy and other trained people who could read the written texts, and as history shows us, this power garnered from reading and interpreting religious texts was used for both good and bad.

Although the Western World had not seen a printing press until 1440, there is evidence to suggest that the Chinese had experimented with the art of printing approximately 5,000 years before Gutenberg. Nevertheless, the Gutenberg Press revolutionized printed materials by making them producible in mass quantity instead of having to write out each copy of a book by hand. As manuscripts became more readily available, the need for a literate public also became the norm.

History of Technology

Very recently, within far less than one-sixteenth of an inch on our imaginary twelve-inch ruler, we humans have developed what many believe to be an incredibly improved system of recording the oral language, one that may make writing obsolete. The advances in electronic recording and transmission have been extremely rapid—radio, film, television, imaging, holography, fax, computers, the Internet, and who knows what next.

Written descriptions of what your grandmother looked like, sounded like, and walked like can never compete with the holographic representation of your grandmother in your own living room talking to you. And a hologram cannot compete with a virtual reality program designed to let humans communicate with their great, great, great grandfathers—an advance that many see as coming in the very near future. Although only a dream a few years ago, these technologies now exist, and most are either already economically feasible or projected to be so in the reasonably near future. As much as we who take pride in being authors might wish it otherwise, the handheld video camera and its relatives and descendants are making texts as obsolete as horse and buggies were after the invention of the automobile. Although writing most likely will continue to exist for many more generations, particularly as an art form, its central role in passing information from one generation to another may soon end.

VIEWING COMMUNICATION MULTIDIMENSIONALLY

As we have described the evolution of communication above, you may have noticed that we proceeded from communication that is primarily dyadic to that which involves potentially millions of people. At the same time, we moved from live interaction to mediated communication. It is important that we keep these two ideas distinguished from each other. The first is concerned with the number of receivers, either real or potential. The second is concerned with live, face-to-face interaction as opposed to communication that is mediated through space and/or time.

An examination of Figure 14.1 will help keep these two ideas distinct. As is illustrated in this figure, media are designed to overcome problems related to separation of

FIGURE 14.1   Communication Dimensions and Media Forms

Potential Receivers	Level of Mediation			
	Interactive			Monologic
Dyadic interaction	Live conversation	Telephone Computer-mediated communication Video phone CB radio	Memo/letter E-mail Voice mail Art	Memo/letter E-mail Voice mail Virtual reality
Small-group interaction	Live group discussion	Teleconference Videoconference Chat rooms Interactive computer	E-mail with copies Letter with copies	E-mail with copies Letter with copies
Large-group meeting	Formal meeting speeches and questions	Interactive TV Interactive computer	Videotape Film	Videotape Film
Mass audience	Public speech or a series of speeches	Microphone Ham radio Live radio Live TV Chat rooms	Book Newspaper Magazine Film Videotape Billboard CD-ROM	Book Newspaper Magazine Film Videotape CD-ROM

source and receiver(s) by space and/or time. Examples of the types of media that might be used for the various combinations of potential receivers and level of mediation are included. The examples provided are *not* presumed to be exhaustive, only illustrative.

In order to envision the place of media in communication, it is useful to focus first on the impact of communication on the number of potential receivers available. Most of our everyday communication is with one individual at a time, or what we have referred to in this book as "dyadic" or interpersonal communication. Our potential, however, includes communication with an infinite number of people if we are able to command the necessary media. It is not, however, necessary to involve either electronic or print media to engage in "mass communications." Before there were either electronic or print media, there was mass communication in the form of public speeches to large (mass) audiences.

Therefore, it is useful to think of audience size on a continuum. We move from dyadic communication to public communication on the extremes. As we do, our communication becomes more monological. That is, when more people are involved, those who speak tend to "make speeches" rather than interact with short comments made by one person after another. Public communication is primarily monological, although people in the audience are often invited to ask questions or make comments after the formal speech is completed.

Even though public communication is monological, when no print or electronic media are involved, the source and receivers are "live" and feedback is possible. As we noted in Chapter 1, feedback is one of the very important aspects of communication that increase its likelihood of success. Feedback permits speakers to get some sense of how the receiver(s) is responding, and adapt to that response if necessary. Live interaction is more immediate, and therefore more likely to gain and maintain another person's attention and interest, and hence increase the effectiveness of the interaction.

To the extent that any form of communication is mediated, the immediacy of the communication is reduced. Not all media have the same effect on the immediacy of the interaction, however. To examine the impact of media on human communication, we will first look at dyadic communication.

Media and Dyadic Communication

When most people think of mediated communication, they think of television or some other form of mass communication. Mediated dyadic communication, however, is something most of us have been involved with since we were children. One of the earliest forms of mediated dyadic communication was letter writing. Until the last fifty years or so, this was about the only method by which a person could keep in touch with someone who lived a long ways away. Remember, at that time a couple of hundred miles was a very long way for many people. Hence letter writing was very popular. But even with a quite efficient mail service, it still took several days to get a letter across a state, much less to get it across the United States. Then, even if the person to whom we wrote answered immediately, it would take quite a while to get the letter through the system and back to us. Many people simply do not understand the importance of letter writing prior to the more advanced mediated technologies. Two prominent scientists in history, Charles Darwin and Albert Einstein, were avid letter writers. Darwin wrote at least 7,591 (one-half letter per day) letters in his career, whereas Einstein wrote 14,500 (1 letter per day) letters in his career. Oliveira and Barabási (2005) found that whereas the letter mechanism used by Darwin and Einstein may have differed from modern e-mail, the writing patterns of Darwin and Einstein are very similar to those of modern e-mail users. In fact, Darwin and Einstein quickly responded to most letters sent them, but other letters sat around for years before getting a written response. In the same way, modern e-mail users generally respond very quickly to e-mails, but other e-mails sit in people's in-boxes for considerable periods of time before responses are written.

Writing letters, although certainly better than nothing, is very nonimmediate. The average turnaround time from when a letter was received by Darwin and Einstein to when the original sender received a response was at least ten days. Although interaction still occurs between members of the dyad, feedback and response are long delayed, and confusion and misunderstandings are likely to be troublesome because they cannot be cleared up immediately. The arrival of the telephone overcame much of the difficulty presented by letters. At least the time aspect became less of an issue. Telephone communicators are spatially apart, but temporally together. Unfortunately, only the vocal aspect of nonverbal communication is present. All of the other aspects of nonverbal behavior that increase the immediacy of dyadic communication are lost. This is improved markedly by the use of videophones and Internet cameras. However, despite the availability and relatively low cost of this technology, we are still years away from becoming the Jetsons, with a videophone in every house. Let's face it, do you really want people to see what you look like at 2:30 in the morning when it's a wrong number?

Two other forms of media also facilitate dyadic communication: CB radio and ham radio. Essentially these are the same thing as the telephone except they operate through the air rather than via telephone lines. They also are somewhat less private, because anyone with a receiver can tune into the radio messages.

In between writing letters and calling on the videophone also are two electronic media systems that may be thought of as "telephonic letters." Facsimile (fax) transmission and electronic mail (e-mail) speed up the process of getting a letter to someone, but both fax and e-mail are more like letters than videophone. They move complete messages over great distances very quickly (unlike letters), but allow for no feedback during the presentation of that message. Feedback may come soon after transmission and reception, or it may be delayed for a substantial period because the receiver may not be present when the fax or e-mail message is sent.

Media and Group Communication

Group communication is a difficult process when it is live, and it only becomes more difficult when it is mediated. As the size of a group becomes larger, more group members cease to be group participants and become group observers instead. Mediation of group communication facilitates this transformation, and in the process reduces the usefulness of group communication itself. As a result, most group communication today still is conducted by live, face-to-face (FtF) groups.

Group communication is possible, although very difficult, to conduct via written messages (copied to all group members) or audio- or videotaped messages similarly distributed. Of the three, the written form is the least immediate and usually the least effective, even if it is handled as email rather than letter, whereas the videotape would be the most immediate and most effective. In all cases, however, because group communication thrives on feedback and immediate interaction, these mediated approaches are only better than nothing at all, and sometimes not even that.

Interactive computer conferencing, telephone conferencing, and video conferencing are all mediated approaches which have fewer drawbacks than written or taped message transmissions. The big advantage of these media approaches is that feedback and immediate response and adaptation are possible. Of course, the written (computer) mode has fewer advantages, whereas the video mode is closest to the live. The big advantage of these modes over the live group meeting, of course, is the cost necessary for having people travel for a meeting. It should be remembered, however, that there is a cost paid in terms of interpersonal affect among group members when they are separated by great distance. It is a whole lot easier to be unpleasant with a person a long way off than it is to do so when sitting next to that person. Furthermore, the social needs of the group members may be ignored in the attempt to save money by keeping the conference short. Groups normally function best when the members are both task and socially attractive to one another.

Finally, holding mediated meetings for large groups is extremely difficult. About the only use for such an approach is a meeting that is intended to distribute information with little or no questioning or interaction. Essentially, this format takes on a public speaking mode rather than a group interaction mode. Virtually all the group members become observers rather than participants. If group participation is needed, a mediated meeting is not the best approach.

Mediated Public Communication

Public communication is sometimes referred to as *person-to-group communication* or *one-to-many communication*. It is primarily monological, although some questioning and response may be possible depending on the level of mediation involved. As soon as there are enough people in the audience to require a microphone for the speaker, we have moved into the realm of mediated communication, although the intrusion of the medium is minimal at this level.

When the potential receivers of the message are spread over a wide distance, electronic media are very likely to be involved in public communication. From the ham radio operator to the live radio and television stations and networks, to computer bulletin boards and chat rooms, the electronic media have the capacity to get the message live to large numbers of people. If the receivers are not all available at the same time, these same media can deliver the public communication, or parts of it, at various times. So too can the "less instantaneous" print and electronic media—books, magazines, newspapers, films, audio- or videotape, CD-ROM, billboards, et cetera.

The industries we are concerned with at this level are what are commonly referred to as the mass *media.* That is, they serve as a medium to take a message to a large mass of people. In this form of communication little feedback is expected, and very little normally is received. This, of course, means that the public communication can only be as effective as its original design will permit it to be. When there is no feedback, there is no adaptation. When the message is one of news or entertainment, the delayed feedback is in the count of how many people listened to or watched the message. If the message has a more direct goal, such as selling cars or political candidates, the feedback comes in terms of how many cars are sold or how many votes the candidate receives.

 ## THE SWITCH TO INTERACTION

The traditional forms of mass mediated communications (books, magazines, newspapers, radios, and television) clearly fulfill the role of source in the communication model, and consumers of such messages fulfill the role of receivers. However, one of the major limitations of mass mediated communications has been the feedback function of a receiver. Although feedback does occur with all traditional mediated forms, feedback is not quick. Maybe you read an article in the newspaper and you decide to write a letter to the editor stating your disagreement, which would be a form of feedback to the newspaper. Maybe you get to be a Nielsen family and let television producers and executives know which television shows you are watching during a given period of time (how television ratings are compiled). Although feedback may occur, it tends to be very slow when compared to face-to-face interactions. In the early 1990s and through the present day, the Internet has taken on the role of a highly utilized mediated communications device that has the capacity to offer real time interaction between sources and receivers making it truly interactive. In Figure 14.2, is a brief outline of the history of the Internet.

Basically, most of what the public is concerned with on the Internet has really only occurred since the early 1990s. When most of the Internet service providers (ISPs) like AOL, CompuServe, and Prodigy first started enabling the public, costs were $10.95 a month to use the Internet for ten hours and each additional hour ran you $4.95. Back in the mid-1990s, people often ran up Internet bills in the hundreds of dollars. In the late 1990s, AOL went to a $19.95 unlimited access plan, which opened up the Internet market enabling the public to affordably enjoy the benefits of the Internet.

 ## COMPUTER-MEDIATED COMMUNICATION (CMC)

On the Internet, there are two basic forms of computer-mediated communication (CMC): asynchronous and synchronous (Barnes, 2003; Wood & Smith, 2001). Asynchronous communication is communication in which people interact with each other at

FIGURE 14.2   Brief History of the Internet

1957   The USSR launches Sputnik (a satellite) into orbit, causing Americans to fear they were losing the technological war, so the U.S. Department of Defense (DOD) creates the Advanced Research Projects Agency (ARPA) to lead technological developments for the military.

1969   ARPANET, a computer networking tool commissioned by the DOD to enable researchers at remote sites to interact, is initiated starting with four remote sites called *nodes* (University of California, Los Angeles [UCLA]; Stanford Research Institute; University of California, Santa Barbara; & University of Utah).

1971   Ray Tomlinson invents a program to send messages across the network, which is eventually called *electronic mail* or *e-mail* for short.

1972   Ray Tomlinson decides to use the @ sign as a way to determine how e-mail will find its way to the receiver of the message.
A computer-to-computer chat takes place at UCLA.

1973   An ARPA study shows that 75 percent of all traffic on ARPANET is e-mail.

1975   Message lists, which eventually become bulletin boards and news groups, are created by Steve Walker for ARPANET. The primary message list for professionals was MsgGroup. The number one unofficial message list was SF-Lovers, a science fiction list.

1979   The first multiple-user domain, or MUD, is created by Richard Bartle and Roy Trubshaw at the University of Essex.
On April 12, 1979, Kevin MacKenzie e-mails the MsgGroup, suggesting they start adding emotional cues to make the text medium less dry. He suggests symbols like -) for indicating that a sentence was meant to be sarcastic or tongue in cheek. MacKenzie receives a considerable amount of derogatory e-mails in response to the notion that emotion be used in e-mail.

1982   Scott Fahlman suggests that MsgGroup users use :-) and :-(on September 19 in a bulletin board at Carnegie Mellon University.

1987   In response to a congressional request by U.S. Senator Al Gore (D-TN) to create a more public presence on the Internet, Gordon Bell and his colleagues write a report for the Office of Science and Technology suggesting the creation of a U.S. research and education network, which would be established four years later by Congress.

1988   Internet Relay Chat (IRC) is developed by Jarkko Oikarinen.

varying times. For example, bulletin boards or newsgroups allow people to participate at any time of the day. Maybe Jeph will post a message at 3:00 A.M. in the morning, and then Keena will respond to that message at 4:00 P.M. Even your basic e-mail is a form of asynchronous communication. Synchronous communication, on the other hand, is communication that occurs in real time (or approximates real time).

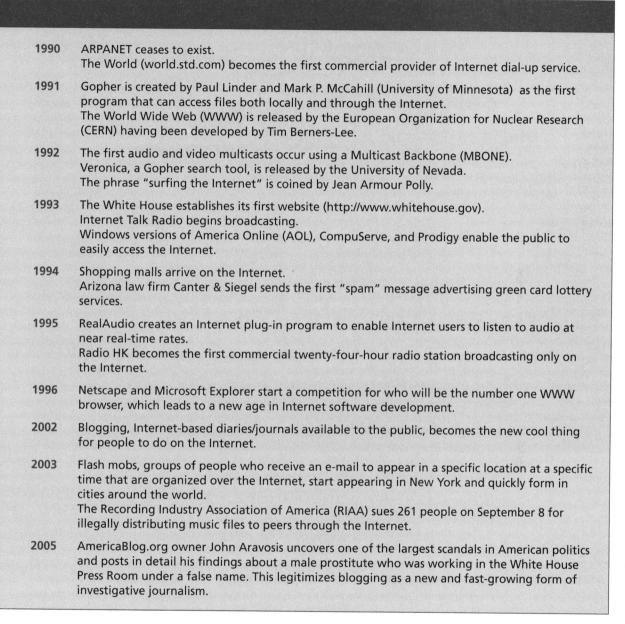

1990	ARPANET ceases to exist. The World (world.std.com) becomes the first commercial provider of Internet dial-up service.
1991	Gopher is created by Paul Linder and Mark P. McCahill (University of Minnesota) as the first program that can access files both locally and through the Internet. The World Wide Web (WWW) is released by the European Organization for Nuclear Research (CERN) having been developed by Tim Berners-Lee.
1992	The first audio and video multicasts occur using a Multicast Backbone (MBONE). Veronica, a Gopher search tool, is released by the University of Nevada. The phrase "surfing the Internet" is coined by Jean Armour Polly.
1993	The White House establishes its first website (http://www.whitehouse.gov). Internet Talk Radio begins broadcasting. Windows versions of America Online (AOL), CompuServe, and Prodigy enable the public to easily access the Internet.
1994	Shopping malls arrive on the Internet. Arizona law firm Canter & Siegel sends the first "spam" message advertising green card lottery services.
1995	RealAudio creates an Internet plug-in program to enable Internet users to listen to audio at near real-time rates. Radio HK becomes the first commercial twenty-four-hour radio station broadcasting only on the Internet.
1996	Netscape and Microsoft Explorer start a competition for who will be the number one WWW browser, which leads to a new age in Internet software development.
2002	Blogging, Internet-based diaries/journals available to the public, becomes the new cool thing for people to do on the Internet.
2003	Flash mobs, groups of people who receive an e-mail to appear in a specific location at a specific time that are organized over the Internet, start appearing in New York and quickly form in cities around the world. The Recording Industry Association of America (RIAA) sues 261 people on September 8 for illegally distributing music files to peers through the Internet.
2005	AmericaBlog.org owner John Aravosis uncovers one of the largest scandals in American politics and posts in detail his findings about a male prostitute who was working in the White House Press Room under a false name. This legitimizes blogging as a new and fast-growing form of investigative journalism.

When computer people talk about *real time*, they are talking about having the ability to have conversations with each other online in a manner that is similar to conversations that one would have in a face-to-face (FtF) interaction. Examples of synchronous communication on the Internet can be found in things like chat rooms, Internet Relayed Chats (IRCs), Multiple-User Dungeons (MUDs), and Instant Messaging (IM) services.

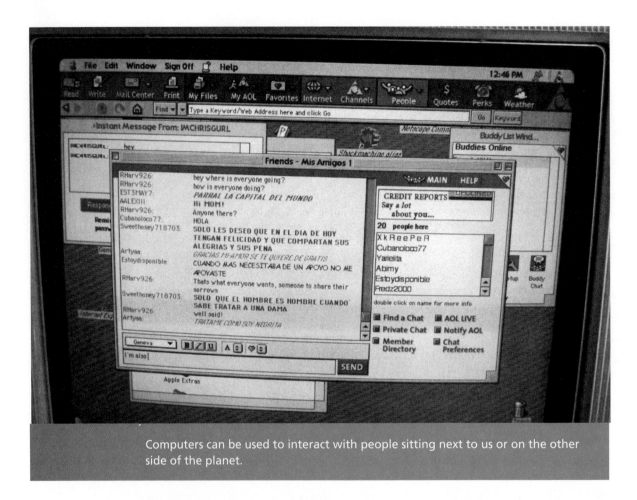

Computers can be used to interact with people sitting next to us or on the other side of the planet.

In Figure 14.3, we see an example of an actual chat room conversation. Notice how the conversation is slightly disjointed.

Learning how to effectively communicate in an online chat room can take a long time. To be effective at CMC, a person must have very good typing and reading skills, learn CMC lingo, and have patience. The entire conversation that you see in Figure 14.3 lasted less than 30 seconds, so you can imagine how many lines of text there would be if we showed you ten minutes of chat. Overall, chat rooms, IRCs, MUDs, and IMs allow people to interact with each other using Internet technology, but do people online communicate in a similar fashion to how they communicate offline?

Joseph Walther was one of the earliest researchers in communication studies to examine the phenomenon of Internet based relationships and chatting. Walther (1996) proposed that CMC and FtF interactions were functional equivalents of each other, but online relationships needed more time to develop. Walther's perspective on CMC relationships is called the social information processing (SIP) theory of CMC relationships.

FIGURE 14.3	Chat Room Conversation
OUEGuy2005:	So, anything interesting going on in here today?
Dusty99:	no
Dusty99:	:)
RoyBoy:	KAT SEND ME SOME PICS
JarHead:	**um**
SpiceGirrl:	***KAT HOW OLD IS THIS DUSTY***
Dusty99:	'cept for me and Kat being in here
KatHouse:	maybe if I find something in hubbys collection I will send it LOL
JarHead:	**IM me to talk 19/f w/pics in profile**
Dusty99:	other than that... nadda
KatHouse:	Well Dusty and Norma are here too Dee
FriendofBW:	wat's up
BoredNTexas:	**DEEDRA~~*~*~***
Dusty99:	:::looks::: where's Norma!?!?!?!?
BoredNTexas:	**hiyaas**
KatHouse:	Thizz he is older ;)
KatHouse:	There she is
Dusty99:	Norma!!!!!!!!!!!!! LoL heya lady~*~*~*
MOORNINGUY:	hello, how is everyone doing this morning?
Dusty99:	hello Ready... we're just peachy....thanks for asking

In essence, SIP theorizes that individuals interacting online will adapt existing communicative cues to replace the lack of cues in the CMC situations caused by a lack of nonverbal communication (touch, feel, taste, smell, proximity, etc.).

Walther's SIP theory has three primary assumptions. The first assumption of Walther's (1996) SIP theory is that people interacting online are motivated to do so because of a drive for affiliation, impression management, or the need for dominance. In other words, people who are interacting online want to interact online, so they are motivated to learn to do so to the best of their ability. The second assumption of Walther's (1996) SIP theory is that individuals communicating in a CMC environment must learn how to transmit relational content despite the limitations of the available channels. In other words, people online must learn how to encode relational messages and goals, while being able to decode another person's relational messages and goals. One of the biggest problems with CMC is that it relies primarily on text. Just like we discussed above when talking about the problems understanding written text in book form, many of those same problems are also inherent in CMC. CMC inherently is limited because it lacks the nonverbal component of communication, so people in the CMC environment have created extensive lists of emoticons like :-) and :-(in an effort to help alleviate some of this ambiguity. The final assumption of Walther's (1996) SIP theory is that individuals interacting online, as compared to FtF interactions, take longer to learn the medium and longer to get to know each other and build up trusts and friendships. In essence, self-efficacy becomes a very important part of the CMC process. If a person is not comfortable with her or his skill either at using the computer or the Internet, he or she will have problems communicating online. Social information processing theory provides researchers a framework for understanding how and why people adapt existing communicative cues to replace the lack of cues in the CMC situations caused by a lack of nonverbal communication.

One area of recent concern in CMC has examined the impact that communication apprehension has on people's likelihood to use the technology. In an unpublished study by Wrench, Fiore, and McCroskey (2006), the researchers found that communication apprehension (CA) and willingness to communicate (WTC) did not relate to an individual's perception of her or his CMC competence (the ability to be personally effective and socially appropriate in a CMC environment). However, extraverts were shown to perceive themselves as more competent communicators than introverts in the CMC environment. Furthermore, extraverts were more likely to take their CMC interactions and turn them into FtF interactions. In fact, a lot of research has noted that many people enjoy taking their Internet-based relationships and making them FtF relationships after a period of time, whether these relationships are friendship or romantically based.

One possible reason for this phenomenon could be due to the fact that people innately prefer to interact with each other in an environment in which we can fully use nonverbal cues to understand the meaning of another person's communication. The Wrench et al. (2006) study also found that highly communicative apprehensive people were more comfortable communicating in the online environment than they were in FtF interactions. Although this finding is still being studied, the CMC environment could provide High CA people with a new medium through which they can meet friends and potential romantic partners outside the traditional methods for doing so, which would not be as traumatic and anxiety causing as FtF interactions.

In addition to basic research on the impact of CA on the CMC environment, Wrench and Punyanunt (2005) have also studied communication apprehension that specifically relates to CMC. Before reading further, please fill out the CMC Apprehension Scales 32-34 in the appendix.

All three forms of CMC CA (e-mail, chat, and IM) were shown to be positively related to each other. Wrench and Punyanunt also found that people who had higher levels of all three forms of CMC CA did not perceive themselves to be very competent communicators online. Furthermore, although knowing how to use the Internet was negatively related to all three forms of CMC CA, the negative relationships were not very strong. What was strong, however, was the negative relationship between computer efficacy, or an individual's perception about her or his computer skills, and all three forms of CMC CA. In essence, this study illustrates that an individual's level of CA in a CMC environment is related to her or his ability to use a computer.

Overall, the real depth and extent to which CMC will revolutionize how individuals communicate with each other is still not known. The Internet has only been in the public hands for a little over fifteen years at the time this book was published, so making long term estimates about how CMC will impact human communication just isn't appropriate yet. In fact, there is always the possibility that future technologies will come in and make the Internet as we know it today obsolete.

 FUTURE CONSIDERATIONS

New media will certainly be created and implemented in society, for our need to "reach out and touch someone," as the telephone company has told us, never ceases. We are likely always to seek to communicate farther and faster, although the speed level of our media today already is extremely high. Our goals in the future will likely focus more on the quality of the communication than on its quantity or speed.

As we noted above, introducing media to the communication process does not improve the quality of the communication, but it does what it is supposed to, namely, it establishes the linkage between source and receiver. It does so imperfectly. It is never "just like being there." Important facets of the communication process are lost, particularly nonverbal and affective aspects. As a result, farther and faster are not enough. Let us draw on two phenomena that are virtually certain to get more attention in the future to illustrate our communication concerns: distance education and telecommuting.

Distance Education

Distance education is a term used to reference mediated instruction which is used to replace live instruction in a classroom. Ever since the advent of radio, and particularly in the early days of television, media buffs have argued that use of whatever new media was available would be the savior of education—and reduce its costs. A current fad is the use of satellite links, microwaves, and the Internet to transmit video lectures from one campus or school to others where students can see the instruction, and in many cases ask questions of the televised teacher. Earlier forms of distance education included correspondence courses, televised lecture courses, telephone lecture courses, radio lecture courses, and, the earliest of all—books. Other versions have included programmed instruction texts, tapes, films, and videos. More recently, interactive computer-mediated videos have been used with considerable success.

One should be very careful before jumping on this mediated bandwagon. The concern should be "What is being substituted for what?" Generally, a mediated instructor is being substituted for a live one—that is it. The question then is whether the amount of money saved is worth any amount of learning lost. In most cases, the satellite instruction, for example, is far more expensive than just sending the instructor to the student—or sending the student to the instructor. Although basic content learning has been found to be quite achievable with well-programmed interactive video cassettes, development of higher levels of cognitive learning and shaping positive attitudes usually requires an effective live teacher. Going to the wrong media, or inserting media when live instruction is necessary, will not advance education in this society.

It should also be mentioned that students do not find distance education nearly as fulfilling as the traditional classroom. Although this technology may make things easier for students who work full time or are otherwise engaged during normal school hours, the traditional education model is still preferable.

Telecommuting

Telecommuting is a new term for working at home—but being connected to the office via computer link, fax machine, phone links, and so on. This option is very attractive to people who have other reasons to be at home—young children, disabled person to care for, and the like—or simply want to avoid long commutes and still be able to live where they want to live or are constrained to live.

For some positions in organizations, this option may be very reasonable. If the work to be done is primarily solitary and not dependent on collaboration with others, it may be that this option is best for both the employee and the employer—who would not have to expend money to provide the employee expensive office space. It is also likely that many people who do not work for a single organization, but "freelance," can exercise this option.

Unfortunately, in most organizations, there are not very many jobs that fit this description. Communication is central to most positions in organizations, particularly those above the entry level. People with higher positions often have supervisory responsibilities, and most people in organizations today function as part of teams that require frequent interpersonal communication.

Bottom line: the media make many positive contributions to our everyday lives. However, mediated communication is always an alternative to live, face-to-face communication. Although in many cases the mediated choice is the intelligent one, that is not always the case.

 **KEY TERMS**

asynchronous computer-mediated communication (CMC) 311	emoticons 315	synchronous computer-mediated communication (CMC) 311
	monological 308	

REFERENCES

Barnes, S. B. (2003). *Computer-mediated communication: Human-to-human communication across the Internet.* Boston: Allyn & Bacon.

McCroskey, J. C. (1992). *An introduction to communication in the classroom.* Edina, MN: Burgess.

Oliveira, J. G, & Barabási, A. L. (2005). Human dynamics: Darwin and Einstein correspondence patterns. *Nature, 437* (7063), 1251–1251.

Richmond, V. P. (1992). *Nonverbal communication in the classroom.* Edina, MN: Burgess.

Richmond, V. P., & McCroskey, J. C. (2003). *Nonverbal behavior in interpersonal relations* (5th ed.). Boston: Allyn & Bacon.

Richmond, V. P., McCroskey, J. C., & Thompson, C. A. (1992). *Communication problems of children.* Edina, MN: Burgess.

Walther, J. B. (1996). Computer-mediated communication: Impersonal, interpersonal, and hyperpersonal interaction. *Communication Research, 23,* 1–43.

Wood, A. F., & Smith, M. J. (2001). *Online communication: Linking technology, identity, & culture.* Mahwah, NJ: Lawrence Erlbaum.

Wrench, J. S., Fiore, A. M., & McCroskey, J. C. (2005, April). *The relationship between human temperament, communication apprehension, willingness to communicate, and computer-mediated communication competence and behaviors.* Paper presented at the Eastern Communication Association's Convention, Philadelphia.

Wrench, J. S., & Punyanunt-Carter, N. M. (2005, October). *The relationship between computer-mediated communication competence, apprehension, self-efficacy and presence.* Paper presented at the Ohio Communication Association's Convention, Dayton, OH.

DISCUSSION QUESTIONS

1. What are the basic problems related to translating documents from thousands of years ago into modern languages?

2. Why is mass communications considered monological? Do you think this will continue to be the case as new forms of media are invented?

3. What was the relationship between Einstein and Darwin's letter-writing techniques and modern e-mail usage?

4. Explain the difference between synchronous and asynchronous computer-mediated communication. Give examples of each.

5. How can Walther's social information processing theory be used to explain people who meet on the Internet and become romantically involved without having ever had face-to-face interactions?

15

Individual Differences in Organizations

Organizational Orientations • Sociocommunicative Orientations/Styles • Immediacy • Communication Apprehension and Talkaholism • Affinity Seeking

Perceptions of People in Organizations

Attraction • Homophily • Source Credibility

Management Communication Styles

Tell • Sell • Consult • Join • Research and Management Communication Style • Power and Influence in Organizations

Work Teams in Organizations

Organizational Communication

OBJECTIVES

- Define and explain *organization*.

- Describe and distinguish between the profit and nonprofit organizations.

- List and explain the three organizational orientations.

- Explain how sociocommunicative styles/orientations impact organizational communication.

- Explain the consequences of immediacy in an organization.

- Understand how communication apprehension and talkaholism affect organizational communication and organization practices.

- Understand how subordinate use of affinity seeking affects supervisor perceptions of their subordinates.

- Explain the importance of attraction, homophily, and source credibility in organizational communication.

- List and explain the four types of management communication styles.

- Understand the relationship between power and influence in an organization.

- Describe the nature of work teams.

- Understand the different types of work teams.

- Understand the five characteristics of effective teams.

As sad as it may seem at this point in your life, almost everyone will spend the rest of their natural lives in some type of organization. In fact, you've already spent most of your life working for or in some form of organization. According to Richmond and McCroskey (2001), an *organization* is "an organized collection of individuals working interdependently within a relatively structured, organized, open system to achieve common goals" (p. 2). Before we start examining how the communication principles we've discussed throughout this book relate to organizations, let's break down this definition. The basic premise of this definition is that you have a group of individuals working together in an organized manner to complete a common goal. Every organization has some basic goal that it is trying to accomplish. Many organizations' primary goal is the acquisition of money. We all like money. In fact, most people who ultimately work in the corporate world will work in an organization that has, at its most basic level, the goal to make money. Even in the health care industry, most people are truly more interested in making money than they are in healing the sick. Now, we are not making a value judgment here; we are just stating the fact that for-profit companies (whether they are health companies or toy companies) have to make money or cease to exist.

Many people do not work in the traditional corporate world. Many work in the "nonprofit" sector instead. Even nonprofit organizations have basic goals, and most nonprofit organizations' basic goal is centered on money. Instead of making money, many nonprofit organizations have a goal of raising money by getting people within the community to donate money, or convincing governments to assign tax money to them. One of the authors of this book does consulting work with a large wellness program. Even though the organization's basic goal is to help people become healthier in their day-to-day lives, the organization still has to face accountants and creditors at the end of the day. We live in a world that cares about how much good you are doing, but cares more about whether you can pay your bills. For this reason, many of the top "nonprofit" organizations have overhead expenditures that rival those of for-profit organizations. Let's face it: as the song from the musical *Cabaret* goes, "Money makes the world go around." Overall, almost everyone is going to work in some form of organization that will have explicit goals, and most of us will have to deal with the goal of money at some point in our adult lives.

This chapter examines the world of organizational communication or, more explicitly, how the communication variables we have examined throughout the first section of this book can be applied in the organizational setting. In order to see how communication knowledge can be applied in the contemporary organization, this chapter examines individual differences in organizations, the influence of perceptions in organizations, the impact of management styles in organizations, and the influence of work teams.

People often deliver formal presentations in the organizational setting.

▣ INDIVIDUAL DIFFERENCES IN ORGANIZATIONS

Go to any organization and you will find many different types of people attempting to work together to accomplish that organization's goal(s). Often these different types of people can work in harmony with each other, making goal accomplishment very easy, but most of the time the people within organizations can act as stumbling blocks preventing the accomplishment of the organization's goal(s). Research in organizational communication has noticed a number of specific communication patterns that influence organizations. This section is going to examine just a handful of these individual differences: organizational orientations, sociocommunicative orientation, nonverbal immediacy, communication apprehension, and affinity seeking.

Organizational Orientations

Organizational communication research has found that there are three basic orientations that people can exhibit in how they approach their roles within organizations. The three organizational orientations are called *upward mobiles, indifferents*, and *ambivalents*. Research suggests that these three orientations toward work and organizational life are probably traitlike. Individuals exhibit these organizational orientations at work, and if they change jobs, they exhibit them in the new job. You will find the Organizational Orientations Scale in the appendix in Scales 35–37. Take a few moments to fill out the scale and score yourself before proceeding to the next section.

All three of these organizational types are found within any organization. Typically speaking, individuals who fill out the Organizational Orientations Scale usually score high on only one or two of its three subscales. It's also possible to not score highly on any of them. Let's examine each of the organizational orientations separately.

Upward Mobiles. If the world were full of upwardly mobile employees, managers everywhere would be rejoicing. The most dedicated and hardworking people within any organization are the upwardly mobile members of the organization. These individuals will give 100 percent of themselves in order to help the organization thrive in a competitive environment. It is not uncommon for upward mobiles to completely identify with the goals of the organization so that it becomes a personal goal for them to help the organization succeed. Upward mobiles are almost entirely self-motivated and are task oriented in the workplace.

The only problem that can occur with upwardly mobile individuals is when they are required to work with someone who they perceive is below them or just a big loser (people who are not as dedicated or self-motivated as they are). In fact, upwardly mobile individuals can be quite demanding and critical of personnel who are simply not up to the upwardly mobile's fairly high standards of dedication and motivation.

When communicating with an upwardly mobile individual, it is important that supervisors remember to give credit and praise to the upwardly mobile individual for her or his accomplishments. One mistake that supervisors can make when working with upwardly mobile individuals is to assume that they do not need credit and/or praise for the work they do. If an upwardly mobile individual works for too long without this encouragement, it is possible that the upwardly mobile individual will find a job elsewhere. The authors of this book know a man who did just that. The organization that this man was working for got so used to this upwardly mobile individual just doing great work that they forgot to give him credit and praise. This man quickly found a better job and took it without anyone in the organization knowing he was even looking. When he submitted his letter of resignation, everyone was stunned because they did not know anything was wrong.

If you want to positively influence an upward mobile in an organization, it is important to explain to the upward mobile about how specific behaviors will be good for the organization. By emphasizing the "good of the organization," supervisors can demonstrate their own loyalty to the organization, and therefore influence the upward mobile on the "loyalty to the organization" level. It is also important to stress to the upward mobile how behavior will influence her or his ability to move up in rank and title within the organization. Upward mobiles are named such because they don't want to be stagnant in an organization; they do want to eventually move up to the top layers within the organization. Upward mobiles try to avoid working for an organization that they cannot picture running themselves one day.

Indifferents.   Whereas upward mobiles are blazing the trail to the upper ranks of the corporations, indifferents simply have no desire to go any farther than where they are. Whereas upward mobiles live to work, indifferents simply work to live. Unless your parents are very wealthy and have given you a sizeable trust fund, chances are you're going to have to work somewhere. Indifferents simply see the work they are doing within an organization as a necessary evil so they can do what they really want to do in life, which has nothing to do with their work. Indifferents are much more interested in what happens with their friends and family than by anything that happens at work. This is not to say that indifferents are bad people; they just have very different priorities when compared to the upwardly mobile. Most organizations would collapse if they lost all their indifferent workers.

You will never get indifferents to do more than what is absolutely necessary. If you start piling too much on these individuals, they are very likely to find another job that does not involve as much work. Every organization needs indifferents because they will complete the menial, routine tasks that the upward mobiles would find boring and dreadful. When communicating with indifferents, it is important to realize that no amount of reward or punishment is going to make them more or less dedicated to the organization's goal(s). Typical conversations with indifferents generally revolve around topics like family, friends, television, and other mundane topics not related to work.

Ambivalents.   The final organizational orientation, *ambivalents,* is the most difficult to work with because they are generally very unpredictable. Ambivalents can be nice one day and hate everything about the organization the next. Ambivalent individuals generally take issue with every little thing within the organization and make sure that *everyone* knows about their complaints. Ambivalents tend to be very moody and get disgruntled with "office politics" in every organization they are in. In essence, there is nothing you can do to truly satisfy ambivalents in your organization.

Although many of their concerns within the organization are real, these concerns are often ignored by others because they do not consider them important. Ambivalents also tend to have problems with organizational hierarchies. It is not uncommon for ambivalents to attempt to overthrow the organizational hierarchy. Most "whistle-blowers" are ambivalents, so they actually can be very helpful to the organization. But they generally are not popular with either their colleagues or their supervisors. In fact, most offices rejoice when the person finally leaves the organization for good (their going-away party is held the day after they leave!).

Communicating with ambivalents can be hard. Because you can never predict how an ambivalent is going to react during communication, most people just get used to tiptoeing around anything that could cause the person to "fly off the handle." Ultimately, it is usually best to simply avoid any controversial conversations with an ambivalent. The best advice is to simply avoid them if you can, but if you can't avoid them, attempt to keep casual conversation limited to "small talk."

Sociocommunicative Orientations/Styles

In Chapter 2, we examined the concepts of sociocommunicative orientations and styles. *Sociocommunicative orientation* refers to the way we perceive ourselves in terms of being responsive and/or assertive during interpersonal interactions, whereas *sociocommunicative style* refers to how others perceive us as being responsive or assertive during interpersonal interactions. McCroskey and Richmond (2000) examined the impact that sociocommunicative orientations and styles had on subordinate–supervisor communication. They asked the participants in the study to take the Sociocommunicative Orientation Scale and then fill out the Sociocommunicative Style Scale for their supervisors. Then the participants filled out the generalized attitude measure (as discussed in Chapter 7) for both their attitude toward their supervisor and their attitude toward the supervisor's communication. The results indicated that subordinates had much more positive attitudes toward their supervisors and their supervisor's communication if their supervisor exhibited a responsive sociocommunicative style.

At the same time, the study also showed that supervisors tend to reciprocate their subordinate's sociocommunicative orientation. In other words, if an employee is responsive, then her or his supervisor will generally be more responsive toward that employee when communicating. However, if an employee is not responsive, then her or his supervisor also will be not responsive toward her or him.

Immediacy

Another important difference often seen between individuals within various organizations is the degree to which they are nonverbally immediate within the organization. As we discussed in Chapter 5, *immediacy* is defined as the perceived physical and/or psychological closeness between two individuals. The research outcomes in the area of immediacy within organizations are similar to the findings with sociocommunicative orientation and style within organizations. In other words, immediacy within organizations appears to be reciprocal in nature (Richmond & McCroskey, 2000). If a subordinate is immediate, then her or his supervisor is also going to exhibit more immediate behaviors. One study actually found that a subordinate's level of immediacy influenced her or his supervisor's immediacy. A supervisor's immediacy influenced the subordinate's attitude toward her or his supervisor, which in turn influenced the subordinate's job satisfaction. This sounds somewhat convoluted, but the diagram in Figure 15.1 is somewhat easier to understand.

Communication Apprehension and Talkaholism

The next major area of research that has been examined in the realm of organizational communication has been in the arena of communication apprehension and talkaholism. As was discussed in Chapter 3, communication apprehension and talkaholism are basically two polar ends of one continuum of communication. On the communication apprehension end of the continuum, you have individuals who simply do not communicate because of apprehension and anxiety; and on the other end, you have people who

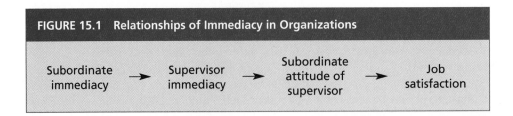

FIGURE 15.1   Relationships of Immediacy in Organizations

Subordinate immediacy → Supervisor immediacy → Subordinate attitude of supervisor → Job satisfaction

could talk to a tree stump and have fun doing it. Both of these orientations to communication have explicit implications for organizational communication.

A lot of the original research on organizational communication looked at how communication apprehensive individuals function within organizations. Research has shown that even the types of jobs that communicative apprehensive people are drawn to are different than those of the general public (McCroskey & Richmond, 1979). Generally speaking, individuals who had high levels of communication apprehension gravitate toward occupations that involve lower levels of communication when compared with those of average or low levels of communication apprehension. High communication apprehensives were also shown to be less satisfied with their occupations when compared to people who have low levels of communication apprehension (Falcione, McCroskey, & Daly, 1977). Additionally, people who have high levels of communication apprehension stay at their jobs for a 50 percent shorter period of time when compared to their low-apprehensive counterparts, and are not as likely to advance within the organizational hierarchy (McCroskey & Richmond, 1979). Needless to say, communication apprehension clearly impacts an individual's work life.

Although talkaholics clearly have an easier time communicating and advancing within the organizational hierarchy, they too can run into a few pitfalls as well. Talkaholics, or compulsive communicators, will talk about anything at any time anywhere. Talkaholics are often seen as pushy by those who are not talkaholics, which can be a negative impression to make within an organization. No one wants to be known as too pushy, so talkaholics have to be aware of how others might perceive them in the organizational setting. For the most part, though, talkaholics in the workplace are generally well-respected and well-liked individuals who have lots of friends and acquaintances.

Affinity Seeking

Affinity seeking was first examined in this book in Chapter 10 in how individuals manage interpersonal relationships. Because most organizational communication initiates at the interpersonal level, examining how affinity-seeking behavior is exhibited in organizations can be very useful. All of the affinity-seeking strategies have been shown to be effective ways of building affinity in some interpersonal relationships. In the organizational context, not all strategies will increase affinity between subordinates and supervisors, but most will. If you employ the majority of the positive affinity-seeking strategies noted in Figure 15.2, then you will have supervisors that will form more positive impressions of you when compared to other subordinates who do not employ the positive affinity-seeking strategies. At the same time, subordinates have to determine which affinity-seeking strategies are the most useful depending on a specific superior's personality.

Overall, there are many individual differences that exist within organizations that communicators must be aware of to have effective communication. Although organizational orientations, sociocommunicative orientation/style, immediacy, communication

FIGURE 15.2	Subordinate Use of Affinity-Seeking Strategies and the Impact on Supervisors	
	Subordinate Use of Affinity-Seeking Strategies	**Impact on Supervisor**
1.	Altruism	1
2.	Assume control	–
3.	Assume equality	–
4.	Comfortable self	1
5.	Concede control	1
6.	Conversational rule keeping	1
7.	Dynamism	1
8.	Elicit others' disclosures	–
9.	Facilitate enjoyment	Depends
10.	Inclusion of other	Depends
11.	Influence perceptions of closeness	–
12.	Listening	1
13.	Nonverbal immediacy	1
14.	Openness	–
15.	Optimism	1
16.	Personal autonomy	–
17.	Physical attractiveness	1
18.	Present interesting self	Depends
19.	Reward association	–
20.	Self-concept confirmation	1
21.	Self-inclusion	Depends
22.	Sensitivity	1
23.	Similarity	1
24.	Supportiveness	1
25.	Trustworthiness	1

Source: Based on the research of Richmond, V. P., McCroskey, J. C., & Davis, L. M. (1986). The relationship of supervisor use of power and affinity-seeking strategies with subordinate satisfaction. *Communication Quarterly, 34,* 178–193.

apprehension, talkaholism, and affinity seeking are not the only individual differences that organizational members need to be aware of, they provide an insight into the vast array of communication issues that exist within an organization. Let's now switch our focus to perceptions of people in organizations.

PERCEPTIONS OF PEOPLE IN ORGANIZATIONS

Anytime you are participating in an organization you are going to run into a lot of different types of people. Depending on how you personally view the world around you, it is entirely possible that you are going to develop very different perceptions of those people within the organization when compared to anyone else's perception within the organization. Person perception, or making judgments of those people you come in contact with, is a very normal thought process. We all make perceptions of people everyday. One of the coauthors of this book had a student on the first day of class who walked into the classroom with a T-shirt that read, "@%°# Authority." Trust us, this left an impression, but not exactly a positive one.

Although our perceptions can change with time, more often than not, our perceptions of individuals actually get strengthened over time. In the long run, we will develop very consistent perceptions of those people around us. We start to expect that people will behave in specific ways, and when they don't, we immediately assume that something is wrong, which often is correct. In this section, we are going to look at three different perceptions that individuals within organizations can make: perceptions about attraction, homophily, and credibility.

Attraction

Interpersonal attraction, as was discussed in Chapter 2, is the degree to which we are drawn to another individual. This section examines the impact that individual perceptions of physical, task, and social attraction can have on organizations.

Physical Attraction.   When people start discussing attraction, most people immediately think about physical attraction and forget about social and task attraction (or are unaware of them). Although physical attraction is important in organizations, especially during initial interactions, physical attraction really is not that important in the long run. In organizations, high physical attraction can definitely be a benefit in highly visible, short-term communicative positions. For example, salespeople are often very physically attractive. Pharmaceutical companies have known the impact of physically attractive sales men and women. Physically attractive sales representatives spend more time discussing various medications with physicians. However, even in a market in which physical attraction can get you in the door, if the physicians do not find the sales representatives as both socially and task attractive their interactions will be superficial and short. So yes, physical attraction can often get people in the door, but usually it cannot keep them there.

Social Attraction. Social attraction is the degree to which individuals perceive other individuals as people with whom they would like to spend time with just hanging out doing social kinds of things (e.g., having lunch together, just getting together to chat, and going to a movie with). Being socially attractive is extremely important because it gives the impression to others that you are a good fit in the organization. When you enter into a new organization, you may seek out other individuals that you find to be socially attractive. Often these people will have interests related to yours or come from similar backgrounds. In the realm of supervisor and subordinate relationships, research has shown that supervisors who are more responsive in their sociocommunicative style are also seen as more socially attractive. Additionally, supervisees who viewed themselves as having a more responsive sociocommunicative orientation also view themselves as being more socially attractive to others (McCroskey & Richmond, 2000).

Task Attractiveness. The last dimension of attractiveness, task attractiveness, is the dimension that is clearly the most relevant dimension for organizations. There are many factors that go into our perceptions of task attractiveness in organizations. Richmond and McCroskey (2001) noted these task attractive behaviors: "competence in performing work-related tasks, a willingness to share responsibility and workload, a commitment to successfully completing tasks, and a willingness to engage in goal-directed communication" (pp. 87–88). In organizations, most people simply want to be surrounded by people who are willing to work together to accomplish the organization's goal(s). In the realm of supervisor and subordinate relationships, research has shown that supervisors who are more responsive in their sociocommunicative style are also seen as more task attractive, and individuals who view themselves as having a more responsive sociocommunicative orientation also view themselves as being more task attractive to others (McCroskey & Richmond, 2000). Although these relationships have been shown to exist, they are not as strong as the relationships that we saw between responsiveness and social attraction.

Ultimately, attraction is an important perception to be understood in any organization. People are going to perceive your attractiveness on all three levels, and you are going to subconsciously and consciously view those individuals around you and their attraction. It is possible to find people attractive on all three types of attraction, and it's also possible to find people completely nonattractive on all three types of attraction. Of course, one can be perceived as attractive on one dimension and not the other two, or attractive on two dimensions, but not on the other one.

Homophily

Homophily, or perceived similarity, is yet another perception that can worm its way into organizations and impact the way people interact. We originally explored the realm of homophily in Chapter 2 when we were looking at individual perceptions, and how perceptions impact interactions. The three dimensions of homophily are demographic, background, and attitude.

Demographic Homophily.   Demographic homophily, although important during initial interactions, usually does not have a long lasting effect on communication. During initial interactions, we tend to keep a lot of our self-disclosure to a bare minimum, so we really do not open ourselves up to determining background and attitudinal homophily. In fact, when people in organizations disclose too much information too quickly, we generally think there is something very wrong with those people. Often when working in organizations in which a lot of diversity exists, people tend to naturally communicate more with people who have larger demographic similarities initially.

Background Homophily.   Background homophily simply refers to individuals who have similar life experiences. One of our coauthors is from Texas. While teaching on the East Coast, he ran into an individual driving a car with a Texas license plate. Even though the two lived eight hours from each other in Texas, when they met on the East Coast the two became close friends. This is an example of background homophily. Both of the Texans became friends because they had a commonality that those around them on the East Coast simply did not have because the two individuals shared similar experiences growing up in Texas. Often people within organizations are attracted to people with whom they perceive as having similar background experiences. U.S. citizens working overseas for long periods of time often create "American ghettos," in which a group of U.S. citizens will live together simply because they're all from the United States. In smaller organizational situations, various groups of people will interact with others they perceive to be on their level. In most organizational cafeterias, you will find administrators eating with other administrators and secretaries eating with other secretaries. We just naturally gravitate toward those individuals that we perceive as having similar backgrounds.

Attitudinal Homophily.   The last form of homophily is attitudinal homophily, or homophily that is a result of an individual's perception that another person shares the same attitudes, values, and beliefs. In organizations, attitudinal homophily is more important than either demographic or background homophily. Attitudinal homophily provides the groundwork for building strong working relationships between subordinates with their peers and subordinates with their supervisors. If individuals within an organization share attitudes, values, and beliefs related to the organization's goals, it will make everyone in the organization work harder to accomplish those goals. At the same time, attitudinal homophily can foster interpersonal trust, effective teamwork, and collaboration.

Overall, homophily is an extremely important perception to be aware of in the organizational setting. If everyone in the organization perceives everyone else as being different, organizations will become stagnant and the organization's goal(s) will not be met. Instead, fostering a sense of homophily within an organization is an easy way to help build motivation for achieving the organization's goal(s).

Source Credibility

The last of the three perceptions that we are discussing in this section is one that keeps popping up in almost every chapter. Perceived credibility is a concept that has been shown to impact a lot of perceptions related to communication. We first examined credibility in Chapter 2. As previously mentioned, credibility as we understand it today is related to Aristotle's original concept of ethos. Through research done by McCroskey and Teven (1999), we have determined that credibility, as we currently understand it, is comprised of three factors: competence, caring/goodwill, and trustworthiness. Perceived credibility has been shown to impact a number of organizational communication variables. Because the three factors of credibility are often closely related to each other, it makes more sense to examine how all three factors of credibility work together to influence organizational communication.

One variable that perceived credibility relates to is sociocommunicative orientations/styles. In the realm of supervisor and subordinate relationships, research has shown that supervisors who are more responsive in their sociocommunicative style are also seen as more credible on all three factors of credibility (competence, caring/goodwill, and trustworthiness), and individuals who view themselves as having a more responsive sociocommunicative orientation also view themselves as being more credible (McCroskey & Richmond, 2000). Richmond and McCroskey (2000) also noted that subordinates who perceived their superiors as being credible (competence, caring/goodwill, and trustworthiness) also had higher levels of job motivation and overall job satisfaction. Ultimately, individual perceptions of the credibility of those around them in organizations impacts how people interact with others in organizations.

In a study that was conducted by Porter, Wrench, and Hoskinson (2007), the researchers found that supervisors who reported high levels of extraversion and low levels of neuroticism and psychoticism were more credible on all three levels. Furthermore, employees were more satisfied with work and were more motivated when they had a supervisor who was highly extraverted and not neurotic or psychotic. Overall, this study indicates that a supervisor's temperament has a clear impact on how subordinates function within the organizational context.

Overall, individual perceptions of those around them within organizations impacts an array of different communicative behaviors. Although attraction, homophily, and credibility are not the only perceptions that impact communication within organizations, the three communication variables are good examples of how individual perceptions do impact communication in organizations. The first two sections in this chapter have primarily focused on how subordinates respond to their organizations; the last two sections are going to examine how management communication styles affect communication and how power affects organizations.

 ## MANAGEMENT COMMUNICATION STYLES

Because large organizations and academics have become interested in finding more effective approaches to management, people have attempted to understand what managers do that enables organizations to do great things or crumble to pieces under their leadership. In 1979, Richmond and McCroskey put forth a simplistic scheme for understanding how managers actually communicate within organizations. Their framework is referred to as *management communication styles*. This section is going to examine the four management communication styles and discuss how they impact organizational communication.

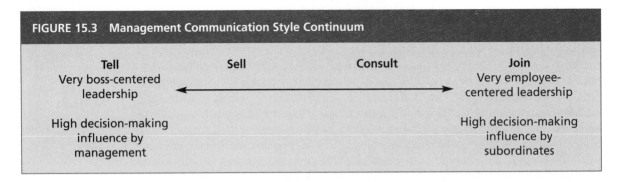

FIGURE 15.3   Management Communication Style Continuum

Tell	Sell	Consult	Join
Very boss-centered leadership			Very employee-centered leadership
High decision-making influence by management			High decision-making influence by subordinates

The framework itself exists on a continuum (see Figure 15.3). At one end of the management communication styles, we see managers who are very boss centered and tend to focus on communication that is top-down and most of the decisions are made by management and then disseminated to their subordinates. At the other end to the continuum, we see managers who believe in employee-centered leadership, and a lot of the decision-making power is influenced directly by their subordinates. To better understand the management communication styles framework, let's examine each of the four communication styles independently.

Tell

The first type of manager that we see in organizations is the manager that we call the *tell manager*. These managers tend to act like their subordinates are marionettes without the ability to think and act on their own. When decisions need to be made within the organization, the manager will personally make the decision and then inform her or his subordinates of that decision. If the manager does not make the decision her or himself, but rather gets the message from above them, the dispersion of the edict will occur in the same way. When the tell manager makes a decision or passes down a decision, he or she expects that the decision will be carried out without challenge.

From a communication perspective, tell managers tend to engage in communication that is top-down and unidirectional. In other words, tell managers believe that communication should only come from the top of the organizational hierarchy and never from the bottom of the organization. The only type of questioning that is permitted is for clarification of how the job should be done. Frankly, these types of managers are only concerned with task at hand and never the social aspects of organizational life.

Sell

The next management communication style is the *sell* style. This type of manager exhibits many of the same behaviors that the tell manager has, but takes communication a step further. The sell manager still believes that all decisions should be made top-down. However, the sell manager actually believes that it is her or his job to persuade her or his subordinates that the decision made is desirable. You could even go so far as to say that the sell manager is a persuader for decisions he or she makes and those made by people above her or him.

Communicatively, sell managers use primarily downward forms of communication, but not exclusively. There are times when sell managers will use bidirectional and interactive communication. Sell managers encourage their subordinates to ask questions related to decisions made, but any disagreement with those decisions will be met with persuasive counterarguments. On a more positive note, sell managers are more explicit in their desire for employee satisfaction.

Consult

The *consult manager* is a manager who attempts to gain input from all invested parties before making a decision her or himself. If a decision has to be made, a consult manager will gather all invested parties and elicit their advice, information, and suggestions before taking it on her or himself to make the tough decision. Often the actual problem will stem from situations above the manager, but the decision to be made lies with the manager.

Communication for the consult manager is primarily upward, bidirectional, and interactive. The consult manager attempts to make sure that an adversary (I'm the manager and you're the subordinate) relationship is not created. Employees are encouraged and expected to help the manager weigh all of the possible advantages and disadvantages of a decision while taking into account the needs of both her or his subordinates and the organization. Consult managers are concerned for their subordinates' well-being, so extra care and energy are put into every decision to make sure it will be the best decision for everyone.

Join

The final management communication style is the *join manager*. The join manager does not make decisions her or himself. Instead, the join manager delegates the authority to make decisions to her or his subordinates. These decisions can be made either in cooperation with the manager or in the manager's absence. The manager will define the problem for her or his subordinates, and then place specific limitations on how the decision must be made. For example, a manager may tell her or his subordinates that they have to redesign a specific product, but the new product cannot cost more than $50,000. In these situations, the consensus or majority opinion will determine the actual course of action after an open discussion(s) has occurred.

Communication with join managers is primarily horizontal, bidirectional, and highly interactive. In other words, the manager does not place her or himself above her or his subordinates in the decision making process. Instead, the manager and the subordinates attempt to work as a collaborate team when attempting to solve specific problems. In this specific management style, employee desires become a primary criterion when making and discussing actual decisions within the organization.

Research and Management Communication Style

Now that we have examined the four different types of management communication styles, let's examine how management communication styles have been researched in the area of organizational communication. Richmond and McCroskey (1979) found a positive relationship between a subordinate's perception of her or his superior's management communication style and their own satisfaction with supervision, satisfaction with work, and satisfaction with promotions. It was also in this study that a subordinate's perception of her or his immediate supervisor's management communication style impacted the way that subordinate viewed senior management as well. In other words, supportive and caring lower-level managers impact how upper-level administration is viewed.

Power and Influence in Organizations

Power is a basic concept in interpersonal situations. Instead of rehashing what was already written, you might want to take a moment to refamiliarize yourself with the concepts of power explored in Chapter 8 before reading how power and influence are enacted in organizations. The relationship between the five basic types of power (legitimate, coercive, reward, referent, and expert power) and management communication styles has been examined.

Power and Management Communication Styles.   Richmond, McCroskey, Davis, and Koontz (1980) examined the relationship between a management communication style and her or his tendency to use the specific types of powers with her or his subordinates. The results of this study demonstrated that those subordinates who rated their superiors higher on the Management Communication Style Scale saw their superiors as primarily using referent and expert power during their interactions. At the same time, those subordinates who rated their superiors lower on the Management Communication Style Scale saw their superiors as primarily using coercive and legitimate power during their interactions. The use of reward power during interactions between subordinates and superiors was not found to be either positively or negatively related to a subordinate's perception of her or his superior's management communication style.

If one looks at the results from the Richmond et al. (1980) study in light of the levels of influence, some interesting trends emerge. Only managers who scored high on the Management Communication Style Scale would have the ability to influence their subordinates at the identification and internalization levels of influence because only referent and expert power are associated with these levels of influence. On the flip side of this, superiors who score on the low end of the Management Communication Style Scale will only be able to achieve compliance from their subordinates.

 ## WORK TEAMS IN ORGANIZATIONS

The word *group* is one of those terms that can conjure up many different definitions. For our discussion of work teams, we are going to use the following definition of *group*, three or more individuals who, through informational and persuasive communication,

Teams are often important to an organization's success.

interact for the achievement of some common purpose(s) (Rothwell, 1995). Notice that the most important aspect of Rothwell's perspective on the word *group* is that the individuals within the collection of people must have some common purpose that needs to be achieved. In other words, five people standing in line at a fast-food restaurant do not form a group; instead, a collection of people without a common purpose are referred to as an aggregation. For a group to be considered a group, there must be some purpose that is driving the group forward. We spent the first part of this section defining the word *group* because groups are the cornerstone of all teams. Devine, Clayton, Philips, Dunford, and Melner (1999) define the word *team* as a group "that interacts intensively to provide an organizational product, plan, decision, or service" (p. 681). When we look at this definition of the word *team,* we can see that in this use of the word *team* we are specifically referring to the modern business conceptualization of the word and not the use of the word commonly associated with athletics. Although athletic and work teams may act similarly at times, the goals of athletic teams are to win a specific game or series of games, whereas the goals of work teams are to help improve the position of the organization through four possible outputs: products, plans, decisions, and services.

The first possible organizational team output are products. Often organizations use teams to help design and/or redesign products to help the organization take over more of the market share. In today's corporate world, rarely is a single product the sole creation of one person. Everything from toothpaste to fighter jets is the product of various work teams. Some final products will actually be the combined result of dozens of work teams. Your average automobile has many work teams that focus on the various parts: mechanics, safety, look, and so on. In other words, work teams have helped create most of the products we use in our daily lives.

Other work teams will focus on plans, or a tentative project or course of action. Organizations often use work teams to develop three types of plans: project plans, tactical plans, and strategic plans. A *project plan* consists of detailed activities, responsible individuals, and the time required to complete a specific organizational project (Wills, 1997). Maybe your organization needs to conduct an internal survey of employee satisfaction. To complete this project, an administrator may put together a work team of people from various divisions and have them create and administer the survey of employee satisfaction within an allotted time. The second type of plans that a work team may put together is a *tactical plan*, or "the overall activities, measurable outcomes, responsible individuals, and targeted completion dates required to succeed during a relatively short period of time" (p. 4). Typically, tactical plans are useful for a twelve- to fifteen-month cycle. Most organizations put together work teams before the beginning of the fiscal year (generally, July 1) to help create the tactical plan for the new work year. In other words, the work team is tasked with deciding what the organization needs to do over the next twelve months to stay competitive and make money. The last type of plan that work teams may be tasked with are *strategic plans*. Strategic plans are often very similar to tactical plans, but whereas tactical plans last twelve to fifteen months, a strategic plan may last five to ten years. An organization's strategic plan should provide the necessary direction an organization needs to consistently grow, make a profit, and stay competitive.

The third type of work teams are decision-based work teams, or work teams that are tasked with making the day-to-day decisions within the organization. In the previous section on management communication style, we discussed the four different ways in which managers may make decisions (tell, sell, consult, and join). The first three are not very team oriented in their decision making, but individuals with join manager communication styles are team oriented. Join managers establish work teams to help foster decision making within the organization. One issue that is always a concern for small group decision making is how many people to add to a group. Research has shown that diversity within a work team is extremely important. If everyone within a work team are similar, they will often have similar ideas about how to approach a problem, so the best decision may not be available to the group. By increasing the number and types of people within a work team, the work team increases the number of ideas available to the work team, which will often lead to better decisions. However, there is a fine line between work team diversity and diversity overkill. Often if a work team is too diverse, there will be too many ideas and the work team will come to decisions very slowly and not be very effective as a result. Hare (2003) put it this way: "More people will be a disadvantage if the different opinions in the large group make it difficult to achieve the consensus necessary for action" (p. 134); so if you need to make quick decisions, a large amount of diversity within the decision-making work team could be a hindrance.

The final type of work teams are service-oriented work teams. Workplace service teams are solely focused on working with people and organizations external to the organization and providing the people with help and information. Often service teams are tasked with the job of keeping customers and suppliers satisfied and happy. Service teams will periodically meet to determine the overall effectiveness of the organization's service to customers and suppliers, and make appropriate recommendations for improvement in the service process.

Devine et al. (1999) also noted that workplace teams often fall into one of two categories: short term and long term. Short-term teams, or ad hoc teams, are teams that are created to fulfill a specific objective. In the example of a satisfaction survey of employees discussed above, the team members are brought together for a onetime employee satisfaction survey, so this team is a short-term team. Short-term teams are in contrast to long-term teams, which are ongoing teams that are continually assigned new tasks to perform or other tasks that need to be repeated periodically. For example, if an administrator decides to survey employee satisfaction every six months, the administrator may establish a long-term work team that will analyze the data every six months over a number of years. In this case, we have taken the concept from a one-shot task to a task that is being repeated on a regular cycle and is overseen by the same group of team members.

Beyond the basic types of work teams that are out there, Salas, Sims, and Burke (2005) argued there are five characteristics necessary for teams to be effective: team leadership, mutual performance monitoring, backup behavior, adaptability, and team orientation. The first characteristic for effective teams is leadership. Team leaders must be able to complete three basic tasks: organize the team, interact with the external environment, and establish behavioral and performance expectations. The team leader is ultimately first responsible for organizing the team and making sure that the team runs smoothly. To enable the smooth running of a team, team leaders must balance two competing team member needs: relational and task. People within teams need to feel that they are part of a team, and the only way to foster this feeling is by encouraging team members to develop working interpersonal relationships with each other. However, the team must also accomplish the team's task(s), which can sometimes be overshadowed by the team's social needs. Ultimately, the team leader needs to help the team balance social and task needs. Team leaders are also responsible for interacting with the external environment. Team leaders need to be interacting with people above them in the decision hierarchy of an organization to ensure that the team has the most current and best information to use when making team decisions. The more a team leader knows what is going on outside of her or his team, the less likely the team will be caught off guard by new developments within the organization or marketplace. Lastly, team leaders need to establish behavioral and performance expectations. Ultimately, a team is only as good as its leader's direction, so team leaders need to establish how team members will behave and to what level the leader expects her or his team members to perform at during the life cycle of the team.

Team leaders are also impacted by their communication traits. In a study by Limon and La France (2005), the researchers examined the relationship among leadership emergence in a small group, argumentativeness, verbal aggression, and communication apprehension. Leader emergence is the tendency for an individual to become a leader within a small group or team. Some people just naturally gravitate toward leadership positions, whereas others naturally avoid leadership positions. Limon and La France found that individuals who are highly argumentative are more likely to emerge as leaders in small groups, whereas people with high levels of communication apprehension are not likely to emerge as leaders within a small group. There was no relationship between leader emergence and verbal aggressiveness in the Limon and La France study.

The second characteristic for effective teams is mutual performance monitoring. Effective teams have people within them that "maintain an awareness of team functioning by monitoring fellow members' work in an effort to catch mistakes, slips, or lapses prior to or shortly after they have occurred" (Salas et al., 2005, p. 575). In other words, effective teams are teams in which everyone has everyone else's back to make sure that mistakes don't happen. If teammates become jealous, they may allow fellow teammates to fall flat on their faces, which will ultimately lead to excessive conflict and the team will no longer function effectively. Teammates should help each other, not compete with each other.

The third characteristic for effective teams is backup behavior. Backup behavior is a team's insurance policy when another teammate does not have adequate information to perform a task, needs help performing a task, or is overwhelmed with other tasks. Often, people on a team may not have the necessary skills to effectively complete a task. Fournies (1999) collected responses from 25,000 supervisors and managers from around the world about one question, "Why don't employees do what they are supposed to do?" The results of this simple study were quite intriguing. The top four responses to Fournies' question were (1) they don't know what they are supposed to do, (2) they don't know how to do it, (3) they don't know why they should do it, and (4) they think they are doing it (lack of feedback). In fact, the first two answers occurred 99 percent of the time (Fournies, 2000). For this reason, teammates are often tasked with the job of coaching other teammates to teach them how to effectively complete necessary team tasks. Other times teammates may simply need someone's help because the task requires multiple people. For example, maybe your team is given the task of putting together the company's annual appreciation picnic. People may complete various parts of the overall task so the picnic doesn't completely take up one person's time. Lastly, teammates are there for you when you are overburdened with other work. All employees will eventually get to the point where they are completely swamped with work, so having teammates that can help take up part of the work load can be very useful.

The fourth characteristic for effective teams is adaptability. The modern business world is one that is rarely stable, so adapting to various internal and external stimuli is extremely important. Internal stimuli are factors that exist within an organization that cause a team to need to adapt. The hiring of a new chief executive officer (CEO) or the pushing up of a deadline from next year to next week can cause teams to panic. For this reason, teams must be flexible and adapt to the changing situations within the organizational environment. Teams should also be able to adapt to what is happening external to the organization within the marketplace. Often, new innovations and ideas will require a team to need to adjust its current thinking or direction on a project. For example, maybe you're on a software design team that's working on a product that will run alongside another company's software. If the other company releases a new version of the compatibility software, your team will need to upgrade as well if your organization's software will not be seen as obsolete.

The last factor of successful teams is a team orientation, or "a preference for working with others [and] a tendency to enhance individual performance through the coordination, evaluation, and utilization of task inputs from other members while performing group tasks" (Salas et al., 2005, p. 584). In other words, for teams to be effective, people must desire to work in teams and must see the benefit of working in teams. Even one member who does not see the benefit of the team process can actually be a big detriment to the success of the team.

Earlier in this section, we talked about the relationship between the communication traits argumentativeness, verbal aggression, and communication apprehension with leadership emergence. Other personality traits have also been shown to be important in the small group context. Hare (1976) found that people who are assertive are more likely to participate in small groups than people who are responsive. Bochner, di Salvo, and Jonas (1975) found that Machiavellians participate more often in groups, offer important information, and are more influential during critical decision making. Bonner (2000) also noted that extraverted people tended to have more influence on small groups than introverted people. Along this same line of thinking, Frey (1997) also discussed the negative impact that communication apprehension can have on small groups. Overall, people with high levels of communication apprehension talk less in small groups, are more dissatisfied with small groups, and are not generally effective group members. In fact, McCroskey and Richmond (1992) conclude, "In no communication situation is CA more important than in the small group context. It is not an exaggeration to suggest that CA may be the single most important factor in predicting communication behavior in a small group" (p. 368).

CONCLUSION

This chapter has explored the realm of organizational communication by examining how individual differences affect organizational communication, how individual perceptions affect organizational communication, how management communication styles affect organizational communication, and how communication affects work teams. Although this chapter has attempted to examine what we know about organizational communication in light of the communication variables discussed in the first section of this book, the study of organizational communication is much larger than could ever be placed in one single chapter. If you are interested in learning more about organizational communication, use the references at the end of this chapter as a launching point for your exploration of organizational communication.

We started this chapter by giving the definition for *organization*. Although all of the nuances of organizations can often prevent us from seeing the broader picture, we must keep ourselves aware of the ultimate goal(s) within our organizations. As both subordinates and superiors who work in organizations, it's up to all of us to create a more effective communication environment to better achieve these goals.

KEY TERMS

aggregation 335
ambivalents 323
consult 333
group 334
indifferents 323

join 333
nonprofit organizations 321
organization 321
organizational orientation 322
sell 332

team 335
tell 332
upward mobile 323

REFERENCES

Bochner, A. P., di Salvo, V., & Jonas, T. (1975). A computer-analysis of small group process: An investigation of two Machiavellian groups. *Small Group Behavior, 6,* 187–203.

Bonner, B. L. (2000). The effects of extroversion on influence in ambiguous group tasks. *Small Group Research, 31,* 225–244.

Devine, D. J., Clayton, L. D., Philips J. L., Dunford, B. B., & Melner, S. B. (1999). Teams in organizations: Prevalence, characteristics, and effectiveness. *Small Group Research, 30,* 678–711.

Falcione, R. L., McCroskey, J. C., & Daly, J. A. (1977). Job satisfaction as a function of employees' communication apprehension, self-esteem, and perceptions of their immediate supervisor. In B. D. Ruben, Ed. *Communication Yearbook I* (pp. 263–276). New Brunswick, NJ: Transaction.

Fournies, F. F. (1999). *Why employees don't do what they are supposed to do and what to do about it* (rev. ed.). New York: McGraw-Hill.

Fournies, F. F. (2000). *Coaching for improved work performance: How to get better results from your employees!* (rev. ed.). New York: McGraw-Hill.

Frey, L. R. (1997). Individuals in groups. In L. R. Frey & J. K. Barge (Eds.), *Managing group life: Communicating in decision-making groups* (pp. 52–79). Boston: Houghton Mifflin.

Hare, A. P. (1976). *Handbook of small group research* (2nd ed.). New York: Free Press.

Hare, A. P. (2003). Roles, relationships, and groups in organizations: Some conclusions and recommendations. *Small Group Research, 34,* 123–154.

Limon, M. S., & La France, B. H. (2005). Communication traits and leadership emergence: Examining the impact of argumentativeness, communication apprehension, and verbal aggressiveness in work groups. *Southern Communication Journal, 70,* 123–133.

McCroskey, J. C., & Richmond, V. P. (1979). The impact of communication apprehension on individuals in organizations. *Communication Quarterly, 27,* 55–61.

McCroskey, J. C., & Richmond, V. P. (1992). Communication apprehension and small group communication. In R. S. Cathcart & L. A. Smovar (Eds.), *Small group communication: A reader* (6th ed., pp. 361–374). Dubuque, IA: William C. Brown.

McCroskey, J. C., & Richmond, V. P. (2000). Applying reciprocity and accommodation theories to supervisor/subordinate communication. *Journal of Applied Communication Research, 28,* 278–289.

McCroskey, J. C., & Teven, J. J. (1999). Goodwill: A reexamination of the construct and its measurement. *Communication Monographs, 66,* 90–103.

Porter, H., Wrench, J. S., & Hoskinson, C. (2007). *The influence of supervisor temperament on subordinate job satisfaction and perceptions of supervisor sociocommunicative orientation and approachability. Communication Quarterly, 55,* 129–153.

Richmond, V. P. (1977). *Communication apprehension and success in the job applicant screening*. Paper presented at the International Communication Association Convention, Berlin, West Germany.

Richmond, V. P., & McCroskey, J. C. (1979). Management communication style, tolerance for disagreement, and innovativeness as predictors of employee satisfaction: A comparison of single-factor, two- factor, and multifactor approaches. In D. Nimmo (Ed.), *Communication Yearbook 3* (pp. 359–373). New Brunswick, NJ: Transaction Books.

Richmond, V. P., & McCroskey, J. C. (2000). The impact of supervisor and subordinate immediacy on relational and organizational outcomes. *Communication Monographs, 67,* 85–95.

Richmond, V. P., & McCroskey, J. C. (2001). *Organizational communication for survival: Making work, work.* Boston: Allyn & Bacon.

Richmond, V. P., McCroskey, J. C., Davis, L. M., & Koontz, J. A. (1980). Perceived power as a mediator of management communication style and employee satisfaction: A preliminary investigation. *Communication Quarterly, 28,* 36–46.

Rothwell, J. D. (1995). *In mixed company: Small group communication* (2nd ed.). Fort Worth, TX: Harcourt Brace.

Salas, E., Sims, D. E., & Burke, C. S. (2005). Is there a "Big Five" in team work? *Small Group Research, 36,* 555–599.

Wills, J. (1997). *The ASTD trainer's sourcebook: Strategic planning.* New York: McGraw-Hill.

DISCUSSION QUESTIONS

1. Which organizational orientation do you have? How has your organizational orientation affected your ability to perform in the organization?

2. Why do you think there is a reciprocal nature in nonverbal immediacy between supervisors and their subordinates?

3. What are some of the negative outcomes of communication apprehension in the organizational context?

4. Which type of attraction do you think is the most important in an organizational environment? Does this change over time?

5. Which management communication style do you prefer from your supervisors? Which management communication style do you use (or think you would use) with your subordinates? Why?

16

Student Communication

Types of Learning • Anxiety in the Classroom • Student Motivation

Teacher Communication

Communicator Clarity • Immediacy Behaviors in the Classroom • Humor in the Classroom • Teacher Misbehaviors in the Classroom

Instructional Communication

OBJECTIVES

- Explain the three types of student learning.

- Understand the issues involved in measuring learning.

- Understand the effects of communication apprehension, teacher apprehension, and evaluation apprehension in the classroom.

- Understand why student motivation is important for learning.

- Understand why communicator clarity is important in the classroom.

- Differentiate between structural and verbal communicator clarity.

- Explain the effects of teacher immediacy in the classroom.

- Understand how humor positively influences a classroom environment and learning.

- Differentiate among the three types of teacher misbehaviors.

- Understand the ramifications of teacher misbehaviors on education.

Most of what we have examined up to this point in the book has been originally studied in the instructional environment. Since communication scholars started to move away from the traditional focus on rhetoric to interpersonal communication, one of the areas that has received major attention has been instructional communication. In fact, one of the major journals in the field of communication is called *Communication Education*. *Communication Education* broadly examines both how teachers and students communicate within the classroom environment and how communication professionals teach communication in the classroom. It should also be mentioned that when we refer to "the classroom," we are not always talking about the traditional elementary, middle school, high school, or college classroom. The information we have learned in instructional communication can be applied much broader than that. Effective instructional communication skills are just as useful in the boardroom and in training and development situations as they are in the more traditional classroom. For this reason, we felt that the last chapter in the book should be instructional communication because so much research time and effort has gone into learning about the instructional communication process. This chapter will not attempt to be an exhaustive explanation of everything we know about instructional communication. However, there are books available that serve this purpose.

As you have read through this entire book, you may have noticed that we have already applied many of the topics in this book to the instructional communication context. This chapter is not going to rehash all of those same topics again. For example, when we talked about power and influence in Chapter 8, we discussed the research on behavior alteration methods (BAMs) and behavior alteration techniques (BATs). The original research in these two areas was completed examining how teachers control behavior within their classrooms. In fact, an entire series of articles known as the "Power in the Classroom Studies" were conducted looking at how teachers use power in the classroom. The resultant work from this research was published in a book called *Power in the Classroom: Communication, Control, and Concern* (see Chapter 8 for more information). We give you this example to make you aware that everything we have talked about so far in this book has been applied in the instructional communication context. Because this is just one chapter out of sixteen, we cannot attempt to examine every nuance of instructional communication. In fact, there is an entire series of books that have been written examining instructional communication in a number of the areas we have discussed already: communication problems with children (Richmond, McCroskey, & Thompson, 1992), communication apprehension and avoidance (Booth-Butterfield & Booth-Butterfield, 1992), nonverbal communication (Richmond, 1996), influence and control (S. Booth-Butterfield, 1992), interpersonal communication (M. Booth-Butterfield, 1992), intercultural communication (Klopf & Thompson, 1992), media (Gorham, 1992), and organizational communication (Richmond & McCroskey, 1992). If that looks a little daunting, we would recommend reading *An Introduction to*

Instructional communication can occur interpersonally, or to 500 students at once.

Communication in the Classroom: The Role of Teaching and Training (McCroskey, Richmond, & McCroskey, 2006), or the *Handbook of Instructional Communication: Rhetorical & Relational Perspectives* (Mottet, Richmond, & McCroskey, 2006), to see how many communication variables discussed in this book have been applied in the instructional communication context.

The remainder of this chapter is going to apply just a handful of communication variables that we believe are extremely important within the instructional communication context. We are going to examine these variables in two categories: student communication and teacher communication.

▣ STUDENT COMMUNICATION

All of us function as students throughout our lives. When we're going through formal education (elementary through graduate school), these lines are very clearly drawn for us. When we enter the workforce, we often forget that we still engage in student behaviors on a regular basis. Anytime an individual goes through a training program, he or she is functioning as a student again. This section is going to examine the types of learning that occur, the impact of anxiety in instructional communication, and student motivation.

Types of Learning

Education occurs because individuals lack specific knowledge, skills, and attitudes about specific subjects. The learning process ideally helps individuals fill these information gaps. Learning, according to Bloom, Englehart, Furst, Hill, and Krathwohl (1956), is composed of three distinct domains: affective, behavioral, and cognitive (i.e., the ABCs of learning). Each of these domains of learning is important to understanding how communication can be used in the instructional setting.

Affective Learning.

Affective learning is the acquisition of likes and attitudes, values, and beliefs related to various aspects of knowledge. In Chapter 7, we discussed how attitudes, values, and beliefs related to human communication. That discussion applies here as well. Affective learning examines the individual perceptions of the content and teacher as a value judgment, not physical or mental learning. Affective learning exists along a continuum with various degrees of internalization: from the point at which a student is aware that an academic subject exists; to being willing to read about that subject; to reading about that subject and liking it; to making an effort to seek out more information about that subject; and, finally, to adopting that subject's content in daily life. All of us find certain subject areas absolutely fascinating and other areas unbelievably boring. The way that we respond to knowledge either positively or negatively has occurred through affective learning.

Behavioral Learning.

Behavioral learning, or psychomotor learning, involves the mastery of a motor act or skill. This learning domain has not been as extensively analyzed as the others, perhaps because it is not relevant to all areas of study. It is also perhaps that most people believe that teaching skills is very straightforward. If you want to teach someone to drive a car, there is only one acceptable way to drive in our culture. Although there may be slight variations in how we drive, the basic driving process is the same. The gas is on right, and the brake is on the left. When learning behavior skills, repetition and rehearsal are the necessary ways of doing so. If someone wanted to learn how to fly an airplane, he or she would have to practice using all types of simulators before he or she ever leaves the ground. However, it is one thing to learn the physical process or behavior, and it's a completely different thing to enjoy that process. The authors of this book know someone who spent seven years in piano lessons as a child. After seven years of constant piano lessons and long practice periods, he began to resent the piano and eventually stopped playing altogether. Although he had the behavioral knowledge to perform and was quite good, the affective learning eventually took over and caused him to just simply stop because playing the piano was no longer seen as a positive experience.

Cognitive Learning.   The last domain of learning, cognitive, involves the recall and recognition of knowledge and the development of intellectual abilities and skills. When most people think of learning, this is the form of learning that is the most often imagined. We all spent our childhoods focusing primarily on cognitive learning. We learned to recite information and regurgitate it for tests. Some of us had to learn how to conjugate verbs and recite all of the prepositions in the English language from memory. Eventually, we will travel from simply knowing a subject, to being able to identify with the content, to applying that content in areas beyond basic learning. Throughout this book, we have discussed communication apprehension. Chances are that most of you reading this book were not familiar with the concept of communication apprehension before reading this book. Hopefully after our explanation of communication apprehension, you were able to identify with the content and know whether or not you are a high communication apprehensive, a low communication apprehensive, or somewhere in between. The ultimate goal of learning is for you to be able to identify communication apprehension in people in situations we haven't explained here in this text.

It should be mentioned that we run into the same problem with cognitive learning that we did with behavioral learning. If an individual does not have positive affect for the content or teacher in a classroom, it will be very hard for that person to learn or retain on a cognitive level. For this reason, the authors of this text strongly believe that affective learning is by far the most important domain of learning because it is the foundation for the other two types of learning.

Measuring Learning.   For the most part, measuring behavioral and cognitive learning is fairly simple. In behavioral learning, did the individual complete the specified behavior correctly? If not, learning hasn't occurred. With cognitive learning, does an individual recall and use knowledge at a specific level? Although measuring both behavioral and cognitive learning is fairly easy, measuring a student's level of affect in a classroom is not. A number of different measures have been developed by researchers to examine affect in the classroom. For the purposes of this textbook, the measure designed by McCroskey (1994) will be used (Scale 38 in the appendix). This instrument measures students' attitudes toward (1) the instructor of the course (teacher evaluation); (2) the content of the course (affective learning), along with measures of higher order levels of student affect; (3) taking additional classes in the subject matter; and (4) taking additional classes with the teacher. Dimensions 2 and 3 are in congruence with Krathwohl, Bloom, and Masia's (1964) conceptualization of the affective domain in learning. Dimensions 1 and 4 represent teacher evaluation.

Overall, this measure is useful when attempting to determine how students affectively feel in a classroom setting. This measure can be used in a number of different ways. This measure can be used for teacher evaluation. Another idea is to use the content sections (future classes and affective learning) to determine initial content affect and previous affective learning at the beginning of the school year. Sadly, if a student enters into a classroom with low affective learning initially, it is going to be a constant struggle to teach cognitive and behavioral content if the affective component is not treated. Research examining the impact that affective learning has on the classroom is quite conclusive. Students who have higher levels of affect in a classroom are going to learn more both cognitively and behaviorally.

Anxiety in the Classroom

In any given classroom, teachers are going to be faced with a number of different anxiety-related issues. Some students have specific types of anxiety, like public speaking apprehension, and other students just experience general anxiety in the classroom setting. This section is going to examine three specific types of anxiety that are often found in instructional settings: communication apprehension, teacher apprehension, and evaluation apprehension.

Communication Apprehension.   In Chapter 3, we focused on the basic principles of communication apprehension. We now know that people with very high levels of communication apprehension, or trait communication apprehension, are probably suffering from a neurological problem. Nevertheless, the cause is not the focus of this section, but how individuals with high levels of apprehension function within the classroom setting. It is estimated that 20 percent of students in schools may suffer from high levels of communication apprehension.

The student who is highly communicatively apprehensive tends to have a low tolerance for ambiguity, lacks self-control, is not adventurous, lacks emotional maturity, is introverted, has low self-esteem, is not innovative, has a low tolerance for disagreement, and is unassertive. On the other hand, the student who has a low level of communication apprehension likes to talk, is usually outgoing, tends to have low general anxiety, tolerates ambiguous situations, has a high degree of selfcontrol, is adventurous, is emotionally mature, is extroverted, has high self-esteem, is innovative, is able to tolerate relatively high levels of disagreement, and is assertive. In the classroom environment, students who are highly apprehensive and low apprehensive are as different as night and day.

In the classroom environment, communication apprehension can cause a student who is quiet to be perceived in a less positive way than the student who is outgoing. Students who do not talk in school are perceived to be less competent, less intelligent, less likely to get into trouble, less likely to do well in school, and less likely to be called on to respond. These students tend to have less opportunities to correct learning mistakes, receive less attention from the teacher, receive less reinforcement when they do something well, ask for assistance less frequently, volunteer to participate less, and receive lower grades on class participation reports. In a very real sense, this group of students is discriminated against in the school environment. Consequently, by the time they complete high school, their learning, as measured by standardized achievement tests, is impacted negatively. In addition, the high communication apprehensive's peer groups often see her or him as less approachable, less friendly, less talkative, less outgoing, less pleasant, and less intelligent than the low communication apprehensive student.

Research has shown that highly apprehensive students suffer many negative impacts because of their apprehension. Highly apprehensive students receive lower grades in classes in which communication is required, lower participation grades, and lower over-all grade point averages (from elementary through college); they are more likely to be held back in kindergarten, and ultimately more likely to drop out of school. Ultimately, highly apprehensive students are suffering a form of academic discrimination. Research has shown that IQ and CA are not related to each other, so high CA individuals can learn just as well as low CA individuals, but the design of education is against them doing so.

Teacher Apprehension.   At some point in our educational careers, we have all faced the "teacher from hell." This individual probably did not like teaching and did not like you either. We may have dreaded going to that class and having to interact with that individual. Now imagine if you perceived all of your teachers that way. There is a seg-ment of students who are truly apprehensive when having to interact with their teachers in the classroom environment. The Teacher Apprehension Test (TAT) is Scale 39, lo-cated in the appendix. Think of a teacher you had when you were in school that you just did not like, and fill out the scale.

Students who have teacher apprehension generally show visible distress or signs of apprehension when being approached by or communicated with by any teacher. These students will look visually sick or even tremble when having to interact with their teacher. It is not uncommon for all of us to have a fear of communicating with one teacher during our academic careers (e.g., situational apprehension about communicating with the toughest teacher in school). This is a perfectly normal reaction.

However, the students who have a general anxiety or fear about receiving communi-cation from teachers or talking with teachers are clearly at a disadvantage in the educa-tional system because the one person who can help them succeed is the one person they fear the most. Teacher apprehension can have far-reaching implications on student academic performance and communication. For example, students with teacher appre-hension are often perceived by their instructors as unapproachable, unfriendly, unpleas-ant, and uninterested. Although the student may or may not feel this way, this teacher perception will impact how the teacher interacts with that student. As you might have guessed, the student who is perceived in a negative light is less likely to receive commu-nication, assistance, and guidance from the teacher. If a student does receive such atten-tion, however, they still are less likely to do well on assignments and projects than those students who are not afraid of the teacher.

Evaluation Apprehension.   Have you ever been up all night studying for a test, and the closer that test gets, the more anxious you get? This form of anxiety or apprehension is referred to as *evaluation apprehension*. Evaluation apprehension is the fear or anxiety associated with either real or anticipated evaluative situations in the classroom. Evalua-tion apprehension can also occur anytime a student is being evaluated in the classroom. Some students have anxiety when writing papers because of the evaluative dimension of writing. One form of evaluation apprehension is test anxiety.

About 20 percent of students have an abnormal fear or anxiety about test or exam situations in the classroom. These students have high evaluation apprehension. Although some students can control their test taking anxiety, students with evaluation apprehension have anxiety that increases dramatically before, during, and after a test or exam. Scale 40 in the appendix is a copy of the Evaluation Apprehension Measures (EAM). Take a minute and fill out the EAM, and then we will examine some of the consequences of evaluation apprehension in the classroom.

Students with evaluation apprehension often perform poorly in formal testing situations. Their anxiety gets so high and out of control that it prevents the student from being able to fully remember what he or she studied. It is not uncommon for students with high evaluation apprehension to fully know the material going into the testing situation and then blank completely.

Many teachers only use tests as assessment devices in their classrooms. For students with evaluation apprehension who end up in these classes, they simply won't perform as well as their fellow students. Before, during, and after a test, their systems are overactivated and their anxiety is so high they simply do not function well. They may become physically ill before, during, or after an exam.

In conclusion, students with high evaluation apprehension will have high anxiety before, during, and after exams. In extreme cases, the students with evaluation apprehension may skip class or have so much anxiety that they become physically ill and have to miss the test. Many teachers perceive students with high evaluation apprehension as unintelligent, slow, uninterested, and uneducated, when in fact these students may know as much as the other students; they simply cannot recall it at test time due to their anxiety.

Overall, anxiety in the classroom can have a number of negative effects. Across the board, students who exhibit abnormal levels of anxiety either in communication, toward their teachers, or during evaluation periods will have a harder time succeeding in education than those students who do not have high levels of apprehension.

Student Motivation

Sir Christopher Ball in his presidential address to the North of England Education Conference in 1995 said, "There are only three things of importance to successful learning: motivation, motivation, and motivation . . . any fool can teach students who want to learn." Millette and Gorham (2002) define motivation as "a force or drive that influences behavior to achieve a desired outcome" (p. 141). In essence, motivation in instructional settings is that little light bulb that just seems to go off in some students' heads that causes them to want to learn. Before we discuss motivation, take a minute and fill out the Student Motivation Measure, which is Scale 41 in the appendix.

In Chapter 8, we discussed the different types of power that you can use during interpersonal encounters. Motivation is not the same thing as power, yet it is related to power. In a study conducted by Richmond (1990), she found that student motivation was positively related to referent power used by the teacher and negatively related to coercive power used by the teacher. In other words, it appears that student motivation is actually associated with the internalization level of influence. Additionally, Richmond found that students who were motivated had higher affective and cognitive learning. Other research in the area of student motivation among college students has found that motivated students prepare more for class, show up to class more often, turn in assignments on time, study more for exams, ask questions during class, have a better grasp of the material, and earn better grades (Millette & Gorham, 2002).

So what motivates students to do well in their classes? Motivation exists in one of two forms: intrinsic and extrinsic. Intrinsic motivation originates from within a student. If I am intrinsically motivated to excel in school, I'm doing it for myself and no one else. Many students just want to do well in school. They are not doing it for their parents, a prize, or even a grade; they are just internally driven to do well. People who exhibit high levels of intrinsic motivation have trait motivation. Some people are just more motivated to do better and have higher achievement levels.

Extrinsic motivation, on the other hand, is motivation that exists outside of the student. Many students are motivated to do well in school because they know that doing well will reward them in some fashion. Many kids do well in school because their parents will reward them in some fashion for good work. At the same time, those things that are initially seen as rewards can eventually become expectations and lose their motivating potential. It should also be known that what extrinsically motivates one student may not motivate another student.

This section of the chapter has focused on student learning, anxiety, and motivation and how all three impact the classroom environment. The next section examines how teacher communication can impact the classroom environment.

TEACHER COMMUNICATION

It is impossible to separate teaching from communication. Teaching is fundamentally dependent on an individual's ability to communicate with her or his students. Some people tend to have much better skills at communicating in the classroom. In this section, we are going to examine how a handful of communication variables (clarity, nonverbal immediacy, humor assessment, and teacher misbehaviors) exhibited by teachers can impact student affect and learning in the classroom.

Communicator Clarity

One of the biggest complaints that university officials get from new students across the United States is that they often cannot understand their professors. Sometimes these complaints are ethnocentric in orientation. However, many students actually like their foreign teachers better than some of their domestic teachers. Most students entering college are not used to listening to vastly different dialects from English speakers around the world. Some students simply cannot adjust. However, there are some college professors that were born and raised in the United States with excellent English, and their students still have no idea what they are saying. One of the biggest problems for new teachers to overcome is learning how to present their lessons in a clear and concise manner. Chesebro and McCroskey (1998) defined communicator clarity as "the process by which an instructor is able to effectively stimulate the desired meaning of course content and process in the minds of students through the use of appropriately-structured verbal and nonverbal messages" (pp. 262–263). Ideally, students should be able to understand the meaning of a message her or his teacher is sending. Unfortunately, it does not always work this way in the classroom environment.

Have you ever had the experience when a teacher said something in class and you could have sworn that he or she had just spoken another language? Imagine sitting in a classroom when a teacher throws out these two phrases: "tintintibulation of the metallic cylinders" and "exuberance on the celestial sphere." Know what that teacher means? Although these two phrases may seem a little daunting at first, the actual meanings are quite simplistic. The first phrase simply means "Jingle Bells," and the second phrase is "Joy to the World." These two common Christmas carols can serve as a good example of the problem of teacher clarity. Too many teachers try to demonstrate their knowledge of the English language in the classroom to the detriment of their students' learning. There is no reason to use huge polysyllabic words while teaching just to demonstrate that you can.

Chesebro (2002) broke down communication clarity in the classroom into two major categories of clarity: verbal and structural. Verbal clarity is a teacher's ability to lecture in a fluent manner (few verbal surrogates like *uhs* and *umms*), clearly explain course content, and use appropriate and meaningful illustrations to help students further understand the content. One of the authors of this text had a professor in college who actually said the verbal surrogates *uhh* and *umm* 167 times in a thirty-minute period (as counted by three students in the class). The students in the professor's class had been driven crazy to the point where they started keeping track of her verbal surrogates in a gamelike fashion. One day, they took bets.

Structural clarity relates to the teacher's ability to maintain and inform her or his students about the structure of lesson before, during, and after the lesson. In reality, structural clarity is closely related to the simple speech structure you probably learned in your first writing or public speaking class. A good lecture has all of the components of a good speech or paper. Teachers need to preview what will be learned during that class period. Teachers need to organize the material in a manner that makes sense and does not seem to jump around a lot. When switching topics during a lecture, a teacher needs to make sure that he or she clearly transitions from one topic to the next to avoid leaving any students behind. When the lecture is over, the teacher needs to go back over the lecture and hit the highlights again to reiterate what has happened during the lecture. One idea to help with overall structural clarity is to provide students with skeletal outlines of a lecture. This allows students to stay on top of where the teacher is located in the lecture notes and know where the lecture is going. And trust us, if a teacher by chance skips a section on her or his outline, the students will be right there to point out the mistake.

The last part of structural clarity involves the use of visual aids. Students will take more away from a lecture when they are able to both see and hear content. This does not mean that teachers should go overboard and turn every lecture into a computer slide presentation, but if you are talking about the various sections of the human brain, students will remember more of your presentation if they can see either a model of a brain or a real one.

Scale 42 in the appendix is the Teacher-Clarity Short Inventory created by Chesebro and McCroskey (1998). If you're like us, chances are if you thought the teacher you thought about in Scale 42 was a bad teacher you probably indicated he or she was not clear. In fact, you probably did not have very high affect for the bad teacher or that class. This is exactly what Chesebro and McCroskey (2001) found in a study that examined a teacher's clarity in the classroom. Teacher clarity was found to be positively related to student motivation, affect for the instructor, affect for the course, and cognitive learning.

Immediacy Behaviors in the Classroom

We have all had teachers that we have connected with in the classroom. Maybe it was their animated style, or the way that they knew everyone's name in the classroom. Somehow we just felt psychologically and/or physically closer to these teachers than to our other teachers. Though immediacy is strictly a perceptual concept, it has been shown to be very important in the learning environment. In a study conducted by Richmond, Gorham, and McCroskey (1987), it was found that "moderate immediacy is necessary for

This picture illustrates a form of nonverbally immediate behavior in the classroom (physical closeness).

cognitive learning and low immediacy may suppress such learning. However, high immediacy may not increase cognitive learning over that generated by moderate immediacy" (p. 587). Overall, a teacher's ability to be at least moderately immediate with her or his students has been shown to greatly impact the learning environment.

Immediacy can come in one of two basic forms: verbal and nonverbal. Verbal immediacy behaviors, in part, include behaviors like using a student's name in class; using inclusive language like *we* and *us*, instead of exclusive language like *you* and *them*. Communicator clarity has also been shown to be positively related to perceptions of immediacy (Chesebro & McCroskey, 1998). A teacher's sociocommunicative style in the classroom has also been shown to positively impact student perceptions of immediacy. Thomas, Richmond, and McCroskey (1994) found that both assertiveness and responsiveness were positively related to immediacy (although assertiveness and responsiveness are not correlated with each other).

Although a lot of research has shown the benefits of both verbal and nonverbal immediacy, Richmond and McCroskey (2004) believe that nonverbal immediacy is by far more important in a learning situation. Scale 43 in the appendix is a version of the Other Report of Nonverbal Immediacy (ONRI-26), a scale very similar to the one that you filled out on yourself in Chapter 5.

To understand how immediacy impacts the learning environment, let's examine a number of the nonverbal messages that we discussed in Chapter 4 and see how they can impact teacher immediacy in the classroom: proxemics, haptics, vocalics, kinesics, eye contact, chronemics, and physical appearance.

Proxemics.   Immediate teachers have been shown to decrease the physical distance between themselves and their students. Immediate teachers will avoid having barriers between themselves and their students such as desks and podiums. Immediate teachers will also move in and around their students while teaching.

Haptics.   Immediate teachers know how to use appropriate touch with their students. A slight pat on the shoulder or upper back can be a sign of immediacy for most students. Teachers must be careful when they are touching students for fear of sexual harassment allegations. Before touching any student, think of the benefits and possible costs, and then touch only with common sense.

Vocalics.   Immediate teachers can use their entire vocal range effectively. The opposite of vocal variety is the infamous monotone teacher whose very voice can put anyone to sleep. To be immediate, teachers should use a range of vocal behaviors that make the lecture varied and more pleasant to listen to during class. Teachers should attempt to find a verbal style that is pleasant and effective.

Kinesics.   Immediate teachers have been consistently found to have very specific kinesic patterns. Immediate teachers have faces that are animated and fun to watch while speaking—think of Robin Williams. Immediate teachers also do not cross their arms in front of them while lecturing. Crossing your arms in front of you has the same effect on nonverbal immediacy as standing behind a podium; it decreases student perceptions of immediacy. Having an open body orientation allows students to connect with their teachers on a more psychologically close level. Immediate teachers also use more gestures than nonimmediate teachers. Nonimmediate teachers tend to stand very stiff and do not move very much. Immediate teachers use appropriate gestures as a way to emphasize points and demonstrate what they are saying during class. Lastly, immediate teachers are more relaxed and in control of a teaching situation. Who would you be more interested in listening to during class, an animated lively teacher or a teacher that has about as much personality and kinesic immediacy as a tree stump?

Eye Contact.   Immediate teachers are teachers who look their students in the eyes. Students want to know that their teachers know that they are sitting there in the classroom. The easiest way to communicate that you know a student is there is to look at her or him. Eye contact is also important because it lets the teacher know how the classroom is responding to the course content.

Chronemics.   Immediate teachers are teachers who are seen spending more time with students, arriving early, staying late, and just making themselves more accessible to their students. At the same time, teachers have to be careful not to make themselves completely open to their students or they will begin to lose personal time that is necessary for sanity.

Physical Appearance.   Physical appearance is the most important aspect of initial attraction as was discussed in Chapter 4. Teachers that are attractive are perceived as more immediate. This does not mean that a teacher has to be a super model to be an immediate and affective teacher, but it is important that a number of characteristics are adhered to when concerned with dress. First, informal but socially appropriate attire that is not conservative is important to be seen as immediate. One of the authors remembers being in high school during the 1990s and having a teacher who only wore polyester clothing and wore a bad toupee. This teacher was not the poster child for immediacy. A clean-cut and modern appearance is helpful in creating immediacy in the classroom. Additionally, teachers should be careful not to wear clothing or accessories that are distracting. If your clothing or accessories clings, clangs, or jingles while you teach, your clothing will be a distraction and will decrease immediacy.

Humor in the Classroom

Researchers have examined humor from a variety of different vantage points, attempting to see how individuals differ in production of and response to humorous messages. When students are asked to generate a list of characteristics that are seen as positive teacher attributes, a strong sense of humor has consistently been one of the primary responses.

Humor is a beneficial and naturally occurring part of the learning environment, but this is not to say that humor cannot be improved and made better. Although humor studies may sound like a lot of fun, to those who do research in this area, it's anything but a laughing matter. Humor is serious business, and when used appropriately, it can have amazing results in the classroom. Avner Ziv (1988), a professor at the University of Jerusalem in Israel and former president of the International Society of Humor Studies, is one of the foremost researchers on humor in the classroom. Dr. Ziv has found that teachers can actually be taught to integrate humor into their classrooms with positive results. He also found that when teachers integrate humor into one section of a class and kept their other section to a traditional style, the students in the humor section scored significantly higher on a standardized test at the end of the semester. In Chapter 5, we discussed the natural way some individuals incorporate humor on a daily basis. Some people are just more attuned to the usage of humor in interpersonal situations.

So, by this point, you're hopefully wondering how humor can be beneficial in the learning environment. Although studies are not completely clear on what is actually happening when students are exposed to humor in a classroom, the following biological basis probably has something to do with this phenomenon. When students are exposed to something they find humorous, endorphin levels rise creating a natural rush. When students are later required to recall information associated with the humor that created the natural rush, they have higher recall rates than students who are not exposed to humor. In essence, the addition of humor to a teaching situation allows for better storage in long-term memory and faster recall and retrieval from long-term memory because of the increased endorphin levels at the time the knowledge was stored inside the brain. Although this is a physiological explanation for why humor is important in the classroom, think of the benefits teachers get from using humor in the classroom.

Scale 44 in the appendix is the Teacher version of the Humor Assessment created by Wrench and Richmond (2004). A number of studies have shown humor to be very positive in the learning environment. Teacher use of humor has been correlated with student affect, cognitive learning, perceived teacher credibility (Martin, Preiss, Gayle, & Allen, 2006; Wrench & Richmond, 2004; Wrench & Punyanunt-Carter, 2005), classroom compliance and level of behavioral problems (Punyanunt, 2000), perceived teacher nonverbal immediacy (Wanzer & Frymier, 1999), and lower evaluation apprehension (Tamborini & Zillmann, 1981). Furthermore, use of humor has been shown to be negatively correlated with use of verbal aggression in academic settings (Wrench & Punyanunt-Carter, 2005).

Teacher Misbehaviors in the Classroom

The first three variables that we have examined in this section were all positively related with creating an effective and affective learning environment. Unfortunately, not all teachers create an effective and affective learning environment. This section examines the communicative behaviors that many teachers use that destroy affect in the learning environment. There are many reasons why teachers communicate in ways that hurt the affective nature of the learning environment (Richmond, Wrench, & Gorham, 2001).

Some teachers get bored with teaching and just stop caring about their students. Other teachers never liked teaching in the first place. Sadly, many teachers get into teaching because they did not know what they wanted to do with their lives, and in the long run these unmotivated teachers are a detriment on the system. Yet other teachers get out of date, develop ridiculously high expectations, don't know how to teach, and eventually succumb to burnout. In Figure 16.1, you will see a list of the three types of teacher misbehaviors that are seen in classrooms, which is based on the research by Kearney, Plax, Hays, and Ivey (1991).

The first category of teacher misbehaviors is teacher *incompetence.* Teacher incompetence exists to the extent to which a teacher does not know her or his content and/or how to present that content effectively in the classroom. Sadly, many teachers are not equipped to teach when they first start teaching. This is true in the lowest levels of education all the way through the highest levels of education. Although a greater effort is now being made to make sure teachers are more prepared to actually teach, there is still room for growth. Often teachers are placed into classrooms outside their specialization. In some school districts, it is not uncommon to have completely unqualified teachers teaching classes, which sets the teacher up to misbehave. Most teachers have learned their content and their pedagogy, but many have no education in effective communication in the classroom at all.

The second category of teacher misbehaviors is teacher *offensiveness.* We have all had the experience of running into offensive people at one point or another in our lives. We do not expect to run into offensive people in our classrooms, however. Yet there are many teachers who seem to get perverse pleasure out of ridiculing their students in front of their peers. Other offensive teachers will regularly use sexist, heterosexist, ageist, or racist language during class. Typically speaking, students feel powerless against teachers who are offensive. If you ever find yourself in a situation with an offensive teacher, make sure that someone in authority knows that it is going on. Often, school administrators do not even know the offensive teacher acts that way in her or his classroom until someone files a complaint or a lawsuit.

The final type of teacher misbehavior is teacher *indolence.* Teacher indolence is basically the traditional perspective of the absent-minded professor. This is the type of teacher who assigns books that are never used, changes test dates without telling anyone, and never picks up assignments—or if he or she does pick up assignments, they may never get graded and returned. Indolent teachers also may miss class regularly and have flimsy excuses for why they missed. If the indolent teacher does show up for class, chances are he or she may not know where the class is in the content. Although on the outside these teachers appear fairly harmless, indolent teachers are not preparing their students for future classes. Many courses grow on each other, so if you have an indolent teacher in an introductory course, you are not likely to be prepared for the next level course.

The authors of this book know a man who had a misbehaving teacher in high school Spanish. She was on the verge of the nervous breakdown all year long, and the students knew this. She sporadically graded assignments and only taught to the white kids in class. She was from Spain and did not like having to teach the students of Mexican ancestry in class because she saw them as inferior and would ridicule their use of the

FIGURE 16.1 Teacher Misbehaviors

Teacher Incompetence

1. An incompetent teacher often exhibits misbehaviors such as giving confusing or unclear lectures, presentations, or notes. Here the teacher often is vague, jumps randomly from one point to another, and has lectures or notes that are often inconsistent with the assigned readings.
2. An incompetent teacher is often apathetic to students. He or she doesn't seem to care about the class or the students, doesn't learn students' names, rejects students' opinions and questions, and rarely allows for class discussions.
3. An incompetent teacher uses unfair testing techniques or strategies. He or she will ask trick questions, have exams or tests that do not relate to notes or lectures, give tests that are too difficult, ask ambiguous questions, and provide no review for tests.
4. An incompetent teacher will give boring lectures and presentations. Such teachers are boring and unenthusiastic, speak in a monotone voice, ramble, repeat too much, drone on, and provide no variety.
5. An incompetent teacher will often have students who have information or communication overloads. For example, he or she talks too fast, rushes the content, talks over students' heads, uses obscure terminology, ignores students' queries, ignores students' confusion and keeps giving information, and assigns excessive busywork.
6. An incompetent teacher does not know her or his subject matter or primary content teaching area. For example, he or she doesn't understand the subject, cannot answer questions, gives incorrect information, cannot extend the subject matter, and often isn't current or up-to-date.
7. An incompetent teacher may have a foreign or regional accent or dialect different from that of the students, which interferes with the students' processing of information. For example, such teachers are hard to understand, enunciate poorly, and don't attempt to adapt their speech to the students, or their accent or speech is so strong or different from the region in which they teach that it interferes with information processing and effective communication.
8. An incompetent teacher uses inappropriate volume. He or she does not speak loudly enough (speaks too softly) to be heard, or he or she speaks too loudly.
9. Lastly, an incompetent teacher uses poor grammar and has poor spelling. Such teachers often use poor grammar, misspell words, and generally use poor English.

Teacher Offensiveness

1. Teachers who behave offensively use sarcasm, putdowns, and hurtful or harmful comments. They are sarcastic, are rude, make fun of students, humiliate students, and insult, pick on, or embarrass students in front of others.
2. Teachers who behave offensively use verbal abuse. They are verbally abusive. They use profanity; are often angry, mean, and hostile; yell, scream, rant, and rave; and will often intimidate students. Sometimes they will interrupt students and verbally harass them in the classroom.
3. Teachers who behave offensively use unreasonable and arbitrary rules. They refuse to accept late work, give no breaks in long classes, punish an entire class for the misbehavior of one student, and are often rigid, inflexible, authoritarian, and hostile.
4. Teachers who behave offensively use sexual harassment techniques. They will make offensive, sexual remarks to or about students. They will make inappropriate comments about their clothing and dress. They will flirt, make sexual innuendoes, and be chauvinistic.

(Continued)

FIGURE 16.1 Teacher Misbehaviors (*Continued*)

5. Teachers who behave offensively have a negative personality. They are impersonal, impatient, cold, self-centered, complaining, and whiny. They act superior, unpredictable, and moody.
6. Lastly, teachers who behave offensively show favoritism, partiality, bias, or prejudice. They play favorites, act prejudiced against others, and are narrow-minded or close-minded.

Teacher Indolence

1. An indolent or lazy teacher is often absent from class. Such teachers simply do not show up for class, use substitutes a lot, and have flimsy, vague excuses for why they were absent.
2. An indolent teacher is often tardy for class. He or she rarely shows up on time and rarely has good excuses for being late.
3. An indolent teacher is often unprepared, disorganized, or sloppy in their preparation. He or she is not prepared, loses notes, forgets test dates, forgets where he or she is in regard to content coverage, makes assignments and does not collect them, and generally seems sloppy, uncoordinated, or unorganized.
4. An indolent teacher is one who will deviate substantially from the syllabus or course outline. For example, such teachers change dates and assignments without any warning or reason, are often behind schedule, do not follow guidelines stated on a syllabus, and assign books, materials, and readings but never refer to them.
5. An indolent teacher is often late in returning work to students. He or she is late in returning papers, projects, assignments, tests, exams, and exercises. He or she often forgets to bring in graded papers and projects.
6. Lastly, an indolent teacher is often guilty of information underload. Such teachers are too easy, do not give enough content to satisfy student needs, seem to skim the content surface, and give light and easy assignments.

Spanish Language. She would occasionally break down crying during the middle of class for no reason. By the end of that year, our friend had learned no Spanish at all. When he entered into the Spanish class the next year, he was terrified because he knew he did not know anything. His next teacher was retiring that year and just didn't care either. To this day, the only Spanish our friend knows is *hola* and *adios*.

A teacher must have a high number of teacher misbehaviors to be considered a real misbehavior problem in the classroom. There could also be other misbehaviors that teachers display that impact student learning such as keeping students overtime, early dismissal, unresponsiveness to students' needs, inaccessibility to students outside of class, not giving students extra help, not answering students' questions outside of class, and giving exams that do not relate to the content or reading. Before we label anyone a *misbehavior problem*, let's be sure they have a number of the above misbehaviors. Usually, good teachers will realize when they are becoming misbehavior problems and correct the situation, but poor teachers often don't realize they are misbehavior problems. Very few teachers went into the profession so they could make students' lives miserable. Unfortunately, however, many do just that.

While there is little current research examining the impact that teacher misbehaviors have on the classroom, Thweatt and McCroskey (1998) found a negative relationship between student perceptions of a teacher's credibility (competence, trustworthiness, and caring/goodwill) and student perceptions of teacher misbehaviors. Furthermore, they also noted a negative relationship between nonverbal immediacy and student perceptions of teacher misbehaviors. Toale (2001) found a negative relationship between student perceptions of teacher clarity and student perceptions of teacher misbehaviors. Clearly, how a teacher communicates in the instructional contexts impacts student perceptions of teacher misbehaviors.

 ## CONCLUSION

This chapter has focused on applying communication variables within the instructional communication context. Specifically, we have examined how student communicative behaviors (learning domains, anxiety, and student motivation) and teacher communicative behaviors (clarity, nonverbal immediacy, humor assessment, and teacher misbehaviors) impact the instructional environment. As researchers, we are a long way off from understanding every facet of the impact that communication has in the instructional context. What we are learning is that the instructional communication competence of teachers is the key factor in the educational success of the teacher, of the student, and of the system.

 ## KEY TERMS

affective learning 345
behavioral/psychomotor
learning 345

cognitive learning 346
evaluation apprehension 347
motivation 349

teacher apprehension 348
teacher clarity 351

 ## REFERENCES

Ball, Sir Christopher. (1995). Presidential Address to the North of England Education Conference, England, cited in D. Galloway, C. Rogers, D. Armstrong, & E. Leo (1998), *Motivating the difficult to teach* (p. 3). White Plains, NY: Longman.

Bloom, B. S., Englehart, M. D., Furst, E. J., Hill, W. H., & Krathwohl, D. R. (1956). *Taxonomy of educational objectives—the classification of educational goals, handbook I: Cognitive domain.* New York: David McKay.

Booth-Butterfield, M. (1992). *Interpersonal communication in instructional settings.* Edina, MN: Burgess.

Booth-Butterfield, M., & Booth-Butterfield, S. (1992). *Communication apprehension and avoidance in the classroom.* Edina, MN: Burgess.

Booth-Butterfield, S. (1992). *Influence and control in the classroom.* Edina, MN: Burgess.

Chesebro, J. L. (2002). Teaching clearly. In J. Chesebro and J. C. McCroskey (Eds.), *Communication for teachers* (pp. 93–103). Boston: Allyn & Bacon.

Chesebro, J. L., & McCroskey, J. C. (1998). The development of the teacher clarity short inventory (TCSI) to measure clear teaching in the classroom. *Communication Research Reports, 15,* 262–266.

Chesebro, J. L., & McCroskey, J. C. (2001). The relationship of teacher clarity and immediacy with student state receiver apprehension, affect, and cognitive learning. *Communication Education, 50,* 59–68.

Gorham, J. (1992). *Commercial media and classroom teaching.* Edina, MN: Burgess.

Kearney, P., Plax, T. G., Hays, E. R., & Ivey, M. J. (1991). College teacher misbehaviors: What students don't like about what teachers say and do. *Communication Research Reports, 39,* 309-324.

Klopf, D. W., & Thompson, C. A. (1992). *Communication in the multicultural classroom.* Edina, MN: Burgess.

Krathwohl, D. R., Bloom, B. S., & Masia, B. B. (1964). *Taxonomy of educational objectives—the classification of educational goals, handbook II: Affective domain.* New York: David McKay.

Martin, D. M., Preiss, R. W., Gayle, B. M., & Allen, M. (2006). A meta-analytic assessment of the effect of humorous lectures on learning. In B. M. Gayle, R. W. Preiss, N. Burrell, & M. Allen (Eds.), *Classroom communication and instructional processes: Advances through meta-analysis* (pp. 295-313). Mahwah, NJ: Lawrence Erlbaum.

McCroskey, J. C. (1994). Assessment of affect toward communication and affect toward instruction in communication. In S. Morreale & M. Brooks (Eds.), *1994 SCA summer conference proceedings and prepared remarks: Assessing college student competence in speech communication.* Annandale, VA: Speech Communication Association.

McCroskey, J. C., Richmond, V. P., & McCroskey, L. L. (2006). *An introduction to communication in the classroom: The role of communication in teaching and training.* Boston: Allyn & Bacon.

Millette, D. M., & Gorham, J. (2002). Teacher behavior and student motivation. In J. Chesebro and J. C. McCroskey (Eds.), *Communication for teachers* (pp. 141–153). Boston: Allyn & Bacon.

Mottet, T. P., Richmond, V. P., & McCroskey, J. C. (2006). *Handbook of instructional communication: Rhetorical & relational perspectives.* Boston: Allyn & Bacon.

Punyanunt, N. M. (2000). The effects of humor on perceptions of compliance-gaining in the college classroom. *Communication Research Reports, 17,* 30–38.

Richmond, V. P. (1996). *Nonverbal communication in the classroom* (2nd ed.). Edina, MN: Burgess.

Richmond, V. P., Gorham, J. S., & McCroskey, J. C. (1987). The relationship between selected immediacy behaviors and cognitive learning. In M. McLaughlin (Ed.), *Communication yearbook 10* (pp. 574–590). Beverly Hills, CA: Sage.

Richmond, V. P., & McCroskey, J. C. (Eds.). (1992). *Power in the classroom: Communication, control, and concern.* Hillsdale, NJ: Lawrence Erlbaum.

Richmond, V. P., & McCroskey, J. C. (2004). *Nonverbal behavior in interpersonal relations* (4th ed.). Boston: Allyn & Bacon.

Richmond, V. P., McCroskey, J. C., & Thompson, C. A. (1992). *Communication problems of children.* Edina, MN: Burgess.

Richmond, V. P., Wrench, J. S., & Gorham, J. (2001). *Communication, affect, and learning in the classroom.* Acton, MA: Tapestry Press.

Tamborini, R., & Zillmann, D. (1981). College students' perception of lectures using humor. *Perceptual and Motor Skills, 52,* 427–432.

Thomas, C. E., Richmond, V. P., & McCroskey, J. C. (1994). The association between immediacy and socio-communicative style. *Communication Research Reports, 11,* 107–114.

Thweatt, K. S., & McCroskey, J. C. (1998). The impact of teacher immediacy and misbehaviors on teacher credibility. *Communication Education, 47,* 348-358.

Toale, M C. (2001). *Teacher clarity and teacher misbehaviors: Relationships with student's affective learning and teacher credibility.* Unpublished doctoral dissertation, West Virginia University, Morgantown.

Wanzer, M. B., & Frymier, A. B. (1999). The relationship between student perceptions of instructor humor and students' reports of learning. *Communication Education, 48,* 48–62.

Wrench, J. S., & Punyanunt-Carter, N. M. (2005). Advisor-advisee communication two: The influence of verbal aggression and humor assessment on advisee perceptions of advisor credibility and affective learning. *Communication Research Reports, 22,* 303–313.

Wrench, J. S., & Richmond, V. P. (2004). Understanding the psychometric properties of the Humor Assessment instrument through an analysis of the relationships between teacher humor assessment and instructional communication variables in the college classroom. *Communication Research Reports, 21,* 92–103.

Ziv, A. (1988). Teaching and learning with humor: Experiment and replication. *Journal of Experimental Education, 57,* 5–13.

DISCUSSION QUESTIONS

1. Why is affective learning the most important form of learning in the classroom?

2. According to the chapter, what is the relationship between student motivation and learning? Are you more internally or externally motivated as a student?

3. What are the tools teachers can use to ensure that they are clear in the classroom?

4. How does humor affect learning in the classroom?

5. From your own educational experience, generate an example for each of the three types of teacher misbehaviors.

Appendix

Scales for the Measurement of Communication Phenomena

SCALE 1   Source Credibility: Competence

Directions: The questionnaire below lists 6 characteristics that we often perceive in other people. Please indicate the degree to which you believe each of the characteristics applies to: **Current President of the United States.** Numbers "1" and "7" indicate a very strong feeling. Numbers "2" and "6" indicate a strong feeling. Numbers "3" and "5" indicate a fairly weak feeling. Number "4" indicates you are undecided or do not understand the adjectives themselves. There are no right or wrong answers. Please record your responses on the line before each item:

1. Intelligent	7	6	5	4	3	2	1	Unintelligent
2. Untrained	1	2	3	4	5	6	7	Trained
3. Inexpert	1	2	3	4	5	6	7	Expert
4. Informed	7	6	5	4	3	2	1	Uninformed
5. Incompetent	1	2	3	4	5	6	7	Competent
6. Bright	7	6	5	4	3	2	1	Stupid

Scoring:
Add the number you circled above for each row. _____

Result: Score for Competence.
Possible score range 6–35. If your score is above 35 or below 6 you have made an error in scoring. Higher scores indicate higher levels of perceived competence.

Source: This instrument is based on research reported by McCroskey, J. C., and Teven, J. J. (1999). Goodwill: A reexamination of the construct and its measurement. *Communication Monographs*, *66*, 90–103; and the earlier work by McCroskey, J. C., and Young, T. J. (1981). Ethos and credibility: The construct and its measurement after three decades. *Central States Speech Journal, 32*, 24–34.

SCALE 2 Source Credibility: Trustworthiness

Directions: The questionnaire below lists 6 characteristics that we often perceive in other people. Please indicate the degree to which you believe each of the characteristics applies to: **Current President of the United States.** Numbers "1" and "7" indicate a very strong feeling. Numbers "2" and "6" indicate a strong feeling. Numbers "3" and "5" indicate a fairly weak feeling. Number "4" indicates you are undecided or do not understand the adjectives themselves. There are no right or wrong answers. Please record your responses on the line before each item:

1. Honest	7	6	5	4	3	2	1	Dishonest
2. Untrustworthy	1	2	3	4	5	6	7	Trustworthy
3. Honorable	7	6	5	4	3	2	1	Dishonorable
4. Moral	7	6	5	4	3	2	1	Immoral
5. Unethical	1	2	3	4	5	6	7	Ethical
6. Phony	1	2	3	4	5	6	7	Genuine

Scoring:
Add the number you circled above for each row. _____

Result: Score for Trustworthiness.
Possible score range 6–35. If your score is above 35 or below 6 you have made an error in scoring. Higher scores indicate higher levels of perceived trustworthiness.

Source: This instrument is based on research reported by McCroskey, J. C., and Teven, J. J. (1999). Goodwill: A reexamination of the construct and its measurement. *Communication Monographs, 66,* 90–103 and the earlier work by McCroskey, J. C., and Young, T. J. (1981). Ethos and credibility: The construct and its measurement after three decades. *Central States Speech Journal, 32,* 24–34.

SCALE 3   Source Credibility: Caring/Goodwill

Directions: The questionnaire below lists 6 characteristics that we often perceive in other people. Please indicate the degree to which you believe each of the characteristics applies to: **Current President of the United States.** Numbers "1" and "7" indicate a very strong feeling. Numbers "2" and "6" indicate a strong feeling. Numbers "3" and "5" indicate a fairly weak feeling. Number "4" indicates you are undecided or do not understand the adjectives themselves. There are no right or wrong answers. Please record your responses on the line before each item:

1.	Cares about me	7	6	5	4	3	2	1	Doesn't care about me
2.	Has my interests at heart	7	6	5	4	3	2	1	Doesn't have my interests at heart
3.	Self centered	1	2	3	4	5	6	7	Not self centered
4.	Concerned with me	7	6	5	4	3	2	1	Not concerned with me
5.	Insensitive	1	2	3	4	5	6	7	Sensitive
6.	Not Understanding	1	2	3	4	5	6	7	Understanding

Scoring:
Add the number you circled above for each row. _____

Result: Score for Caring/Goodwill.
Possible score range 6–35. If your score is above 35 or below 6 you have made an error in scoring. Higher scores indicate higher levels of perceived caring/goodwill.

Source: This instrument is based on research reported by McCroskey, J. C., and Teven, J. J. (1999). Goodwill: A reexamination of the construct and its measurement. *Communication Monographs*, *66*, 90–103 and the earlier work by McCroskey, J. C., and Young, T. J. (1981). Ethos and credibility: The construct and its measurement after three decades. *Central States Speech Journal, 32*, 24–34.

SCALE 4   Interpersonal Attraction: Physical

Directions: The questionnaire below lists 12 characteristics that we often perceive in other people. Please indicate the degree to which you believe each of the characteristics applies to: **Your supervisor in the most recent job you have had.** Please record your responses on the line before each item:

Strongly Disagree	Disagree	Neutral	Agree	Strongly Agree
1	2	3	4	5

_____   1. I think he/she is handsome/pretty.

_____   2. He/She is sexy looking.

_____   3. I don't like the way he/she looks.

_____   4. He/She is ugly.

_____   5. I find her/him attractive physically.

_____   6. He/She is not good looking.

_____   7. This person looks appealing.

_____   8. I don't like the way this person looks.

_____   9. He/She is nice looking.

_____ 10. He/She has an attractive face.

_____ 11. He/She is not physically attractive.

_____ 12. He/She is good looking.

Scoring:
Step 1. Begin with a score of 30.
Step 2. Add the scores of items 1, 2, 5, 7, 9, 10, and 12.
Step 3. Add the scores of items 3, 4, 6, 8, and 11.
Step 4. Add the score of Step 1 to the score of Step 2.
Step 5. Subtract the score of Step 3 from the score of Step 4.

Result: Score for Physical.
Possible score range 12–60. If your score is above 60 or below 12 you have made an error in scoring.

Source: This instrument is based on research reported by McCroskey, L. L., McCroskey, J. C., & Richmond, V. P. (2006). Analysis and improvement of the measurement of interpersonal attraction and homophily, *Communication Quarterly, 54*, 1–31. And the earlier work by McCroskey, J. C., & McCain, T. A. (1974). The measurement of interpersonal attraction. *Speech Monographs, 41*, 261–266.

SCALE 5   Interpersonal Attraction: Social

Directions: The questionnaire below lists 12 characteristics that we often perceive in other people. Please indicate the degree to which you believe each of the characteristics applies to: **Your supervisor in the most recent job you have had.** Please record your responses on the line before each item:

Strongly Disagree	Disagree	Neutral	Agree	Strongly Agree
1	2	3	4	5

_____   1. I think he/she could be a friend of mine.

_____   2. I would like to have a friendly chat with her/him.

_____   3. It would be difficult to meet and talk with her/him.

_____   4. We could never establish a personal friendship with each other.

_____   5. He/She just wouldn't fit into my circle of friends.

_____   6. He/She would be pleasant to be with.

_____   7. He/She is sociable with me.

_____   8. I would not like to spend time socializing with this person.

_____   9. I could become close friends with her/him.

_____ 10. He/She is easy to get along with.

_____ 11. He/She is unpleasant to be around.

_____ 12. This person is not very friendly.

Scoring:
Step 1. Begin with a score of 36.
Step 2. Add the scores of items 1, 2, 6, 7, 9, and 10.
Step 3. Add the scores of items 3, 4, 5, 8, 11, and 12.
Step 4. Add the score of Step 1 to the score of Step 2.
Step 5. Subtract the score of Step 3 from the score of Step 4.

Result: Score for Social.
Possible score range 12–60. If your score is above 60 or below 12 you have made an error in scoring.

Source: This instrument is based on research reported by McCroskey, L. L., McCroskey, J. C., & Richmond, V. P. (2006). Analysis and improvement of the measurement of interpersonal attraction and homophily, _Communication Quarterly, 54_, 1–31. And the earlier work by McCroskey, J. C., & McCain, T. A. (1974). The measurement of interpersonal attraction. _Speech Monographs, 41_, 261–266.

SCALE 6   Interpersonal Attraction: Task

Directions: The questionnaire below lists 14 characteristics that we often perceive in other people. Please indicate the degree to which you believe each of the characteristics applies to: **Your supervisor in the most recent job you have had.** Please record your responses on the line before each item:

Strongly Disagree	Disagree	Neutral	Agree	Strongly Agree
1	2	3	4	5

_____ 1. If I wanted to get things done, I could probably depend on her/him.

_____ 2. He/She would be a poor problem solver.

_____ 3. I couldn't get anything accomplished with her/him.

_____ 4. I have confidence in her/his ability to get the job done.

_____ 5. He/She is a typical goof-off when assigned a job to do.

_____ 6. I would enjoy working on a task with her/him.

_____ 7. This person is lazy when it comes to working on a task.

_____ 8. This person would be an asset in any task situation.

_____ 9. I would recommend her/him as a work partner.

_____ 10. I could rely on her/him to get the job done.

_____ 11. This person takes her/his work seriously.

_____ 12. He/She is an unreliable work partner.

_____ 13. I could not count on the person to get the job done.

_____ 14. I could not recommend her/him as a work partner.

Scoring:
Step 1.   Begin with a score of 42.
Step 2.   Add the scores of items 1, 4, 6, 8, 9, 10, and 11.
Step 3.   Add the scores of items 2, 3, 5, 7, 12, 13, and 14.
Step 4.   Add the score of Step 1 to the score of Step 2.
Step 5.   Subtract the score of Step 3 from the score of Step 4.

Result: Score for Task.
Possible score range 14–70. If your score is above 70 or below 14 you have made an error in scoring.

Source: This instrument is based on research reported by McCroskey, L. L., McCroskey, J. C., & Richmond, V. P. (2006). Analysis and improvement of the measurement of interpersonal attraction and homophily, *Communication Quarterly, 54,* 1–31. And the earlier work by McCroskey, J. C., & McCain, T. A. (1974). The measurement of interpersonal attraction. *Speech Monographs, 41,* 261–266.

SCALE 7   Homophily: Background

Directions: The questionnaire below lists 10 characteristics that we often perceive in other people. Please indicate the degree to which you believe each of the characteristics applies to: **Your supervisor in the most recent job you have had.** Please record your responses on the line before each item:

Strongly Disagree	Disagree	Neutral	Agree	Strongly Agree
1	2	3	4	5

_____ 1. This person is from a social class similar to mine.

_____ 2. This person's status is different from mine.

_____ 3. This person is from an economic situation different from mine.

_____ 4. This person's background is similar to mine.

_____ 5. This person's status is like mine.

_____ 6. This person is from a social class different from mine.

_____ 7. This person is from an economic situation like mine.

_____ 8. This person's background is different from mine.

_____ 9. This person and I come from a similar geographic region.

_____ 10. This person's life as a child was similar to mine.

Scoring:
Step 1. Begin with a score of 24.
Step 2. Add the scores of items 1, 4, 5, 7, 9, and 10.
Step 3. Add the scores of items 2, 3, 6, and 8.
Step 4. Add the score of Step 1 to the score of Step 2.
Step 5. Subtract the score of Step 3 from the score of Step 4.

Result: Score for Background.
Possible score range 10–50. If your score is above 50 or below 10 you have made an error in scoring.

Source: This instrument is based on research reported by McCroskey, L. L., McCroskey, J. C., & Richmond, V. P. (2006). Analysis and improvement of the measurement of interpersonal attraction and homophily, Communication Quarterly, 54, 1–31. And the earlier work by McCroskey, J. C., Richmond, V. P., & Daly, J. A. (1975). The measurement of perceived homophily in interpersonal communication. Human Communication Research, 1, 323–332.

SCALE 8 Homophily: Attitude

Directions: The questionnaire below lists 17 characteristics that we often perceive in other people. Please indicate the degree to which you believe each of the characteristics applies to: Your supervisor in the most recent job you have had. Please record your responses on the line before each item:

Strongly Disagree	Disagree	Neutral	Agree	Strongly Agree
1	2	3	4	5

_____ 1. This person thinks like me.

_____ 2. This person doesn't behave like me.

_____ 3. This person is different from me.

_____ 4. This person shares my values.

_____ 5. This person is like me.

_____ 6. This person treats people like I do.

_____ 7. This person doesn't think like me.

_____ 8. This person is similar to me.

_____ 9. This person doesn't share my values.

_____ 10. This person behaves like me.

_____ 11. This person is unlike me.

_____ 12. This person doesn't treat people like I do.

_____ 13. This person has thoughts and ideas that are similar to mine.

_____ 14. This person expresses attitudes different from mine.

_____ 15. This person has a lot in common with me.

_____ 16. This person's attitudes are different from mine.

_____ 17. This person's beliefs are like mine.

Scoring:

Step 1. Begin with a score of 48.

Step 2. Add the scores of items 1, 4, 5, 6, 8, 10, 13, 15, and 17.

Step 3. Add the scores of items 2, 3, 7, 9, 11, 12, 14, and 16.

Step 4. Add the score of Step 1 to the score of Step 2.

Step 5. Subtract the score of Step 3 from the score of Step 4.

Result: Score for Attitude.

Possible score range 17–85. If your score is above 85 or below 17 you have made an error in scoring.

Source: This instrument is based on research reported by McCroskey, L. L., McCroskey, J. C., & Richmond, V. P. (2006). Analysis and improvement of the measurement of interpersonal attraction and homophily, _Communication Quarterly, 54,_ 1–31. And the earlier work by McCroskey, J. C., Richmond, V. P., & Daly, J. A. (1975). The measurement of perceived homophily in interpersonal communication. _Human Communication Research, 1,_ 323–332.

SCALE 9   Shyness

Directions: The questionnaire below lists 14 characteristics that we often perceive in other people. Please indicate the degree to which you believe each of the characteristics applies to you. Please record your responses on the line before each item:

Strongly Disagree 1	Disagree 2	Neutral 3	Agree 4	Strongly Agree 5

_____   1. I am a shy person.

_____   2. Other people think I talk a lot.

_____   3. I am a very talkative person.

_____   4. Other people think I am shy.

_____   5. I talk a lot.

_____   6. I tend to be very quiet in class.

_____   7. I don't talk much.

_____   8. I talk more than most people.

_____   9. I am a quiet person.

_____   10. I talk more in a small group (3–6) than others do.

_____   11. Most people talk more than I do.

_____   12. Other people think I am very quiet.

_____   13. I talk more in class than most people do.

_____   14. Most people are more shy than I am.

Scoring:
Step 1. Begin with a score of 42.
Step 2. Add the scores of items 1, 4, 6, 7, 9, 11, and 12.
Step 3. Add the scores of items 2, 3, 5, 8, 10, 13, and 14.
Step 4. Add the score of Step 1 to the score of Step 2.
Step 5. Subtract the score of Step 3 from the score of Step 4.

Result: Score for Shyness.
Possible score range 14–70. If your score is above 70 or below 14 you have made an error in scoring.

Source: This instrument is based on research reported by McCroskey, J. C., & Richmond, V. P. (1982). Communication apprehension and shyness: Conceptual and operational distinctions. Central States Speech Journal, 33, 458–468.

SCALE 10   Willingness to Communicate

Directions: Below are 20 situations in which a person might choose to communicate or not to communicate. Presume you have completely free choice. Indicate the percentage of times you would choose to communicate in each type of situation. Indicate in the space at the left of the item what percent (zero to 100) of the time you would choose to communicate.

_____ 1. Talk with a service station attendant.

_____ 2. Talk with a physician.

_____ 3. Present a talk to a group of strangers.

_____ 4. Talk with an acquaintance while standing in line.

_____ 5. Talk with a salesperson in a store.

_____ 6. Talk in a large meeting of friends.

_____ 7. Talk with a police officer.

_____ 8. Talk in a small group of strangers.

_____ 9. Talk with a friend while standing in line.

_____ 10. Talk with a waiter/waitress in a restaurant.

_____ 11. Talk in a large meeting of acquaintances.

_____ 12. Talk with a stranger while standing in line.

_____ 13. Talk with a secretary.

_____ 14. Present a talk to a group of friends.

_____ 15. Talk in a small group of acquaintances.

_____ 16. Talk with a garbage collector.

_____ 17. Talk in a large meeting of strangers.

_____ 18. Talk with a spouse (or girl/boyfriend).

_____ 19. Talk in a small group of friends.

_____ 20. Present a talk to a group of acquaintances.

General Scoring:
Step 1.   Add the scores of items 3, 4, 6, 8, 9, 11, 12, 14, 15, 17, 19, and 20.
Step 2.   Divide the score of Step 1 by 12.

Result: Score for Willingness to Communicate.
Possible score range 0–100. If your score is above 100 you have made an error in scoring.

Subscale Scoring:
SCORING: The WTC permits computation of one total score and seven subscores. The range for all scores is 0–100. Follow the procedures outlined below.

1. Group discussion—add scores for items 8, 15, and 19; divide sum by 3. Scores above 89 = high WTC, scores below 57 = low WTC in this context.
2. Meetings—add scores for items 6, 11, and 17; divide sum by 3. Scores above 80 = high WTC, scores below 39 = low WTC in this context.

3. Interpersonal—add scores for items 4, 9, and 12; divide sum by 3. Scores above 94 = high WTC, scores below 64 = low WTC in this context.
4. Public speaking—add scores for items 3, 14, and 20; divide sum by 3. Scores above 78 = high WTC, scores below 33 = low WTC in this context.
5. Stranger—add scores for items 3, 8, 12, and 17; divide sum by 4. Scores above 63 = high WTC, scores below 18 = low WTC with these receivers.
6. Acquaintance—add scores for items 4, 11, 15, and 20; divide sum by 4. Scores above 92 = high WTC, scores below 57 = low WTC with these receivers.
7. Friends—add scores for items 6, 9, 14, and 19; divide sum by 4. Scores above 99 = high WTC, scores below 71 = low WTC with these receivers.

To compute the total score for the WTC, add the totals for stranger, friend, and acquaintance; then divide by 3. Scores above 82 = high WTC, below 52 = low WTC.

Group Discussion	> 89 High WTC, < 57 Low WTC
Meetings	> 80 High WTC, < 39 Low WTC
Interpersonal Conversations	> 94 High WTC, < 64 Low WTC
Public Speaking	> 78 High WTC, < 33 Low WTC
Stranger	> 63 High WTC, < 18 Low WTC
Acquaintance	> 92 High WTC, < 57 Low WTC
Friend	> 99 High WTC, < 71 Low WTC
Total WTC	> 82 High Overall WTC
	< 52 Low Overall WTC

Source: This instrument is based on research reported by McCroskey, J. C. (1992). Reliability and validity of the willingness to communicate scale. *Communication Quarterly, 40,* 16–25; and McCroskey, J. C., & Richmond, V. P. (1987). Willingness to communicate. In J. C. McCroskey & J. A. Daly (Eds.), *Personality and interpersonal communication* (pp. 119–131). Newbury Park, CA: Sage.

SCALE 11 Personal Report of Communication Apprehension–24

Directions: This instrument is composed of 24 statements concerning feelings about communicating with other people. Pleased indicate the degree to which each statement applies to you. Please record your responses on the line before each item:

Strongly Disagree	Disagree	Neutral	Agree	Strongly Agree
1	2	3	4	5

_____ 1. I dislike participating in group discussions.

_____ 2. Generally, I am comfortable while participating in group discussions.

_____ 3. I am tense and nervous while participating in group discussions.

_____ 4. I like to get involved in group discussions.

_____ 5. Engaging in a group discussion with new people makes me tense and nervous.

_____ 6. I am calm and relaxed while participating in group discussions.

_____ 7. Generally, I am nervous when I have to participate in a meeting.

_____ 8. Usually, I am comfortable when I have to participate in a meeting.

_____ 9. I am very calm and relaxed when I am called upon to express an opinion at a meeting.

_____ 10. I am afraid to express myself at meetings.

_____ 11. Communicating at meetings usually makes me uncomfortable.

_____ 12. I am very relaxed when answering questions at a meeting.

_____ 13. While participating in a conversation with a new acquaintance, I feel very nervous.

_____ 14. I have no fear of speaking up in conversations.

_____ 15. Ordinarily I am very tense and nervous in conversations.

_____ 16. Ordinarily I am very calm and relaxed in conversations.

_____ 17. While conversing with a new acquaintance, I feel very relaxed.

_____ 18. I'm afraid to speak up in conversations.

_____ 19. I have no fear of giving a speech.

_____ 20. Certain parts of my body feel very tense and rigid while giving a speech.

_____ 21. I feel relaxed while giving a speech.

_____ 22. My thoughts become confused and jumbled when I am giving a speech.

_____ 23. I face the prospect of giving a speech with confidence.

_____ 24. While giving a speech, I get so nervous I forget facts I really know.

General Scoring:

Step 1. Begin with a score of 72.

Step 2. Add the scores of items 1, 3, 5, 7, 10, 11, 13, 15, 18, 20, 22, and 24.

Step 3. Add the scores of items 2, 4, 6, 8, 9, 12, 14, 16, 17, 19, 21, and 23.

Step 4. Add the score of Step 1 to the score of Step 2.

Step 5. Subtract the score of Step 3 from the score of Step 4.

Result: Score for Personal Report of Communication Apprehension–24.
Possible score range is 24–120. If your score is above 120 or below 24 you have made an error in scoring.

Specific Scoring:
SCORING: To compute context subscores, begin with a score of 18 for each context and follow the instructions below.

1. Group discussion—add scores for items 2, 4, and 6. Subtract scores for items 1, 3, and 5. Scores can range from 6 to 30.
2. Meetings—add scores for items 8, 9, and 12. Subtract scores for items 7, 10, and 11. Scores can range from 6 to 30.
3. Interpersonal—add scores for items 14, 16, and 17. Subtract scores for items 13, 15, and 18. Scores can range from 6 to 30.
4. Public speaking—add scores for items 19, 21, and 23. Subtract scores for items 20, 22, and 24. Scores can range from 6 to 30.

Source: This instrument is based on research reported by McCroskey, J. C. (1970). Measures of communication-bound anxiety. *Speech Monographs, 37,* 269–277; McCroskey, J. C., (1977). Oral communication apprehension: A summary of recent theory and research. *Human Communication Research, 4,* 78–96; McCroskey, J. C. (1978). *Communication Monographs, 45,* 193–203; McCroskey, J. C., Beatty, M. J., Kearney, P., and Plax, T. G. (1985). The content validity of the PRCA-24 as a measure of communication apprehension across communication contexts. *Communication Quarterly, 33,* 165–173; and Levine, T. R., & McCroskey, J. C. (1990). Measuring trait communication apprehension: A test of rival measurement models of the PRCA-24. *Communication Monographs, 57,* 62–72.

SCALE 12   Compulsive Communication (Talkaholism)

Directions: This instrument is composed of 16 statements concerning communicating with other people. Please indicate the degree to which each statement applies to you. Please record your responses on the line before each item:

Strongly Disagree	Disagree	Neutral	Agree	Strongly Agree
1	2	3	4	5

——— 1. Often I keep quiet when I should talk.

——— 2. I talk more than I should sometimes.

——— 3. Often, I talk when I know I should keep quiet.

——— 4. Sometimes I keep quiet when I know it would be to my advantage to talk.

——— 5. I am a "talkaholic."

——— 6. Sometimes I feel compelled to keep quiet.

——— 7. In general, I talk more than I should.

——— 8. I am a compulsive talker.

——— 9. I am not a talker; rarely do I talk in communication situations.

——— 10. Quite a few people have said I talk too much.

——— 11. I just can't stop talking too much.

——— 12. In general, I talk less than I should.

——— 13. I am not a "talkaholic."

——— 14. Sometimes I talk when I know it would be to my advantage to keep quiet.

——— 15. I talk less than I should sometimes.

——— 16. I am not a compulsive talker.

Scoring:
Step 1. Begin with a score of 12.
Step 2. Add the scores of items 2, 3, 5, 7, 8, 10, 11, and 14.
Step 3. Add the scores for items 13 and 16.
Step 4. Add the score of Step 1 to the score of Step 2.
Step 5. Subtract the score of Step 3 from the score of Step 4.

Result: Score for Compulsive Communication (Talkaholism).
Possible score range is 10–50. If your score is above 50 or below 10 you have made an error in scoring.

Source: McCroskey, J. C., & Richmond, V. P. (1993). Identifying compulsive communicators: The talkaholic scale. *Communication Research Reports, 11,* 39–52. And McCroskey, J. C., & Richmond, V. P. (1995). Correlates of compulsive communication: Quantitative and qualitative characteristics. *Communication Quarterly, 43,* 39–52.

SCALE 13   Self-Perceived Communication Competence

Directions: Below are 12 situations in which you might need to communicate. People's abilities to communicate effectively vary a lot, and sometimes the same person is more competent to communicate in one situation than in another. Please indicate how competent (ranging from completely incompetent = 0 to completely competent = 100) you believe you are to communicate in each of the situations described below. Indicate in the space provided at the left of each item your estimate of your competence.

Presume 0 = completely incompetent and 100 = completely competent.

_____   1. Present a talk to a group of strangers.

_____   2. Talk with an acquaintance.

_____   3. Talk in a large meeting of friends.

_____   4. Talk in a small group of strangers.

_____   5. Talk with a friend.

_____   6. Talk in a large meeting of acquaintances.

_____   7. Talk with a stranger.

_____   8. Present a talk to a group of friends.

_____   9. Talk in a small group of acquaintances.

_____   10. Talk in a large meeting of strangers.

_____   11. Talk in a small group of friends.

_____   12. Present a talk to a group of acquaintances.

Scoring:
Step 1.   Add the scores for all 12 situations.
Step 2.   Divide the score of Step 1 by 12.

Result: Score for Self-Perceived Communication Competence.
Possible score range 0–100. If your score is above 100 you have made an error in scoring.

Source: McCroskey, J. C., & McCroskey, L. L. (1988). Self-report as an approach to measuring communication competence. *Communication Research Reports, 5,* 108–113.

SCALE 14   Assertiveness and Responsiveness

Directions: The questionnaire below lists 20 characteristics of peoples' communication with others. Please indicate the degree to which you believe each of these characteristics applies to you. Please record your responses on the line before each item:

Strongly Disagree	Disagree	Neutral	Agree	Strongly Agree
1	2	3	4	5

_____ 1. Helpful

_____ 2. Defends own beliefs

_____ 3. Independent

_____ 4. Responsive to others

_____ 5. Forceful

_____ 6. Has strong personality

_____ 7. Sympathetic

_____ 8. Compassionate

_____ 9. Assertive

_____ 10. Sensitive to the needs of others

_____ 11. Dominant

_____ 12. Sincere

_____ 13. Gentle

_____ 14. Willing to take a stand

_____ 15. Warm

_____ 16. Tender

_____ 17. Friendly

_____ 18. Acts as a leader

_____ 19. Aggressive

_____ 20. Competitive

Scoring:

For your *assertiveness* score, add responses to items: 2, 3, 5, 6, 9, 11, 14, 18, 19, 20.

For your *responsiveness* score, add responses to items: 1, 4, 7, 8, 10, 12, 13, 15, 16, 17.

Possible score range is 10 to 50 on each measure. If your score is above 50 or below 10 you have made an error in scoring.

Source: Richmond, V. P., & McCroskey, J. C. (1990). Reliability and separation of factors on the assertiveness-responsiveness scale. *Psychological Reports, 67,* 449–450.

SCALE 15   Nonverbal Immediacy Scale–Self-Report (NIS-S)

Directions: The following statements describe the ways some people behave while talking with or to others. Please indicate in the space at the left of each item the degree to which you believe the statement applies to you.

Never	Rarely	Occasionally	Often	Very Often
1	2	3	4	5

_____ 1. I use my hands and arms to gesture while talking to people.

_____ 2. I touch others on the shoulder or arm while talking to them.

_____ 3. I use a monotone or dull voice while talking to people.

_____ 4. I look over or away from others while talking to them.

_____ 5. I move away from others when they touch me while we are talking.

_____ 6. I have a relaxed body position when I talk to people.

_____ 7. I frown while talking to people.

_____ 8. I avoid eye contact while talking to people.

_____ 9. I have a tense body position while talking to people.

_____ 10. I sit close or stand close to people while talking with them.

_____ 11. My voice is monotonous or dull when I talk to people.

_____ 12. I use a variety of vocal expressions when I talk to people.

_____ 13. I gesture when I talk to people.

_____ 14. I am animated when I talk to people.

_____ 15. I have a bland facial expression when I talk to people.

_____ 16. I move closer to people when I talk to them.

_____ 17. I look directly at people while talking to them.

_____ 18. I am stiff when I talk to people.

_____ 19. I have a lot of vocal variety when I talk to people.

_____ 20. I avoid gesturing while I am talking to people.

_____ 21. I lean toward people when I talk to them.

_____ 22. I maintain eye contact with people when I talk to them.

_____ 23. I try not to sit or stand close to people when I talk with them.

_____ 24. I lean away from people when I talk to them.

_____ 25. I smile when I talk to people.

_____ 26. I avoid touching people when I talk to them.

Scale 15 Scoring:
Step 1.   Begin with a score of 78.
Step 2.   Add the scores of items 1, 2, 6, 10, 12, 13, 14, 16, 17, 19, 21, 22, and 25.
Step 3.   Add the scores of items 3, 4, 5, 7, 8, 9, 11, 15, 18, 20, 23, 24, and 26.
Step 4.   Add the score of Step 1 to the score of Step 2.
Step 5.   Subtract the score of Step 3 from the score of Step 4.

Result: Score for Self-Reported Nonverbal Immediacy.
Possible score range is 26 to 130. If your score is above 130 or below 26 you have made an error in scoring.

Source: Richmond, V. P., McCroskey, J. C., & Johnson, A. D. (2003). Development of the Nonverbal Immediacy Scale (NIS): Measures of self- and other-perceived nonverbal immediacy. *Communication Quarterly, 51,* 504–517.

SCALE 16 Nonverbal Immediacy Scale–Observer-Report (NIS-O)

Directions: The following statements describe the ways some people behave while talking with or to others. Please indicate in the space at the left of each item the degree to which you believe the statement applies to: **Your supervisor in the most recent job you have had.** Please record your responses on the line before each item.

Never	Rarely	Occasionally	Often	Very Often
1	2	3	4	5

_____ 1. He/she uses her/his hands and arms to gesture while talking to people.

_____ 2. He/she touches others on the shoulder or arm while talking to them.

_____ 3. He/she uses a monotone or dull voice while talking to people.

_____ 4. He/she looks over or away from others while talking to them.

_____ 5. He/she moves away from others when they touch me while we are talking.

_____ 6. He/she has a relaxed body position when he/she talks to people.

_____ 7. He/she frowns while talking to people.

_____ 8. He/she avoids eye contact while talking to people.

_____ 9. He/she has a tense body position while talking to people.

_____ 10. He/she sits close or stands close to people while talking with them.

_____ 11. Her/his voice is monotonous or dull when he/she talks to people.

_____ 12. He/she uses a variety of vocal expressions when he/she talks to people.

_____ 13. He/she gestures when he/she talks to people.

_____ 14. He/she is animated when he/she talk to people.

_____ 15. He/she has a bland facial expression when he/she talks to people.

_____ 16. He/she moves closer to people when he/she talks to them.

_____ 17. He/she looks directly at people while talking to them.

_____ 18. He/she is stiff when he/she talks to people.

_____ 19. He/she has a lot of vocal variety when he/she talks to people.

_____ 20. He/she avoids gesturing while he/she is talking to people.

_____ 21. He/she leans toward people when he/she talks to them.

_____ 22. He/she maintains eye contact with people when he/she talks to them.

_____ 23. He/she tries not to sit or stand close to people when he/she talks with them.

_____ 24. He/she leans away from people when he/she talks to them.

_____ 25. He/she smiles when he/she talks to people.

_____ 26. He/she avoids touching people when he/she talks to them.

Scoring:

Step 1. Begin with a score of 78.
Step 2. Add the scores of items 1, 2, 6, 10, 12, 13, 14, 16, 17, 19, 21, 22, and 25.
Step 3. Add the scores of items 3, 4, 5, 7, 8, 9, 11, 15, 18, 20, 23, 24, and 26.
Step 4. Add the score of Step 1 to the score of Step 2.
Step 5. Subtract the score of Step 3 from the score of Step 4.

Result: Score for Other-Reported Nonverbal Immediacy.
Possible score range is 26 to 130. If your score is above 130 or below 26 you have made an error in scoring.

Source: Richmond, V. P., McCroskey, J. C., & Johnson, A. D. (2003). Development of the Nonverbal Immediacy Scale (NIS): Measures of self- and other-perceived nonverbal immediacy. *Communication Quarterly, 51,* 504–517.

SCALE 17   Generalized Attitude Measure

Directions: Below are 6 bipolar scale items relating to one's attitude toward: **Capital Punishment.** Please indicate your attitude toward capital punishment by circling one number for each bipolar scale item. Numbers "1" and "7" indicate a very strong feeling. Numbers "6" and "2" indicate a strong feeling. Numbers "5" and "3" indicate a fairly weak feeling. Number "4" indicates you are undecided, or you do not understand the adjectives themselves. Be sure to circle one, and only one, number for each scale item.

1. Good	7	6	5	4	5	2	1	Bad
2. Wrong	1	2	3	4	5	6	7	Right
3. Harmful	1	2	3	4	5	6	7	Beneficial
4. Fair	7	6	5	4	5	2	1	Unfair
5. Wise	7	6	5	4	5	2	1	Foolish
6. Negative	1	2	3	4	5	6	7	Positive

Scoring:
Add the number you circled above for each row. _____

Result: Score for General Attitude Measure/Capital Punishment.
Possible score range 6–42. If your score is above 42 or below 6 you have made an error in scoring.

Earlier Research:
McCroskey, J. C. (1966). *Experimental studies of the effects of ethos and evidence in persuasive communication.* Unpublished doctoral dissertation. Pennsylvania State University.

McCroskey, J. C., & Richmond, V. P. (1989). Bipolar scales. In P. Emmert & L. L. Barker (Eds.), *Measurement of Communication Behavior* (pp. 154–167). New York: Longman.

Source: McCroskey, J. C. (2006). Reliability and validity of the Generalized Attitude Measure and Generalized Belief Measure. *Communication Quarterly, 54,* 265–274.

SCALE 18   Attitude toward Capital Punishment

Directions: Below are 8 statements about capital punishment. Please indicate the degree to which you agree with each statement on the line before the statement. Please use the possible responses noted below.

Strongly Disagree	Disagree	Neutral	Agree	Strongly Agree
1	2	3	4	5

_____ 1. Capital punishment is nothing but legalized murder.

_____ 2. Capital punishment should be abolished in all states and territories.

_____ 3. There is no crime which justifies capital punishment.

_____ 4. In most cases when the death penalty is enforced it is justified.

_____ 5. Capital punishment is a justifiable means for society to use to protect itself from certain types of criminals.

_____ 6. Capital punishment gives a murderer just what he/she deserves.

_____ 7. States which have abolished capital punishment should reestablish it.

_____ 8. Vicious criminals deserve capital punishment.

Scoring:

Step 1.   Begin with a score of 24.

Step 2.   Add the scores of items 4, 5, 6, and 8.

Step 3.   Add the scores of items 1, 2, 3, and 7.

Step 4.   Add the score of Step 1 to the score of Step 2.

Step 5.   Subtract the score of Step 3 from the score of Step 4.

Result: Score for Attitude toward Capital Punishment.

Possible score range 8–40. If your score is above 40 or below 8 you have made an error in scoring.

Source: McCroskey, J. C. (1966). Experimental studies of the effects of ethos and evidence in persuasive communication. Doctoral dissertation, Pennsylvania State University, State College. http://www.jamescmccroskey.com/publications/jim.pdf.

SCALE 19   Generalized Belief Measure

Directions: On the 5 bipolar scale items below, please indicate the degree to which you believe the following statement: I am very satisfied with the job I have. Circle the number between the adjectives which best represents your beliefs. Numbers "1" and "7" indicate a very strong belief. Numbers "2" and "6" indicate a strong belief. Numbers "3" and "5" indicate a fairly weak belief. Number "4" indicates you are undecided, or you do not understand the adjectives. Circle one, and only one, number for each item.

1. Agree	7	6	5	4	5	2	1	Disagree
2. False	1	2	3	4	5	6	7	True
3. Correct	7	6	5	4	5	2	1	Incorrect
4. Wrong	1	2	3	4	5	6	7	Right
5. No	1	2	3	4	5	6	7	Yes

Scoring:
Add the number you circled above for each row. _____

Result: Score for Generalized Belief Scale/Job Satisfaction.
Possible score range 5–25. If your score is above 25 or below 5 you have made an error in scoring.

Earlier Research:
McCroskey, J. C. (1966). Experimental studies of the effects of ethos and evidence in persuasive communication. Doctoral dissertation, Pennsylvania State University, State College. http://www.jamescmccroskey.com/publications/jim.pdf.

McCroskey, J. C., & Richmond, V. P. (1989). Bipolar scales. In P. Emmert & L. L. Barker (Eds.), *Measurement of Communication Behavior* (pp. 154–167). New York: Longman.

Source: McCroskey, J. C. (2006). Reliability and validity of the Generalized Attitude Measure and Generalized Belief Measure. *Communication Quarterly, 54,* 265–274.

SCALE 20   Willingness to Listen (WTL)

Directions: The following 24 statements refer to listening. Please record your responses on the line before each item.

Never	Rarely	Occasionally	Often	Very Often
1	2	3	4	5

_____ 1. I dislike listening to boring speakers.

_____ 2. Generally, I can listen to a boring speaker.

_____ 3. I am bored and tired while listening to a boring speaker.

_____ 4. I will listen when the content of a speech is boring.

_____ 5. Listening to boring speakers about boring content makes me tired, sleepy, and bored.

_____ 6. I am willing to listen to boring speakers about boring content.

_____ 7. Generally, I am unwilling to listen when there is noise during a speaker's presentation.

_____ 8. Usually, I am willing to listen when there is noise during a speaker's presentation.

_____ 9. I am accepting and willing to listen to speakers who do not adapt to me.

_____ 10. I am unwilling to listen to speakers who do not do some adaptation to me.

_____ 11. Being preoccupied with other things makes me less willing to listen to a speaker.

_____ 12. I am willing to listen to a speaker even if I have other things on my mind.

_____ 13. While being occupied with other things on my mind, I am unwilling to listen to a speaker.

_____ 14. I have a willingness to listen to a speaker, even if other important things are on my mind.

_____ 15. Generally, I will not listen to a speaker who is disorganized.

_____ 16. Generally, I will try to listen to a speaker who is disorganized.

_____ 17. While listening to a nonimmediate, nonresponsive speaker, I feel relaxed with the speaker.

_____ 18. While listening to a nonimmediate, nonresponsive speaker, I feel distant and cold toward that speaker.

_____ 19. I can listen to a nonimmediate, nonresponsive speaker.

_____ 20. I am unwilling to listen to a nonimmediate, nonresponsive speaker.

_____ 21. I am willing to listen to a speaker with views different from mine.

_____ 22. I am unwilling to listen to a speaker with views different from mine.

_____ 23. I am willing to listen to a speaker who is not clear about what he or she wants to say.

_____ 24. I am unwilling to listen to a speaker who is not clear, not credible, and abstract.

Scoring:

Step 1. Begin with a score of 64.

Step 2. Add the scores of items 2, 4, 6, 8, 9, 12, 14, 16, 17, 19, 21, and 23.

Step 3. Add the scores of items 1, 3, 5, 7, 10, 11, 13, 15, 18, 20, 22, and 24.

Step 4. Add the score of Step 1 to the score of Step 2.

Step 5. Subtract the score of Step 3 from the score of Step 4.

Result: Score for Willingness to Listen.

Possible score range is 24 to 120. If your score is above 120 or below 24 you have made an error in scoring.

Scores above 80 indicate a high willingness to listen.

Scores below 50 indicate a low willingness to listen.

Source: Richmond, V. P., & Hickson, M. III. (2001). *Going public: A practical guide to public talk.* Boston: Allyn & Bacon.

SCALE 21 Tolerance for Disagreement

Directions: This questionnaire involves people's feelings and orientations. Hence, there are no right or wrong answers. We just want you to indicate your reaction to each item. All responses are to reflect the degree to which you believe the item applies to you. Please indicate your response in the space before each item.

StronglyDisagree	Disagree	Neutral	Agree	Strongly Agree
1	2	3	4	5

_____ 1. It is more fun to be involved in a discussion where there is a lot of disagreement.

_____ 2. I enjoy talking to people with points of view different than mine.

_____ 3. I don't like to be in situations where people are in disagreement.

_____ 4. I prefer being in groups where everyone's beliefs are the same as mine.

_____ 5. Disagreements are generally helpful.

_____ 6. I prefer to change the topic of discussion when disagreement occurs.

_____ 7. I tend to create disagreements in conversations because it serves a useful purpose.

_____ 8. I enjoy arguing with other people about things on which we disagree.

_____ 9. I would prefer to work independently rather than to work with other people and have disagreements.

_____ 10. I would prefer joining a group where no disagreements occur.

_____ 11. I don't like to disagree with other people.

_____ 12. Given a choice, I would leave a conversation rather than continue a disagreement.

_____ 13. I avoid talking with people who I think will disagree with me.

_____ 14. I enjoy disagreeing with others.

_____ 15. Disagreement stimulates a conversation and causes me to communicate more.

Scoring:
Step 1.   Begin with a score of 48.
Step 2.   Add the scores of items 1, 2, 5, 7, 8, 14, and 15.
Step 3.   Add the scores of items 3, 4, 6, 9, 10, 11, 12, and 13.
Step 4.   Add the score of Step 1 to the score of Step 2.
Step 5.   Subtract the score of Step 3 from the score of Step 5.

Result: Score for Tolerance for Disagreement.
Possible score range is 15–75. If your score is above 75 or less than 15 you have made an error in scoring.

Source: Teven, J. J., Richmond, V. P., & McCroskey, J. C. (1998). Measuring tolerance for disagreement. _Communication Research Reports, 15,_ 209–217.

SCALE 22   Personal Report of Intercultural Communication Apprehension

Directions: This instrument is composed of 16 statements concerning feelings about communicating with people from cultures other than your own. Please indicate the degree to which each statement applies to you. Please record your responses on the line before each item.

Strongly Disagree	Disagree	Neutral	Agree	Strongly Agree
1	2	3	4	5

_____ 1. I dislike interacting with people from different cultures.

_____ 2. Generally, I am comfortable interacting with a group of people from different cultures.

_____ 3. I am tense and nervous while interacting with people from different cultures.

_____ 4. I like to get involved in group discussions with others who are from different cultures.

_____ 5. Engaging in a group discussion with people from different cultures makes me nervous.

_____ 6. I am calm and relaxed while interacting with a group of people who are from different cultures.

_____ 7. While participating in a conversation with a person from a different culture, I get nervous.

_____ 8. I have no fear of speaking up in a conversation with a person from a different culture.

_____ 9. Ordinarily I am very tense and nervous in a conversation with a person from a different culture.

_____ 10. Ordinarily I am very calm and relaxed in conversations with a person from a different culture.

_____ 11. While conversing with a person from a different culture, I feel very relaxed.

_____ 12. I'm afraid to speak up in conversations with a person from a different culture.

_____ 13. I face the prospect of interacting with people from different cultures with confidence.

_____ 14. My thoughts become confused and jumbled when interacting with people from different cultures.

_____ 15. I enjoy interacting with people from different cultures.

_____ 16. Communicating with people from different cultures makes me feel uncomfortable.

Scoring:
Step 1. Begin with a score of 48.
Step 2. Add the scores of items 1, 3, 5, 7, 9, 12, 14, and 16.
Step 3. Add the scores of items 2, 4, 6, 8, 10, 11, 13, and 15.

Step 4. Add the score of Step 1 to the score of Step 2.
Step 5. Subtract the score of Step 3 from the score of Step 4.

Result: Score for Personal Report of Intercultural Communication Apprehension.
Possible score range is 16 to 80. If your score is above 80 or below 16 you have made a scoring error.

Source: Neuliep, J. W., & McCroskey, J. C. (1997). The development of intercultural and inter-ethnic communication apprehension scales. *Communication Research Reports, 14,* 385–398.

SCALE 23 Personal Report of Interethnic Communication Apprehension

Directions: This instrument is composed of 16 statements concerning feelings about communicating with people from ethnic/racial groups other than your own. Please indicate the degree to which each statement applies to you. Please record your responses on the line before each item.

Strongly Disagree	Disagree	Neutral	Agree	Strongly Agree
1	2	3	4	5

_____ 1. I dislike interacting with people from different ethnic/racial groups.

_____ 2. Generally, I am comfortable interacting with a group of people from different ethnic/racial groups.

_____ 3. I am tense and nervous while interacting with people from different ethnic/racial groups.

_____ 4. I like to get involved in group discussions with others who are from different ethnic/racial groups.

_____ 5. Engaging in a group discussion with people from different ethnic/racial groups makes me nervous.

_____ 6. I am calm and relaxed while interacting with a group of people who are from different ethnic/racial groups.

_____ 7. While participating in a conversation with a person from a different ethnic/racial group, I get nervous.

_____ 8. I have no fear of speaking up in a conversation with a person from a different ethnic/racial group.

_____ 9. Ordinarily I am very tense and nervous in a conversation with a person from a different ethnic/racial group.

_____ 10. Ordinarily I am very calm and relaxed in conversations with a person from a different ethnic/racial group.

_____ 11. While conversing with a person from a different ethnic/racial group, I feel very relaxed.

_____ 12. I'm afraid to speak up in conversations with a person from a different ethnic/racial group.

_____ 13. I face the prospect of interacting with people from different ethnic/racial groups with confidence.

_____ 14. My thoughts become confused and jumbled when interacting with people from different ethnic/racial groups.

_____ 15. I enjoy interacting with people from different ethnic/racial groups.

_____ 16. Communicating with people from different ethnic/racial groups makes me feel uncomfortable.

Scoring:
Step 1. Begin with a score of 48.
Step 2. Add the scores of items 1, 3, 5, 7, 9, 12, 14, and 16.

Step 3. Add the scores of items 2, 4, 6, 8, 10, 11, 13, and 15.

Step 4. Add the score of Step 1 to the score of Step 2.

Step 5. Subtract the score of Step 3 from the score of Step 4.

Result: Score for Personal Report of Interethnic Communication Apprehension.

Possible score range is 16–80. If your score is above 80 or below 16 you have made a scoring error.

Source: Neuliep, J. W., & McCroskey, J. C. (1997). The development of intercultural and inter-ethnic communication apprehension scales. *Communication Research Reports, 14*, 385–398.

SCALE 24   Ethnocentrism

Directions: Below are items that relate to the cultures of different parts of the world. Work quickly and record your first reaction to each item. There are no right or wrong answers. Please indicate the degree to which you agree or disagree with each item using the following five-point scale:

Strongly Disagree	Disagree	Neutral	Agree	Strongly Agree
1	2	3	4	5

_____   1. Most other cultures are backward compared to my culture.

_____   2. My culture should be the role model for other cultures.

_____   3. People from other cultures act strange when they come to my culture.

_____   4. Lifestyles in other cultures are just as valid as those in my culture.

_____   5. Other cultures should try to be more like my culture.

_____   6. I am not interested in the values and customs of other cultures.

_____   7. People in my culture could learn a lot from people in other cultures.

_____   8. Most people from other cultures just don't know what's good for them.

_____   9. I respect the values and customs of other cultures.

_____ 10. Other cultures are smart to look up to our culture.

_____ 11. Most people would be happier if they lived like people in my culture.

_____ 12. I have many friends from different cultures.

_____ 13. People in my culture have just about the best lifestyles of anywhere.

_____ 14. Lifestyles in other cultures are not as valid as those in my culture.

_____ 15. I am very interested in the values and customs of other cultures.

_____ 16. I apply my values when judging people who are different.

_____ 17. I see people who are similar to me as virtuous.

_____ 18. I do not cooperate with people who are different.

_____ 19. Most people in my culture just don't know what is good for them.

_____ 20. I do not trust people who are different.

_____ 21. I dislike interacting with people from different cultures.

_____ 22. I have little respect for the values and customs of other cultures.

Scoring:
Step 1.   Begin with a score of 18.
Step 2.   Add the scores of items 1, 2, 5, 8, 10, 11, 13, 14, 18, 20, 21, and 22.
Step 3.   Add the scores of items 4, 7, and 9.
Step 4.   Add the score of Step 1 to the score of Step 2.
Step 5.   Subtract the score of Step 3 from the score of Step 4.

Result: Score for Ethnocentrism.
Possible score range is 15 to 75. If your score is above 75 or below 15 you have made a scoring error.

Source: Neuliep, J. W., & McCroskey, J. C. (1997). The development of a U.S. and generalized ethnocentrism scale. *Communication Research Reports, 14,* 385–398.

SCALE 25   Homonegativity

Directions: Below are several descriptions of how some people feel about homosexuals. Please use the scale below to rate the degree to which each statement applies to you. Please be completely honest. Otherwise your score will be meaningless. Please indicate the degree to which you agree or disagree with each item using the following five-point scale:

Strongly Disagree	Disagree	Neutral	Agree	Strongly Agree
1	2	3	4	5

_____ 1. Gay and lesbian people make me nervous.

_____ 2. Homosexuality is perfectly normal.

_____ 3. I wouldn't want to have gay or lesbian friends.

_____ 4. I would trust a gay or lesbian person.

_____ 5. I fear homosexual persons will make sexual advances towards me.

_____ 6. I would have no problem living with someone who is gay or lesbian.

_____ 7. Homosexual behavior should be perfectly legal.

_____ 8. I would have a serious problem if I saw two men or women kissing in public.

_____ 9. I think that gay and lesbian people need civil rights protection.

_____ 10. When I see a gay or lesbian person I think, "What a waste."

Scoring:

Step 1. Begin with a score of 30.
Step 2. Add the scores of items 1, 3, 5, 8, and 10.
Step 3. Add the scores of items 2, 4, 6, 7, and 9.
Step 4. Add the score of Step 1 to the score of Step 2.
Step 5. Subtract the score of Step 3 from the score of Step 4.

Result: Score for Homonegativity.
Possible score range is 10 to 50. If your score is above 50 or below 10 you have made a scoring error.

Source: Wrench, J. S. (2005). Development and validity testing of the homonegativity short form. *Journal of Intercultural Communication Research, 34,* 152–165. Wrench, J. S. (2001). *Intercultural communication: Power in context.* Acton, MA: Tapestry Press.

SCALE 26   Sexual Communication Style Scale

Directions: Below are a series of statements that describe the ways some people communicate while having a sexual relationship. You are asked to indicate how well each statement applies to your current or most recent sexual partner's communication behavior. For each statement, choose the number that most closely describes your perception of your partner's behavior. Indicate your perception on the line before each statement.

Strongly Disagree	Disagree	Neutral	Agree	Strongly Agree
1	2	3	4	5

_____ 1. My partner does not verbally tell me when he/she is sexually satisfied.

_____ 2. My partner demonstrates what he/she likes sexually through her/his nonverbal communication.

_____ 3. My partner verbally tells me when he/she is sexually satisfied.

_____ 4. My partner demonstrates nonverbally what "turns them on" during sex.

_____ 5. My partner verbally communicates during sex.

_____ 6. I can tell when my partner is sexually satisfied through her/his nonverbal communication.

_____ 7. My partner does not verbally communicate during sex.

_____ 8. I cannot tell when my partner is sexually satisfied through her/his nonverbal communication.

_____ 9. My partner talks during sex.

_____ 10. I can tell from my partner's nonverbal behavior whether he/she is enjoying sex.

_____ 11. My partner does not verbally tell me what he/she finds pleasing during sex.

_____ 12. My partner does not nonverbally demonstrate what turns him/her on during sex.

_____ 13. My partner is verbally communicative during sex.

_____ 14. My partner does not communicate nonverbally that he/she is sexually satisfied.

_____ 15. My partner does not verbally tell me when he/she is enjoying sex.

_____ 16. My partner does not show me nonverbally when he/she is sexually satisfied.

_____ 17. My partner does not verbally demonstrate what he/she likes sexually.

_____ 18. My partner nonverbally communicates that he/she is sexually satisfied.

Scoring for Verbal Sexual Communication Style:
Step 1.   Begin with a score of 30.
Step 2.   Add the scores of items 3, 5, 9, and 13.
Step 3.   Add the scores of items 1, 7, 11, 15, and 17.

Step 4.   Add the score of Step 1 to the score of Step 2.
Step 5.   Subtract the score of Step 3 from the score of Step 4.

Scoring for Nonverbal Sexual Communication Style:
Step 1.   Begin with a score of 24.
Step 2.   Add the scores of items 2, 4, 6, 10, and 18.
Step 3.   Add the scores of items 8, 12, 14, and 16.
Step 4.   Add the score of Step 1 to the score of Step 2.
Step 5.   Subtract the score of Step 3 from the score of Step 4.

Result: Score for Nonverbal Sexual Communication Style.
Possible score range for both Verbal and Nonverbal Sexual Communication Style is 9 to 45. If your score is above 45 or below 9 you have made a scoring error.

Source: Wrench, J. S., Brogan, S. M., & Fiore, A. M. (2005, November). *Understanding the psychometric properties of the Sexual Communication Style Scale.* Paper presented at the National Communication Association Annual Convention, Boston.

SCALE 27 Satisfaction with Physician

Directions: Below are 3 bipolar scale items relating to how you feel about interactions with your physician. Please indicate how you feel about interacting with your physician by circling one number for each bipolar scale item. Numbers "1" and "7" indicate a very strong feeling. Numbers "6" and "2" indicate a strong feeling. Numbers "5" and "3" indicate a fairly weak feeling. Number "4" indicates you are undecided, or you do not understand the adjectives themselves. Be sure to circle one, and only one, number for each scale item.

1. Pleased	7	6	5	4	5	2	1	Displeased
2. Unsatisfied	1	2	3	4	5	6	7	Satisfied
3. Comfortable	7	6	5	4	5	2	1	Uncomfortable

Scoring:
Add the number you circled above for each row. _____

Result: Score for Satisfaction with Physician.
Possible score range is 3 to 21. If your score is above 21 or below 3 you have made a scoring error.

Source: Richmond, V. P., Smith, R. S., Jr., Heisel, A. M., & McCroskey, J. C. (1998). The impact of communication apprehension and fear of talking with a physician on perceived medical outcomes. *Communication Research Reports, 15,* 344–353.

SCALE 28   Perceived Quality of Medical Care

Directions: Below are 6 bipolar scale items relating to how you feel about the kind of medical care that you get from your physician. Please indicate how you feel about your medical care by circling one number for each bipolar scale item. Numbers "1" and "7" indicate a very strong feeling. Numbers "6" and "2" indicate a strong feeling. Numbers "5" and "3" indicate a fairly weak feeling. Number "4" indicates you are undecided, or you do not understand the adjectives themselves. Be sure to circle one, and only one, number for each scale item.

1.	High Quality	7	6	5	4	5	2	1	Low Quality
2.	Personable	7	6	5	4	5	2	1	Impersonal
3.	Uncaring	1	2	3	4	5	6	7	Caring
4.	Unconcerned	1	2	3	4	5	6	7	Concerned
5.	Beneficial	7	6	5	4	5	2	1	Not Beneficial
6.	Unsatisfactory	1	2	3	4	5	6	7	Satisfactory

Scoring:
Add the number you circled above for each row. _____

Result: Score for Perceived Quality of Medical Care.
Possible score range is 6 to 42. If your score is above 42 or below 6 you have made a scoring error.

Source: Richmond, V. P., Smith, R. S., Jr., Heisel, A. M., & McCroskey, J. C. (1998). The impact of communication apprehension and fear of talking with a physician on perceived medical outcomes. *Communication Research Reports, 15,* 344–353.

SCALE 29   Fear of Physician

Directions: Below are 5 items that relate to how people feel about interacting with their physician. Please indicate the degree to which you agree or disagree with each item using the following five-point scale. Indicate your response on the line before each item.

Strongly Disagree	Disagree	Neutral	Agree	Strongly Agree
1	2	3	4	5

_____ 1. When communicating with my physician, I feel tense.

_____ 2. When communicating with my physician, I feel calm.

_____ 3. When communicating with my physician, I feel jittery.

_____ 4. When communicating with my physician, I feel nervous.

_____ 5. When communicating with my physician, I feel relaxed.

Scoring:

Step 1.   Begin with a score of 12.

Step 2.   Add the scores for items 1, 3, and 4.

Step 3.   Add the scores for items 2 and 5.

Step 4.   Add the score of Step 1 to the score of Step 2.

Step 5.   Subtract the score of Step 3 from the score of Step 4.

Result: Score for Fear of Physician.

Possible score range is 5 to 25. If your score is above 25 or below 5 you have made a scoring error.

Source: Richmond, V. P., Smith, R. S., Jr., Heisel, A. M., & McCroskey, J. C. (1998). The impact of communication apprehension and fear of talking with a physician on perceived medical outcomes. _Communication Research Reports, 15,_ 344–353.

SCALE 30   Health Locus of Control

Directions: The following questions are concerned with how you perceive yourself across a variety of issues. Please indicate the degree to which each of these statements applies to you by using the following five-point scale. Indicate your response on the line before each item.

Strongly Disagree	Disagree	Neutral	Agree	Strongly Agree
1	2	3	4	5

_____ 1. When I get sick, I can control how long it takes me to heal.

_____ 2. I am not in control of my own health.

_____ 3. I can stay healthy by taking good care of myself.

_____ 4. If I get sick, there's nothing I can do about it.

_____ 5. When I am sick, I'm generally the one to blame.

_____ 6. There is nothing I can do to ensure my health.

_____ 7. If I take care of myself, I can avoid getting sick.

_____ 8. Getting sick is a matter of bad luck.

_____ 9. When I get sick, I know it's because I was not taking care of my health.

_____ 10. Most things that affect my health happen by accident.

_____ 11. Good and bad luck control the state of my health.

_____ 12. I control the destiny of my health.

_____ 13. When I'm sick, I just let nature run its course because there's nothing I can do.

_____ 14. If I take care of myself, I will pretty much stay healthy.

_____ 15. I am responsible for my own health.

_____ 16. Being healthy or being sick is simply a matter of fate.

Scoring:

Step 1. Begin with a score of 48.

Step 2. Add scores for items 1, 3, 5, 7, 9, 11, 13, and 15.

Step 3. Add scores for items 2, 4, 6, 8, 10, 12, 14, and 16.

Step 4. Add the score of Step 1 to the score of Step 2.

Step 5. Subtract the score of Step 3 from the score of Step 4.

Result: Score for Health Locus of Control.

Possible score range is 16 to 80. If your score is above 80 or below 16 you have made a scoring error. Higher scores indicate an internal locus of control.

Source: Wrench, J. S. (2005). Health locus of control. In. J. Hladek (Ed.), _The Wellness Bridge manual_ (p. 80). St. Clairsville, OH: Wellness Bridge.

SCALE 31 Risk Communicator Style Scale

Directions: Below are several descriptions examining the way your primary care physician may educate you about health risks. Please the following scale to rate the degree to which each statement applies to the way your primary care physician explains risk(s). Indicate your response on the line before each item.

Strongly Disagree	Disagree	Neutral	Agree	Strongly Agree
1	2	3	4	5

_____ 1. The risk communicator(s) used statistics during the presentation about the risk.

_____ 2. The risk communicator(s) was concerned with my perception of the risks involved.

_____ 3. The risk communicator(s) did not use statistical information while discussing the risk.

_____ 4. The risk communicator(s) tried to understand our concerns about risks.

_____ 5. The risk communicator(s) used statistics to communicate risks.

_____ 6. The risk communicator(s) wanted me to feel satisfactorily informed about the risks involved.

_____ 7. The risk communicator(s) presented the risks scientifically.

_____ 8. The risk communicator(s) did not listen to my point of view about the risks involved.

_____ 9. The risk communicator(s) presented a scientific analysis of the risk.

_____ 10. The risk communicator(s) cared about my perceptions of the risks involved.

_____ 11. The risk communicator(s) did not present the risks scientifically.

_____ 12. The risk communicator(s) did not care if I was informed or not.

_____ 13. The risk communicator(s) used statistical information while discussing the risk.

_____ 14. The risk communicator(s) did not care about my perceptions of the risks involved.

_____ 15. The risk communicator(s) used mathematical information to explain the risk.

_____ 16. The risk communicator(s) did not care about our concerns about the risks involved.

_____ 17. The risk communicator(s) did not discuss the risk using scientific information.

_____ 18. The risk communicator(s) listened to my point of view about the risks involved.

_____ 19. The risk communicator(s) did not use statistics during the presentation about the risk.

_____ 20. The risk communicator(s) did not want me to participate in the decision-making process.

Scoring (Two Scores Are Generated):
For Technical Risk Communication

Step 1.   Begin with a score of 24.
Step 2.   Add scores for items 1, 5, 7, 9, 13, and 15.
Step 3.   Add scores for items 3, 11, 17, and 19.
Step 4.   Add the score of Step 1 to the score of Step 2.
Step 5.   Subtract the score of Step 3 from the score of Step 4.

For Democratic Risk Communication
Step 1.   Begin with a score of 30.
Step 2.   Add scores for items 2, 4, 6, 10, and 18.
Step 3.   Add scores for items 8, 12, 14, 16, and 20.
Step 4.   Add the score of Step 1 to the score of Step 2.
Step 5.   Subtract the score of Step 3 from the score of Step 4.

Result: Score for Technical and Democratic Risk Communication.
Possible score range for both technical and democratic communicator style is 10 to 50. If your score on either is above 50 or below 10 you have made a scoring error.

Source: Wrench, J. S. (2005). *The development and validity testing of the Risk Communicator Style Scale and the Risk Knowledge Index.* Unpublished doctoral dissertation, West Virginia University, Morgantown.

SCALE 32 CMC Communication Apprehension Scale (E-mail)

Directions: This set of questions asks you about how you feel while communicating using e-mail. If you have never used e-mail, do not respond to this scale. Please indicate the degree to which each of these statements applies to you by using the following five-point scale. Indicate your response on the line before each item.

Strongly Disagree	Disagree	Neutral	Agree	Strongly Agree
1	2	3	4	5

_____ 1. When communicating using e-mail, I feel tense.

_____ 2. When communicating using e-mail, I feel calm.

_____ 3. When communicating using e-mail, I feel jittery.

_____ 4. When communicating using e-mail, I feel nervous.

_____ 5. When communicating using e-mail, I feel relaxed.

Scoring:

Step 1. Begin with a score of 12.

Step 2. Add the scores for items 1, 3, and 4.

Step 3. Add the scores for items 2 and 5.

Step 4. Add the score of Step 1 to the score of Step 2.

Step 5. Subtract the score of Step 3 from the score of Step 4.

Result: Score for E-mail.
Possible score range is 5 to 25. If your score is above 25 or below 5 you have made a scoring error.

Source: This measure is based on the Fear of Physician Scale and was first utilized by: Wrench, J. S., & Punyanunt-Carter, N. M. (2005, October). _The relationship between computer-mediated communication competence, apprehension, self-efficacy and presence._ Paper presented at the Ohio Communication Association's Convention, Dayton.

SCALE 33   CMC Communication Apprehension Scale (Chat Room, IRC, or MUD)

Directions: This set of questions asks you about how you feel while communicating in online chat rooms, IRCs, or MUDs. If you have never used chat rooms, IRCs, or MUDs, please do not complete this measure. Please indicate the degree to which each of these statements applies to you by using the following five-point scale. Indicate your response on the line before each item.

Strongly Disagree	Disagree	Neutral	Agree	Strongly Agree
1	2	3	4	5

_____   1. When communicating in a chat room, IRC, or MUD, I feel tense.

_____   2. When communicating in a chat room, IRC, or MUD, I feel calm.

_____   3. When communicating in a chat room, IRC, or MUD, I feel jittery.

_____   4. When communicating in a chat room, IRC, or MUD, I feel nervous.

_____   5. When communicating in a chat room, IRC, or MUD, I feel relaxed.

Scoring:

Step 1. Begin with a score of 12.
Step 2. Add the scores for items 1, 3, and 4.
Step 3. Add the scores for items 2 and 5.
Step 4. Add the score of Step 1 to the score of Step 2.
Step 5. Subtract the score of Step 3 from the score of Step 4.

Result: Score for Chat Room, IRC, or MUD.
Possible score range is 5 to 25. If your score is above 25 or below 5 you have made a scoring error.

Source: This measure is based on the Fear of Physician Scale and was first utilized by: Wrench, J. S., & Punyanunt-Carter, N. M. (2005, October). The relationship between computer-mediated communication competence, apprehension, self-efficacy and presence. Paper presented at the Ohio Communication Association's Convention, Dayton.

SCALE 34   CMC Communication Apprehension Scale (Internet Messaging)

Directions: This set of questions asks you about how you feel while communicating using **Internet Messaging Programs** like AOL Instant Messenger, Yahoo Messenger, or MSN Messenger. If you have never used Internet Messaging Programs, please do not complete this measure. Please indicate the degree to which each of these statements applies to you by using the following five-point scale. Indicate your response on the line before each item.

Strongly Disagree 1	Disagree 2	Neutral 3	Agree 4	Strongly Agree 5

_____ 1. When communicating using an Internet messaging program, I feel tense.

_____ 2. When communicating using an Internet messaging program, I feel calm.

_____ 3. When communicating using an Internet messaging program, I feel jittery.

_____ 4. When communicating using an Internet messaging program, I feel nervous.

_____ 5. When communicating using an Internet messaging program, I feel relaxed.

Scoring:
Step 1.   Begin with a score of 12.
Step 2.   Add the scores for items 1, 3, and 4.
Step 3.   Add the scores for items 2 and 5.
Step 4.   Add the score of Step 1 to the score of Step 2.
Step 5.   Subtract the score of Step 3 from the score of Step 4.

Result: Score for Internet Messaging.
Possible score range is 5 to 25. If your score is above 25 or below 5 you have made a scoring error.

Source: This measure is based on the Fear of Physician Scale and was first utilized by: Wrench, J. S., & Punyanunt-Carter, N. M. (2005, October). _The relationship between computer-mediated communication competence, apprehension, self-efficacy and presence._ Paper presented at the Ohio Communication Association's Convention, Dayton.

SCALE 35   Organizational Orientations (Upward Mobile)

Directions: Please indicate the degree to which you agree or disagree with each of the statements below by recording your response in the space before each item. Use the following response options:

Strongly Disagree	Disagree	Neutral	Agree	Strongly Agree
1	2	3	4	5

_____ 1. I generally try my best to do what an organization I work for wants me to do.

_____ 2. If I had the choice, I would take a promotion over the acceptance of my peers any time.

_____ 3. One of my goals is to get a good job and excel at it.

_____ 4. Eventually, I would like to be the "big boss" in an organization.

_____ 5. I firmly believe that if I work hard enough, one day I will be right up at the top.

_____ 6. I am good at my job and I love it.

_____ 7. Most of all, I really want to be recognized for the excellent work I do.

_____ 8. Moving up in an organization is worth all the work you have to do.

_____ 9. Sometimes I think I am a "workaholic."

_____ 10. I want a job where what I do really counts for something.

_____ 11. Everyone tells me I am a really good worker.

_____ 12. I want work which has a lot of intangible rewards.

_____ 13. Ordinarily, I feel good about what I have accomplished when I am done with my day's work.

_____ 14. I would be willing to work hard to be the top person in an organization.

_____ 15. Since I am really good at what I do, I will move up in the organization.

_____ 16. What I want most in a job is the possibility of really doing something important.

_____ 17. Any job worth doing is worth doing as well as I can.

_____ 18. I am a very creative worker.

Scoring:
Step 1: Add the scores for items 1 through 18.

Result: Score for Upward Mobile.
Possible score range is 18 to 90. If you score is above 90 or below 18 you have made a scoring error.

Source: McCroskey, J. C., Richmond, V. P., Johnson, A. D., & Smith, H. T. (2004). Organizational orientations theory and measurement: Development of measures and preliminary investigations. _Communication Quarterly, 52,_ 1–14.

SCALE 36　Organizational Orientations (Ambivalent)

Directions: Please indicate the degree to which you agree or disagree with each of the statements below by recording your response in the space before each item. Use the following response options:

Strongly Disagree	Disagree	Neutral	Agree	Strongly Agree
1	2	3	4	5

———— 1. Other than a paycheck, the organizations I have worked for have had little to offer me.

———— 2. The product/service produced by organizations where I have worked are of very low quality.

———— 3. I have generally not been satisfied with the jobs I have had.

———— 4. The organizations I have worked for couldn't care less whether I live or die—and I feel the same way about them.

———— 5. I really dislike the rules and regulations I am forced to live with in organizations.

———— 6. I am usually unhappy wherever I work.

———— 7. Everywhere I have worked, I have had an incompetent supervisor.

———— 8. Wherever I work, I wish I were working somewhere, almost anywhere, else than where I am.

———— 9. The procedures and regulations of organizations I have worked for have not generally been reasonable.

———— 10. I find it difficult to adapt to the demands of most organizations.

———— 11. Generally, I don't like the rules that organizations make me follow.

———— 12. I don't really like most of the people I have worked with.

———— 13. I have not worked for really good organizations.

———— 14. Most organizations have unreasonable expectations for workers like me.

———— 15. Most of the time, a halfhearted effort is all I feel I need to give in a job.

———— 16. I really hate most organizations I have worked for.

———— 17. One supervisor is about like any other, a pain in the backside.

———— 18. What I want most in a job is to be left alone.

———— 19. Frankly, I am smarter than most of the people I have worked for.

———— 20. I have been unhappy just about everywhere I have worked.

Scoring:
Step 1: Add the scores for items 1 through 20.

Result: Score for Ambivalent.
Possible score range is 20 to 100. If your score is above 100 or below 20 you have made a scoring error.

Source: McCroskey, J. C., Richmond, V. P., Johnson, A. D., & Smith, H. T. (2004). Organizational orientations theory and measurement: Development of measures and preliminary investigations. *Communication Quarterly, 52,* 1–14.

SCALE 37   Organizational Orientations (Indifferent)

Directions: Please indicate the degree to which you agree or disagree with each of the statements below by recording your response in the space before each item. Use the following response options:

Strongly Disagree	Disagree	Neutral	Agree	Strongly Agree
1	2	3	4	5

_____ 1. My life begins when I get off work.

_____ 2. If I were offered a job that paid better, I would take it in a "New York minute."

_____ 3. A job is a job—everyone has to work somewhere.

_____ 4. I am generally indifferent to where I work. One job is about the same as another.

_____ 5. Generally, I just do as much as is required by my job.

_____ 6. Since I am entitled to them, I take all of my sick days whether I am sick or not.

_____ 7. I don't much care where I work, so long as the pay is good.

_____ 8. When work is over, life begins.

_____ 9. One job is pretty much like any other job.

_____ 10. If I found out the organization I worked for was in trouble, I would quickly look for a job in another organization.

_____ 11. Work is something I have to do, not something I want to do.

_____ 12. When it comes to choosing a job, "Show me the money!"

Scoring:
Step 1: Add the scores for items 1 through 12.

Result: Score for Indifferent.
Possible score range is 12 to 60. If your score is above 60 or below 12 you have made a scoring error.

Source: McCroskey, J. C., Richmond, V. P., Johnson, A. D., & Smith, H. T. (2004). Organizational orientations theory and measurement: Development of measures and preliminary investigations. _Communication Quarterly, 52,_ 1–14.

SCALE 38 Affective Learning and Affect toward Instructors Measures

Directions: Below are 4 sets of bipolar scale items relating to one's attitude toward a class and teacher. Please indicate your attitude toward the content and teacher you have **in the class you have just before the one you are in now.** Circle one number for each bipolar scale item. Numbers "1" and "7" indicate a very strong feeling. Numbers "6" and "2" indicate a strong feeling. Numbers "5" and "3" indicate a fairly weak feeling. Number "4" indicates you are undecided, or you do not understand the adjectives themselves. Be sure to circle one, and only one, number for each scale item.

I feel the content of the class is:

1. Bad	1	2	3	4	5	6	7	Good
2. Valuable	7	6	5	4	3	2	1	Worthless
3. Unfair	1	2	3	4	5	6	7	Fair
4. Positive	7	6	5	4	3	2	1	Negative

My likelihood of taking future courses in this content (presuming I have that opportunity) are:

5. Unlikely	1	2	3	4	5	6	7	Likely
6. Possible	7	6	5	4	3	2	1	Impossible
7. Improbable	1	2	3	4	5	6	7	Probable
8. Would	7	6	5	4	3	2	1	Would not

Overall, the instructor I have in this class is:

9. Bad	1	2	3	4	5	6	7	Good
10. Valuable	7	6	5	4	3	2	1	Worthless
11. Unfair	1	2	3	4	5	6	7	Fair
12. Positive	7	6	5	4	3	2	1	Negative

Were I to have the opportunity, my likelihood of taking future courses with this specific instructor would be:

13. Unlikely	1	2	3	4	5	6	7	Likely
14. Possible	7	6	5	4	3	2	1	Impossible
15. Improbable	1	2	3	4	5	6	7	Probable
16. Would	7	6	5	4	3	2	1	Would not

Scoring—Affect for Content:
Add the number you circled above for row 1, 2, 3, and 4. _____

Scoring—Taking another Class in the SAME SUBJECT MATTER:
Add the number you circled above for row 5, 6, 7, and 8. _____

To obtain a score for "affective learning," add scores of Scales 37 and 38.

Scoring—Affect for Teacher:
Add the number you circled above for row 9, 10, 11, and 12. _____

Scoring—Taking another Class with the Teacher:
Add the number you circled above for row 13, 13, 14, and 16. _____

To obtain a score for "teacher evaluation," add scores of Scales 39 and 40.

Source: McCroskey, J. C. (1994). Assessment of affect toward communication and affect toward instruction in communication. In S. Morreale & M. Brooks (Eds.), *1994 Summer Conference proceedings and prepared remarks: Assessing college student competence in speech communication.* Annandale, VA: Speech Communication Association.

SCALE 39 Teacher Apprehension Test

Directions: Please indicate the degree to which you agree or disagree with each of the statements below by recording your response in the space before each item. Use the following response options:

Strongly Disagree	Disagree	Neutral	Agree	Strongly Agree
1	2	3	4	5

_____ 1. I feel uncomfortable receiving communication from my teacher.

_____ 2. I feel disturbed when my teacher communicates with me.

_____ 3. I have no fear when my teacher communicates with me.

_____ 4. I am comfortable when my teacher communicates with me.

_____ 5. I feel uneasy when my teacher talks to me.

_____ 6. I feel relaxed when listening to my teacher.

_____ 7. I feel fearful when my teacher talks.

_____ 8. I feel ruffled when my teacher talks to me.

_____ 9. I am jumpy when my teacher talks.

_____ 10. I feel composed when listening to my teacher.

_____ 11. I am bothered when my teacher talks.

_____ 12. I feel satisfied when my teacher is talking and teaching.

_____ 13. I feel safe when my teacher communicates.

_____ 14. I feel nervous when listening to my teacher.

_____ 15. I am cheerful when my teacher is talking.

_____ 16. I feel happy when my teacher is communicating ideas to the class.

_____ 17. I feel dejected or hurt when my teacher is communicating.

_____ 18. I feel pleasure when my teacher talks to me.

_____ 19. I feel good when my instructor is teaching a lesson to us.

_____ 20. I feel happy when he or she is talking to us.

Scoring:
Step 1. Begin with a score of 60.
Step 2. Add scores for items 1, 2, 5, 7, 8, 9, 11, 14, 17, and 20.
Step 3. Add scores for items 3, 4, 6, 10, 12, 13, 15, 16, 18, and 19.
Step 4. Add the score of Step 1 to the score of Step 2.
Step 5. Subtract the score of Step 3 from the score of Step 4.

Result: Score for Teacher Apprehension Test.
Possible score range is 20 to 100. If your score is above 100 or below 20 you have made a scoring error.

Source: Richmond, V. P., Wrench, J. S., & Gorham, J. (2001). *Communication, affect, and learning in the classroom.* Acton, MA: Tapestry Press.

SCALE 40   Evaluation Apprehension Measure

Directions: This measure is composed of statements students have used to describe how they feel in evaluation/examination/testlike situations in their class. Please indicate the degree to which you agree or disagree with each of the statements below by recording your response in the space before each item. Use the following response options:

Strongly Disagree	Disagree	Neutral	Agree	Strongly Agree
1	2	3	4	5

_____ 1. I feel apprehensive while preparing for a test.

_____ 2. I feel tense when I am studying for a test or exam.

_____ 3. I am calm when I am studying for a test.

_____ 4. I feel peaceful when I am studying for a test.

_____ 5. I feel fear and uneasiness when taking an exam or being evaluated.

_____ 6. I feel self-assured when taking an exam.

_____ 7. I feel fearful when preparing for a test.

_____ 8. I feel ruffled when the test is handed to me.

_____ 9. I am jumpy and nervous while taking a test.

_____ 10. I feel composed and in control while taking an exam.

_____ 11. I am bothered and tense when I am being evaluated.

_____ 12. I feel satisfied when my exam is completed.

_____ 13. I feel safe during evaluative situations.

_____ 14. I feel flustered and confused when I start a test.

_____ 15. I am cheerful after I turn in my test.

_____ 16. I feel happy about how I did in evaluation situations.

_____ 17. I feel dejected and humiliated an hour before an exam.

_____ 18. I feel pleased and comfortable while taking a test.

_____ 19. I feel confident while taking a test.

_____ 20. I feel unhappy throughout an exam period.

Scoring:

Step 1. Begin with a score of 60.

Step 2. Add scores for items 1, 2, 5, 7, 8, 9, 11, 14, 17, and 20.

Step 3. Add scores for items 3, 4, 6, 10, 12, 13, 15, 16, 18, and 19.

Step 4. Add the score of Step 1 to the score of Step 2.

Step 5. Subtract the score of Step 3 from the score of Step 4.

Result: Score for Evaluation Apprehension Measure.

Possible scale range is 20 to 100. If your score is above 100 or below 20 you have made a scoring error.

Source: Richmond, V. P., Wrench, J. S., & Gorham, J. (2001). _Communication, affect, and learning in the classroom._ Acton, MA: Tapestry Press.

SCALE 41   Student Motivation Scale

Directions: Below are 5 bipolar scale items relating to how you feel about being in the class **just before the one you are in now**. Please indicate how you feel about that class by circling one number for each bipolar scale item. Numbers "1" and "7" indicate a very strong feeling. Numbers "6" and "2" indicate a strong feeling. Numbers "5" and "3" indicate a fairly weak feeling. Number "4" indicates you are undecided, or you do not understand the adjectives themselves. Be sure to circle one, and only one, number for each scale item.

1. Unmotivated	1	2	3	4	5	6	7	Motivated
2. Excited	7	6	5	4	3	2	1	Bored
3. Interested	7	6	5	4	3	2	1	Uninterested
4. Involved	7	6	5	4	3	2	1	Uninvolved
5. Dreading It	1	2	3	4	5	6	7	Looking Forward to It

Scoring:
Add the number you circled above for each row. _____

Result: Score for Student Motivation Scale.
Possible scale range is 5 to 35. If your score is above 35 or below 5 you have made a scoring error.

Source: Richmond, V. P. (1990). Communication in the classroom: Power and motivation. *Communication Education, 39,* 181–184.

SCALE 42   Teacher Clarity Short Inventory

Directions: Below are a series of descriptions of how some teachers have been observed communicating in their classrooms. Please respond to the statements in terms of how well they apply to the teacher you are describing (the teacher you have in the class you take just before this one). Please use the following scale to respond to each of the statements:

Strongly Disagree	Disagree	Neutral	Agree	Strongly Agree
1	2	3	4	5

_____ 1. My teacher clearly defines major concepts.

_____ 2. My teacher's answers to student questions are unclear.

_____ 3. In general, I understand my teacher.

_____ 4. Projects assigned for the class have unclear guidelines.

_____ 5. My teacher's objectives for the course are clear.

_____ 6. My teacher is straightforward in her/his lecture.

_____ 7. My teacher is not clear when defining guidelines for out of class assignments.

_____ 8. My teacher uses clear and relevant examples.

_____ 9. In general, I would say that my teacher's classroom communication is unclear.

_____ 10. My teacher is explicit in her/his instruction.

Scoring:
Step 1. Begin with a score of 36.
Step 2. Add scores for items 1, 3, 5, 6, 8, and 10.
Step 3. Add scores for items 2, 4, 7 and 9.
Step 4. Add the score of Step 1 to the score of Step 2.
Step 5. Subtract the score of Step 3 from the score of Step 4.

Result: Score for Teacher Clarity Short Inventory.
Possible scale range is 10–50. If your score is above 50 or below 10 you have made a scoring error.

Source: Chesebro, J. L., & McCroskey, J. C. (1998). The development of the teacher clarity short inventory (TCSI) to measure clear teaching in the classroom. _Communication Research Reports, 15,_ 262–266.

SCALE 43   Teacher Nonverbal Immediacy

Directions: The following statements describe the ways some people behave while talking with or to others. Please indicate in the space at the left of each item the degree to which you believe the statement applies **to the teacher you have in the class you take just before this one.** Please use the following 5-point scale:

Never	Rarely	Occasionally	Often	Very Often
1	2	3	4	5

———— 1. My teacher uses her or his hands and arms to gesture while talking to people.

———— 2. My teacher touches others on the shoulder or arm while talking to them.

———— 3. My teacher uses a monotone or dull voice while talking to people.

———— 4. My teacher looks over or away from others while talking to them.

———— 5. My teacher moves away from others when they touch her or him while talking.

———— 6. My teacher has a relaxed body position when talking to people.

———— 7. My teacher frowns while talking to people.

———— 8. My teacher avoids eye contact while talking to people.

———— 9. My teacher has a tense body position while talking to people.

———— 10. My teacher sits close or stands close to people while talking with them.

———— 11. My teacher's voice is monotonous or dull when talking to people.

———— 12. My teacher uses a variety of vocal expressions when talking to people.

———— 13. My teacher gestures when talking to people.

———— 14. My teacher is animated when talking to people.

———— 15. My teacher has a bland facial expression when talking to people.

———— 16. My teacher moves closer to people when talking to them.

———— 17. My teacher looks directly at people while talking to them.

———— 18. My teacher is stiff when talking to people.

———— 19. My teacher has a lot of vocal variety when talking to people.

———— 20. My teacher avoids gesturing while talking to people.

———— 21. My teacher leans toward people when talking to them.

———— 22. My teacher maintains eye contact with people when talking to them.

———— 23. My teacher tries not to sit or stand close to people when talking with them.

———— 24. My teacher leans away from people when talking to them.

———— 25. My teacher smiles when talking to people.

———— 26. My teacher avoids touching people when talking to them.

Scoring:
Step 1. Begin with a score of 78.
Step 2. Add scores for items 1, 2, 6, 10, 12, 13, 14, 16, 17, 19, 21, 22, and 25.
Step 3. Add scores for items 3, 4, 5, 7, 8, 9, 11, 15, 18, 20, 23, 24, and 26.
Step 4. Add the score of Step 1 to the score of Step 2.
Step 5. Subtract the score of Step 3 from the score of Step 4.

Result: Score for Teacher Nonverbal Immediacy.
Possible scale range is 26 to 130. If your score is above 130 or below 26 you have made a scoring error.

Source: Richmond, V. P., McCroskey, J. C., & Johnson, A. D. (2003). Development of the nonverbal immediacy scale (NIS): Measures of self- and other-perceived nonverbal immediacy. *Communication Quarterly, 51,* 504–517.

SCALE 44 Humor Assessment

Directions: The following statements apply to how people communicate humor when relating to others. Indicate the degree to which each of these statements applies to: **Your teacher in class you have just before the one you are in.** Please use the following scale responses.

Strongly Disagree	Disagree	Neutral	Agree	Strongly Agree
1	2	3	4	5

———— 1. My teacher regularly communicates with others by joking with them.

———— 2. People usually laugh when my teacher makes a humorous remark.

———— 3. My teacher is not funny or humorous.

———— 4. My teacher can be amusing or humorous without having to tell a joke.

———— 5. Being humorous is a natural communication orientation for my teacher.

———— 6. My teacher cannot relate an amusing idea well.

———— 7. My friends would say that my teacher is a humorous or funny person.

———— 8. People don't seem to pay close attention when my teacher is being funny.

———— 9. Even funny ideas and stories seem dull when my teacher tells them.

———— 10. My teacher can easily relate funny or humorous ideas to the class.

———— 11. I would say that my teacher is not a humorous person.

———— 12. My teacher cannot be funny, even when asked to do so.

———— 13. My teacher relates amusing stories, jokes, and funny things very well to others.

———— 14. Of all the people I know, my teacher is one of the "least" amusing or funny persons.

———— 15. My teacher uses humor to communicate in a variety of situations.

———— 16. On a regular basis, my teacher communicates with others by being humorous or entertaining.

Scoring:

Step 1. Begin with a score of 48.

Step 2. Add scores for items 1, 2, 4, 5, 7, 10, 13, and 15.

Step 3. Add scores for items 3, 6, 8, 9, 11, 12, 14 and 16.

Step 4. Add the score of Step 1 to the score of Step 2.

Step 5. Subtract the score of Step 3 from the score of Step 4.

Result: Score for Humor Assessment.

Possible scale range is 16 to 80. If your score is above 80 or below 16 you have made a scoring error.

Source: Wrench, J. S., & Richmond, V. P. (2004). Understanding the psychometric properties of the Humor Assessment instrument through an analysis of the relationships between teacher humor assessment and instructional communication variables in the college classroom. *Communication Research Reports, 21,* 92–103.

Glossary

accenting: Nonverbal messages that highlight, stress, or enhance the verbal message.

accidental communication: When a source communicates a message to a receiver that is unintentional and happens outside the source's conscious control.

acculturation: Directly and indirectly influencing newcomers to a culture to adopt new ways of thinking and doing things—the ways of the host culture.

action-oriented listening style: Listening style marked by listening behaviors that are focused on the desired action a source is asking for in her or his message.

actual reason for coming (ARC): The real reason a patient or client visits a physician or psychologist.

adaptors: Unintentional behaviors that are usually responses to boredom or stress, or responses closely linked with negative feelings toward ourselves or others.

adventurousness: The desire to try new things.

affect displays: Cues that involve primarily facial expressions but also include a person's posture, gait, limb movements, and other behaviors that provide information about her or his emotional state or mood.

affective learning: The acquisition of likes and attitudes, values, and beliefs related to various aspects of knowledge.

affinity seeking: The degree to which we feel social needs for affection and inclusion; often manifests itself in our attempts to get other people to like and appreciate us.

agentic friendships: Friendships marked by an activity orientation.

aggregation: A collection of people without a common purpose (as opposed to a group).

ambivalents: Organizational orientation exhibited by individuals who tend to be disgruntled with the status quo within an organization and despise the hierarchy within the organization.

argumentativeness: The tendency to approach communicative interactions in which one must advocate positions on controversial issues and to attack verbally the positions that other people hold on these issues.

artifacts: Accessories used to adorn our bodies and clothing.

assertiveness: The capacity to make requests; actively disagree; express positive or negative personal rights and feelings; initiate, maintain, or disengage from conversations; and stand up for oneself without attacking another (factor of sociocommunicative orientation/style—see also *responsiveness*).

asynchronous computer-mediated communication (CMC): Form of mediated communication in which people interact with each other at varying times.

attitude: A predisposition to respond to people, ideas, or objects in an evaluative way.

attitude homophily: The degree to which a receiver perceives her or his attitudes, beliefs, and values to be similar to those of a source.

audience-oriented behavior: Personality characteristics that surface depending on the audience with whom an individual is communicating.

authoritarianism: Having an orientation toward power in social relationships.

background homophily: Perceptions of similarity in similarities of life experience.

bad mood: Factor of exhilaratability that measures the tendency of individuals to be generally in a bad mood, sad (despondent and distressed), ill-humoredness (sullen and grumpy or grouchy feelings), and displeasure in situations related to cheerfulness-evoking situations.

basic attribution error: When we attribute the causes of our own behavior to external factors and the causes of another person's behavior to internal causes.

behavior alteration messages (BAMs): Messages a source uses in an attempt to alter a receiver's behavior.

behavior alteration techniques (BATs): General techniques a source uses in an attempt to alter a receiver's behavior (they correspond with specific behavior alteration messages).

behavioral biology: The attempt to understand both the genetic and environmental contributions to individual variations in human behavior.

behavioral/psychomotor learning: The mastery of a motor act or skill.

belief: Our perception of reality about whether something is true or false.

biological time: How people feel and react physically to time, and the effects of time on physical well-being.

caring/goodwill: Aspect of source credibility related to the degree to which a source is perceived as caring about the receiver.

causal attribution: The perception process by which we make sense out of the behavior of others.

channel: The means by which a message is carried from one person to another.

cheerfulness: Factor of exhilaratability that measures the tendency to be happy and have a low threshold for smiling and laughter, a composed view of adverse life circumstances, a broad range of active factors that make us cheerful and smile, and a generally cheerful interaction style.

chronemics: The ways in which different cultures perceive and use time.

co-culture: Cultural groups not necessarily below or suppressed by the larger culture, but existing inside of a larger culture.

codes: Series of letters that represents a known concept or thing.

coercive power: Form of power based on French and Raven's five bases of power in which an individual's expectations that he or she will be punished by another if he or she does not conform to that person's influence attempt.

cognitive learning: The recall and recognition of knowledge and the development of intellectual abilities and skills.

communal friendships: Friendships marked by intimacy, personal/emotional expressiveness, amount of self-disclosure, quality of self-disclosure, confiding, and emotional supportiveness.

communibiology: The study of human communication from a behavioral biological focus.

communication: The process by which one person stimulates meaning in the mind(s) of another person (or persons) through verbal and nonverbal messages.

communication apprehension: The fear or anxiety associated with either real or anticipated communication with another person or persons.

communication competence: The degree to which a person has the ability to make ideas known to others by talking or writing.

communications: Transferring messages from place to place (e.g., mass communications—television, radio, and print media).

competence: Aspect of source credibility related to the degree to which a source is perceived to be knowledgeable or expert in a given subject.

complementing: Nonverbal function of adding to, clarifying, enriching, emphasizing, or supplementing a verbal message.

compliance: Level of influence at which a person accepts another's request because he or she can see either potential reward for complying or potential punishment for not complying.

compliance gaining: Goal of communication focused on getting another person (the receiver) to engage in some behavior that is wanted by the source.

composure: The degree to which a source is poised, relaxed, and confident as opposed to nervous, tense, and uptight.

connotative definition: How a word is perceived and is actually used; attitude about a word.

consensus: Whether the individual acts in a way similar to the way other people act in a given situation.

consistency: Whether the individual behaves the same way in the same situation at different times.

consult: Management communication style in which managers make the ultimate decisions, but not until the problem has been presented to subordinates and their advice, information, and suggestions have been obtained.

content-oriented listening style: Listening style marked by listening behaviors that analyze the content and logical flow of a source's message.

context: The circumstances within which communication takes place.

contextual behavior: When personality characteristics are demonstrated by individuals within specific contexts (interpersonal, group, meeting, public, and mediated).

contradicting: Use of nonverbal messages that are opposite to verbal messages.

courtship-readiness cues: Nonverbal behaviors that are exhibited in a courtship situation and includes displays of courtship readiness, preening behavior, positional cues, and actions of appeal or invitation.

cross-cultural communication: Comparisons of communication behaviors across different cultures and the study of specific communication issues on a comparative basis in two or more cultures.

cultural level: Level of communication in which adaptation of our message-sending and -receiving processes occur to enable accurate predictions of our interactant's behavior based on her or his cultural background.

culture: A group of people who through a process of learning are able to share perceptions of the world that influences their beliefs, values, norms, and rules, which eventually affect behavior.

decoding: The translation of a message into ideas or information.

decoding process: Process a receiver goes through in sensing the source's message, interpreting it, evaluating it, and responding to it.

demographic homophily: Physical or social characteristics of an individual that are real and objectively identifiable: age, sex, height, socioeconomic status, educational level, religion, culture, and ethnicity.

denotative definition: Specific dictionary use of a word.

disagreement: A difference of opinion about facts, on what the facts imply, or on what we might wish to do about those facts.

distinctiveness: Whether the individual behaves the same way in different situations.

dogmatism: Tendency to be rigid in one's thinking; can best be described as "close-minded."

emblems: Gestures and movements that have a direct verbal translation and can be used to stimulate specific meanings in the minds of others in place of verbal communication.

emoticons: Typed symbols intended to illustrate emotional states and nonverbal behavior in a computer-mediated environment.

emotional maturity: Personality trait that distinguishes between people who are changeable, dissatisfied, and easily annoyed and those who are stable, calm, and well-balanced.

empathy: The capacity of an individual to put her- or himself into the shoes of another person; to see things from the other person's vantage point.

encoding: The process of creating messages that we believe represent the meaning to be communicated and are likely to stimulate similar meaning in the mind of a receiver.

encoding process: Process a source goes through to create a message, adapt it to the receiver, and transmit it across some source-selected channel.

ethnocentrism: The view of one's culture as the center of the universe.

evaluation apprehension: The fear or anxiety associated with either real or anticipated evaluative situations in the classroom.

exhilaratability: Concept created by Willibald Ruch to measure the extent to which an individual exhibits a cheerful state.

expert power: Form of power based on French and Raven's five bases of power, based on an individual's perceptions of another's competence and knowledge in specific areas.

expressive communication: Messages sent by a source that expresses an internal emotional state.

external attribution: When we attribute a person's behavior to that individual's psychological or physiological causes.

external locus of control: The degree to which individuals perceive that reward for actions stems from outside forces.

external noise: Noise in the physical surrounding that prohibits effective rhetorical communication from occurring.

extraversion: One of Hans Eysenck's three supertraits related to the biologically based desire to be sociable, have stimulation around them, and have an easygoing nature.

feedback: A receiver's observable response to a source's message.

formal time: The way in which a culture keeps track of time.

friendship-warmth touch: Lets another person know that we care for, value, and have an interest in her or him.

functional-professional touch: Impersonal, businesslike touch used to accomplish or perform some task or service.

gain understanding: Goal of communication focused on the acquisition of information.

general anxiety: This personality trait distinguishes between those who tend to be tense, restless, and impatient most of the time, and those who generally tend to be calm, relaxed, and composed.

group: Three or more individuals who, through informational and persuasive communication, interact for the achievement of some common purpose(s).

haptics: The study of the type, amount, uses, and results of tactile behavior.

health communication: The process by which one person stimulates meaning in the mind(s) of another person (or persons) through verbal, nonverbal, and mediated messages specifically related to the physical and psychological well-being of another person (or persons).

homophily: Perceived similarity between two people.

identification: Level of influence in which a person accepts another's request because he or she identifies with and wants to establish a relationship with that particular person or group.

illustrators: Gestures and movements that are closely linked with spoken language and help to illustrate what is being said.

immediacy: The degree of perceived physical or psychological distance between people in a relationship.

indifferents: Organizational orientation exhibited by individuals who work out of necessity, but see their life as something that occurs outside of work.

influence: When we cause that person to alter his or her thinking or behavior as a result of accidental, expressive, or rhetorical communication.

informal time: The casual time employed by a culture, which is often unconscious and determined by the situation or context in which it is used.

intensity: The strength of attitudes, beliefs, or values about people, ideas, or objects.

intercultural communication: Communication between members of two co-cultures within a larger culture, particularly when the co-culture differences as seen as quite substantial.

interethnic communication: Communication between members of more than one ethnic subculture.

internal attribution: When we attribute a person's behavior to external factors that explain her or his behavior as caused by certain situational influences, which may include other people with whom they are associated.

internal locus of control: The degree to which individuals perceive that reward for actions follows from their own behavior.

internal noise: Noise within the receiver that prohibits effective rhetorical communication from occurring.

internalization: Level of influence in which a person accepts another's request because he or she has adopted a way of thinking or behaving because it is intrinsically rewarding and is similar to that person's value system.

international communication: Communication between individuals from different countries often the communication between governmental representatives of different countries.

interpersonal conflict: The breaking down of attraction and the development of repulsion; the dissolution of perceived homophily (similarity) and the increased perception of incompatible, irreconcilable differences; and the loss of perceptions of credibility and the development of disrespect.

interracial communication: Communication between individuals from different racial backgrounds.

intimacy: The perceived depth of a relationship between people.

intracultural communication: Communication between individuals within the same culture.

investigation process: Process a source goes through to conceive an idea, decide her or his intent, and select some meaning to be stimulated (intentionally) in the mind of the receiver.

join: Management communication style in which managers do not make decisions; rather, the authority to make the decision is delegated to the subordinates, either in cooperation with the manager or in her or his absence.

kinesics: The study of the communicative aspects of gestures and bodily movements.

language: System of symbols or codes that represent certain ideas or meanings.

learning theory: Problematic social scientific theory for human behavior that alleges that humans are born as "blank slates" with no personality characteristics, so humans must learn their personalities.

legitimate power: Form of power based on French and Raven's five bases of power in which an individual's perceptions of another's right to influence or prescribed behavior for her or him has been granted by some person or body of people outside the immediate relationship.

love-intimacy touch: Touch that expresses emotional and affective attachment and caring; usually a hug, caress, or stroke.

Machiavellianism: Personality type that views other people as objects to be manipulated for her or his own purposes.

medical interview: The process a physician uses when he or she asks a patient questions and the patient responds with answers related.

message: Any verbal or nonverbal stimulus that stimulates meaning in a receiver.

monochronic (M-time): The norm in the North American culture; it emphasizes the scheduling of activities one at a time, the segmentation of work, and the promptness of work.

monological: When a source's message becomes unidirectional and not interactional.

moral responsibility power: Form of power that rests on an individual's perceptions of responsibility to others.

motivation: A force or drive that influences behavior to achieve a desired outcome.

neuroticism: One of Hans Eysenck's three supertraits related to the biologically based tendency toward mania (being really happy) and depression (being really sad).

noise: Part of the rhetorical model of communication that is concerned with anything that prohibits effective rhetorical communication from occurring.

nonprofit organizations: Organizations that are concerned with providing products or services without the goal of making money while doing so.

nonverbal messages: Any stimuli other than words that can potentially elicit meaning in the mind of a receiver.

nonverbal sexual communication: The process of one person stimulating meaning in the mind of another person or persons their sexual desires by means of nonverbal messages.

norms: Expected guidelines that govern our interactions that are not explicitly established.

not-for-profit organizations: Organization that is able to sell goods and services at higher rates than are needed for organizational stability without the desire to truly make a profit; all funds that exceed organizational stability (salaries, supplies, property, etc.) are then donated to a true nonprofit organization.

oculesics: The study of eye behavior, eye contact, eye movement, and the functions of eye behavior.

olfactics: The study of scents and smells and how people perceive and process information about them.

organization: Organized collection of individuals working interdependently within a relatively structured, organized, open system to achieve common goals.

organizational orientation: An individual's predisposition toward work, motivation to work, job satisfaction, and ways of dealing with peers, subordinates, and supervisors on the job.

owls: People who are at their peak in late afternoon and evening and at their worst in early morning.

people-oriented listening style: Listening style marked by listening behaviors that attend to and are concerned with a source's emotional state.

perception: The process of attributing meaning to messages.

personal space: An invisible bubble that surrounds us and expands or contracts depending on personalities, situations, and types of relationships.

personality: A person's phenotype, or the interaction between an individual's genotype (see temperament) and her or his environment (nurture, diet, socialization, etc.), which is a reflection of her or his experiences, motivations, attitudes, beliefs, values, and behaviors.

personality traits: An individual's predispositions for responding in a certain way to various situations.

personality variables: The specific characteristics of the individual that make her or him unique from other individuals.

persuasion: Altering someone's behavior as a result of conscious intent, so persuasion is innately rhetorical.

physical attraction: The degree to which an individual finds another person to be physically appealing and pleasant.

physiological noise: Form of noise that occurs because a person's physical body prevents her or him from attending to a sent message.

polychronic (P-time): The norm for many Latin American cultures; it emphasizes the involvement of many people and is less rigid about the ordering of events and scheduling, and they believe in handling several transactions at once.

power: The degree to which we believe a source can control our thoughts, feelings, or behavior.

primacy: The notion that we are more likely to remember information covered first in a message.

principle of consistency: When two attitudes (or perceptions, or beliefs, or values) are inconsistent with each other, change in one or both occurs because of the mind's efforts to establish and maintain consistency.

principle of homophily: The more similar two communicators are, the more likely they are to interact with one another, the more likely their communication will be successful, and the more similar they are likely to become.

profit-based organizations: Organization that is concerned with how much money a company nets in a given period of time.

proxemics: The study of the ways in which humans use and communicate with space.

psychological gender: A person's level of self-identification with both dominance (instrumentality/assertiveness) and submissiveness (expressiveness/responsiveness) in interactions with others.

psychological level: Level of communication in which we communicate with another person based on our predictions about how a person's beliefs, values, and behavior transcend cultural and social expectations and are derived from the person's unique psychological, emotional, and personality traits.

psychological noise: Form of noise that occurs because a person's psychological state prevents her or him from attending to a sent message.

psychological time: Psychological time orientation determines what a culture's communication will focus on (people tend to be past, present, or future focused).

psychoticism: One of Hans Eysenck's three supertraits related to the biologically based tendency to be tend to be a loner, unempathetic (uncaring about other people's emotions), and antisocial (violating social rules and norms).

receiver: The person who gets the source's message.

receiver apprehension: The fear of misinterpreting, inadequately processing, and/or not being able to adjust psychologically to messages sent by others.

recency: The notion that we are more likely to remember information covered last in a message.

referent power: Form of power based on French and Raven's five bases of power in which an individual grants another individual the ability to influence her or him because he or she desires to be like the person who is doing the influencing.

regulating: Nonverbal messages that allow us to control, monitor, coordinate, and manage verbal communication.

regulators: Gestures and movements that, along with eye and vocal cues, maintain and regulate the back-and-forth interaction between speakers and listeners during spoken dialogue.

relational power: Form of power where influence occurs because of the nature of the relationship and the desire to please another within the relationship.

relationship development: Goal of communication focused on the need to develop relationships out of needs of companionship, sharing, and love.

repeating: Nonverbal messages that restate, reinforce, duplicate, or reiterate the verbal message.

responsiveness: The capacity to be sensitive to the communication of others, to be a good listener, to make others comfortable in communicating, and to recognize the needs and desires of others (factor of sociocommunicative orientation/style—see also *assertiveness*).

reward power: Form of power based on French and Raven's five bases of power in which an individual's perception of another's ability to mediate rewards for her or him.

rhetorical communication: Messages sent by a source that are goal directed and are intended to produce a specific meaning in the mind of another individual.

rhetorical criticism: The art of evaluating another person's speech, starting with the rhetorical situation and the speaker's purpose.

rhetorical sensitivity: The degree to which one can alter her or his communicative behaviors to adapt to the rhetorical situation.

rhetorical situation: The situation in which an individual's understanding or behavior can be changed through a communicated message.

roles: Socially prescribed forms of behavior consistent with specific communicative contexts.

rules: Clearly established guidelines that govern our interactions according to the roles we engage in within a communicative context.

salience: Perceived importance of an attitude, a belief, or a value to the individual.

selective exposure: A person's conscious or unconscious decision to place her or himself in a position to receive messages from a particular source.

self-control: A personality variable that separates people who have much control over their emotions from those who have little control over their emotions.

self-disclosure: Messages that reveal information that is private and personal to another.

self-esteem: The view people have of themselves in terms of total worth.

sell: Management communication style in which managers make decisions (or receives them from above), but rather than simply announcing them to subordinates, the manager tries to persuade the subordinates of the desirability of the decisions.

seriousness: Factor of exhilaratability that measures the tendency for serious states; a perception that even everyday happenings are important and deserving of thorough and intensive consideration; the tendency to plan ahead and set long-range goals; the tendency to prefer activities for which concrete, rational reasons can be produced; the belief that rational reasons can be produced; the preference for a sober, object-oriented communication style; and a humorless or dull attitude about cheerfulness-related matters.

sex-typed orientations: When people whose biological sex is female have a feminine gender orientation and when people whose biological sex is male have a masculine gender orientation.

sexual-arousal touch: Touch that can be a part of love and intimacy, but can also be distinct; sexual-arousal touch can include the use of a person as an object of attraction or lust, or even monetary gain.

shyness: The behavioral tendency to not initiate communication and/or respond to the initiatives of others.

situational behavior: When personality characteristics surface for no reason; during a situation, we just naturally start communicating in a pattern that is not normal for us.

SOAP note: The note taking completed by a physician during a medical interview (subjective, objective, assessment, and plan).

sociability: The degree to which a source is perceived as likable, friendly, and pleasant.

social attraction: The degree to which an individual finds another person to be entertaining and fun to be around.

social-polite touch: Affirms or acknowledges the other person's identity; this type of touch follows strict cultural codes, and in North America, social-polite touch is exemplified by the classic handshake.

sociological level: Level of communication in which we communicate with another person based on our predictions about other persons, which we use to make our encoding and decoding decisions that are based on our perceptions of the sociological subgroups to which people belong.

source: The person who originates a message.

sparrows: People who are at their best in the early morning and at their worst in the late evening.

sponsorship effect: When an unknown source is introduced by someone known and the receiver transfers much of the introducer's image to that unknown source.

sprowls: People who are a mixture of owl and sparrow, and never seem to be run down.

status: A person's position in some hierarchy.

stereotype: A generalization about a group based on our perception that a group of people from a culture or co-culture as sharing one or several common characteristics.

substituting: Nonverbal message that can be used instead of a verbal message.

synchronous computer-mediated communication (CMC): Form of mediated communication that occurs in real time (or approximates real time).

talkaholic (compulsive communicator): Personality trait in which individuals are driven to communicate.

task attraction: The degree to which an individual finds another person to be a desirable one with whom to establish a work relationship.

teacher apprehension: Generally visible distress or signs of apprehension when being approached by or communicated with by any teacher.

teacher clarity: The process by which an instructor is able to effectively stimulate the desired meaning of course content and process in the minds of students through the use of appropriately structured verbal and nonverbal messages.

team: A group that interacts intensively to provide an organizational product, plan, decision, or service.

technical time: Refers to precise, scientific measurements of time; has the least correlation with interpersonal communication.

tell: Management communication style in which managers habitually make decisions (or receive them from above) and announce them to subordinates with the expectation that the subordinates will carry out those decisions without challenge.

temperament: An individual's genotype, characteristics present early in life caused by human biology.

territory: A semifixed or fixed space whose perceived owners can move in and out of it without giving up their claim to it; it is claimed, staked out in some way, and defended against encroachment.

time-oriented listening style: Listening style marked by listening behaviors that are focused on specified internal or external time limitations for a source's message.

tolerance for ambiguity: Personality variable that distinguishes people who can operate effectively in communication situations in which there is a great deal of uncertainty from those who cannot operate effectively in such situations.

tolerance for disagreement: An individual's ability to openly discuss opposition arguments to their own arguments without feeling personally attacked or confronted.

trustworthiness: Aspect of source credibility related to the degree to which a source is perceived as being honest.

uncertainty reduction theory: Theory of communication created by Berger and Calabrese that theorizes that humans do not like uncertainty so they try to get to know another person very quickly after first meeting to reduce uncertainty that comes from a new person.

upward mobile: Organizational orientation exhibited by individuals within an organization who actively desire advancement within the hierarchy of the organization and see their work as a central part of their life.

values: Our enduring conceptions of the nature of right and wrong, good and bad.

verbal aggression: The tendency to attack a person's self-concept in order to deliver psychological pain.

verbal messages: Form of messages that are composed of words.

verbal sexual communication: The process of one person stimulating meaning in the mind of another person or persons their sexual desires through the use of verbal symbols or words.

versatility: An individual's ability to adapt her or his communication behavior to the context, situation, and other person(s) involved in a communication event.

vocalics (paralanguage): The study of the communicative value of vocal behavior and includes all oral cues in the stream of spoken utterances except the words themselves.

willingness to communicate: A person's general level of desire to initiate communication with others.

willingness to listen: A person's general level of desire to listen to others.

Index

427